THEIR FAIR SHARE

TAXING THE RICH IN THE AGE OF FDR

Also of interest from the Urban Institute Press:

War and Taxes, by Steven A. Bank, Kirk J. Stark, and Joseph J. Thorndike

Tax Justice: The Ongoing Debate, edited by Joseph J. Thorndike and Dennis J. Ventry Jr.

Taxing Capital Income, edited by Henry J. Aaron, Leonard E. Burman, and C. Eugene Steuerle

Contemporary U.S. Tax Policy, second edition, by C. Eugene Steuerle

THEIR FAIR SHARE

TAXING THE RICH IN THE AGE OF FDR

JOSEPH J. THORNDIKE

THE URBAN INSTITUTE PRESS
WASHINGTON, DC

THE URBAN INSTITUTE PRESS
2100 M Street, N.W.
Washington, D.C. 20037

Library of Congress Cataloging-in-Publication Data

Thorndike, Joseph J.
 Their fair share : taxing the rich in the age of FDR / Joseph J. Thorndike.
  pages cm
 Includes bibliographical references and index.
 ISBN 978-0-87766-771-1 (paper : alk. paper) — ISBN (invalid) 978-0-87766-782-7 (ePub) 1. Taxation—United States—History—20th century. 2. Tax incidence—United States—History—20th century. 3. New Deal, 1933-1939. 4. Roosevelt, Franklin D. (Franklin Delano), 1882-1945—Political and social views. 5. United States. Congress—History—20th century. 6. Taxation—Law and legislation—United States—History—20th century. 7. Social classes—United States—History—20th century. 8. United States—Economic policy—1933-1945. I. Title.
 HJ2377.T46 2012
 336.2'009730904—dc23

                                                          2012045283

Printed in the United States of America

17 16 15 14 13   1 2 3 4 5

THE URBAN INSTITUTE is a nonprofit, nonpartisan policy research and educational organization established in Washington, D.C., in 1968. Its staff investigates the social, economic, and governance problems confronting the nation and evaluates the public and private means to alleviate them. The Institute disseminates its research findings through publications, its web site, the media, seminars, and forums.

Through work that ranges from broad conceptual studies to administrative and technical assistance, Institute researchers contribute to the stock of knowledge available to guide decisionmaking in the public interest.

Conclusions or opinions expressed in Institute publications are those of the authors and do not necessarily reflect the views of officers or trustees of the Institute, advisory groups, or any organizations that provide financial support to the Institute.

For Frances

Contents

Acknowledgments

I am indebted to a long list of teachers and mentors, including Nelson Lichtenstein of the University of California, Santa Barbara; Melvyn Leffler and Charles McCurdy of the University of Virginia; and Robert Dalzell of Williams College. W. Elliot Brownlee, also at UCSB, deserves special thanks, not only from me but from anyone working on the history of U.S. public finance. Through his own work he has reshaped the historiography of American taxation, while also encouraging a new generation of fiscal historians.

My colleagues at Tax Analysts, both past and present, have been extraordinarily generous in their support of this project. I owe particular thanks to Chris Bergin and David Brunori, who offered crucial guidance (and no small measure of forbearance). The entire project was inspired, moreover, by Tax Analysts' founder Tom Field, who taught me that the 1930s and 1940s held the key to understanding our current tax system.

Other institutions have also provided valuable and often crucial support, including the George W. Bush Institute, the Urban-Brookings Tax Policy Center, the Corcoran Department of History at the University of Virginia, and the Northwestern University School of Law (where my students ensured that I never forgot the "tax" in tax history).

At various points, I have benefited from the advice and counsel of many readers and academic colleagues, especially Steven Bank, Andrea Campbell, Robin Einhorn, Dan Ernst, Eisaku Ide, David Cay Johnston, Carolyn Jones, Marjorie Kornhauser, Mark Leff, Andrew Lewis, Isaac Martin, Ajay Mehrotra, Monica Prasad, Satoshi Sekiguchi, Amity Shlaes, Kirk Stark, Dennis Ventry, and Larry Zelenak.

I am grateful to Tax Analysts for permission to republish elements of several chapters that previously appeared in the pages of *Tax Notes* magazine. Thanks also to Cambridge University Press for permission to republish parts of chapters five and six. And finally, a special thanks to my coauthors for *War and Taxes*, who improved my treatment of World War II enormously.

1

A Nation of Taxpayers

Americans hate taxes, right?

We vote for candidates who promise to cut them and punish politicians who agree to raise them. We tell pollsters we don't want to pay them, and we teach our children that the nation was founded to resist them. From the Boston Tea Party to Shay's Rebellion to Proposition 13, we're a nation of tax revolters. Hand us a pitchfork, and we'll march on Washington.

It's a good story, that tale of the antitax American. And a convenient one for a certain kind of politician. But it's also wrong. Yes, Americans hate taxes. But so do people all over the world—our aversion to forced extraction is hardly unique. And while we may not whistle happily as we hustle to the post office on April 15 (or ask a computer to do the hustling for us), we generally pay up with minimal fuss. Oliver Wendell Holmes once observed that "taxes are what we pay for civilized society," and for more than 200 years, Americans have been remarkably willing to foot the bill.[1]

To be sure, American history is peppered with tax revolts. But they are the exception, not the rule. And the *meaning* of those revolts is not unitary and timeless. Some have been sparked by the simple financial hardship of paying taxes. During the 1930s, for instance, large swaths of the nation were plagued by property tax revolts as hard-pressed farmers and homeowners struggled to make ends meet.[2] But other protests have been driven by complaints about tax avoidance and distributional justice. Loopholes, favors, and special privileges in the tax law have fed a powerful sense of injustice, as has overreliance on certain revenue tools—like the protective tariff—that have burdened some groups more than others.

Consider the Boston Tea Party, the creation myth for today's antitax activists. That totemic revolt was actually a protest against tax loopholes, not high taxes. The colonists who dumped tea into Boston Harbor certainly disliked paying the British tax on tea. But they were moved to action by a special tax exemption that Parliament had granted to the East India Company, a well-connected enterprise that happened to be in dire need of a government bailout. It was a loophole, not a tax, that prompted a band of ersatz Indians to toss the tea in Boston harbor.[3]

The Tea Party of 1773, in other words, has something in common with the Tea Party of 2011. But the connection is not a shared aversion to high taxes. Rather, it's a keen sensitivity to issues of fairness and political equity. When Rick Santelli, a political commentator for CNBC, ignited the modern Tea Party in 2009, his chief complaint was about favoritism—specifically, a proposal to have the federal government rescue debt-ridden homeowners. "This is America!" he shouted in his famous televised rant. "How many of you people want to pay for your neighbor's mortgage?"[4] As soon became clear, not many. And it's that rejection of favoritism and special privilege that ties the Tea Parties together and situates both within a longer tradition of American fiscal protest.

Americans, it turns out, have been willing to pay the price for civilization. But they've objected when anyone has tried to get their civilization on the cheap.

Fairness and Progressive Taxation

Historically, tax avoidance has been a key element in larger debates about tax fairness. Since the founding, the federal government has been funded by a series of fiscal regimes, each defined, in the words of historian W. Elliot Brownlee, by a "system of taxation with its own characteristic tax bases, rate structures, and social intentions."[5] The arrival of each new regime (and the disappearance of its predecessor) has always been prompted by a crisis of some sort—usually a war, but sometimes an economic collapse. At these inflection points in our fiscal history, policy debates have featured practical questions about revenue adequacy and fiscal infrastructure. But they have often turned on grander issues, including questions of social justice, distributional equity, and civic responsibility.[6]

Our current regime is an old one, dating to the 1940s. World War II forced lawmakers to cast about for new sources of federal revenue, and the solutions they hit upon—a broad-based, progressive tax on individual income, a moderate tax on corporate profits, and a flat-rate levy on wage income—remain central to federal finance even today. This regime also embodied a bargain of sorts—a deal hashed out between politicians and their constituents about who should pay for national priorities. Ultimately, middle-class Americans agreed to shoulder much of the fiscal burden, chiefly through the income and payroll taxes. In return, however, they were promised that rich Americans would pay higher rates on their incomes, as well as special taxes on large estates.

This bargain lies at the heart of progressive taxation in the modern American tradition. It rests on the notion that rich people should contribute not just proportionally to the nation's treasury, but somewhat more than proportionally. That proposition—that tax rates should climb along with income—has long enjoyed broad (if sometimes only implicit) popularity with voters.[7] Even today, when antitax ideology seems to course through the electorate, it still commands majority support. In 2008, for instance, pollsters found that 63 percent of respondents believed making taxes more progressive was a "very good" or "somewhat good" expression of American patriotism.[8]

Such poll results are consistent with historical attitudes toward progressive taxation. Over the decades, progressive taxes have sometimes been advanced as a means to remake society along more egalitarian lines. On June 19, 1935, for instance, Franklin Roosevelt defended to Congress his sweeping plan for tax reform by highlighting the failures of the existing system. "Our revenue laws have operated in many ways to the unfair advantage of the few," he declared, "and they have done little to prevent an unjust concentration of wealth and economic power."[9]

More often, however, progressive taxes have been defended as a means to redistribute not wealth, but the *tax burden.* Rep. Cordell Hull of Tennessee, a leading proponent of the income tax during the early 20th century, repeatedly stressed the need to reallocate fiscal responsibilities, not economic power. "I have no disposition to tax wealth unnecessarily or unjustly," he said, "but I do believe that the wealth of the country should bear its just share of the burden of taxation and that it should not be permitted to shirk that duty."[10]

A "just share," a "fair share"—such phrases are a rhetorical fixture of American tax politics. But what do they mean? Often almost nothing. The notion of a "fair share" certainly doesn't require, in any scientific or technical sense, that Americans adopt a graduated tax on personal income. And it certainly doesn't provide much guidance in determining how much graduation in the rate structure will best serve the cause of fiscal justice. That question—one of the most intractable facing policymakers— is deeply political, its answers inherently arbitrary.

Nonetheless, the notion of a fair share has propelled the drive for tax reform during crucial moments in American history. It has, moreover, given a particular cast and content to the policies emerging from these moments. Politicians have deployed the notion of a fair share to advance progressive taxes, including individual and corporate income taxes, as well as the estate tax. They have also used it to deflect calls for other kinds of taxation, including broad-based taxes on consumption. As a result, the United States stands alone among large industrialized nations in resisting the global popularity of the value-added tax. The absence of such a tax from our fiscal infrastructure is every bit as distinctive as our heavy reliance on more progressive alternatives.[11]

Perhaps most notably, the notion of a "fair share" has resonated strongly with arguments about tax avoidance. Americans have long demanded a measure of fair dealing in the operation of their tax system. Movements for sweeping tax reform have often been driven by a popular suspicion that some people—usually, but not always, *rich* people—are shirking their fiscal responsibilities. In 2003, for instance, only 14 percent of respondents to a national survey said their chief complaint about federal taxation was the large amount they had to pay. By contrast, 51 percent cited a worry that "wealthy people get away not paying their fair share."[12]

And there's that phrase again: arguably the most powerful trope in American tax politics. It represents contested terrain, with champions of disparate policies vying to claim it as their own. But if legislation is a measure of success, then advocates of progressivity—and the income tax in particular—have been the victors in this battle. Fairness-as-progressivity has been the ascendant definition for decades, and it lies at the heart of our current tax system.

The Rise of the Income Tax

The proximate origin of our modern fiscal regime—including its dependence on income taxes and its lack of any broad-based consumption levy—can be found in a series of policy decisions made during the Great Depression and World War II. A path-dependent policy process has imbued those decisions with lasting importance for American state and society.

The roots run deeper, of course. The American penchant for progressive taxation can be discerned in the revenue debates of the Early Republic, when lawmakers struggled to pay the new nation's bills. Its effects were evident during the Civil War, when Union leaders imposed the nation's first income tax to ensure that rich Americans were sharing in the war's crushing cost. And in the late 19th and early 20th centuries, Populists and Progressives honed their arguments for income taxation by insisting that rich people were shouldering too little of the nation's fiscal burden.

But ratification of the Sixteenth Amendment in 1913, which clarified the federal government's authority to levy and collect a tax on income, was hardly the end of the story. It took another 30 years for the income tax to assume its durable and dominant position in the nation's revenue structure. Until World War II, only rich people paid the levy. Indeed, that was the point. Lawmakers had traditionally confined it to the upper strata of American society, using it to balance more regressive taxes on consumption. When first enacted in 1913, the individual tax affected fewer than 2 percent of U.S. households.[13] Thanks to a large exemption—that portion of an individual's income that falls below the threshold for taxation—most people remained well outside the taxman's grasp. The income tax was a rich man's burden.

Critics of this arrangement were legion, and they insisted that narrow taxes were inherently dangerous. Democratic nations required democratic taxes, they maintained, if only to keep the grasping majority from robbing the pocketbooks of a well-heeled minority. "When men once get the habit of helping themselves to the property of others," warned the *New York Times* in 1909, "they are not easily cured of it."[14]

The editors were right; it took more than a quarter-century for the income tax to reach the middle class. Within a few years of its 1913 statutory debut, the levy grew somewhat broader, as World War I prompted lawmakers to lower exemptions (and raise rates) in a bid for cash. But the tax remained narrow, burdening about 15 percent of American families in 1918.[15] In the 1920s, the tax base even reversed course and started to shrink. By 1930, roughly 12 percent of American households were paying the income tax.[16]

Meanwhile, GOP leaders of the 1920s pushed through a series of rate cuts, softening the redistributive edges of this controversial levy and robbing its opponents of their best argument for repeal. As the nation teetered on the edge of the Great Depression, the income tax was narrower, flatter—and, consequently, more politically secure—than it had been at the end of World War I.

And then disaster struck. The Great Depression caused incomes to plummet, especially among the rich, and revenue from the income tax fell dramatically. Faced with a soaring deficit, Congress broadened the tax in 1932 by lowering exemptions across the board. But it wasn't enough to stanch the bleeding, and lawmakers used excise taxes to slow the coursing red ink. A few years later, Roosevelt convinced lawmakers to raise rates, chiefly as a matter of social justice. But the tax still applied to a relatively narrow slice of the American public, and its yields remained anemic (at least compared to what they might have been and what they would later become). Not until 1938 would revenue from personal and corporate income taxes return to its 1931 level.[17]

World War II eventually brought dramatic and lasting change to the individual income tax; between 1939 and 1943, Congress transformed it from a "class tax" to a "mass tax." Exemptions fell dramatically and the number of taxpayers increased more than sixfold.[18] Almost overnight, it was later said, the income tax "changed its morning coat for overalls."[19] Meanwhile, lawmakers pushed rates upward, with the top bracket eventually peaking at 94 percent.[20] Together, these changes made the income tax a fiscal workhorse, boosting revenue from $1.0 billion in fiscal year 1939 to $18.4 billion in 1945.[21] By war's end, the tax was raising more than 40 percent of total revenue, displacing excise taxes—which dominated the tax system through the mid-1930s—as the principal source of federal funds.[22]

The transformation of the individual income tax arose from a confluence of factors, including politics, conviction, and necessity. Historians have emphasized the last, giving the story a functional and teleological cast.[23] But while necessity was certainly the mother of fiscal invention, other factors—including ideas and political institutions—were vital, too.[24] The modern, broad-based income tax did not spring fully formed from the minds of wartime lawmakers. Nor was it ever a sure thing. Rather, it emerged from a vigorous debate over the meaning of tax justice. Beginning at least a decade before the war, this argument pit conservatives against liberals—and liberals against themselves.

Ideas, Institutions, and Leadership

Over the course of the 1930s, President Franklin Roosevelt championed a variety of important tax reforms, including the so-called Wealth Tax of 1935, the undistributed profits tax of 1936, and the anti-loophole Revenue Act of 1937. All three did much to alienate Roosevelt from business leaders, and they probably slowed the nation's recovery from the Great Depression, too. But whatever their short-run effect, none worked lasting change on the tax system. Federal taxes in the 1930s looked a lot like federal taxes in the 1920s. In particular, the system continued to depend heavily on narrow consumption taxes, including levies on alcohol, tobacco, and a wide range of consumer goods. During this decade, these taxes raised between a quarter and half of all federal revenue.[25] To be sure, Democrats pushed income tax rates sharply higher, eager to ensure that rich Americans were paying their fair share. But they left the income tax as narrow as they found it, ensuring that *only* the rich would have to pay it.[26]

The modest short-run impact of New Deal tax reform should not, however, obscure its long-run importance. If we broaden the analytical horizon beyond the artificial confines of the 1930s, two factors emerge as especially important. First, Roosevelt developed a moralistic approach to tax policy that emphasized the fiscal responsibilities of wealthy Americans. With support from a cohort of administration lawyers, he championed narrow tax hikes on the very rich. These efforts had only modest redistributive effect in the short term, but they ensured that wartime reforms—and the durable postwar tax regime they spawned—would feature high marginal rates.

New Deal lawyers also highlighted the issue of tax avoidance, harnessing it to the larger project of progressive tax reform. On the one hand, they believed that rampant tax avoidance was making a mockery of the graduated rate structure (and progressive taxation more generally), and they repeatedly urged lawmakers to close egregious loopholes. But they also understood that outrage over tax avoidance might be used to muster support for grander types of tax reform, including rate hikes and even entirely new revenue tools. Indeed, one of the New Deal's most ambitious tax reforms, the creation of a new tax on undistributed corporate profits, was defended chiefly as a way to curb tax avoidance among shareholders.

The second aspect of New Deal taxation with vital long-run implications was the development of a new policy community around taxation. Politicized White House lawyers were not the only ones working on tax policy during the 1930s. Alongside them toiled a growing community of tax professionals, including academic experts, lobbyists, Treasury officials, congressional staff, and even a few members of Congress.[27] This community advanced a version of progressive reform that diverged from the soak-the-rich program popular in the White House. While FDR and his New Deal lawyers sought to raise taxes on the rich, this nascent policy network—dominated by liberal economists but home to a new generation of tax lawyers, too—proved more interested in cutting taxes on the poor. In particular, they stressed the redistributive potential of broader income taxation: by extending this progressive levy to the underburdened middle class, lawmakers could find room in the budget to cut regressive consumption taxes on the overburdened poor.

It would take the fiscal shock of World War II to make the broad-based income tax a reality. And when lawmakers *did* finally agree to expand the tax base (as the economists urged), they were careful to keep rates high (as the lawyers insisted). This compromise bridged the gap between soak-the-rich New Deal lawyers and save-the-poor New Deal economists. It also proved durable, fostering a political dynamic that made room for partisan rivalry around taxation while ensuring that many fundamentals of the wartime revenue structure would remain unchallenged for decades to come.

In fact, the New Deal tax regime outlived the political system from which it sprang. What historians call the "New Deal Order"—a political regime that was established in the early years of the depression and lasted for more than 40 years—drew sustenance from the revenue system that emerged during Roosevelt's presidency.[28] Even after the New Deal Order began to collapse in the 1970s and 1980s, its tax regime—including a broad-based income tax with meaningfully graduated rates—proved resilient.

Which isn't to say that nothing has changed in more than half a century. The "mass tax" of World War II has shrunk considerably near the bottom of the income scale, as lawmakers have chosen to exempt more and more Americans from paying the tax (in part because Congress has chosen to use the tax system to implement antipoverty programs like the earned income tax credit). Today, nearly half of us don't pay any income tax at all. Rates, moreover, are nothing like their wartime predecessors, at least for those near the top of the economic pyramid. Lawmakers have dramatically reduced both the number of brackets and their associated rates. Indeed, over the past quarter-century or so, effective rates have fallen alongside statutory ones, substantially reducing the overall burden on rich taxpayers.[29] Perhaps most important, payroll taxes have become a crucial element of the federal tax system, financing a large and growing welfare state, but since the tax only applies to roughly the first $100,000 in income, it remains more or less trivial for many of the nation's richest taxpayers.

Such changes notwithstanding, however, the American federal tax system of the early 21st century bears more than a passing resemblance to its predecessor of the mid-20th century. Despite long-running campaigns to scrap the progressive income tax and replace it with some alternative (including a flat tax, a national sales tax, or some other consumption-based system), our existing tax regime still seems secure. The Republican resurgence of the late 20th century may have transformed the landscape of American politics, ending decades of Democratic hegemony in Washington. But it left the New Deal tax regime largely intact—no small irony for a movement rooted in the politics of tax resentment.[30]

Organization of the Book

This book explores the emergence of the modern tax regime, focusing especially on the vital years between 1934 and 1943. Chapters 2–4 consider the precursors, beginning with tax policy during the Republican ascendancy of the 1920s. It then examines Franklin Roosevelt's tax policies while governor of New York, since FDR's personal influence was pivotal in shaping the fiscal watershed of his presidency. Finally, this part concludes with a discussion of early New Deal tax policy, including the impact of Ferdinand Pecora's investigation of Wall Street and the resulting campaign against loopholes.

Chapters 5–7 explore the high tide of New Deal tax reform, including the Revenue Acts of 1935, 1936, and 1937. As a group, these laws established new norms and political expectations that would guide federal taxation for years to come. Part II also outlines the ideas advanced by New Deal economists and New Deal tax lawyers. While never starkly at odds, these two bureaucratic camps differed fundamentally over the proper focus of progressive reform: the latter were eager to soak the rich, while the former were determined to save the poor.

Chapters 8–10 examine the New Deal's retreat from ambitious tax reform. Bedeviled by political and economic problems, the Roosevelt administration was hard pressed to defend past victories, let alone strive for new ones. But the onset of World War II changed the political and economic dynamics once again, opening the door to sweeping reform. From the crucible of war emerged a new tax system that proved remarkably durable, even after the emergency.

The book concludes with a survey of that durability, evaluating postwar tax reform in light of New Deal precedents. It concludes that a path-dependent policy process kept the essentials of Roosevelt-era tax reform largely intact. In particular, Republicans proved willing to leave the broad outlines of the wartime regime unchallenged, while Democrats remained steadfast in their opposition to any reform that threatened the primacy of progressive income taxation.

The Republican Roots of New Deal Taxation

The New Deal tax regime was not a product of the New Deal. At least not entirely or initially. Several of its key elements—including its broad, regressive consumption taxes and its narrow but progressive income tax—were enacted five months before Franklin Roosevelt won his bid for the White House. The Revenue Act of 1932 was an ironic capstone to a decade of Republican fiscal stewardship, establishing the durable framework for 1930s tax policy. For the next eight years, every tax debate would unfold against the backdrop of this landmark revenue law.

Throughout the 1920s, Republicans had led a popular campaign to slash federal taxes. Under the guiding hand of Treasury Secretary Andrew Mellon, Congress abolished the excess profits tax, gutted the estate levy, and cut income tax rates. The Republican ascendancy did not go wholly unchallenged. Democrats spent much of the decade trying to fend off conservative reforms, and in the process, they managed to put their stamp on fiscal policy. Party leaders forged a pivotal compromise with Mellon over the individual income tax, arguing consistently, and almost unanimously, that it should be focused narrowly on the rich. Against GOP resistance, they managed to push through a major increase in exemptions. The number of taxpayers fell accordingly, plummeting more than 40 percent in just one year.[1] Meanwhile, Mellon got his cherished rate cuts, easing the burden on those few Americans still paying the tax. This bargain left the income tax enfeebled; the narrower, flatter levy was far from robust, its revenue highly sensitive to economic conditions.

The onset of the Great Depression made these flaws all too evident. The weakened income tax proved unequal to the task of Depression finance, its revenues falling precipitously as the economy tumbled downward. Faced with a ballooning deficit, President Herbert Hoover asked Congress for a tax hike, including new excise levies on consumption and a broader, steeper income tax. And eager to cast themselves as the party of fiscal discipline, Democrats agreed. Widely considered both prudent and distasteful, the Revenue Act of 1932 imposed the largest peacetime tax increase to that point in the nation's history. For Republicans, it brought an unhappy end to Mellon's long campaign for tax reduction. For Democrats, it established the regressive starting point for New Deal tax reform.

Taxation for Prosperity

Tax cuts were the order of the day—and the decade—throughout the 1920s. Taken together, the Revenue Acts of 1921, 1924, 1926, and 1928 lightened the burden for almost everyone. Corporations engineered repeal of the excess profits tax—the most progressive, productive, and burdensome revenue innovation to emerge from World War I. Rich individuals saw the top marginal rate on personal income drop from 77 percent to just 24 percent. The effective rate for the top 1 percent of households fell from 15.8 percent in 1920 to just 8.1 percent in 1929.[2] Major cuts in the estate tax further eased the burden on wealthy taxpayers. But millions of middle-class taxpayers got the ultimate prize: complete exemption from the income tax. These taxpayers continued to pony up a large share of federal revenue, shouldering a host of consumption taxes. But lawmakers moved decisively to narrow the scope of the income tax, raising exemptions even as they reduced rates. The tax ended up much flatter and much narrower.

Democrats and progressive Republicans played a vital role in crafting these tax reforms, but Andrew Mellon was the towering figure of 1920s public finance. He moved into his Treasury office in 1921 and stayed there until 1932. As one wag later remarked, "three presidents served under Mellon."[3] Over the course of this long tenure, Mellon managed to reshape the tax system along new, distinctly less progressive lines.

Andrew Mellon on Taxation

Mellon believed that tax burdens were too high. In his 1924 essay on tax policy, *Taxation: The People's Business,* he insisted that steep rates stifled incentive and fostered tax evasion. "Any man of energy and initiative in this country can get what he wants out of life," he wrote. "But when initiative is crippled by legislation or by a tax system which denies him the right to receive a reasonable share of his earnings, then he will no longer exert himself and the country will be deprived of the energy on which its continued greatness depends."[4]

Worse yet, high rates didn't even raise money. By encouraging both legal tax avoidance and illegal tax evasion, Mellon argued, they eroded the tax base and reduced overall revenue. Lower rates would actually raise money by spurring economic growth and reducing the incentive for tax avoidance. "It seems difficult for some to understand," he complained, "that high rates of taxation do not necessarily mean large revenue to the government, and that more revenue may actually be obtained by lower rates."[5] In particular, Mellon contended that high rates distorted investment decisions, boosting the popularity of tax-free state and local government bonds. Absent tax considerations, most of the money invested in such securities would be more productively employed elsewhere.[6]

Mellon's case for tax reduction was consistent, passionate, and politically compelling. Even his opponents were impressed. "There was a mystical righteousness about tax reduction," observed Randolph Paul, a leading tax lawyer who would soon become a key Treasury official in the Roosevelt administration.[7] That sense of righteousness even extended to specialized tax breaks and loopholes. The revenue laws passed during the 1920s included a variety of narrow provisions designed to benefit specific industries or corporations. In 1921, for instance, lawmakers enacted oil and gas percentage depletion allowances, much to the delight of these extractive industries. Depletion allowances permitted companies to deduct the investment costs associated with a mineral reserve, such as an oil well. Since extraction necessarily depleted the mineral reserve over time, companies had been permitted since 1918 to take deductions reflecting the declining market value of their mineral reserve. Percentage depletion, by contrast, allowed lucky companies to deduct an arbitrary, statutorily defined percentage of gross sales from their corporate income tax. In some cases, percentage depletion allowed companies to deduct much, much more than their original acquisition and exploration costs. It was a very generous gift from lawmakers to the oil and gas industry. A convenient side effect of such tax breaks was the power they conferred on policymakers, who could use them to reward friends and political allies.[8]

Lawmakers weren't the only ones handing out favors. As Mellon critics pointed out, the Treasury was in a generous mood as well. Throughout the 1920s, the Bureau of Internal Revenue (BIR) cut sweetheart deals with well-connected corporate taxpayers, allowing them to slash their tax bills though friendly negotiation with the bureau. "There has been a great deal of evidence tending to show that it is the policy of the bureau to fix taxes by bargain rather than by principle," observed a Senate investigating committee. "The best and most persistent trader gets the lowest tax and gross discrimination is the inevitable result of such a policy."[9] Bargaining not only allowed Treasury officials to grant tax preferences where and when they wished, it also paved the way for subsequent private-sector employment. Bureau officials complained that the agency's best employees were routinely poached by corporate taxpayers and well-heeled law firms. The market value of these Bureau employees derived from their secret stash of knowledge; the agency failed to publish many of its rulings, and negotiated deals with corporate taxpayers were treated confidentially. Only BIR employees had access to the agency's working law. The revolving door for agency personnel was not illegal. Indeed, it was a time-honored tradition at the agency. And negotiated tax deals were a necessary part of administering the tax system. But handing out favors to lucky taxpayers was unseemly, and the close relationship between bureau employees and corporate taxpayers only made matters worse. The Mellon Treasury had something of an image problem, at least on Capitol Hill, where critics, including some Republicans, were quick to point the finger of suspicion.[10]

For all his tax-cutting zeal, Mellon was not quite single-minded in his pursuit of lower taxes. He split with some of his GOP colleagues to support the retention of both corporate and individual income taxes. In 1921, a group of conservative Republicans, led by Sen. Reed Smoot (R-UT), advanced a plan for a national sales tax. Smoot had enormous support among business leaders, although spokesmen for retail industries were leery of the effect such a tax might have on consumer purchasing. Nonetheless, a major contingent of business leaders longed desperately to use sales tax revenue as a replacement for the excess profits tax. Mellon resisted the idea, quashing it before Smoot could gather sufficient support on Capitol Hill.[11] Mellon, too, sought to repeal the profits tax, but he wanted to pay for it with a hike in regular corporate income taxes.

Mellon was all about rate reduction, but he was cautious when it came to sweeping structural reform. "It would not seem either wise or necessary to change from our present system of taxation to new and untried plans," he told Congress. "The income tax is firmly embedded in our system of taxation and the objections made are not to the principle of the tax but only to the excessively high rates."[12] Mellon understood the economic and political realities of his day. His version of fiscal conservatism was methodical and cautious. He was not one to support abrupt breaks with the past, especially when reform might threaten the stability and adequacy of federal revenue. Proven revenue tools were never to be abandoned lightly.

Mellon even had a few distinctly progressive ideas. He argued, for instance, that "earned" income from wages and salaries should be taxed more lightly than "unearned" income from investments. "The fairness of taxing more lightly income from wages, salaries, or from investments is beyond question," he wrote. "In the first case, the income is uncertain and limited in duration; sickness or death destroys it and old age diminishes it; in the other, the source of income continues; the income may be disposed of during a man's life and it descends to his heirs."[13]

This was a striking contention, especially coming from one of the richest people in America. But it was not out of character. Mellon believed that some degree of progressivity was necessary to forestall more radical attacks on capital. Such an argument did not sit well with many of his Republican colleagues, like Smoot, who longed to eliminate income taxes entirely. But Mellon remained committed to taming, not destroying, the income tax, saving progressive taxation from the excesses of its more ardent supporters, as well as its most bitter critics.

Indeed, for die-hard opponents of the federal income tax, the Mellon reforms of the 1920s were a mixed blessing. While they reduced the redistributive qualities of the federal tax system, they also ensured that the income tax would remain a fixture of national finance. First enacted in 1913, the income tax had grown dramatically during World War I, emerging with a highly progressive rate structure and a controversial cousin in the excess profits tax. Mellon tamed this system, reducing rates and abolishing the profits levy. In doing so, he stole the thunder of his more conservative colleagues. Mellon's tax ideology might be described as a form of corporate liberalism, with the secretary seeking to accommodate the reformist impulse so evident in wartime taxation.[14] Woodrow Wilson may have made the world safe for democracy, but Andrew Mellon made it safe for progressive taxation.

Excess Profits Taxation

The tax debates of the 1920s touched on any number of specific topics, but three dominated the decade: corporate income taxes, and the excess profits tax in particular; the estate tax; and the personal income tax. Mellon and the GOP establishment dispatched with the first issue immediately, engineering swift repeal of this controversial tax. But debate over excess profits taxation raised vital and persistent questions about what role, if any, the federal government should have in the disposition of corporate profits. Over the short term, Mellon and his Republican legislative majority answered this question decisively. But the issue did not disappear. In fact, corporate tax reform figured prominently in the fiscal debates of the interwar period, coming to a head during the New Deal and World War II.

The excess profits tax was the most important fiscal innovation to emerge from World War I. In general, of course, the war had worked dramatic change on the tax system. Revenue climbed from $512.7 million in fiscal 1916 to $5.4 billion in fiscal 1920.[15] The United States managed to cover nearly a third of its war costs with taxation, a feat unmatched by other combatants.[16] Steep rates on personal income helped produce this revenue, with the top marginal rate soaring from 15 percent in 1916 to 77 percent in 1918. Meanwhile, the number of taxpayers increased, too, with Congress lowering exemptions to broaden the base of this highly productive tax.[17] But excess profits taxation was the centerpiece of wartime finance, providing roughly two-thirds of total revenue during the fighting.[18] Originally levied on both corporations and individuals, it was designed as a bulwark against war profiteering. Liberals hoped, however, that it would become much more. Specifically, they sought to retain the tax after the war as a tool for regulating business and promoting social equity.

Over the course of the war, 27 countries adopted some form of excess profits taxation. The tax proved to be a prodigious source of revenue, and many countries, including the United States, expanded its scope to tax away not simply war profits but "excess" profits that might or might not be the direct result of war.[19] Rep. Claude Kitchin (D-NC) was an outspoken advocate of excess profits taxation, and as chairman of the House Ways and Means Committee from 1915 to 1919, he was in a position to do something about it. Kitchin and a group of like-minded Democrats insisted that war taxes serve progressive ends. Specifically, they sought to use the federal tax system as a tool for regulating business and constraining monopoly power. President Wilson cast his lot with this progressive coalition, cooperating to fashion what Elliot Brownlee has called a "democratic-statist" tax system. Marked by steep levies on wealth and income, this tax regime survived the war, even as its centerpiece, the excess profits tax, fell victim to a conservative onslaught.[20]

First enacted in 1917, the excess profits tax imposed a graduated rate structure on all corporate profits above a predetermined "normal" rate of return on invested capital. The rate of tax increased with the rate of return, ensuring that highly profitable companies paid more than less profitable ones. This invested capital standard for measuring excess profits was controversial. In fact, leading officials in the Treasury Department came to oppose it, arguing that wartime profits should instead be measured against an average of prewar profits. Using invested capital as a benchmark, they contended, allowed overcapitalized businesses to escape much of their rightful burden, while small, lightly capitalized companies often paid dearly. But despite administration pleas, Kitchin remained firm in his support for the invested capital standard. Although he eventually agreed to a hybrid design that incorporated elements of both measures, Kitchin believed the invested capital standard was necessary if the tax were to survive in the postwar era.[21]

Even before the war ended, a broad cross-section of American political leaders began to reconsider steep wartime taxes, eagerly anticipating a return to peacetime levels of revenue extraction. Two of Wilson's Treasury secretaries, Carter Glass and David Houston, suggested the need for cuts. And even Wilson held out the possibility of relief: "The Congress might well consider," he suggested, "whether the higher rates of income and profits taxes can in peace times be effectively productive of revenue and whether they may not, on the contrary, be destructive of business activity and productive of waste and inefficiency."[22] And while the president endorsed retention of the excess profits tax, many critics were determined to see it repealed.[23]

Business leaders had never reconciled themselves to the excess profits tax, and with hostilities over, they began to lobby hard for repeal. One contemporary observer likened their efforts to a "crusade," and so it seemed.[24] The U.S. Chamber of Commerce, the National Retail Dry

Goods Association, the Tax League of America, the Association of Credit Men, the Merchant's Association of New York, and many other business groups urged repeal.[25] One somewhat dubious survey by the Fidelity & Deposit Company of Maryland found that repeal was "favored in every state," as was imposition of a new federal sales tax.[26] The National Economic League—an organization of leading figures in academia, government, and the business community—reported that 75 percent of its members opposed retention of the excess profits tax.[27]

Critics of the profits tax insisted that it was arbitrary in incidence and complex in administration. Business leaders resented its heavy burden, and they insisted that consumers were picking up the tab in the form of higher prices. Left unchecked, these higher prices would impoverish millions of Americans. "Present conditions are grinding these people down, using up their savings, and rushing them to pauperism," declared one business speaker. Such privation was a breeding ground for communism, leaving the United States in grave peril. "For economic reasons, for patriotic reasons, and for the sake of unification of national thought and purpose, we must do away with the present law," the speaker declared.[28]

In the hallowed halls of the Treasury, Andrew Mellon heard such complaints with a sympathetic ear. He was already convinced that excess profits taxation was a drag on business—no small issue as the country struggled with a postwar recession. Moreover, Mellon resented the very qualities that made the tax popular among progressives: its tendency to shift the burden to corporations and their wealthy shareholders. In his annual report for 1921, Mellon paid lip service to the wartime necessity of taxing excess profits. During the emergency, he wrote, the levy had generated much-needed revenue. In peacetime, however, its capricious incidence and extraordinary complexity made it an albatross around the neck of American business.[29]

On April 30, 1921, Mellon asked Congress to repeal the profits tax.[30] Most Republicans on Capitol Hill were eager to comply, but "farm bloc" Republicans from the Midwest required some coaxing. Many Senate GOP members were particularly reluctant to sign on. Since the end of World War I, the old-line Republican leadership in the Senate, once dominated by northeastern warhorses like Sen. Nelson Aldrich (R-RI), had lost much of its control in the chamber. A new group of progressive, western Republicans had captured key positions in the leadership, including the chairmanship of several important committees. Often allied with Democrats on various issues, most notably agriculture policy, the farm bloc Republicans were substantially more progressive than Mellon and old-line colleagues. In fact, they were often sympathetic to progressive tax reforms, including proposals for relatively steep taxes on wealth and income.[31]

Democrats were broadly opposed to Mellon's proposed tax cuts, but their opposition was futile once GOP members fell into line with the Treasury program. Meanwhile, the excess profits tax was under attack from some of the same fiscal experts who had once championed it. Thomas S. Adams, arguably the most influential tax expert of his day, offered a stinging critique. A trusted adviser to Treasury officials in both the Wilson and Harding administrations, Adams had helped design the profits tax. But by 1918, he had lost faith, unhappy with its real-world administration if not its theoretical justification. Having once defended the levy as a means to "allay hostility to big business," Adams now decried it as burdensome, complicated, and inequitable. Business leaders, he warned, understandably resented its "intricacy and capricious inequalities." Government officials, moreover, had found the tax hard to administer.[32]

Columbia University economist Edwin R. A. Seligman was another vocal critic. More conservative than Adams, Seligman was a leading light of the economics profession and a pioneer in the modern study of taxation. With strong support from the business community, Seligman argued that the excess profits tax posed a threat to corporate autonomy and economic efficiency. While supporting progressive taxation generally, he insisted that the excess profits tax was an unwise instrument of tax fairness. The invested capital standard of measuring excess profits had none of the advantages inherent in less convoluted taxes on either income or capital. It was an unfortunate hybrid, he argued, that served no purpose other than to "penalize enterprise and ingenuity." As an alternative, Seligman endorsed broader use of the federal income tax, perhaps even including a graduated rate structure for corporate taxpayers.[33]

Not every economist was a critic. Robert Murray Haig, a Seligman protégé and colleague at Columbia, offered a compelling case for retention. The tax, insisted this adviser to the Roosevelt Treasury, was both just and practical—or at least it might be, if Congress would enact several key reforms to simplify its administration. Compared with its alternatives, including higher income taxes or a national sales tax, the profits tax was far superior. Policymakers should "continue the policy of skimming the richer crocks of milk," he counseled, rather than opting for less progressive alternatives.[34] Similarly, economist David Friday offered argued that the tax was fair and efficient. "The excess profits tax or some other form of tax on differential profits should be continued not merely because it is just and furnishes a much-needed correction to the workings of our price system," he wrote. "It is the tax that least impedes enterprise and business activity." By falling most heavily on companies with the largest profits, the tax also allocated the burden to those entities best able to pay.[35]

But the forces arrayed against the excess profits tax were irresistible. Even some Democrats joined the campaign for repeal. Wilson's Treasury secretary Carter Glass, never a loud voice for progressive taxation but still a Democrat, insisted in 1919 that the tax "encourages wasteful expenditure, puts a premium on overcapitalization and a penalty on brains, energy, and enterprise, discourages new ventures, and confirms old ventures and their monopolies."[36] Most Democrats, however, remained firmly opposed. Claude Kitchin, hobbled by a stroke in 1920, offered a passionate objection. "Why in the name of right and justice should these big profiteering corporations and the millionaires and multimillionaires who filled their rapacious maw with these fabulous billions of blood money be relieved of taxation?" he asked.[37]

Republican leaders engineered quick approval in the House, but in the Senate, a debate over sales taxation slowed the move for repeal. Sen. Smoot proposed a national retail sales tax, and he had considerable support among Senate leaders as well as the business community. Sen. George Higgins Moses (R-NH) offered a colorful, if intemperate, appeal, insisting that a sales tax would "strike down the vicious principle of graduated taxation which appears in the pending [House] tax bill, and which is but a modern legislative adaptation of the Communistic doctrine of Karl Marx." Moses failed to persuade his colleagues, especially when Mellon sided with opponents of the sales tax. Meanwhile, a strong coalition of Democrats and progressive Republicans challenged the bill on the Senate floor, resisting the sales tax and insisting on higher income tax rates. This "agricultural block"—derided as the "wild asses of the desert" by their enemies—also pushed for steeper estate tax rates, as well as higher corporate income taxes.[38]

Outside the Capitol, farm and labor groups continued to agitate against the Mellon reforms; the American Farm Bureau Federation, the National Grange, and the American Federation of Labor (AFL) were particularly vocal. And they reserved special animus for Smoot's sales tax. Farm groups had long been reliable advocates of progressive taxation—and vituperative opponents of any reforms they considered regressive. Grange spokesman R. T. C. Atkeson declared that Smoot and his like-minded supporters wanted to lift the burden from a small minority "and saddle it on many who are less able to pay."[39] Similarly, J. R. Howard of the Farm Bureau told supporters that "strenuous efforts are being made to place the burden of taxation on farmers and homeowners" by repealing excess profits taxes and reducing rates for the personal and corporate income levies.[40] The AFL, meanwhile, added its voice to those skeptical of Mellon's plan. Notably, the group endorsed retention of existing excise taxes, characterizing most of them as "luxury taxes" and comparing them favorably with a general sales tax. Any move to enact the latter, the group warned, would constitute an attempt to shift the tax burden from capital to labor. Taken together, such vigorous opposition from farm and labor groups had a sobering effect on lawmakers, prompting most to abandon serious interest in a sales tax.[41]

In fact, opposition to the sales tax emerged in the business community as well, with the National Industrial Conference Board, the National Association of Credit Men, the U.S. Chamber of Commerce, and other groups joining the opposition. These business groups worried that a sales tax would slow economic recovery, raising prices and depressing demand. Ultimately, these sales tax opponents triumphed. Nearing the end of the session, harried lawmakers agreed to a relatively moderate package of reforms, with no sales tax in sight. But the excess profits tax was firmly dispatched. Lawmakers replaced some of its lost revenue with a hike in corporate income tax rates, much as Mellon had requested.[42]

Critics of the 1921 revenue act complained that it was a pastiche of unrelated, politically driven compromises. Republicans were disappointed in its modest rate reductions. "When the bill becomes law it will be the present revenue baby merely dressed in pink instead of red," Sen. Smoot observed bitterly. But at least one contemporary observer thought the country had dodged a bullet. "The leaders of each of the contesting parties," observed economist Roy Blakey, "as well as the nation at large, had cause to be thankful that the law was no worse than it was."[43]

Estate Taxes

Lawmakers of the 1920s just couldn't decide what to do with the estate tax. Andrew Mellon argued repeatedly for its reduction and repeal. But Republican members of Congress were far from unanimous in supporting such a move, and Democrats opposed it consistently. As a result, the

tax had a rough ride for the first half of the decade, with legislators raising it dramatically, only to slash it severely a couple of years later. Ultimately, they left it close to where they found it: heavier than Mellon had
hoped, but lighter than progressives had urged.

In his first major tax initiative, Mellon did not ask Congress for changes
to the estate tax. But he made clear his distaste for the levy, insisting that
its wartime rates, which reached a peak of 25 percent on the largest fortunes, were "fundamentally wrong." The tax was a levy upon capital, he
said, and it tended to destroy what capital it collected by using it for the
regular operating expenses of the government. Moreover, the tax was
more destructive of economic value than its revenues would suggest.
Forced to liquidate property and other less-than-liquid assets in order to
pay the tax, heirs found the value of their inheritances plummeting. "It
has become notorious in recent years," Mellon told lawmakers, "whenever a man of means dies, leaving his estate to pay a large amount by way
of taxes or debts, or both, that there is an immediate decline in all classes
of securities in which he is known to be interested." By requiring fire-sale
liquidations, the tax served the interests of neither heirs nor the fisc;
"the effect of this breaking down of values," Mellon contended, "tends
directly toward making the tax less productive of revenue." By depressing the value of the estate, forced liquidations reduced the tax base for
the estate levy.[44]

In 1924, Mellon got a nasty surprise when Congress abruptly raised
estate tax rates. Western Republicans in the House of Representatives
had added the hike to Mellon's package of income tax cuts, which was
then sailing easily through the chamber. Democrats, of course, were only
too happy to help, and a similar bipartisan coalition managed to keep the
Senate on board. Lawmakers also tacked on a gift tax, designed to prevent evasion of the estate levy. Absent a gift tax, many taxpayers would
be able to avoid the estate tax by disposing of the bulk of their property
during the latter days of their life.

When the bill finally arrived on the desk of President Calvin Coolidge,
this very conservative Republican held his nose and signed it. Both he
and Mellon were extremely displeased with the estate provisions, which
hiked the top rate from 25 percent to 40 percent. They also detested the
bill's provision for income tax publicity; Sen. Robert M. La Follette Jr.
(D-WI), long a champion of making returns public, had convinced his
colleagues that the BIR should annually release a list of taxpayers, includ-

ing their incomes and taxes paid. But Coolidge reasoned that some tax relief was better than none, and since the bill included a cut in marginal income tax rates, he reluctantly decided to approve it.[45]

Progressives had reason to celebrate, but Mellon soon came roaring back with another plan to slash taxes, and this time he put the estate tax at the top of his list. In October 1925, he asked the Ways and Means Committee to repeal the tax entirely. This field of taxation should be left to the states, he insisted. It was defensible on the federal level only as a wartime emergency measure. "We ought not to use our reserves in time of peace," he said. "We may need them badly when the next emergency arises."[46]

As a rule, tax experts dismissed these arguments, as well as Mellon's complaints about the destruction of capital. "This whole outcry against an estate tax because of the destruction of capital idea seems to me to be bordering on the absurd," said Edwin Seligman in testimony before the Ways and Means Committee.[47] "The estate tax is the result of one of the modern democratic movements of the world. When you have a democracy you have an income tax and an estate tax."[48] Thomas Adams, while not comfortable with existing estate rates as high as 40 percent, insisted that the federal tax could and should impose an estate levy of some sort.[49] Indeed, economists, including the conservative ones, tended to view the estate tax sympathetically. It was clearly consistent with ability-to-pay standards of tax fairness, and it raised significant revenue.

Congress was in the mood to cut taxes, but lawmakers eventually struck a compromise of sorts. Rep. John Nance Garner, a rising Democratic star, managed to fend off outright repeal of the estate tax, aided by the independent-minded GOP chairman of the Ways and Means Committee, William Green (R-IA). As eventually signed into law, the Revenue Act of 1926 slashed the top estate tax rate to 20 percent, below where it had been when lawmakers chose to increase it just two years earlier. Congress also granted a rebate to taxpayers for revenue collected under the 1924 estate rates that exceeded what would have been collected had the 1921 rates been in effect. In other words, the heirs of anyone who had died over the previous two years got quite a windfall, in many cases totaling several million dollars.[50] In a final blow against this most progressive of modern taxes, lawmakers acceded to Mellon's request that they repeal the gift tax. With no restriction on inter vivos gifts, the estate tax was reduced to a mere shell: 1926 was not a good year for advocates of wealth taxation.

Income Taxes

Ultimately, the most important revenue debates of the 1920s centered on individual income taxes. For Mellon, cutting surtaxes was of paramount importance, since he believed that steep rates served to hinder the economy and depress tax revenues. But for Democrats and progressive Republicans, these surtax rates were central to the fairness of the overall federal tax system. In addition, Mellon and his ideological opponents squared off over exemptions, with Democrats agitating for a dramatic increase and Mellon opposing the move. Ultimately, lawmakers would settle on a compromise that gave Mellon his rate cuts and Democrats their exemption hike. The bargain was politically expedient but fiscally disastrous.

In 1921, Mellon convinced Congress that wartime surtaxes were too steep, and lawmakers cut the top rate from 65 percent to 50 percent. Taxpayers in lower brackets also got a cut, helping boost the political appeal of the Mellon agenda.[51] In 1924, the Treasury secretary reprised his argument, and lawmakers agreed to further reductions, cutting both normal rates and surtaxes. This time, however, Democrats advanced a plan to raise exemptions, arguing that the income tax should remain a narrow burden for the rich; middle-class taxpayers should, they insisted, be exempt. Democrats lost the argument in 1924, but two years later they got the narrow tax they wanted.

Mellon began the 1924 debate by urging lawmakers to cut income taxes, restating his 1921 case that lower rates would raise revenue and promote economic growth. Existing taxes were simply too high, he told congressional taxwriters. "Ways will always be found to avoid taxes so destructive in their nature," he wrote the chairman of the House Ways and Means Committee, "and the only way to save the situation is to put the taxes on a reasonable basis that will permit business to go on and industry to develop." Failure to do so would have dire consequences, he warned. "The alternative is a gradual breakdown in the system and a perversion of industry that stifles our progress as a nation," he declared. Mellon suggested a top rate of 25 percent, insisting that lower surtaxes would reduce the incentive for tax avoidance.[52] He also proposed a special tax break for earned income, amounting to a 25 percent reduction for wages and salaries.

The secretary encountered significant resistance among legislators. With a smaller congressional majority than they had enjoyed in 1921,

Republicans had less room to maneuver. Rep. Garner seized the opportunity to launch a Democratic attack.

Garner is best remembered for his later assessment of the vice presidency; the office, he reportedly sneered in 1932, "isn't worth a pitcher of warm spit." The quote may be apocryphal, but one thing is certain: Garner deserves a better epitaph. The plain-spoken Democrat from Uvalde, Texas, played a vital role in crafting fiscal policy during the latter half of the 1920s.

"Cactus Jack" Garner was born November 22, 1868, in Red River County, Texas. After a comfortable childhood, he ventured off to college at the University of Tennessee. But Garner was no scholar, and he soon returned home and began working in a local law office. Apprenticeship was a popular route to law practice in the late 19th century, and Garner soon passed the bar and launched his political career.

After brief stints as a county judge and state lawmaker, Garner won election to the House of Representatives in 1902. For years thereafter, he was a loyal soldier in the chamber's Democratic ranks. His constancy earned him a spot on the Ways and Means Committee, and by 1921 he was the ranking minority member.

Garner believed that the Mellon tax cuts were grossly lopsided. "This is the time to determine the policy of who is going to pay the taxes," he told one observer. "The crux of the fight is the surtax. The Mellon 25 percent maximum is at least 10 or 15 per cent too low."[53] Garner stressed the uneven incidence of the Mellon plan, insisting that a coterie of economic giants would reap enormous benefits while the vast majority of taxpayers would get a relative pittance. Just six taxpayers, Garner said, would split among themselves a tax cut of almost $10 million. Meanwhile, 1 million taxpayers in the lower brackets would have to share a cut of less than $1.3 million.[54]

As an alternative, Garner suggested a smaller cut in surtaxes coupled with a substantial boost in exemptions. Under his plan, Americans of modest means would see their income tax burden vanish. "Would any of you say, or would anyone on God's green earth except [current representative and future Treasury secretary] Ogden Mills and Andrew Mellon say, that a married man is not entitled to an exemption of $3,000 before you start to tax him?" he asked his colleagues. The income tax was never intended to burden such people. "When you adopted the income tax amendment to the Constitution you did it in order to tax the rich," Garner said. Existing exemptions—$2,500 for families and $1,000 for individuals—ignored this obvious intent. The only reason to tax small incomes, Garner charged, was to destroy the income tax by undermining its popular appeal. "You want to break down the income-tax system," he scolded GOP colleagues, "and as long as you have him [the taxpayer] paying taxes on an income of from two to three thousand dollars a year he is dissatisfied with the law."[55]

Garner mustered a good head of steam in his denunciation of low exemptions, but he had a very narrow sense of what it meant to be rich in America. An exemption of $3,000 would have left the vast majority of the population beyond the taxman's grasp.[56] The income tax was already narrow, affecting only a small percentage of the population. Garner's plan was to make it narrower still, restricting the levy to the very top echelon of American society.

Republican leaders attacked Garner's substitute bill, declaring it a mishmash of bad economics and political opportunism. "You have heard of great musicians sitting down at a piano and improvising a tune," declared Rep. Ogden L. Mills Jr. (R-NY). "Mr. Garner sits down at a table in this chamber and improvises a tax bill."[57] But Garner was gaining ground, securing the votes of virtually all Democrats and even some progressive Republicans. Within three weeks, Republican leaders capitulated, with House Speaker Nicholas Longworth (R-OH) agreeing to higher surtax rates, and even a dramatic hike in estate taxes.[58]

The exemption hike, however, did not survive partisan wrangling over the 1924 revenue bill; Garner sacrificed it in favor of higher rates. But neither did the idea disappear. Support ran deep among Democrats, and Mellon worried that it would quickly reappear on the congressional agenda. He took pains to attack the proposal. "If taxation is to be successful as a revenue producer in times of depression as well as in times of business prosperity," he told legislators in November 1925, "it must have a broad base as a foundation." Raising exemptions would rob the income tax of its stability and revenue productivity. While the economy continued to chug along, the effect of such a cut was minor. But when the business cycle turned, lawmakers would suddenly find themselves with a deeply inadequate revenue system. "From a revenue standpoint alone it is exceedingly dangerous to take out the lower tiers of this pyramid of taxation, since it is upon this broad base that a continuous source of revenue must rest," he wrote.[59]

Mellon also believed that levying income taxes on people of modest means had salutary political effects. "As a matter of policy," he contended, "it is advisable to have every citizen with a stake in his country. Nothing brings home to a man the feeling that he personally has an interest in seeing that Government revenues are not squandered, but intelligently expended, as the fact that he contributes individually a direct tax, no matter how small, to his Government."[60] Critics pointed out that indirect taxes, including excises on various consumer goods, might have a similar effect on fiscal vigilance. But Mellon believed that direct taxes played a unique role in the nation's fiscal health, not just for the revenue they provided, but for the visibility they gave to the federal tax burden.

Such arguments did nothing to sway Democrats, who revived their argument for higher exemptions in 1926. The 1924 tax law had amounted to half a loaf for Mellon; modest surtax cuts had come at the steep price of a major estate tax hike. So two years later, the secretary made another try, proffering his familiar argument that lower rates would raise more revenue by boosting the economy.[61] And this time, the secretary got enormous help from private-sector lobbyists, who organized "tax clubs" to lobby members of Congress. The clubs claimed to be grassroots organizations, but critics considered them ill-informed, partisan mouthpieces for the rich.[62] As one liberal Republican complained,

> Men of wealth are naturally interested in tax reduction that will benefit themselves, and no one gainsays the right or the desire to relieve them from tax burdens; but the blackjack method of intimidating Congress to relieve a handful of wealthy men, to the exclusion of the rest of the country, is perilous to any system of representative government.[63]

As it happened, Congress needed little convincing; lawmakers of both parties rushed to sweeten the Mellon proposals. With the progressive wing of the Republican party in disarray and many Democrats throwing in their lot with GOP tax cutters, the success of the Mellon proposals was never in much doubt. Garner, however, took the opportunity to resurrect his plan for higher income tax exemptions, and this time his colleagues agreed. The Revenue Act of 1926 raised exemptions across the board, removing from the rolls more than a third of the nation's 7.3 million income taxpayers in one fell swoop.[64]

The exemption hikes were not part of Mellon's plan. Indeed, he had opposed the idea consistently and emphatically. But the buoyant economy robbed Mellon of his most compelling argument: that narrow income taxes were a dangerously unstable source of revenue. And his insistence that broader taxes were the only way to promote fiscal vigilance among the middle and lower classes struck many progressives as outrageous. "Surely the Secretary of the Treasury can not intend, with a stroke of his mighty pen, to expatriate 96 per cent of us," noted the *Omaha World-Herald:*

> We pay taxes on our coats, on our shoes and socks, on our hats, on our shorts and underwear, on the food on the breakfast-table, on the materials of which are homes are constructed, on the furniture in them, on the vehicles we ride in, on the amusements wherein we seek surcease—on practically everything, indeed, that we have and do. Do not these payments entitle us to feel equally with Mr. Mellon, that we have a stake in our country?[65]

Poor Americans did, indeed, pay a host of taxes, most of them on consumption. Many excise taxes enacted during World War I remained on the books, imposing their regressive burden on a wide range of consumer goods and services.

Rep. Cordell Hull (D-TN) was an original champion of the modern income tax, playing a key role in the debate over the Sixteenth Amendment and helping shape the wartime tax system. He was certainly an advocate for progressive revenue policy, and for that very reason, he too opposed any move to narrow the scope of the income tax. "A tax system vitally important as is the income tax should apply to a respectable number of persons," he warned his colleagues.[66] Narrowing it too much would endanger the very existence of the income tax, leaving it vulnerable to charges that it was class legislation.

Moreover, Hull pointed out, leaving exemptions unchanged would make room in the budget to cut consumption taxes. Taxes on shoes and socks, and hats, and underwear were remnants of the wartime tax system. By keeping the income tax reasonably broad, lawmakers would have enough money to repeal these levies. Eliminating them "would afford not only a greater measure of tax relief to the small-income taxpayers, whose exemption is proposed, but to some two or three million other persons with small incomes who pay automobile taxes but no income taxes."[67]

It was a powerful argument, and it had some limited support among Democrats. Rep. Henry Rainey (D-IL) argued vigorously against higher exemptions, insisting that they actually served the interests of rich taxpayers. "This bill expresses a tender solicitude for the very rich in which I do not share," he declared. Higher exemptions would apply to everyone, lowering the average tax rate for all income taxpayers, not just those removed from the rolls. "In order to exempt these 3,000,000 taxpayers, we have, of course, exempted every income-tax payer," he complained.

"It is a horizontal exemption clipped off of the taxes paid by the entire bloc of income-tax payers." As an alternative, Rainey suggested repeal of the federal automobile excise tax. The Ways and Means Committee had rejected that idea as too expensive. The tax was "immensely productive," the committee explained, making it impossible to eliminate. While agreeing to cut taxes on auto parts—the so-called tax on misfortune since it burdened people with broken cars—the committee refused to abolish the larger tax. Rainey was unsatisfied. "We are not rendering much of a favor to men of small incomes," he complained, "when we relieve them of the income tax they now pay of about $7.50 and impose a tax of from $15 to $30 on the cheap automobiles they buy."[68]

The Hull-Rainey argument cut across political lines, uniting a small contingent of Democrats with a much larger group of conservative Republicans. But the argument never caught on. Traditional divisions on the income tax persisted, with Democrats supporting a narrow, steep levy and Republicans endorsing a broader, flatter tax.

Outside Congress, opinions on the exemption hike were mixed. Farm groups endorsed the idea. "In many sections of the country," observed E. B. Reid of the American Farm Bureau Federation, "the income tax law is an unfathomable mystery to the man of small income." Business spokesmen, by contrast, generally opposed the move. Some echoed Mellon's argument that the income tax gave people a stake in their government. L. R. Gottlieb of the National Industrial Conference Board suggested that exemptions were already too generous. "Any movement toward freeing larger numbers of our population from the obligation of supporting to some extent the Federal Government in a tangible, conscious manner would be inconsistent with the sound development of representative government," he said. Similarly, Edward P. Doyle of the Real Estate Board of New York insisted that poor people were already getting a good deal. Without specifying exactly what largesse they enjoyed, Doyle contended that poor Americans got more than their fair share of government benefits. "The poor man gets everything and he spends $3,500,000,000 for prize fights and baseball games and chewing gum and beauty parlors, and yet he objects to paying any tax at all." Not surprisingly, Doyle endorsed excise taxes, like those on entertainment, gum, and cosmetics.[69]

Academics tended to agree with conservative leaders, resisting higher exemptions. Edwin Seligman told the Ways and Means Committee that taxes must remain reasonably broad. "It will not do," he said, "to have all the rights on one side and all the obligations on the other side. If you are developing a community where only one class pays the taxes, and the other class, because of its immense numbers, votes the expenditures, you are opening the door for all sorts of political abuses."[70] Like Hull, Seligman believed deeply in the income tax, even endorsing a progressive rate structure. But in his view, high exemptions were a threat to the tax, inviting political trouble. If the tax were to survive, then it should be getting broader, not narrower.

Nonetheless, 1926 was a year for tax cuts, and Garner's exemption hike became part of the package. Mellon swallowed hard and accepted the change as the price of his marginal rate cuts. In a few years, the Treasury chief would have cause to regret that decision, but for the time being, it seemed a reasonable expedient.

As Mellon surveyed his seven years in office at the end of the 1920s, he must have been pleased. To be sure, he had compromised prodigiously with Democrats, as well as more liberal members of his own party. The income tax had grown more central to the federal revenue system, especially after Prohibition dried up alcohol excise revenue. But rates had declined dramatically since 1921. And while Mellon never succeeded in his quest to eliminate the estate tax, he did manage to keep its rates relatively modest. All in all, taxes were less burdensome for many Americans, particularly those in the upper strata of society. These were happy years for tax policymakers of both parties. They had the pleasant task of choosing among various tax cuts, their deliberations buoyed by a fat and happy Treasury. As Franklin Roosevelt later pointed out, "it was all very merry while it lasted."[71]

Taxation for Depression

The Great Depression wreaked havoc on the federal budget. By 1930, Andrew Mellon was warning Congress that declining revenues would produce a deficit of $200 million. His projection proved optimistic, and lawmakers watched the fiscal gap soar to more $900 million. As one observer recalled, "The sun was sinking in a cloudy western sky."[72]

Despite the prospect of even larger deficits to come, Mellon and President Herbert Hoover continued to resist tax increases. But with national income falling from $87.8 billion to $42.5 billion between 1929 and 1932—and tax revenues falling at an even faster rate, thanks to the progressive rate structure of the individual income tax—such intransigence could not last.[73] Early in 1932, Mellon appeared before the House Ways and Means Committee to ask for a tax hike. It was a painful request for this inveterate tax cutter, but one dictated by fiscal orthodoxy. Like almost all national political leaders of his time, Mellon believed firmly in the importance of a balanced budget. Since the Civil War, Republicans had championed fiscal balance as a means to keep tariff rates high; determined to protect manufacturers from foreign competition, they had used budget balance as a justification for steep import duties. In the 1920s, income taxes replaced the tariff as the principal source of federal revenue. GOP commitment to balanced budgets, however, remained constant.

The orthodox commitment to balanced budgets was not simple-minded, nor was it rooted entirely in some inchoate cultural commitment to thrift. While the latter was important for many policymakers, especially on Capitol Hill, more sophisticated thinkers also believed that excessive government borrowing was dangerous to the nation. Too much could imperil the nation's credit system, destabilizing markets, worsening the depression, and making recovery all but impossible. In light of later economic theory, such arguments seem badly misguided. And even at the time, many policymakers worried that slavish devotion to an annually balanced budget could lead to dangerous tax hikes that might make the depression even worse. But most political leaders, and many of the economists who advised them, were concerned that unchecked red ink posed a bigger threat. Some sort of revenue increase, they counseled, was necessary.[74]

For much of the 1920s, balance had been easy to achieve. A steady flow of tax dollars, coupled with spending restraint under a series of GOP presidents, had made for a comfortable surplus. But in the face of depression, the GOP commitment to balanced budgets required painful choices. Specifically, it demanded a major tax hike. Democrats, meanwhile, were trying to cast themselves as the party of fiscal discipline, and soaring deficits under a GOP administration gave them ample partisan fodder. As a result, Mellon, his allies, and even his opponents joined forces to staunch the flow of red ink—even if it meant raising taxes.[75]

In a sign of things to come, Mellon asked Ogden Mills, appointed undersecretary of the Treasury in 1927, to read the department's statement on tax reform. Within a month, Mellon would be eased out of the Treasury, dispatched to London as an ambassador. This towering figure of the 1920s was being put out to pasture. Hoover named Mills to replace the fiscal titan, and the new secretary offered the administration his financial expertise and political acumen. An upper-class New York Republican of orthodox fiscal inclinations, Mills believed deeply in the need to shrink the federal deficit. During his early career in the House of Representatives, Mills had served on the Ways and Means Committee. "Little Oggie," as he was known in the liberal press, had developed a reputation as a tax expert.[76]

Amid the sales tax furor of 1921, Mills had proffered a novel, if short-lived, proposal for a "spendings" tax. Like a traditional sales tax, the spendings tax was to be levied on the money that taxpayers spent on various goods. Unlike a sales tax, however, its rates would increase along with the amount spent. The point, Mills explained, was to promote thrift and saving, while avoiding the regressive pitfalls associated with a traditional sales tax. "It can fairly claim the virtues of the sales tax, being in effect a tax on money spent for consumption, without being regressive in character or laying a disproportionate burden on those least able to bear it," he explained.[77] It was a provocative idea, but not a new one. John Stuart Mill had proposed something similar in 1848. As Mills pointed out, that proposal had been criticized as a sop to the rich, but the utilitarian philosopher had insisted that it only benefited those who saved, rather than those who spent their money. And since saved money was generally invested in productive enterprise, society as a whole benefited from a preferential treatment of saved income. In the 1920s, the spendings tax had found important intellectual support, especially from Thomas Adams. But it was still an idea ahead of its time, and Mills's proposal went nowhere. Some twenty years later, a Democratic administration would propose a similar tax—with similar, disappointing results.[78]

But in 1932, Mills was not proposing his spendings tax. In fact, he avoided recommending any sort of broad-based consumption tax. Before addressing the Ways and Means Committee, Mills had already done much of the hard work, convincing President Hoover that balancing the federal budget amidst economic depression was, in fact, a reasonable, if improbable, goal. With support from several other fiscal conservatives in the administration, he convinced the president to endorse a large package of tax increases. In his 1931 annual message to Congress, Hoover warned lawmakers that they must cut expenses and raise taxes. He stressed, however, that tax increases (and spending cuts) should be of limited size and duration. Excessive tax hikes, he declared, would "destroy confidence, denude commerce and industry of its resources, jeopardize the financial system, and actually extend unemployment and demoralize agriculture rather than relieve it."[79]

In presenting the administration's proposals, Mills warned that the deficit was soaring above $2 billion. Excessive expenditures, coupled with falling tax revenues, had opened a huge hole in the budget. The decline in tax revenue was particularly dramatic. Corporate income taxes, which had yielded $1.1 billion in fiscal 1930, were likely to raise only $550 million in 1932. Individual income tax rates were plummeting even more dramatically, from just over $1 billion in 1930 to $370 million in 1932. The only relatively bright spot was excise revenue, which Mills expected to decline from $628 million to $544 million over the same period; the moderate decline, he pointed out, was due largely to the stable revenues of the federal tobacco tax.[80]

Altogether, the revenue shortfalls were nothing short of cataclysmic. The problem, Mills declared, was inherent in the revenue structure. "The truth of the matter is that our revenue system rests on a comparatively narrow base," he explained, "and that our tax receipts are susceptible to the widest variations in accordance with variations in business conditions. This is particularly true of current individual income-tax collections." The progressive nature of the income tax made the problem worse; large incomes were the first to rise in good times and the first to fall in bad ones. The graduated rate structure ensured that revenues would rise faster than overall income when the economy was doing well. But it also guaranteed that when depression struck, revenues would fall faster than most incomes.[81]

Given this reality, Mills counseled against steep increases in the rate structure, predicting that they would not raise adequate revenue. While acknowledging that rates must necessarily rise, especially on the richest Americans, he emphasized the need for an increase in the number of people paying income taxes in the first place. Congress must recognize, he said, that "the weakness in our revenue system is, as I have already stated, the narrowness of the base on which it rests." Broadening that base was crucial to securing adequate, and dependable, revenue. It was also, he said, manifestly fair. "Many not now taxed are very definitely in a position to make some contribution to the support of Government," he declared. "They should be asked to do so, taking into consideration ability to pay."[82]

Mills made a point of not suggesting a general sales tax. Republicans had lost this battle in the twenties, and he was not about to saddle the

Hoover administration with this contentious issue. He did, however, lay out in some detail the success of Canada's broad-based sales tax, implicitly inviting lawmakers to consider the levy. While warning that such a tax could be difficult to administer in the United States, he had many favorable things to say about it. Nonetheless, when push came to shove, Mills counseled lawmakers to opt for more familiar taxes. "Instead of embarking on new and untried ventures in taxation," he suggested, "it is wiser to utilize a known general plan with such changes as may be appropriate in the light of altered conditions." While most observers took him at his word, others questioned his sincerity; many suspected that the Treasury would embrace a sales tax proposal were it to come from Congress.[83]

To close the budget gap, Mills suggested a package of tax hikes that would together raise about $920 million. First and foremost, he asked legislators to restore income tax rates to their 1924 levels. Surtax rates, he said, should increase across the board, topping out at 40 percent—twice their existing level. Even more important, Congress should reduce exemptions to $1,000 for individuals and $2,500 for married couples (down from $1,500 and $3,500, respectively). These reductions would broaden the tax base substantially, bringing 1.7 million new taxpayers into the system. The tax, Mills emphasized, would still be confined to a narrow slice of American society. "There would be only some 3,600,000 Federal taxpayers in a Nation of 120,000,000 people, and of this number less than 300,000 would contribute 90 percent of the tax." Indeed, Mills's plan would have left the tax much as it was before the 1926 exemption hike. Together, the higher rates and broader base would raise $83 million in the remainder of fiscal 1932, Mills predicted, and $185 million in fiscal 1933.[84]

Corporation income taxes should also rise, Mills said, climbing from 12 percent to 12.5 percent. Exemptions for the tax should be eliminated entirely. These changes would raise $60 million annually. And finally, Mills asked Congress to return estate tax rates to their 1921 level. While declaring his general dislike for the levy, he asked for a tax ranging from 1 percent on the first $50,000 up to 25 percent on amounts over $10 million. Estate tax hikes would bring in $22 million.[85]

These were dramatic recommendations, and a bitter pill for this scion of the Mellon regime. Ultimately, however, these plans proved less momentous than a host of smaller changes to what the Treasury called miscellaneous taxes. Noting that the depression had savaged individual and corporate income tax receipts, which were highly sensitive to economic fluctuations, Mills recommended a variety of new or increased excise levies, including taxes on tobacco, stock transfers, admissions, radio and phonograph equipment, bank checks, telephone calls, and telegrams. He also suggested additional taxes on the sale of automobiles and trucks. Altogether, Treasury predicted these increases would raise $514 million in fiscal 1933.[86]

A Broader, Steeper Income Tax

Hearings on the Treasury's revenue plan featured a running debate on income tax exemptions. Several business groups, including the U.S. Chamber of Commerce and the National Association of Manufacturers (NAM), endorsed the idea, arguing that it would raise revenue and promote tax consciousness. The latter effect, they maintained, would promote governmental thrift. As NAM representative James A. Emery put it, broadening the tax base would "arouse the tax consciousness of the individual citizen and excite his interest through his contribution so that he may realize the purposes for and the manner in which public funds are expended, and examine anew the function, objectives, and capacity of government to render service with the expenditures made." It was a familiar argument. But it found at least a few unfamiliar champions. In particular, the American Farm Bureau Federation, generally allied with partisans of a narrow tax, embraced the idea, though without much fervor. Leaders of the organization apparently worried that other, even less desirable taxes, were gaining too much political momentum. Broader income taxes, in other words, might head off plans for a sales tax. A spokesman for the National Grange offered similar, grudging support.[87]

Some committee members worried that lower exemptions would cost more to administer than they could ever raise in new revenue. Ways and Means chairman James Collier (D-MS) asked Mills whether a broader tax were even worth collecting:

> I recall that several years ago, there was a disputed tax item of less than $6, and on two different occasions the return was sent back by the Washington office to the taxpayer, and the revenue collector came 50 or 60 miles to a town where the taxpayer lived. His railroad fare, I suppose, was $3 or $4, and I do no know what his hotel bill was, but they finally got the $6.

Mills took the bait. "It seems to me," he responded dryly, "that that is a tribute to the efficiency of the department."[88] Mills assured the committee that broadening the income tax was both practical and necessary.

Critics of the broader income tax included liberal members of Congress, as well as labor leaders. Rep. Fiorello LaGuardia (R-NY) argued that low- and middle-income taxpayers already paid their fair share of state and local taxes, as well as federal excise levies. Rep. Charles Crisp (D-GA) pressed LaGuardia on whether broader income taxation might be defended as a means to promote governmental economy:

> Now, as a public policy, is it or is it not advisable to have as many citizens as can economically do so contribute to the maintenance of the Government? Will they not have more interest in the expenditures and affairs of the Government if they are directly contributing something, no matter how small, toward its maintenance?

This was a classic restatement of the tax visibility argument that conservatives advanced to defend a broader income levy. But LaGuardia would have none of it. "I think Mr. Average Citizen knows he is paying his share of the maintenance of government," LaGuardia said.[89]

Other witnesses agreed. Carlos B. Clark of the National Retail Dry Goods Association, for instance, argued that trying to balance the budget on the backs of taxpayers would damage the economy. He criticized a host of Mills's proposed increases, including the lower income tax exemptions. "I cannot bring myself to the belief that the lowering of the exemptions would be a good thing," he told the lawmakers, questioning whether the new revenue would be worth the administrative cost of collecting it. In addition, he agreed with committee members who argued that people with smaller incomes were already stretched thin. "It is only another burden on the man of small income, who is doing his best to help the other fellow."[90] Spokesmen for organized labor also opposed lower exemptions, with the AFL offering a strident critique. "The plan of the Treasury Department," the AFL spokesmen declared, "proposes that those who have suffered the most during this depression must pay the taxes of those who have neither hungered nor wanted for any of the necessaries of life."[91]

Fairness and Excise Taxation

Ways and Means members heard endless testimony from business groups seeking to avoid excise levies on their goods and services. Affected industries were quick to organize, claiming undue hardship. In fact, the issue arose during Mills's testimony, when Rep. Allen T. Treadway (R-MA) spoke up for the paper manufacturers. Treadway challenged the fairness of the administration's proposed tax on bank checks, suggesting that its flat rate made it unfair; the stamp would cost 2 cents whether a check were written for $1 or $1,000. Mills was unmoved: "Mr. Treadway, you have wrestled with these tax problems long enough to know that there is no tax devised by man that works with exact justice." Nonetheless, Mills said, the check tax came close. It would be levied at a low rate on a very broad base. In addition, the use of checks implied an ability to pay. Taken together, these qualities were the essence of a fair, practical, and economically efficient tax. It was an instructive response, encapsulating the Hoover administration's stance on excise levies. Taxing items of "wide use but not of first necessity" was a popular notion among Republicans and even many Democrats.[92]

Treadway then took a different tack, complaining that the check tax would hurt the paper industry. The argument also held no water with Mills. "Mr. Treadway, that is just the beginning of the stories you are going to hear over the next 10 days," he predicted. "I have seen the legion gathering and I could almost recite the story that each industry is going to tell. But the only way to raise money is to increase taxes, and some one has got to pay them."[93]

Several members pressed Mills on the absence of "luxury" taxes from his package of revenue proposals. Mills offered the Treasury Department's stock answer: taxes on furs, cosmetics, or other "luxuries" would raise little revenue but cause many problems. "All these luxury taxes are difficult and costly to collect, and the dealer or manufacturer who is honest pays them, and the dishonest one does not," Mills said. He pointed to his proposed automobile tax as an alternative, again outlining his definition of a good excise tax. The car tax, he said, "is easy to administer, can be imposed at a very low rate, that rests on a very broad base, and therefore imposes no particular hardship on anyone." Moreover, he added, anyone able to buy a car clearly had some ability to pay, making the tax fair.[94]

In general, affected industries were vocal in their efforts to deflect new taxes on their products. Often, they justified their position as a defense of progressivity, insisting that regressive excises would be passed on to consumers, including those least able to pay. At other times, however, they simply complained that the tax was too much for the industry to bear, particularly in hard economic times. Without offering specifics, they urged lawmakers to find other sources of new revenue.[95] Forty years later, another lawmaker would aptly describe this political dynamic: "don't tax you, don't tax me, tax that man behind the tree."[96]

Sales Tax

Business leaders unhappy with narrow excises often suggested a different revenue source to fill the gap: a general sales tax. NAM representatives approached the subject elliptically, urging that excise taxes be levied as broadly as possible. In case the committee missed the hint, they added, "We suggest, in this connection, exploration for new sources of income capable of yielding additional revenue, without being either burdensome to the taxpayer or expensive to collect." Other industry groups were less coy. The American Petroleum Institute spoke out against a new federal gas tax and in favor of a general sales levy. The American Hotel Association agreed, adding by way of justification that "the singling out of one commodity for tax exaction to the exclusion of another is not fair to business."[97]

But businesses did not all line up on the side of a sales tax. Indeed, even closely allied industries differed on the subject. Spokesmen for the American Manufacturers of Toilet Articles predictably opposed new excise levies on cosmetics, and when asked about a sales tax, demurely noted that "we ourselves are not particularly opposed to it." By contrast, the National Association of Retail Druggists opposed the sales tax, predicting that politically driven exemptions would quickly turn it into a less-than-comprehensive collection of excises.[98] Generally speaking, retailers were most likely to oppose the sales tax, while businesses in other sectors often found much to like. Manufacturers, while sometimes wary of the impact a sales tax might have on consumer purchasing, tended to prefer the levy to its most likely alternative: selective excises.

Outside the business community, sales tax support was harder to find. The American Farm Bureau Federation strenuously rejected the idea, noting that "a general sales tax is constantly opposed by the Farm Bureau for the broad reason that it is based on the necessity to consume rather than on the ability to pay." And the AFL attacked the levy as a cruel addition to the burden of working Americans. The proposal would shift the tax burden down the income ladder, spokesmen insisted. They compared its effect to a cold-hearted biblical injunction: "for unto everyone that hath shall be given, and he shall have abundance, but from him that hath not shall be taken away even that which he hath."[99]

Despite such objections, the committee showed considerable interest in a sales tax. Lawmakers listened attentively to Thomas Adams, who outlined details of the Canadian sales levy. While not precisely endorsing the tax, Adams gave it a warm review. Similarly, members entered into the record a report on the Canadian tax produced after publisher William Randolph Hearst arranged an all-expenses-paid trip for U.S. policymakers to meet with their Canadian counterparts and discuss the sales tax.[100]

Indeed, Hearst carried on a vigorous campaign against the income tax, promoting the sales tax as a workable alternative. He implored readers in a March 1932 editorial to "please carry on a sustained crusade Morning, Evening, and Sunday against the present Bolshevist system of income taxation." Meanwhile, other influential Democrats, most from the party's conservative wing, also lined up behind the sales tax bill, including Bernard Baruch, John J. Raskob, and Jouett Shouse, chairman of the Democratic National Executive Committee.[101]

When the Ways and Means Committee finally issued its report on the revenue bill, the influence of business arguments was clear to see. The panel recommended a general manufacturers' sales tax of 2.25 percent on all items except food. Arguing that a broad levy was fairer than one on selected items, the panel also insisted that it would not be regressive. The tax, according to the majority, would be so small as to be almost negligible. Moreover, a substantial portion of it would almost certainly be absorbed by manufacturers, rather than passed on to consumers in the form of higher prices. Not surprisingly, the committee noted with approval the Canadian sales tax of similar design.[102]

The Democratic majority offered a traditionally Republican argument for the tax, insisting that it would be progressive, not regressive in its operation. "It should also be pointed out," the panel contended, "that the more one spends the greater his tax under this manufacturers' excise tax. The poor man with small living expenses will pay much less than the wealthy man who lives in great luxury."[103] This argument hinged on the notion of free will; taxpayers could simply choose to consume less, thereby limiting their tax burden. It was a powerful argument, at least among Democratic leaders and their Republican bedfellows.

But these were also strange arguments for a Democratic committee; the party had a long history of opposing general sales taxes in any form. The fiscal crisis had apparently convinced party leaders that they had no alternative. "In these times of doubt and uncertainty, even more than in normal times, the unimpaired credit of the Federal Government is of paramount importance," the committee declared. "In the opinion of your committee the preservation, unimpaired, of the national credit is the most important single issue facing this country to-day, and it is con-fidently stated that this is only possible by taking those steps necessary to balance the Budget for 1933."[104] Such comments represented a strik-ing success for the Hoover administration, which had managed to make fiscal soundness a new touchstone for Democratic politics.

The most vigorous champions of the bill were Ways and Means senior Democrat Charles Crisp of Georgia and Majority Leader Henry Rainey of Illinois. Speaker of the House John Garner provided critical, if lukewarm, support for the Ways and Means bill, including its sales tax. His willing-ness to embrace the idea no doubt pleased William Randolph Hearst, who earlier in the year had launched a Garner for President campaign.[105] Pres-ident Hoover was probably pleased as well. Although he insisted that the sales tax was a Democratic idea, skeptics were unconvinced by his mod-esty.[106] Treasury Secretary Mills had already signaled his approval to House Democrats, and he applauded the House bill after its release.

Rebellion and Compromise

Not every Democrat was eager to cooperate with Hoover. Progressive leg-islators of both parties were appalled. In the Senate, Tom Walsh (D-MT) and Elmer Thomas (D-OK) were quick to oppose the sales tax, while in the House, Rep. Robert L. Doughton (D-NC)—known as "Muley" to the Washington cognoscenti—took the lead in a brewing rebellion. Doughton dissented from the Ways and Means report, and his stance against the sales tax grew stronger by the day. An outpouring of constituent com-plaints prompted his opposition, and many other lawmakers reported similar constituent opinion. Despite leadership assurances that the bill was highly progressive—Crisp insisted that "Wealth will say this bill is confiscatory"—outspoken Democrats began to denounce it.[107] One mem-ber of the House felt moved to offer his critique in verse:

> He was taxed on boots, was taxed on shoes, was taxed on suits and taxed on booze,
> Was taxed on socks, was taxed on hose, was taxed on everything that grows.
> A tax attacked him when he was born, attacked him till he felt forlorn.
> If they increase, as in this bill, it won't be long until they will
> Impose a tax on growing corn and on the toots of Gabriel's horn.[108]

Working closely with insurgent Republicans like Rep. Fiorello LaGuardia, Doughton helped orchestrate a series of votes that eventually killed the sales tax idea. It was a major setback for Democratic leaders, especially Garner, who found his presidential prospects considerably less bright in the wake of the sales tax fight. Garner eventually appealed to the House to pass some sort of tax bill raising new revenue. Failure to raise adequate revenue would imperil the nation, he declared. The speaker challenged every House member who agreed with the principle of a balanced budget to rise in their seats; no one remained seated. Lawmakers soon agreed on a compromise measure, featuring an array of new excise levies. Indeed, the sales tax rebellion prompted the House to embrace a collection of "miscellaneous" taxes not unlike the Treasury Department's original proposal. As passed by the House, the bill included taxes on luxuries like furs, jewelry, and yachts, as well as stock transfers and safety deposit boxes. It also hiked taxes on a range of more common goods.[109]

The House bill included higher income and estate tax rates, and it reimposed the federal gift tax. Significantly, it also reduced personal exemptions in line with administration proposals. The exemption cut was generally uncontroversial; in the midst of a revenue crisis, the idea seemed reasonable, especially since it still left the income tax very narrow in an overall sense. The tax emerging from the 1932 debate was certainly not broad-based. Indeed, with its higher rates on upper-income Americans, it was still very much the narrow, steep tax that Democrats had long championed.

As it left the chamber, the House bill was broadly viewed as inadequate, and senators were determined to write something better. Majority Leader Joe Robinson (D-AR) took a more pragmatic approach to the legislation than his House counterparts. In no hurry to throw in his lot with the Hoover administration, he heeded Democratic colleagues when they warned him against trying to revive the sales tax. Several progressive Republicans, including George Norris of Nebraska, William Borah of Idaho, Arthur Capper of Kansas, and John Blaine of Wisconsin, also signaled their opposition. In hearings before the Finance Committee, Treasury Secretary Mills attacked the numerous excises that emerged from the House debacle. Without endorsing a sales tax, he hinted broadly that the administration would welcome the idea. Senate conservatives began to marshal support for the idea, with Sen. Reed Smoot reprising his long-standing arguments for sales taxation. And when the Finance Committee—under the conservative but pragmatic leadership of chairman Pat Harrison (D-MS)—declined to reinstate the levy, its champions took the fight to the Senate floor. But there it died, as Democrats and progressive Republicans lined up against the levy. House Democrats had demonstrated that the party rank and file would never support the idea, and the Senate acquiesced in a package of miscellaneous excise taxes.[110]

The sales tax debate in both Houses revealed some persistent sectional divisions over revenue policy. Indeed, sectional interests, even more than party lines, seemed to dictate positions on the revenue bill. In the House vote of April 1, 1932, 80 percent of southern representatives voted against the sales tax levy. Such sentiment implied a preference for steeper income tax rates, which was unsurprising, given the region's long-standing support for the levy. Meanwhile, almost all eastern representatives supported the sales tax, reflecting the disproportionate share of the income tax burden shouldered by states like New York and Massachusetts. Similarly, in the Senate vote on May 31 to kill the sales tax, no easterners voted against the levy, and no southerners voted for it.[111]

As ultimately passed by Congress, the Revenue Act of 1932 was predicted to raise $1.1 billion in new revenue. A substantial chunk of this money—some $178 million—was expected to come from a combination of steeper rates and lower exemptions in the personal income tax. The higher corporation income tax also raised some new revenue. But fully $457 million was expected from new or increased excise taxes. The list of consumption levies was long, including taxes on lubricating oil, malt syrup, brewer's wort, tires, toilet articles, furs, jewelry, automobiles, trucks, radio and phonograph equipment, refrigerators, sporting goods, cameras, firearms, matches, candy, chewing gum, soft drinks, and electricity.[112] Taxed goods were disparate, their selection dependent on a variety of factors, including the political influence of affected industries. Most important, however, was a preference for articles of wide consumption, with a secondary concern for their relative necessity. Lawmakers preferred to tax items that people had some choice about consuming, rather than, say, table salt or flour. Some levies were selected because they clearly seemed to indicate a capacity to pay—hence the tax on jewelry, for instance. Others, like the car tax, were selected at least as much for the revenue they promised. Long the target of progressive tax reformers, the car tax survived the legislative battle because it promised to raise money.

Indeed, revenue was the name of the game in 1932. All other concerns were secondary. The pitched battle over the sales reflected not so much an argument about whether to increase taxes—that was never in doubt— but exactly how to get the additional funds necessary in the face of economic collapse. The rank and file Democrats who shaped the debate made clear their preference for isolated excise taxes, strongly preferring them to a more general sales tax. In large part, this preference reflected a conviction that people could choose whether to consume taxed goods. Under a general sales tax, no such choice was possible. Of course, the excise taxes were highly regressive. But regressivity was only one measure of fairness, and in the face of a gaping deficit, it was not the most important one. Democrats made consumer choice a central aspect in their definition of fair taxation.

The 1932 revenue act also worked important change on the income tax. The lower exemptions so earnestly sought by the Hoover administration found their way into the final bill. Indeed, this aspect of the legislation proved relatively uncontroversial; the Senate Finance Committee report noted the expansion of the tax base only in passing.[113] Lawmakers were too distracted by the sales tax debate to argue much over the exemption changes. Higher rates on the nation's richest taxpayers did receive some attention. House Majority Leader Henry Rainey, who had denounced the 1926 revenue act for its "tender solicitude" for the rich, now turned his wrath on his Democratic colleagues. When the House turned down the sales tax and replaced some of the lost revenue with higher income tax rates, he warned that "we have made a longer step in the direction of communism than any country in the world ever made except Russia." In the press of legislative debate, Rainey was always more vigorous than consistent.[114]

Just five months after the 1932 revenue act was signed into law, Franklin Roosevelt won his campaign for the presidency. When he took the oath of office in 1933, he inherited a tax system largely defined by this last revenue bill of the Hoover administration. The law represented a triumph for fiscal orthodoxy, albeit at the expense of tax fairness. Even supporters recognized that it put a heavy new burden on the lower class.

The Republican era of tax policymaking would have long-lasting effects, if not quite the ones that Mellon had hoped for. The low taxes of the 1920s were a distant memory in 1932. But the tax system of 1933 was certainly nothing like the revenue system emerging from World War I. Republicans had managed to limit the scope of progressive taxation, keeping the income tax reasonably limited and placing more of the tax burden on consumption. While sales tax proponents had reason to be disappointed, the federal revenue system was increasingly dependent on narrow sales taxes of one sort or another. That dependence, moreover, was not imposed by Republicans on their unwilling Democratic colleagues. Indeed, Roosevelt's party had crafted this system in close cooperation with the Hoover administration. Regressive taxation was a bipartisan achievement.

3

The State Roots of New Deal Taxation

During his 12 years in the White House, Franklin Roosevelt played a vital personal role in shaping federal tax policy. While never one for technical details, he consistently displayed a keen sensitivity to questions of tax justice. His commitment to vertical equity—and especially the heavy taxation of the rich—defined the most important tax reforms of his presidency. But to understand FDR's ideas on tax justice, we can't begin with his arrival in the Oval Office. Roosevelt cut his tax teeth while governor of New York, and his years in Albany reveal the origins of his fiscal philosophy.

As governor of New York, Franklin Roosevelt took a simple approach to tax policy: make the cuts broad and the hikes narrow. This agenda seemed to have some vague foundation in accepted standards of tax fairness, most notably ability to pay. But for the most part, it was an expression of his inchoate moral commitment to progressive taxation. When it came to taxes, Roosevelt simply believed that rich people should pay more than poor people. And in emergencies, they should pay a lot more.

Roosevelt's years in Albany were also important for their role in shaping the New Deal tax bureaucracy. Many of the advisers who guided Roosevelt across the rocky terrain of gubernatorial finance later joined him in Washington.

Agriculture and Taxes

Soon after taking office in January 1929, Governor Franklin Roosevelt dove headlong into a major debate over agriculture. Farm problems were a fixture of political debate across the nation, and President Herbert Hoover had signaled his interest in providing some measure of farm relief during an upcoming special session of Congress. Plagued by chronic over-production, American farmers never shared in the much-vaunted prosperity of the 1920s, and experts offered a variety of solutions. Most plans drew considerable opposition, attacked on the one hand as inadequate and on the other as radical. Forced by economic and political realities to confront the issue, national politicians tread this ground carefully.[1]

Like their counterparts across the nation, New York farmers struggled during the 1920s. The 1928 state Democratic platform called for a major reevaluation of farm-related tax issues, reflecting a widely held belief that agrarian regions were paying more than their fair share of state and local taxes. But as Roosevelt arrived in Albany, his problems were different—and less intractable—than those facing Washington policymakers. While Midwest farm states struggled with overproduction, many New York farms were only marginally productive. In fact, one of the state's most pressing agricultural dilemmas was a continuing exodus from the land; squeezed between low commodity prices and meager production, New York farmers were heading for town. Clearly, any farm solution for New York would have to account for the state's particular (and peculiar) conditions, making it a poor model for a national program.[2]

A 1929 study by the New York State Tax Commission, a permanent agency charged with economic research on state tax issues, described the problem succinctly. "The shrinkage of the New York farm area that has been going on almost without interruption since 1880 will and must continue," declared economist Ralph Theodore Compton with all the dispassionate conviction of a professional economist. "It has resulted from and will continue to result largely from the free play of natural forces." Still, there was room for government assistance. Compton suggested a reallocation of state tax burdens, with an eye toward reducing dependence on local real estate levies.[3]

Compton's suggestion was no surprise. Across the nation, real estate interests had been agitating for property tax cuts, many of them embellishing their arguments with rhetorical obeisance to the American farmer. "The welkin is made to ring with propaganda for the reduction of real estate taxes," complained one skeptical economist.[4] Farm interests found a key ally in the White House. "The tax burden upon real estate is wholly out of proportion to that upon other forms of property and income," declared President Hoover. "There is no farm relief more needed today than tax relief."[5]

New York politicians were keenly interested in reforming the property tax. Indeed, lawmakers had been debating the subject for decades. In 1916, the state's Joint Legislative Committee on Taxation had complained that real estate taxes were excessive. In 1922, the panel restated its concern that "real property in the State is being much overtaxed." Similar reports in 1925 and 1926 bolstered the case for reform. By 1929, Democrats and Republicans had agreed, at least in principle, to seek tax relief for the New York farmer. But they couldn't agree on how to work this fiscal legerdemain. Everyone agreed that unnecessary spending should be cut, but no one expected economy programs to pay for tax relief. Policymakers needed to find new revenue sources, reallocating the real estate burden to other bases of taxation, such as consumption or income.[6]

Real estate interests had a few suggestions. The New York State Association of Real Estate Boards called for a gasoline tax, urging in high-minded prose that the issue "cease to be a political football and become one of pure justice and equity in the tax problems of the State." Who can argue with calls for "pure justice"? Well, just about anyone opposed to a gas tax, but that argument was still in the future. For the time being, the group also suggested that lawmakers use the state income tax to pay most of the state's bills.[7]

Prominent newspapers agreed. The *New York Times* urged lawmakers to join their colleagues in all but one other state by establishing a gas tax. Urgent needs for road improvement, combined with inequities in the existing system of property taxation, made tax reform imperative.[8] The *Wall Street Journal,* while never eager to suggest any sort of tax, was quick to denounce the existing system of state property taxation. "There can be no real farm relief if the states tax agriculture to death," the editors declared.[9]

By the time Roosevelt arrived in Albany, rural tax reform seemed all but inevitable. Indeed, the governor had campaigned on the issue the previous fall. Newly installed in the executive mansion, he set about crafting a bill, not least because he recognized the partisan utility of enacting a vigorous farm program while Hoover struggled with broader agricultural problems.

In late 1928, just after his election victory, Roosevelt assembled a group of advisers to develop a package of farm relief measures. Composed of 21 prominent farm and political leaders, the panel included 18 Republicans, according to Roosevelt's count, providing at least the appearance of bipartisanship.[10] To lead this advisory group, Roosevelt tapped Henry J. Morgenthau Jr., a close friend and Dutchess County neighbor. Like Roosevelt, Morgenthau was a genuine, if genteel, farmer. Unlike the governor-elect, he had real experience in agricultural policy. The son of a rich New York City developer and Democratic activist, Morgenthau had foresworn the world of business, instead pursuing an avid interest in farming. He operated a small but notably profitable farm in the Hudson River valley and achieved some modest renown as publisher of the *American Agriculturalist*, a leading farm journal. During Roosevelt's campaign for governor, Morgenthau had successfully courted the farm vote, helping drum up Democratic support in the state's traditionally Republican rural regions.[11]

Morgenthau's appointment to head the agriculture panel was the first step on a long official road he would walk with Roosevelt. Over the next 15 years, his ministerial portfolio would shift from agriculture to public finance. As Secretary of the Treasury for virtually all of Roosevelt's presidency, he would preside over a watershed change in American taxation. For the time being, however, his efforts were confined to New York State, and his first run at tax policymaking was cast in terms of farm relief.

Soon after his inauguration, Roosevelt reconstituted his farm panel as the Agricultural Advisory Commission. During his first week in office, he asked the commission to develop a reform program. "What can the State of New York do," he asked Morgenthau, "to aid agriculture, give farmers a square deal, and help make the farm dollar go as far as the dollar of the city man?"[12] It was a rhetorical question, since Morgenthau's commission had already presented the governor with a set of proposals. The commission's program, moreover, had already won the stamp of approval from prominent farm leaders, giving the governor a leg up in his looming battle with Republican lawmakers.[13]

Republicans controlled both houses of the New York legislature, and they were loath to concede the farm issue to Roosevelt. Much of their most loyal support came from rural regions, and they could ill afford to grant Roosevelt the initiative on this pivotal issue. Yet Republicans were committed to the same sort of rural tax relief championed by the governor, and they reluctantly pledged at least limited cooperation. First, however, they appointed their own farm commission, with an eye toward stealing the governor's thunder.[14]

Roosevelt's panel, however, was quicker off the mark, releasing its public report early in the legislative session. Chief among its recommendations, which the governor warmly embraced, was a plan to reallocate the state's overall tax burden, reducing the role of county property taxes and replacing the revenue with a new state gasoline tax. Roosevelt championed the shift as a blow for tax fairness, and his arguments revealed a distinctive understanding of what it meant for a tax to be "fair."[15]

Consumption, User Fees, and Fairness

Roosevelt's argument for the gas tax hinged on its status as a user fee. In general, user fees were taxes dedicated to a specific purpose. This sort of earmarking was politically crucial, for it represented an attempt to match costs with benefits. When operating as planned, a user fee would be paid by those receiving the benefit of associated services. Since New York's local property taxes were used principally to finance road construction, they failed to match benefits with burdens. Replacing the property levy with a gas tax, paid principally by motorists, would bring the two into line.

When Roosevelt took office in 1929, New York counties were required to pay 35 percent of the cost of state highway construction, amounting to some $9 million annually. Counties had raised the money almost exclusively through a property tax, which was manageable for well-to-do counties, with their higher real estate prices and consequently larger tax bases. Poor, largely rural counties, on the other hand, faced a much harder task: they had to raise a similar amount of revenue from a much smaller tax base. Poor counties had been forced to hike rates dramatically in order to make the required highway contribution. The inevitable result? A wide variation in tax burdens. State Tax Commissioner Mark Graves, a member of Roosevelt's farm panel, explained the situation in convincing terms: "A farmer owning a ten thousand dollar farm in Erie County, for example, could pay $5.70 once and would have completed his payment of the cost for the state highway system," Graves explained. "Whereas, if he owned the same farm in Yates County, it would cost him $464.50."[16]

To remedy this situation, the governor's Agricultural Advisory Commission suggested that the state pay all highway construction costs, thereby relieving poor counties of this heavy burden. To keep budgets in balance, the state would pay for the shift by imposing a new gas tax of 2 cents per gallon. At least 40 percent of the resulting revenue, estimated at $20 million to $22 million annually, would be used for state road construction. The remainder would be distributed to the counties to help pay for a system of secondary roads. New York City was specifically allotted 5 percent of the total revenue.[17]

Experts on the permanent State Tax Commission supported the plan. "The striking thing about New York highway finance is the large burden which was placed upon real estate before the gasoline tax was adopted," an economist for the panel wrote in 1929. "In 1927 only 15.8 percent of the total revenue for streets and highways came from owners and operators of motor vehicles, while 82 percent came chiefly from the owners of real estate in the form of taxes and special assessments." Imposing a gas tax would more directly associate the road-building burden with those motorists who benefited from the highway system.[18]

Roosevelt embraced the tax proposal, making it a centerpiece of his farm relief package. Styling himself a farmer, he called on lawmakers to enact a "square deal" for his rural colleagues.[19] Roosevelt stressed the economic integration of city and country. "I am not so sure that those who live in towns and cities realize entirely how much the prosperity of the farmer directly affects their own prosperity," he told listeners to his radio address on farm relief. Or as he pointed out on another occasion, "we are all in the same boat, and if we put too large a burden on the rural sections, the cities must and will inevitably feel the reaction, just as too heavy a burden on the cities will in the long run retard the progress and prosperity of the farms." What was good for farmers, in other words, was also good for New York. Farm reform was everybody's business.[20]

Roosevelt was a well-known champion of the gas tax; he had been tilling the soil for this levy since at least 1927, when he urged it on then-governor Al Smith. After his election, Roosevelt encouraged Tax Commissioner Mark Graves to stump the state on behalf of the new tax. Graves agreed, echoing the governor's promise that the bill would benefit everyone. "It is not a purely farm tax relief measure," he assured one audience. "It will benefit directly every real property taxpayer whether he be a farmer, home owner, merchant, manufacturer, or public utility."[21]

Indeed it would. Taxes are notoriously blunt instruments of public policy. Used to raise money, they can often be designed to do the job efficiently. But when employed in the service of larger, nonrevenue goals—like helping farmers—they can be unwieldy. Incentives and benefits are difficult to target and easy to co-opt. Even the best intentioned tax reform can be manipulated for the personal gain of unintended beneficiaries. Roosevelt's property tax reform, while designed to aid farmers, was certain to be a windfall for every property owner in the state.

Benefits and Burdens

Roosevelt spoke approvingly of the gas tax, having "seen its excellent results in the south." In fact, the tax was popular almost everywhere; by 1929, every state but New York had one. Roosevelt described the tax as both fair and efficient, insisting that it linked benefits with costs. "One of the outstanding features of the proposed tax on gasoline," he explained, "lies in the fact that of all forms of taxation this is one of the most scientifically designed. I know of no other tax which so exactly lays the burden upon those who will derive direct benefit from the expenditure of the money thus raised." User fees, according to Roosevelt, could actually work to the benefit of those who paid them. Car owners, in fact, should welcome the gas tax. "In the last analysis the gasoline tax costs the automobile owner little," he promised. "It is an investment by him in good roads. His automobile lasts longer, the cost of operation is less, the tires will travel many more miles and the repair bills on his automobile will be very considerably smaller."[22]

Roosevelt was so keen on connecting the new tax with its associated highway spending that he called for rebates to gas users who did not rely on public highways, including owners of farm tractors, stationary gasoline engines, boats, and airplanes. Other states used similar rebates to ensure that gasoline taxes remained politically viable, as well as technically fair. The close connection between costs and benefits was central to Roosevelt's defense of the gas tax.[23]

The flip side of Roosevelt's new gas tax was the elimination of local property taxes used for road building. Abolishing the property tax was popular, and Roosevelt made the most of it. He disparaged property taxes as unfair to farmers, using an ability-to-pay argument to support his position. The tax was particularly inequitable during hard times: "The businessman pays a tax on his profits and on his income," Roosevelt explained. "The farmer pays a real estate tax, but he pays it whether he is making any money or not." In other words, paying the annual property tax—the amount of which did not necessarily vary with economic conditions—was difficult when income was scarce. Burdened with a relentless tax bill, farmers often found themselves unable to pay.[24]

Experts agreed. "The ownership of property is not necessarily evidence of tax-paying ability," pointed out the State Tax Commission. "Taxes must be paid out of income, and when they are levied upon property which does not provide its owner with income, they must be paid from some other source." Since New York farmers were struggling in the face of both economic depression and reduced agricultural output, they were hard pressed to pay their tax bills. The result was an inexorable pressure to abandon farming and the property that came with it.[25]

By the late 1920s, property taxes were under broad assault—and not just by farmers. Public finance economists were unhappy with the levy, insisting that it was neither fair nor efficient. Originally, the tax had been levied on all forms of property. But personal property—meaning all forms of property other than real estate—had proven difficult to assess and tax; evasion flourished as people found ways to conceal their ownership of nonreal property.

As a result, economists had become increasingly disenchanted with the tax. It had once enjoyed a reputation for fairness. Since property could be used as a measure of wealth, property taxes held out the promise of progressivity. Properly administered, they would fall most heavily on people with the most property. But economic modernization had undermined this argument for property taxation. The new forms of wealth that proliferated (particularly financial instruments like stock and bonds) were difficult to identify and tax. Taxpayers trying to evade the tax could readily disguise their assets. By the end of the 19th century, the property tax had become a de facto real estate tax, even as it pretended to tax property in all its forms.

Economists decried this arrangement, even as they acknowledged its inevitability. In 1890, Edwin Seligman published a landmark attack on the property tax, describing it as "the worst tax known in the civilized world." The levy, he insisted, was devoid of practical or theoretical merit.

> It puts a premium on dishonesty and debauches the public conscience. It reduces deception to a system and makes a science of knavery. It presses hardest on those least able to pay. It imposes double taxation on one man and grants entire immunity to the next. In short, the general property tax is so flagrantly inequitable that its retention can be explained only through ignorance or inertia. It is the cause of such crying injustice that its abolition must become the battle cry of every statesman and reformer.[26]

Seligman was no rabble rouser, his inflammatory rhetoric notwithstanding. Indeed, his choice of words reflected the disrepute into which property taxes had already fallen. The general sales tax was becoming an object of widespread scorn.

Lawmakers responded by scaling back expectations. In states and localities around the nation, they carved out one exception after another, exempting various sorts of property when they proved difficult to assess. Eventually, these changes brought the law into line with reality. But it left the tax vulnerable to fairness complaints. Critics pointed out that it now burdened certain types of wealth while letting others escape completely; as a result, it no longer taxed people according to their ability to pay. By the 1930s, many experts had long since accepted that the property tax—in any form—was overdue for retirement.[27]

For many experts, the gas tax seemed a reasonable alternative. Paul Studenski, an economist at New York University, endorsed the gasoline levy, pointing out that fuel taxes were popular in other states. The key, he said, was to tie the gas tax with road spending, making the connection obvious to voters. "It is popular because it is used for a popular purpose," he said of the gas levy. "It is paid in the final analysis by the users of the roads in proportion to their use." Studenski warned that political success depended on the proper allocation of revenues. Shifting gas tax receipts to other uses would diminish popular support. The levy, he insisted, was best described as a fee, rather than a tax.[28]

In a related vein, economist M. Slade Kendrick questioned whether gas taxes were actually regressive in their incidence. To the extent that revenue from the levy was used for road improvement, the tax would burden taxpayers lightly or not at all. Highway improvements compensated drivers for the cost of the tax, he said, since they enjoyed the benefits associated with better roads.[29]

In Albany, Roosevelt embraced the user fee argument as he stumped for his farm relief plan. Using a property tax to pay for highway construction made for a mismatch in the source and expenditure of revenue, he explained: it taxed property owners for the sake of road users. Better, he suggested, to levy a tax on gasoline, the benefits of which would accrue directly to the affected taxpayers. "Associations of automobilists as well as individual car owners have, I think, come to realize the justness and real advantages to themselves from this tax," he asserted. "I am convinced that this gasoline tax is proper, sound, and fair."[30] Indeed, the New York Automobile Club chose not to oppose the gas tax. While the group was hardly an outspoken proponent of the tax, they opted not to campaign against it.[31]

Occasionally, Roosevelt strayed from the user fee argument. Seeking to broaden support for the levy, he insisted that its benefits would be widely distributed. "The proposed gasoline tax is not rightly called a farm relief measure," he explained, "because it will benefit the great majority of owners of real property. It really should be termed a fair tax measure." Good roads benefited everyone, in other words, not just the property owners with adjacent land.[32] This sort of "general welfare" argument undermined the "user fee" rationale. If the benefits of new roads were so widely diffused, then why should only road users pay for them? Moreover, by noting the benefits accruing to property owners, Roosevelt seemed to undermine his case for relieving the property tax burden in the first place. In shifting the tax burden to road users, legislators might be undertaxing the property owners who stood to benefit from new roads.

Opinion on the gas tax followed predictable lines. Farm associations endorsed the plan, as did real estate groups like the State Association of Real Estate Boards; both stood to benefit from reductions in the real estate levy.[33] Conversely, auto groups, including the Motor Truck Association of America and the Automobile Merchants Association of New York, opposed the gas tax. The latter group was especially vocal, leading the campaign against the tax. It was unnecessary, the group insisted, and its revenue promised to exceed legitimate highway costs: "the history of the gasoline tax is that it breeds extravagance." States with a gas tax had a penchant for raising it, using revenue to fund general expenses, not just road building. Association chairman George Stowe also pointed out that automobile and truck owners were already saddled with substantial registration and license fees.[34]

Leading newspapers supported the tax. Almost everyone agreed that the rural tax burden was too high, and the gas tax promised to raise substitute revenue with a minimum of administrative difficulty. The *New York Times* endorsed the levy as "eminently fair." The tax was levied on a broad base, and it would be relatively easy to collect. More important, it promised to raise considerable revenue. The paper warned, however, that lawmakers should be careful with such a productive levy. Revenue should be used for road building and maintenance, not general government functions. "Any tendency to place an unreasonably heavy burden on the motorist is likely to end in revolt."[35]

The *Wall Street Journal* offered a similar opinion, predicting that a "reasonable gasoline tax, strictly devoted to the one purpose of highway improvement, would be cheerfully met by motorists." But, again, the paper warned against extravagance. Other states had fallen prey to temptation, using gas tax revenue for a wide variety of unrelated spending needs. New York must stand firm against such fiscal irresponsibility, the editors warned, lest they give the lie to user fee arguments.[36]

After flirting with alternatives, Republicans in the legislature eventually agreed to the gas tax. In fact, this part of Roosevelt's farm plan attracted no serious opposition, despite its regressive quality. Cast as part of the popular farm relief package, and justified as a user fee, the tax proved a political winner. On April 8, Roosevelt signed a budget bill into law, levying a 2 cent tax on every gallon of gas sold after May 1. Observers expected it to raise $26 million in new revenue, which the state would use to pay for highway costs. Localities were relieved of their responsibility to pay for road costs, and land owners around the state breathed a sigh of relief.[37]

An Unlikely Episode in Income Tax Reform

Roosevelt's gubernatorial career included a surprising venture in high-end tax relief. For a politician who would later be reviled by his opponents for trying to "soak the rich," FDR's effort to cut income taxes in 1929 seems a striking anomaly. It was, in any case, short lived. As depression ravaged the state revenue system, Roosevelt would quickly return to his preference for steep but narrow income taxes that forced much of the tax burden onto rich New Yorkers.

An ancillary benefit of the new gas tax was the surplus it promised for the state treasury. New revenue would exceed the cost associated the state's assumption of road building and maintenance.[38] Eager to expand on his political advantage, then, Roosevelt coupled his call for a gas tax with a recommendation for sweeping tax cuts. This time, he targeted his cuts more precisely, suggesting a program that would please most rich New Yorkers. "It is probable that when I send in my recommendation," he told the Albany Chamber of Commerce, "I will go on the theory that I don't know very much about the intricate problem of taxation, but I shall urge a plan that will do the greatest good to the greatest number, and therefore recommend a reduction of 20 percent in the State income tax."[39]

Outflanked on the gas tax, Republicans were unwilling to let Roosevelt preside over an income tax cut, too. As an alternative, they suggested that the state join its counties in reducing the property tax burden.

Republicans offered a plan to repeal the modest property tax imposed directly by the state. While small by comparison with county property taxes, the state levy was still a potent symbol amid the larger debate over farm relief. If Roosevelt could champion the elimination of one property tax, why shouldn't Republicans try to abolish another as well?

Roosevelt rejected the Republican initiative. Cutting the income tax would benefit more New Yorkers, he explained. Displaying a keen— if disputable—interest in tax incidence, he claimed that 35 rural counties would save $250,000 more from his income tax cut than through a state property tax elimination. He declined to specify how those tax savings would be distributed among each county's various residents; they may well have redounded to the benefit of a few rich taxpayers in each locality.

Still, Roosevelt insisted his plan was fairer than the GOP alternative. The major beneficiaries of a property tax elimination would be among the least deserving. "I wonder if those who advocate the elimination of the direct state tax as opposed to a reduction of the income tax realize that the greatest benefit under that plan would be to those who least need reduction. I refer to the fact that the direct State tax is paid in larger amounts by the big holders of real estate, the railroads and large business and industrial plants."[40]

Unlike county property taxes, the state property tax did not over-burden poor counties. County levies were used to pay for the state's road budget, and poor counties had to shoulder their share despite a smaller tax base. But the state property levy was imposed directly on taxpayers, and therefore operated in a more uniform manner. Rates were consistent across geographic regions.

While economically reasonable, however, Roosevelt's argument was politically curious, especially coming from a governor eager to eliminate local property taxes. Republicans made the most of this apparent incon-sistency. They countered Roosevelt's numbers with the observation that only 4,000 taxpayers—just three-quarters of 1 percent of Roosevelt's vaunted 530,000 tax cut beneficiaries—would receive more than 50 per-cent of the benefit from the governor's rate reduction. This sort of com-petitive statistical analysis was typical of tax debates, each side mustering the data in slightly different fashion to make wholly divergent points. According to Republicans, the bottom 335,000 taxpayers, ranked accord-ing to income, would enjoy a reduction of only $1.28 each. Moreover, they pointed out, the state property tax was designed as a temporary tax to help balance the budget, and should therefore be the first levy slated for elimination. (The *New York Times,* however, observed that Republican legislatures had levied the tax more or less continuously since the Civil War, albeit on an annually renewed basis.)[41]

GOP leaders bolstered their claim to the mantle of progressive taxation by agreeing to consider a reduction in the tax on earned incomes, meaning wages and salaries, not investment returns. Under their proposal, taxpayers with earned incomes of $10,000 or less would have enjoyed a 25 percent reduction in their income tax bills. The proposal recalled similar earned income preferences on the national level, which Treasury Secretary Andrew Mellon had championed throughout the 1920s. In New York, the earned income preference was designed to outflank Roosevelt on his left. Republicans said the credit would benefit 450,000 state taxpayers, and the *New York Times* predicted that most of them would see more relief under the Republican plan than under Roosevelt's across-the-board income tax cut. While some observers saw the proposal as a concession to the governor, others pointed out that the GOP plan was designed to protect the party's plan to eliminate the state property tax; they were trying to buy one tax cut with another.[42]

Roosevelt hung tough, threatening to veto the entire farm relief package, including the gas tax, unless lawmakers accepted the income tax cut. He also offered an administrative argument for income tax reduction. The budget surplus, he contended, was a temporary phenomenon, expected to disappear the next year. Consequently, the best way to provide relief was through a rate reduction, not the outright abolition of a tax that might be needed in the future.[43]

Neither Roosevelt nor GOP leaders won the tax debate outright. Instead, they reluctantly agreed on a bill raising the state's income tax exemptions. Single persons enjoyed an increase in their exemption from $1,500 to $2,500, while married persons and heads of household saw a boost from $3,500 to $4,000. The changes were designed to channel most relief to lower-income taxpayers, and as such reflected the GOP effort to target the tax relief measures according to income level. On the other hand, the compromise did not require elimination of the state property tax, giving Roosevelt at least a modest victory.

The exemption increase further sharpened the narrow focus of the state's income tax. Roosevelt, like almost all Democrats, preferred to keep the tax targeted at the well-off. Although exemption cuts had not been his first choice, they were consistent with a general approach to income taxation. Soon, however, the governor would be forced to defend the higher exemptions in a different economic climate. Revenue shortfalls would soon bring calls for broader income taxation. And this time, Roosevelt would take the lead in defending a narrow tax base.

Tax Reform amid Fiscal Crisis

Roosevelt was not entirely pleased with the state tax system, even after his initial round of rural tax reforms. It was, he complained, a "jerry-built tax system" in need of wholesale remaking. Experts agreed, with members of the State Tax Commission complaining that recent changes had moved state exemptions out of line with the federal income tax, making for increased complexity in completing tax returns.[44] In March 1930, Roosevelt called for a general revision of the state tax system. "It is time we consider a complete overhauling of our money-raising and -spending governmental machine," he declared:

> For the most part this machine which we have was never built up according to any particular design. Like Topsy, it just grew. I am suggesting that before our taxes go any higher we should survey the whole situation and see if we wouldn't accomplish more in the way of service to the taxpayers at a lower cost to them by building a new machine capable of doing all the things we demand of it.[45]

At Roosevelt's behest, the legislature established a special tax reform commission, headed by Republican State Senator Seabury C. Mastick, chairman of the Senate's Taxation and Retrenchment Committee. The panel was instructed to consider wholesale tax reform, but they were also charged specifically with further reducing the property tax burden.

Mastick was something of a maverick among New York Republicans. After being elected to the Senate in 1923, he quickly developed substantial expertise in tax matters. Representing a safe Republican district in Westchester County, he was a good candidate for the often contentious job of sorting out state tax policy. Over the years, he had served on various tax and spending commissions. And he had made a name for himself, if only because he espoused a variety of unusual positions for a Republican. In the 1920s, he championed old-age, health, and unemployment insurance. In 1930, he had successfully proposed a law giving small pensions to New Yorkers over age 70.

Roosevelt, notably, had opposed the measure, complaining that it vested too much control with local administrators. Even more important, he attacked the plan for not requiring any sort of contribution from beneficiaries. As he would later insist in the national debate over Social Security, some sort of contribution was necessary to keep the pension from becoming a dole. Better, he argued, to offer a graduated benefits schedule based on the recipient's effort to save for retirement. "In other words," he explained, "a definite premium should be placed on savings, giving to the workers an incentive to save based on the prospect of not only food and shelter, but on comfort and higher living standards than the bare minimum."[46]

Mastick shared with Roosevelt a fondness for farming, which he pursued as a hobby distinct from his legal career. He was no friend of the property tax, at either the state or the local level. And generally speaking, he was a proponent of lower taxation, bringing him in line with most of his party colleagues. As he noted during debate over Roosevelt's commission proposal, "taxes are increasing everywhere and in many cases amount to confiscation."[47]

Mastick's new reform commission included various academic and business luminaries, including Jesse Isidor Straus, president of Macy's department store, and Edwin Seligman, the dean of U.S. tax economists. Commission members were named jointly by the legislature and the governor, and they represented an ideologically heterogeneous mix. Most were business leaders, although all had important political and intellectual ties. A disproportionately large percentage came from upstate regions, rather than New York City—"a recognition of political rather than economic realities," complained the New York Times, "since the metropolitan area pays three-quarters of the tax bill." As the commission's staff director later pointed out, the Mastick Commission was heavily weighted toward real estate interests.[48]

Among commission members, Seligman possessed the most impressive intellectual credentials. In the 1890s, Seligman had taken a position in the vanguard of income taxation, providing intellectual support for a politically vulnerable tax. He was also an outspoken defender of the federal estate tax, opposing Republican moves to eliminate the levy and insisting on its fairness. Perhaps most important, Seligman was well known for his criticism of the general property tax.

Seligman was never a liberal economist, instead finding his political home in the moderate middle, often allied with more progressive members of the business community. By the mid-1920s, he had developed a somewhat conservative reputation, at least compared to many of his colleagues. He was a prominent opponent of the federal excess profits tax in the years after World War I, and business leaders enlisted his help in their successful campaign to repeal the levy. While Seligman continued to support a progressive income tax, he stood for a distinctly moderate flavor of tax policy.

A Cadre of Tax Experts

The Mastick Commission employed a distinguished staff of economists and attorneys. Indeed, the panel was a breeding ground for New Deal economists; several of its staff members would help craft Roosevelt's presidential tax policy.[49] Chief among them was Robert Murray Haig. As executive secretary and research director of the Mastick Commission, Haig played a vital role, shaping the panel's deliberations by controlling its research agenda. The commission granted him remarkable independence, and his analyses sometimes left him at odds with the panel's majority. Indeed, the commission's final report included a separate study by Haig, featuring conclusions and recommendations inconsistent with the panel's formal recommendations.

Haig brought a liberal but solidly mainstream approach to his study of taxation, earning his Ph.D. at Columbia in 1913 under Seligman's guidance. He remained at Columbia as a faculty member, and in 1931 he assumed the McVickar Chair of Political Economy when Seligman retired. Haig pursued an active career in public policy. He served on a variety of local, state, and international tax commissions, authoring studies on the revenue systems of New York City, Colorado, California, Alberta, Saskatchewan, and numerous other jurisdictions. During World War I, he served on the blue ribbon Committee on War Finance, assembled by the American Economic Association to evaluate wartime tax policies. And as a consultant to the U.S. Treasury Department, he helped draft the highly progressive Revenue Act of 1918.[50] After World War I, Haig squared off against Seligman during debate over the excess profits tax. Like Seligman, he was a supporter of income taxation and an advocate for progressivity. But he stood significantly to the left of his mentor. The excess profits tax, in Haig's view, was a salutary component of a progressive tax system, helping shift the tax burden to those most able to pay.[51]

Haig is best known for having contributed his name to the Haig-Simons definition of income, an economic concept undergirding the modern income tax. According to the Haig-Simons definition, "income" should be construed broadly and comprehensively; for individuals, it should equal consumption during a given period (usually a year), plus any change in net worth.[52] This definition implies that capital gains, even unrealized ones, should be treated as income—a theoretically consistent but administratively problematic notion. Haig, however, was an energetic spokesman for the idea, telling one audience that "an income tax which would allow capital gains to escape unscathed would, in this country at least, be an ethical monstrosity." That position placed him at odds with Republicans and business leaders, many of who supported preferential treatment for realized capital gains, and no taxation at all for unrealized capital income.[53]

Haig championed a scientific approach to taxation, seeking to imbue an inherently political process with a more intellectually sensible agenda. He had many allies in the endeavor, including Seabury Mastick, who convinced Haig in 1928 to help him organize the New York State Tax Association. According to the *Wall Street Journal*, the group was "an association of taxpayers of all lines of professional, business, labor, industrial, and farming endeavor" dedicated to a "sound, sensible, and comprehensive fiscal program" for the state. Indeed, the association's members included State Tax Commissioner Mark Graves, a variety of less exalted public finance officials, and numerous business leaders. It was an ideologically diverse group, representing both Republicans and Democrats. Haig was its most prominent academic member.[54]

Haig recruited a variety of distinguished colleagues to join the Mastick staff, including many of his students and colleagues at Columbia University. Economist Mabel Newcomer was one of his choices. Newcomer earned her Ph.D. at Columbia in 1917, writing a dissertation on the coordination of state and local tax systems. She was in the vanguard of a renewed movement to improve the interaction of fiscal systems—an issue that attracted surprising attention in the early 1930s, even appearing in Franklin Roosevelt's campaign rhetoric. Newcomer joined the faculty at Vassar College after her graduation, where she quickly developed a reputation for tax expertise. Beginning in the early 1930s, she served on numerous tax study commissions, assisting Haig with several studies, including one of the California tax system.[55] Indeed, during the 1930s and 1940s, she came to play a central role in state and federal tax policymaking, becoming the most prominent woman in the upper echelon of the tax policy community.[56]

Also joining the Mastick Commission was Carl Shoup, a lawyer and economist with degrees from Stanford and Columbia. His Ph.D., completed in 1930 under Haig's guidance, focused on the French sales tax, making Shoup an expert on the subject just as this levy was sweeping through the states. Perhaps the most promising young economist of his generation, Shoup joined Seligman in publishing a 1932 study of the Cuban tax system, and in 1934, he coauthored with Haig the definitive study of state sales taxation. Throughout the 1930s and 1940s, Shoup played a vital role in federal tax policy, serving as a staff member and consultant to the Treasury Department. Perhaps his most lasting achievement, however, came after World War II, when he spearheaded reform of the Japanese tax system during the postwar occupation.[57]

Haig, Newcomer, and Shoup would all figure prominently in New Deal tax policymaking, as would Louis Shere, another economist on the Mastick staff who would later move to the U.S. Treasury Department. As both staff members and consultants to the Treasury Department, these economists shaped the modern federal tax system. For the time being, however, they focused on New York tax issues, undertaking an intensive study of real estate levies—still a sore spot despite the property tax reductions of 1929.

In February 1931, the Mastick Commission issued a preliminary report suggesting that the state replace some of the money currently coming from real estate taxes with some other source of revenue. It was an obvious restatement of the problem, not a recommendation of any consequence: lawmakers had instructed the commission to design "a system of taxation which shall reasonably distribute the tax burden as widely and evenly as possible and thereby relieve those present sources of revenue, particularly real estate, which now bear a disproportionate part of the whole tax burden of the state."[58] But how should the state raise equivalent revenue? At that time, the commission had no answer.

Over the course of several months, the Mastick Commission had convened a series of hearings around the state. In each, real estate interests called for a reduction in property taxes. Several witnesses even suggested alternatives, including lower income tax exemptions and new sales taxes on retail purchases. As time went on, speculation increased as to what the commission would recommend. Many observers believed they were leaning toward a sales tax, in large part because it would raise so much money. According to Mastick, the panel wanted to shift about $250 million out of the property tax, and a new sales levy promised to raise substantial revenue.[59]

Some key political forces favored a sales tax. Potent support came from the New York State Farm Bureau, which regarded the levy as a reasonable replacement for property tax revenue.[60] Retail interests, however, were predictably hostile, organizing a formal coalition to oppose the idea. At the Mastick Commission's final hearing, held in New York City, more than 100 representatives of the retail industry gathered to voice their concerns. Representing hardware, furniture, jewelry, and other retail interests, the coalition's spokesmen denounced the "expense, difficulties, and injustice" of a sales tax. He also insisted that it would retard economic recovery.[61]

Merchants had a key ally in the governor's office. "I am against a sales tax," Roosevelt declared in December 1931. "I have been in the past and I still am." The sales tax imposed too great a burden on poor New Yorkers, he said; it was simply not fair. For all this progressive vehemence, however, Roosevelt was willing to consider narrow consumption taxes, especially on luxury goods. Such levies enjoyed considerable public support, due in part to their long history at both the federal and the state level. But the governor was never a big fan of these excise taxes either, as he occasionally observed in public. When asked by a reporter whether a luxury tax might be levied on tobacco products, Roosevelt reached for a cigarette. "Many people," he deadpanned, "do not consider tobacco a luxury."[62]

Fairness and Freedom of Choice

Experts were divided on the subject of luxury taxes. Many considered them a nuisance. Tax administrators criticized them for raising too little revenue at too great a cost; levied on the retail level, they were administratively burdensome and tended to encourage evasion. But a few tax specialists believed that certain, limited excise taxes had a legitimate place in the revenue system. In 1931, an economist with the New York State Tax Commission endorsed luxury taxes, just as lawmakers were casting about for new revenue. Ralph Burnett Tower observed that luxury was almost always in the eye of the beholder; practically speaking, it was defined politically. "No exact definition of *luxury* is possible," he stated, "except from the standpoint of society as a whole since superfluity can only be measured in terms of what seems normal for the social group."[63]

But once luxury was defined, it provided a reasonable basis for equitable taxation. Luxury taxes, according to Tower, featured an important element of choice. "They reach goods and services the consumption of which is entirely voluntary," he wrote. "Furthermore, if any person be denied the right to consume the taxed goods or services by reason of the tax, his position as a member of society will in no wise be injured."[64] This was a key point, buttressing the notion that luxury taxes were fair, despite their regressive burden. Tower acknowledged that many luxury taxes were passed on to the ultimate consumer rather than being absorbed by manufacturers. But that pattern of incidence wasn't much of a concern when the taxed item was a diamond ring, fur coat, or motor yacht.

Admittedly, luxury taxes were more problematic when the taxed items were cheap and broadly consumed. Alcohol and tobacco, for instance, were popular targets for luxury taxation. The argument for taxing such items rested on the idea that luxury could be defined not simply by price, but also by necessity. If an item were nonnecessary *enough,* then it might reasonably be called a luxury. This argument was used to justify taxes on a range of goods, including chewing gum, cosmetics, and entertainment admission.

But alcohol and tobacco, while generally considered nonnecessities, were also targeted for taxation because they were socially undesirable. In such cases, the levy was better described as a sumptuary tax. The antisocial quality of many taxed items had long been used to deflect criticism of the regressive burden associated with such taxes. But the fact remained that these sorts of narrow excise duties placed a heavy burden on the poor.[65]

Despite their regressivity, luxury taxes were a desirable source of revenue, according to Tower. They tapped income and wealth otherwise beyond the reach of state tax authorities, promising to raise significant revenue; if levied in New York at rates already common in other states, taxes on tobacco, entertainment admissions, and bottled soft drinks would raise at least $45 million annually, he predicted.[66]

Tower made the classic case for luxury taxation, insisting that the taxes were essentially optional; would-be taxpayers could exempt themselves by simply living more frugally. As long as they targeted superfluous or undesirable goods, luxury taxes could be tolerated, even in an otherwise progressive tax system. Roosevelt seemed to endorse this view, at least halfheartedly, while acknowledging that he might support taxes on "a small number of articles distinctly in the luxury class." But he left his definition of "luxury" conveniently vague. Soon, he would disavow the idea entirely.[67]

Steep New Taxes on the Rich

Meanwhile, the Great Depression was swelling relief rolls across New York, and Roosevelt soon proposed a temporary work relief program. The cost, he argued in August 1931, should be borne by wealthier taxpayers through an increase in the income tax. "It seems logical," Roosevelt declared, "that those of our residents who are fortunate enough to have taxable incomes should bear the burden of supplementing the local governmental and private philanthropic work of assistance." He suggested a proportional increase in state income tax rates, adding "merely half again as much" to each taxpayer's annual liability.[68]

The 50 percent increase, Roosevelt told the state legislature in a special session, would fall lightly on those with small incomes, totaling only $2.50 for a single person with net income of $3,000. Higher incomes, not surprisingly, would be taxed more, with those earning more than $100,000 paying an extra $1,162.50. Such a proportionate increase in tax burden seemed fair to Roosevelt. "It is clear to me," he told lawmakers, "that it is the duty of those who have benefited by our industrial and economic system to come to the front in such a grave emergency and assist in relieving those who under the same industrial and economic order are the losers and sufferers. I believe their contribution should be in proportion to the benefits they receive and the prosperity they enjoy."[69]

Republicans were unhappy with the income tax plan. Senate GOP leader George R. Fearon and Assembly Speaker Joseph A. McGinnies opposed the idea, and they advanced an alternative scheme of strict economy and limited borrowing.[70] Eventually, however, they gave in, cowed by FDR's political skill and the pressing need for revenue.

The 1931 tax hike soon proved insufficient, however, as declining revenues and growing relief demands opened a gaping hole in the state budget. By early 1932, the state faced a serious shortfall, with deficit predictions creeping upward almost weekly. The depression had changed the debate over tax reform. It was no longer enough to simply replace property tax revenue with something else; the state needed money to close its budget gap, and the Mastick Commission began considering the fairest way to do it.

Roosevelt, meanwhile, defined his own path out of the red ink. In his January 1932 budget message to the state legislature, he criticized Washington leaders for their lack of decisive action on the budget front. To underscore the alternative, he offered a host of proposals for New York. In broad strokes, he called for dramatically steeper taxes on income, gasoline, and the sale of securities. All were doubled under Roosevelt's plan, and he even tacked on a retroactive increase in income taxes for 1931. The increased taxes were expected to raise $137 million, more than covering the expected $124 million deficit.[71]

Roosevelt had not entirely forgotten about tax reform; he went out of his way to endorse complaints about real estate taxation. "These taxes on real estate are too high," he declared. But the issue, he insisted, was really a matter of spending, not taxing. "The answer to the problem of excessive real estate taxation is reduction in the cost of local government." [72] Roosevelt had been stressing problems in local government throughout his years in Albany. In July 1931, for instance, he had given a major speech at the University of Virginia outlining the case against profligate local governments. Roosevelt would soon expand such criticism to include the federal government when he began his run for the White House. At this juncture, however, he was unwilling to consider tax cuts as a remedy for overburdened property taxpayers. Short-term revenue problems made reduction impossible.

Technical issues of tax administration played a role in Roosevelt's recommendation for an income tax hike. As he explained to the legislature, new revenue should come from old taxes. He specifically declined to recommend new consumption levies, including taxes on luxury goods. He cited the administrative difficulty of collecting numerous small taxes. The New York Times praised the governor for this approach, noting that his plans had the "merit of simplicity and familiarity."[73]

Ultimately, however, it was fairness, not simplicity, that Roosevelt stressed in rejecting excise taxes. "In the last analysis, these so-called luxury taxes are on the average individual, bearing nearly equally in actual cost on the individual members of our population. They are not based on ability to pay and therefore bear relatively far more heavily upon the poor than upon the rich."[74] It was a persuasive case, and one widely echoed among professional economists. But it might well have been offered against his proposed gas tax hike, as well, especially since gasoline was not a luxury for many people. And Roosevelt had voiced no such qualms in 1929, either, when he championed introduction of the new gas tax.

Nonetheless, it seems clear that Roosevelt understood the regressive pitfalls of any consumption-based tax. As his earlier comments made clear, he was willing to consider such levies, especially if narrowly focused. And he was thoroughly convinced of the fairness of a user fee like the gas tax. But his new gas tax hike was not really a user fee; it was prompted by a general revenue crisis, not a road-building initiative, or even a shortfall in the highway budget. Roosevelt chose the gas tax among his various revenue options because he knew it would raise substantial revenue. It was an entirely pragmatic decision.

Still, the gas tax hike must be viewed in the context of Roosevelt's overall revenue proposal. He asked low- and middle-income New Yorkers to shoulder a regressive tax burden, one bearing more heavily on them than on their richer neighbors. But he also made sure to saddle the wealthy with sharply higher income taxes. It was, on balance, a progressive package, politically if not, perhaps, economically.

Indeed, income taxes were declining in their capacity to provide adequate revenue, and boosting rates higher would not solve the problem as long as the economy sputtered. But high rates had a symbolic role to play, as well as an economic one, boosting the fairness of the overall system. As president, Roosevelt would embrace this argument for progressivity at the top end of the income scale, using it to justify many of the New Deal's most controversial tax reforms.

The Mastick Commission Reports

On February 1, the Mastick Commission issued its long-awaited final report. The panel took as a starting point the legislature's insistence that real estate taxes were too high. In fact, however, the panel was divided over this issue. A majority concurred strongly with the legislative opinion, but two members—Edwin Seligman and Jesse Isidor Straus—were less convinced. Seligman and Straus, along with staff director Robert Murray Haig, questioned the severity of the problem.

All members of the commission agreed, however, that road users should foot more of the state tax bill, reflecting the steep cost of highway maintenance. Consequently, the panel unanimously recommended a hike in the gas tax from 2 cents to 4 cents per gallon. They also endorsed a variety of other car and truck taxes, all designed to allot more of the tax burden to drivers and vehicle owners.[75]

Even more important, the panel called for a substantial broadening of the state income tax. Specifically, they suggested reducing exemptions to the federal level. Politically, it was a controversial idea, at variance with Roosevelt's preference for high exemptions. But the commission pointed out that the 1929 tax cuts had raised exemptions well above the federal level. They called for a return to the earlier numbers: $3,500 for a married couple and $1,500 for a single taxpayer. Even those numbers would have left the vast majority of taxpayers entirely exempt. Indeed, the Mastick panel went on to suggest an even more radical reduction in exemption levels to $2,500 for married filers and $500 for individuals. At the lower end of the single exemption, taxpayers would still be required to file a return and pay a $2 filing fee.[76]

The commission argued that broadening the income tax base was a good thing in its own right, even absent revenue needs. "This proposal springs from a conviction that the personal income tax should be as comprehensive as possible and that everyone not positively destitute should pay at least a nominal sum as a direct contribution toward the costs of the government under which he lives."[77] To many, this seemed a conservative idea, one that sought to shift more of the tax burden to lower-income citizens. But the idea reflected one of the era's canons of good tax policy: visibility. By requiring taxpayers to pay some amount—no matter how trivial—a broad-based income tax would presumably heighten awareness of government finance.

Many tax experts believed tax consciousness would foster good government and fiscal responsibility. "Although little direct evidence bears on the point, it appears that tax consciousness is in general a force for good government," noted one prominent study published in 1937. Moreover, the income tax was almost certainly the best way to foster awareness of the tax burden. "The real problem of lack of tax consciousness is represented by the mass of urban tenants and farm tenants who do not own automobiles and do not have enough income to be taxable under existing income tax laws," the report continued. "They bear a real tax burden, of course, but it is hidden. We see no practicable way of bringing it out in the open except by substituting, for some of the tax they now pay indirectly, some form of income tax."[78]

Over the course of the 1930s, economists of all political stripes would make that argument. But at the decade's start, it was still considered a conservative position, and only a few Democrats were inclined to embrace it. Certainly not Roosevelt. Given an early look at the Mastick

Commission's report, he ignored its suggestions as he prepared his own plan in late 1931. Roosevelt preferred his income taxes narrow and steep. Ultimately, his arguments carried the day, with the legislature quickly approving most of his suggestions. Lawmakers did, however, insist on scaling back the gas tax increase, limiting the hike to 50 percent. Apparently, they, too, understood the regressive burden of such a levy.

Perhaps the most striking aspect of the Mastick Commission report was its accompanying staff memos. Though not endorsed by the commission's appointed members, these memos formed the basis for the official recommendations. But they also went much further. Unconstrained by the political difficulties of trying to build a consensus among disparate political appointees, staff were able to voice their own opinions on a wide variety of issues. Some of these opinions were a sign of things to come, as these same researchers moved from Albany to Washington when Roosevelt won the presidential election.

Robert Murray Haig wrote most of the staff report, although he co-authored large sections with Carl Shoup and Mabel Newcomer. His analysis raised doubts about the severity of the property tax burden. While acknowledging that some readjustment was in order, he cautioned against hasty assumptions. "Although there seems to be widespread acceptance of the proposition which appears in the statute creating the commission that real estate is bearing a disproportionate part of the tax burden, there has been a remarkable paucity of analysis of the character and extent of this disproportion."[79]

Haig pointed out that when trying to gauge tax equity, the prevailing standards were the benefit principle and ability to pay. The former was relevant to the gas tax and other vehicle taxes proposed by the commission. In this case, the connection between a tax and a related government service was fairly certain. In most cases, however, such a connection was impossible to trace. In that situation, Haig argued, ability to pay was the accepted standard of fairness.

Ability to pay, Haig observed, tended to encourage a move away from property taxation. While once considered a suitable measure of ability, property was no longer in good standing among economists. Neither, he pointed out, did consumption seem to be a reasonable measure of ability. Instead, income had emerged as the preferred yardstick.[80]

In an important caveat, Haig stressed that fairness was not the only concern facing tax policymakers. "The canon of equity is not the only canon to be considered," he stated. "Economic and administrative questions enter also." Moreover, even assuming the primacy of fairness concerns, no single measure could tell the whole story; "a combination of several norms may be superior to any one used singly," he suggested. This was a fine exposition of the taxwriter's challenge: confronted with norms and ideals, policymakers also had to grapple with practicalities and imperatives. In calling for property tax cuts, lawmakers had indulged in some thinly veiled political posturing. Haig counseled, however, that sweeping indictments of the tax system were premature. Policy was about compromise and balance, not theoretical or ideological purity. As he phrased it with good bureaucratic concern for dispassionate expertise, "The wise decision is one which represents a balanced judgment arrived at after a full consideration of all the facts which can be marshaled regarding the probable effects."[81]

Finally, Haig pointed out that history was more than just a guide for tax policymakers. Arguments for tax reform often ignored "the fact that what has been done in the past in this field of taxation controls to a very important extent the action which may be wisely taken in the present and the future." Shifting and capitalization prompted economic adjustments, many of them built into asset valuation and business decisionmaking. Such adjustments "may be unjust and foolish to disturb," he suggested, making a case for the status quo.

> Certainly he who ignores history in dealing with tax changes assumes a heavy responsibility. The proponent of a radical change must accept the responsibility for demonstrating that the disturbance of the existing state of affairs will, in the general balance, show a net gain.[82]

Haig was articulating an old maxim of taxation: an old tax is a good tax. Haig was not, by nature, a conservative policymaker. Indeed, his defense of the World War I excess profits tax marked him as something of an innovator. But like most tax professionals, he recognized the pitfalls of sweeping, ill-considered reform; it was not something to undertake lightly or legislate quickly.

The old tax maxim also provided a compelling argument for retaining old, if admittedly imperfect, taxes. New York's property tax was one such levy. While problematic, it was reasonably well understood. Hence, Haig supported moderate reform of the levy, not its abolition or radical reduction. In the future, New Deal economists would use that sort of argument to defend a variety of other flawed taxes, including consumption levies on consumer goods like alcohol and tobacco. While certainly regressive, they were also well-tested and effective. And many old taxes provided a lot of revenue: an important consideration—perhaps the *most* important consideration—when shaping tax policy.

Two other sections of the Mastick staff report deserve special mention. In a discussion of the state income tax, Haig argued that any significant increase in revenue would necessarily come from higher rates on the richest taxpayers. Given existing low rates across the income range, it would be impossible to substantially increase revenue from middle brackets without imposing tax increases of more than 100 percent. That was not the sort of measured reform that Haig could recommend.

The staff report did suggest, however, that lowering the income tax exemptions would have important benefits. While it would not raise significant new revenue, it would boost the visibility of the tax. Indeed, the narrowness of the tax base was often used as an argument against the income tax, endangering a levy that Haig and most other economists considered to be the fairest of all revenue tools. Furthermore, lower exemptions would open the door to future reforms that *would* substantially increase the revenue flowing from this tax; by establishing the administrative foundation for a broader tax, lower exemptions would allow policymakers to increase rates and revenue in the future.[83]

The report endorsed the notion of a filing fee—essentially a minimum tax for those just above the exemption level. The fee would not raise much money, but it, too, would boost tax consciousness. And it would also help bolster enforcement in the lower reaches of the income tax. "The two chief virtues of the filing fee," Haig wrote, "would be its direct message to almost every citizen that the government is a tax-collecting as well as a spending body, and its aid in detecting whatever evasion now occurs among those who are close to the preset exemption limits."[84]

A second important section of the Haig report—written almost entirely by Carl Shoup—took aim at the notion of a state sales tax. While acknowledging the growing popularity of state sales levies, the report raised doubts about their use in New York. A sales tax would mark a major departure for the state, Shoup noted. And it would not necessarily redress any of the revenue system's acknowledged problems. "Although one cannot be certain of its effects," he cautioned, "it does not hold out a promise of correcting whatever wrongs that now exist, but on the contrary would probably be the originator of more injustice."[85]

The sales tax would inevitably weigh on the state's poorest citizens, Shoup contended, even assuming that some of the burden would be offset by a reduction in the property tax. If the revenue were used to off-set reductions in other taxes, such as the inheritance levy, then the over-all tax burden would shift even more decisively downward. "This, of course, is one of the aims of the proponents of the sales tax," Shoup observed coolly, "who wish the masses to pay more tax than at present, on the theory that a more equitable distribution of the burden would result therefrom." But the masses already shouldered a heavy burden, according to Shoup, especially since the real estate tax was almost cer-tainly shifted to apartment dwellers by their landlords.[86]

Shoup warned against luxury taxes, especially when the term was used to describe taxes on items of mass consumption but admitted superfluity—things like cigarettes, soft drinks, entertainment admis-sions, toilet articles, or chewing gum. Moreover, "luxury taxes" were often conflated with "sumptuary taxes."

> Sometimes, in the argument for taxes on tobacco, cosmetics, etc., appears a sumptuary note, e.g., poorly paid stenographers wasting their salaries on lip-stick and soft drinks instead of eating a fair quota of wholesome food should not object if they are shown the way to correct expenditure via an alteration of the tax system.[87]

While boosting the perceived fairness of an excise tax, the sumptuary argument ran counter to revenue imperatives. To the extent that a tax managed to successfully discourage consumption of an undesirable item, it would cease to raise significant money for the state. And while some people would reduce their consumption to avoid the tax, others would not: "those least able to pay will suffer the most by the tax," he complained.

When lawmakers used luxury taxes to raise significant revenue, they were implicitly undermining the sumptuary argument for the levies. If rates were set low enough to actually make money, then they could not be set high enough to discourage use. In practice, sumptuary taxes were not designed to forestall undesirable behavior: they were designed to raise money from those least able top pay.

Overall, the Haig report to the Mastick Commission provided a valu-able window into current thinking among some of the nation's most important tax experts. The Columbia clique that dominated the Mastick Commission staff would soon move to Washington. Just two years later, many of these same economists would be reunited in the Treasury Department to undertake a major, multivolume study of the federal revenue system. Their ideas, in turn, became the foundation for a series of important Roosevelt-era tax reforms.

Conclusion

Taken as a whole, Roosevelt's tax record as governor of New York was clearly a mixed bag. Often, he seemed to sacrifice consistency for expediency. He generally treated tax reform as a means to other, more important ends. His two most significant tax proposals—the 1929 gas tax and the later pair of income tax hikes—were really about agriculture and unemployment relief. And when the Mastick Commission actually focused on tax policy as a subject unto itself, Roosevelt showed little real interest. Indeed, he ignored the panel's most important recommendation—its plan for lower exemptions.

Still, Roosevelt's record as governor did portend some of his later policies as president. His comments and proposals began to describe the outlines of a tax ideology. In general, he supported a system of limited consumption taxation, coupled with steeply progressive income levies. As president, Roosevelt would adopt similar positions. Ultimately, this willingness to compromise on consumption taxes reflected a pragmatic approach to tax policy. Both as governor and later as president, he was prepared to compromise equity for the sake of adequacy.

Roosevelt's fondness for a narrow, heavy income taxation reflected his commitment to progressivity, especially at the upper end of the income scale. He resisted suggestions to broaden the tax. While many Republicans and economists were partial to the idea, neither Roosevelt nor most of his Democratic colleagues were ready to embrace it. They believed the income tax was best restricted to the upper reaches of American society. So contained, it offered a quick and easy way to ensure that rich people paid their fair share, even as poor Americans were saddled with heavy taxes on consumption. This was the fundamental bargain of high-end progressivity.

4

Early New Deal Taxation and the Moral Status of Tax Avoidance

The early New Deal offered scarcely a hint of tax reform. During his first campaign for the White House, Franklin Roosevelt attacked Republican fiscal policies, accusing President Hoover of spending too much and taxing too little. But he offered few alternatives and suggested no major tax reforms. He soon made good on his implicit promise of benign neglect: for the first year of his presidency, Roosevelt all but ignored taxation.

Taxes did play a role in several early New Deal initiatives. The National Industrial Recovery Act and the Agricultural Adjustment Act both included tax provisions; revenue from the latter would be sorely missed when the Supreme Court eventually took it away.[1] By and large, however, taxation was a congressional province in the early 1930s. The White House treated taxes as a means to achieve other, more immediate policy goals.

It would be a mistake, however, to dismiss the importance of federal tax policy in 1933 and 1934. These years were marked by a vigorous debate over tax avoidance and evasion. Congressional investigators revealed that some of America's richest financiers had paid no taxes in the dark years of the early depression. The resulting moral outrage resonated through the rest of the 1930s. Indeed, tax avoidance became a leitmotif of New Deal tax reform.

The Candidate on Taxation

Things were grim in the fall of 1932. The Great Depression had reached its nadir, and observers—editorial, political, and academic—warned darkly of revolution. On the tax front, there already *was* a revolution. Or more precisely, a series of small revolts, as taxpayers throughout the country refused to pay their tax bills. Most tax revolts concerned the property tax, a state and local levy on landowners of every sort. Farmers, urban homeowners, and even some business leaders complained that the tax violated standards of fairness. Specifically, it did not reflect the tax-payer's ability to pay. Levied almost exclusively on real estate, it came due annually, regardless of income fluctuations. And when the depression squeezed personal income, taxpayers had trouble paying their bills.[2]

Throughout the nation, but especially in the Midwest, farmers and homeowners suffered the pain and indignity of tax auctions. Communities organized to challenge such enforcement techniques. As the *Washington Post* reported, "Iowa farmers are attending tax sales in great numbers—to see that nobody bids." In one Ohio auction, a $400 tax debt was settled for just $2.15. And in Chicago, a powerful tax resistance movement left most of the city's property taxes unpaid in 1931 and 1932. Tax resistance some-times took an ugly turn. Bank employees and tax officials found them-selves the target of agitated crowds. One bank representative in Ohio arrived at a foreclosure only to find a noose dangling from the barn.[3]

Federal taxes were less controversial. So much so that both candidates in the 1932 presidential election felt free to ignore the issue, at least for the most part. As a candidate, Franklin Roosevelt rarely addressed issues of substantive tax reform, instead simply bemoaning the heavy burden of existing levies. Building on his gubernatorial record, FDR did call for lower farm taxes, by which he meant property levies. It was a powerful message, especially in light of the tax protests sweeping the heartland. But the property tax was a state, not a federal, issue; Roosevelt had nothing to offer but moral indignation.[4]

When it came to national policy, Roosevelt reached for the mantle of fiscal orthodoxy—after a fashion. As Federal Reserve chairman Marriner Eccles later recalled, "Given later developments, the campaign speeches often read like a giant misprint, in which Roosevelt and Hoover speak each other's lines."[5] FDR chastised Hoover for imposing high taxes. At the same time, he denounced the administration's improvidence and fiscal irrespon-sibility. It was a neat trick, flaying Hoover on both sides of the same issue.

Hoover was a spendthrift, Roosevelt declared. The cost of government had gotten out of hand, spurred on by soaring national income during the 1920s. " 'Come-easy-go-easy' was the rule," FDR told an audience. "It was all very merry while it lasted."[6] But the depression had slashed national income, and with it most tax revenues. Nervous lawmakers had responded with the Revenue Act of 1932, saddling Americans with millions of dollars in new taxes. But still, the red ink grew.

New taxes not only failed to balance the budget, they had also slowed recovery. "That burden is a brake on any return to normal business activity," Roosevelt declared. "Taxes are paid in the sweat of every man who labors because they are a burden on production and are paid through production. If those taxes are excessive, they are reflected in idle factories, in tax-sold farms, and in hordes of hungry people, tramping the streets and seeking jobs in vain."[7] Andrew Mellon couldn't have said it better.

In some respects, Roosevelt seemed to have the makings of a good Keynesian; if tax hikes bred recession, then perhaps tax cuts would spur recovery. In fact, however, Roosevelt was no Keynesian, at least not yet. He wasn't even a proto-Keynesian, as scholars have defined that label.[8] It didn't take a Keynesian to recognize that tax hikes in the midst of depression were a recipe for disaster. Even some Hoover advisers disliked them. "At the treasury," reported the *New York Times* in 1931, "it was pointed out that during a period when business is slack it would appear to be better policy to increase the public debt than to raise taxes."[9]

Mellon and his colleagues had long recognized that tax cuts were an effective means to raise national income. Hoover had actually proposed one in late 1929 and Congress had approved it. Eventually, however, orthodox economic theory seemed to demand both retrenchment and new revenue to help curb swelling deficits. Hoover and his advisers believed that too much government borrowing would imperil the credit system, plunging the nation into even deeper depression. Such beliefs were comfortably in the mainstream of political and economic thought. Balanced budgets, strong national credit, and business confidence were articles of faith among politicians, but they were the product of careful thought among experts, too.[10]

If Roosevelt had been trying to draw a bright line between himself and Hoover, he had failed; when it came to fiscal policy, no such line existed. When Roosevelt indicted the 1932 tax hike, he sounded like many GOP leaders of the 1920s complaining about taxes held over from World War I. And in any case, Roosevelt seemed to accept the budget orthodoxy that had led Hoover to support a tax hike in the first place. The tax increases of 1931 were "two years too late and in far too scanty measure," FDR declared.[11] Such criticism brought a puzzling circularity to FDR's indictment: Hoover had tolerated excessive tax burdens, thereby depressing the economy. At the same time, he had failed to raise taxes high enough, leaving the economy in peril. Roosevelt made this argument work by suggesting that spending cuts might have saved the day. But here, too, he managed to have it both ways. Emergency spending, he warned, might well be necessary, especially to alleviate depression-borne suffering. And this relief would require taxes. "If men or women or children are starving in the United States—anywhere—I regard it as a positive duty of the Government—of the national Government if local and State Governments have not the cash—to raise by taxes whatever sums may be necessary to keep them from starvation," he declared.[12]

Roosevelt offered few specifics about the sort of taxes he might choose to raise, given the chance. But he did make one important suggestion. Repeal of Prohibition would bring many new dollars into the Treasury, he pointed out, since federal alcohol taxes were still on the books. The levy on beer, in particular, would raise "several hundred millions of dollars" annually.[13]

But wouldn't the beer tax add to the nation's fiscal burden? And wouldn't it fall most heavily on the poor? Roosevelt betrayed no such concern, and neither did his audience. In a speech all about fiscal responsibility and the tax burden, neither Roosevelt nor his listeners seemed to find anything to dislike about beer taxes. The *New York Times* even reported a surge of cheering around Roosevelt's suggestion. All this for a tax that economists understood to be regressive.[14]

In fact, the beer tax enjoyed considerable support. With a long history stretching back to the nation's founding, alcohol taxes enjoyed a large measure of historical legitimacy. As president, Roosevelt would continue to rely on alcohol levies, as well as similar taxes on other discretionary goods with a long tax history, including tobacco.

The President-Elect on Taxation

After winning the election, Roosevelt began to engage tax issues more seriously. But he still lacked solid ideas. Indeed, beyond a few key convictions—that sales taxes were bad and that steep, narrow income taxes were good—he brought almost no tax program to his new job. In the months following the election, even these preferences seemed in question. As the president-elect pondered his revenue options, the sky was crowded with trial balloons.

Sales Tax

Congress, meeting in the last months of 1932, was filled with "the lamest of 'lame ducks'," noted one tax specialist.[15] Almost 100 House Republicans had lost their seats in the November election, as had 12 Senate Republicans. Democrats, meanwhile, still had to contend with President Hoover, making legislation tricky. But leaders of both parties paid lip service, at least, to the notion of fiscal responsibility. Many of the 1932 tax hikes had proved disappointing. "The miscellaneous taxes have fallen down almost without exception," noted the *Tax Magazine*, "but they have had the excellent company of the income and customs taxes." A yawning deficit prompted serious discussion of yet another tax increase.[16]

In December, Hoover recommended a sales tax, but his idea found little support. When Ogden Mills suggested it to the House Ways and Means Committee, Democrats attacked viciously. "They shrieked at Mr. Mills and the Secretary of the Treasury shrieked back," reported the *New Republic*.[17] Hoover's plan seemed to be doomed, but the sales tax still haunted discussions of federal revenue. Keeping the issue alive was a careful silence from the office of the president-elect. The *Washington Post* reported that Roosevelt was considering a sales tax as a parting gift for New York State. (The state got one almost immediately after he left the governor's office, but courtesy of his successor.) Other reports suggested that FDR might support a general sales levy on the national level, and a small groundswell of support emerged, even among some Democrats.[18] But Roosevelt quickly quashed the idea. Friends of the governor voiced "amazement and some indignation" over reports that he favored such a regressive levy. In fact, they insisted, Roosevelt considered it an unfair burden on "the forgotten man." Speaker of the House and Vice President elect John Nance Garner, a sometime supporter of the tax, pronounced the idea dead, as did Senate leaders of both parties.[19]

This trial balloon popped.

Excise Taxes

Roosevelt did not forswear consumption taxes entirely. Once again, "friends" of the governor reported that he would tolerate further hikes in excise taxes, especially those on tobacco products. Since tobacco taxes were already on the books, it was a fairly innocuous suggestion. But it hinted at a tolerance for boosting consumption taxes more generally. In a January 10, 1933, meeting with representatives for publisher William Randolph Hearst—a passionate sales tax supporter—Roosevelt delicately avoided any strong opposition to consumption taxes. He did, however, restate his preference for a broad array of excises taxes rather than a general sales levy.[20]

Depending on the specifics, that might have been a distinction without a difference. During the Civil War, for instance, the federal government had imposed such a broad collection of excise taxes as to roughly approximate a general sales tax. But from Roosevelt's perspective, excises had at least one important virtue: they were already enacted. The Revenue Act of 1932 had imposed a slew of new ones, while raising rates on many older excises. Adding a few more, or increasing rates on those already enacted, would be less treacherous than trying to sell a new general sales tax.[21]

Moreover, some tax experts of the 1930s defended the fairness of excise taxation, at least when levied on nonnecessities. Ralph Tower, a one-time consultant to the New York government and a professor at Mount Union College in Ohio, pointed out that excise taxes were gaining favor among lawmakers, even while most tax experts decried them for their regressive incidence. In practice, if not in theory, "the old and established tests of tax-paying ability are declining in importance," he asserted. Tower maintained that excise taxes had a claim to fairness rooted in the power of choice. A consumer could usually avoid an excise tax by choosing not to buy the taxed product. "His standard of living is not so inflexible that if need be he cannot substitute untaxed goods and services for those upon which taxes are levied," he wrote. Of course, when levied on too many goods—or on goods without adequate substitutes, such as tobacco—an excise was quite burdensome. But most narrow consumption taxes were subject to consumer decisionmaking.[22]

One consumption tax getting a lot of attention after Roosevelt's election was the beer tax. The levy was expected to raise considerable revenue, and some Democrats believed it would obviate the need for any other taxes. But skeptics were legion. As the *Washington Post* noted wryly in early 1932,

> There is a magic quality in the very proposal to tax beer. It would be so simple. Let Congress put a levy on 2.75 per cent beer and $350,000,000 would roll into the Treasury amid the rejoicing of the people. There seems to be something about beer that makes those who drink it love to pay taxes to the Government as well as huge profits to saloons. In the form of a levy against manufactured goods taxes are undoubtedly a curse. But when one can drink taxes at a bar they become soothing, comforting, and appetizing.[23]

Some critics questioned the fairness of a beer tax. "If you were a congressman how would you explain opposition to a 2¼ percent sales tax as oppressing the poor, while advocating taxes on bread and beer of six to eight times as much?" asked columnist Paul Hudson. But such questions were rare. Most criticism of the beer tax concerned doubts about its revenue, not complaints about its fairness.[24]

This trial balloon seemed likely to survive the potshots.

Income Taxes

Congress was skittish as Roosevelt continued to mull his options. Some lawmakers, most notably House Majority Leader Henry Rainey (D-IL), were opposed to any revenue hike. "The people," he warned, "will not stand for more taxes and if we vote them we will invite revolution." Rainey was never one to mince words.[25]

Other Democrats were more flexible. After a meeting in New York City with the president-elect, Speaker Garner announced a surprising new plan. Democrats, he said, would seek a renewal of the federal gas tax, as well as a new, higher tax on beer. But in a startling move, they would also seek a reduction in income tax exemptions for married couples, lowering the figure from $2,500 to $2,000. Even more startling, party leaders would seek an increase in the "normal" income tax—the rate applicable to all taxpayers, even those just above the exemption threshold.[26]

These were dramatic proposals, substantially broadening the income tax and focusing rate increases on the lower end of the levy. Most Democrats had resisted efforts to broaden the tax throughout the 1920s. In 1932, Mellon had pleaded with Congress for lower exemptions, and Democrats had reluctantly agreed, but only in the face of fiscal emergency. Now the shoe was on the other foot; Democrats had to find new revenue, and the income tax beckoned as a likely prospect. Since Roosevelt had killed the notion of a sales tax, the income tax seemed the only viable alternative.

Democrats might have tried to raise rates on the richest taxpayers. But steep rates in the upper reaches of the tax were broadly understood to raise little revenue. Only a broader base could close the budget gap, according to most observers. "The decision to increase income taxes in the lower brackets is a courageous move," intoned the *Washington Post*. "Heavier imposts upon moderate incomes are the only practical alternative to the sales tax, if the budget is to be balanced."[27]

But congressional liberals were not happy. Sen. Tom Walsh (D-MT) reluctantly allowed that he would support a modest reduction in exemptions, as well as an increase in lower-bracket rates, but only in exchange for major hikes in the upper brackets. In broad strokes, he was insisting on the sort of bargain that lawmakers had struck in 1932: if the poor were going to pay more, then the rich would too, even if the revenue from steep upper bracket rates was inconsequential. Sen. George Norris (R-NE), a leader of the GOP progressives who had supported Roosevelt during the campaign, warned that he would have to be "absolutely convinced" that lower exemptions were necessary. Rejecting the arguments recently advanced by Republican Treasury officials, including Andrew Mellon and Ogden Mills, he insisted that there was still room for revenue growth in the upper brackets.[28]

In fact, most rank and file Democrats were unwilling to accept Garner's suggestion that exemptions should fall. Rumbles of dissent grew into a roar, and the party had a revolt on its hands, not unlike the rollicking tax debate of early 1932. This time, the leadership was quick to back off. House Majority Leader Rainey reassured voters that the income tax changes were far from settled. "President-elect Roosevelt," he said, "did not for a moment favor the enactment, except as a last resort, of legislation increasing the income tax rates and lowering existing exemptions." Roosevelt issued his own statement, too, refusing to rule out the possibility of broader income taxation, but putting plenty of distance between the Garner proposal and his own thinking.[29]

This trial balloon was losing altitude.

Luxury Taxes

As other tax plans floundered, a group of congressional Democrats advanced yet another idea: a luxury tax. Building on excises enacted in the 1932 revenue act, the luxury tax would apply strictly to expensive, superfluous goods. "Extremely high-priced wearing apparel, certain fancy foods and beverages, luxurious furniture and housefurnishings, and expensive appurtenances of all kinds would be included," the *New York Times* reported. Items of mass consumption would be exempt, even if they might reasonably be called indulgences; gum, cosmetics, and baseball tickets were all presumably in the clear.[30]

But the details of the luxury tax remained murky. It might be imposed on a list of defined luxury goods. Or it might be levied on all goods not included on a free list. The latter approach implied a very broad tax, indeed. Either way, supporters insisted that the new tax would spread the burden more fairly than existing excise duties. "The prospect for success of such a levy," the *New York Times* observed, "was considered enhanced by the demand of manufacturers taxed through the special excises in the 1932 act for a more equitable distribution of taxation throughout their class of manufacturing."[31]

No lawmaker stepped forward to claim responsibility for the luxury tax; the idea remained the province of unnamed sources in various newspaper accounts. Such reticence proved prudent when the luxury tax began to gather enemies. Critics pointed out the implausibility of a luxury tax in the midst of a serious depression. "During a period of hard times people buy few luxuries," noted the *Washington Post;* how could such a levy raise significant revenue when people couldn't afford to buy taxed items? If the tax were heavy, it would discourage consumption, further reducing revenue. If it were light enough—and broad enough—to actually raise money, then it wouldn't really be a luxury tax at all. "When developed in detail it [the luxury tax] would be either a deceptive sales tax or another futile gesture of taking money from empty purses," the *Post* concluded.[32]

This balloon never got off the ground.

None of the tax proposals debated during Roosevelt's transition seemed very promising. "Trial balloons to test public sentiment on new tax levies have become so common that there is no longer much interest in seeing them explode," the *Post* observed.[33] While Democrats were eager to demonstrate their fiscal responsibility, they couldn't get close to agreeing on a tax program. The best they could offer was a beer tax: with happy days here again, Americans could drink themselves into a (slightly) better fiscal future.

Pecora, Morgan, and Tax Avoidance

If Democrats couldn't develop their own tax agenda, then someone was sure to do it for them. That person turned out to be Ferdinand Pecora, chief counsel for the Senate Banking Committee and tormentor of tax avoiders everywhere.

June 1, 1933, was a bad day for J. P. Morgan Jr. Summoned to testify before a Senate committee, this scion of Wall Street's most fabled dynasty wilted visibly under the public scrutiny. For more than a week, he and his partners had been badgered by Pecora, whose prosecutorial style was good headline fodder. Eager to illuminate Wall Street's seamy underside, Pecora had grilled Morgan on his business practices during the first several days of testimony. Now the banker found events moving from bad to worse.

Mesmerized by the humbling of Wall Street's gray eminence, reporters were having a field day. So, too, were hearing spectators, who jammed the Senate Caucus Room in hopes of snaring a front row seat. At least one member of the committee found the whole scene revolting. "We are having a circus," complained Sen. Carter Glass (D-VA), "and the only things lacking now are peanuts and colored lemonade."[34]

Charles Leef, a publicity agent for Barnum and Bailey Circus, seized on Glass's comment. The next day, he appeared at the hearing with Lya Graf, a circus performer of very small stature. Leef dropped Graf, who stood just 27 inches tall, in Morgan's lap, setting the stage for one brief conversation and countless famous photographs of "the Millionaire and the Midget."[35]

Graf and Morgan appeared together on the front pages of newspapers across the country. It was a low point for Wall Street's most famous private banker, who found himself reduced to a public spectacle. The Great House of Morgan, established by Jack Morgan's imperious father, had seldom been the subject of scrutiny, much less ridicule. But the Pecora investigation had brought many embarrassments to the firm, not the least of which concerned Morgan's personal tax returns.

Throughout the first half of 1933, American financial leaders had squirmed under the spotlight of Pecora's investigation. Prompted by the crash of 1929, the Banking Committee had begun a series of hearings on stock exchange practices. Wall Street critics hoped the panel would uncover shady dealings and financial duplicity, pinning responsibility for the depression on lower Manhattan's merchants of greed.

The critics were not disappointed. Under Pecora's leadership, senators built a powerful case for financial regulation. Congress responded with a series of regulatory measures, including the Glass-Steagall Act, the Securities Act of 1933, and the Securities Exchange Act of 1934. It was an impressive political triumph.

History remembers Ferdinand Pecora as the patron saint of Wall Street regulation. But he also deserves a spot in the pantheon of tax reformers. Pecora scored some of his most potent political points when he strayed from narrow questions of banking and securities practices. Indeed, his most explosive revelations concerned Morgan's tax returns.

"J. P. Morgan, head of the international banking firm which bears his name, paid no income tax in 1931 and 1932, nor did any of his partners," reported the *New York Times* on May 24, 1933.[36] It was a stunning revelation, at least to the popular press. How could this giant of American wealth escape the income tax? The question rang through the halls of Congress, galvanizing critics of the federal revenue system and propelling a move for tax reform.

Washington was mesmerized by Morgan's appearance before the Banking Committee. His very presence seemed improbable. The *Richmond Times-Dispatch* spoke for many when it breathlessly observed: "J. Pierpont Morgan, the twentieth-century embodiment of Croesus, Lorenzo the magnificent, Rothschild; the lordly Mr. Morgan, with his impregnable castle at Broad and Wall Streets and his private army of armed guards; the austere Mr. Morgan, to whose presence only the mighty are admitted, in a committee room and upon his bare brow the gaze of the 'peepul.' Truly an extraordinary event."[37]

The scene outside the committee room was chaotic. People clamored to reach the hearing. "Outside in the long corridor is a suffocating crush of men and women, bitterly disappointed at the impossibility of fighting their way into the circus," wrote one observer. "They argue with the doorkeepers. They complain. They crane their necks. Anything for one little peek at the great J. P. Morgan, giant of money." The Senate installed special phone lines to handle to influx of reporters, as well as new lighting to facilitate photography.[38]

Pecora questioned Morgan on a wide range of topics, including sweetheart deals for certain political figures. Treasury Secretary William Woodin found himself under the uncomfortable spotlight, having been the recipient of a few Morgan favors. But Morgan felt the glare of public scrutiny most acutely when questions turned to his personal tax returns.

Pecora quickly established that Morgan had paid no income taxes to the United States during the darkest days of the early Depression. The news rocked the nation.[39] "A cry of anguish ascended to high heavens," observed *Business Week,* "when millions of white collar workers discovered that they had been nicked for a considerable percentage of their earnings for 1930 and 1931 when J. P. Morgan and partners had paid no income tax at all."[40] The liberal press reacted with outrage. "Rich men of the country should not be able to escape income taxes at the very moment when the rest of the country is burdened with increased taxes and when the Government is so desperately in need of revenue," fumed the *Washington Daily News*. It didn't help that Morgan continued to enjoy the fruits of his great wealth, even purchasing a two-and-a-half-million dollar yacht in one of the same years he claimed to have no taxable income.[41]

Pecora, a consummate showman, lingered on the tax issues, milking them for every ounce of political advantage. He kept the focus on Morgan, refusing to let subordinates testify even when Morgan proved unable to answer certain questions. Pecora preferred to elicit a string of admissions from Morgan that the great banker was unfamiliar with his own tax returns.[42]

Soon enough, Morgan got his facts straight, but they did little to burnish his public image. The partners of J. P. Morgan and Co. had, in fact, paid no income taxes for 1931 and 1932. The firm had suffered dramatic losses in the market crash, wiping out every other source of income for the partners. Indeed, the firm's net worth had plunged from $119 million to $53 million between 1929 and 1931. When all was said and done—and all capital loss deductions had been taken—there was simply no taxable income for any of the partners. "I am not responsible for these figures," Morgan insisted wryly. "I viewed them with great regret when they appeared."[43]

Morgan stressed that during the salad days of the 1920s, he and his partners had paid many millions in taxes, most of them on capital gains; between 1917 and 1929, they had collectively ponied up more than $57 million.[44] But that point seemed lost on many reporters and lawmakers—not to mention the general public.

Perhaps most galling, Morgan had paid taxes to Great Britain in years when he had escaped U.S. levies. Britain did not allow deductions for capital losses—nor did it assess tax on capital gains. Morgan's other sources of income, including the imputed rental value of his real estate holdings, had left him subject to the British income tax, which he dutifully paid, even during the worst years of the depression. To hostile observers, Morgan's payment of British taxes smacked of something unpatriotic. It didn't help that the banker spoke with British affectations, referring, for instance, to the assistance he received from his "clark."[45]

Pecora spent much time and energy trying to lay bare one particular tax maneuver. In 1931, he pointed out, the Morgan partners had claimed a $21 million loss. The firm had admitted a new partner, S. Parker Gilbert, on January 2, and the resulting reorganization produced a write-off for depreciated securities. Pecora hammered home the unusual timing. By waiting until January 2, rather than admitting Gilbert on December 31, the firm had been able to carry over the loss until 1933, rather than just through 1932. The maneuver required a tax return covering just two days, but the BIR had accepted it without complaint.[46]

The Bureau, it turned out, had a soft spot for Morgan and his partners. As Pecora gleefully related, the agency had declined to examine certain Morgan-related returns simply by virtue of the firm's reputation. As one auditor scrawled on a return, "Returned without examination for the reason that the return was prepared in the office of J. P. Morgan & Co., and it has been our experience that any schedule made by that office is correct."[47] Such trust seemed misplaced, at least to hostile observers.

In fact, however, Morgan had broken no laws. The only shady activity Pecora was able to uncover concerned one junior partner, Thomas S. Lamont, who had sold depressed securities to his wife and then bought them back three months later in a wash sale. But Morgan himself, as well as all the other partners except Lamont, had done nothing wrong. As one Morgan defender complained, "It is not criminality. Mr. Pecora only makes it seem so."[48]

Indeed, Pecora did make it seem so. By training and inclination, he was a prosecutor, not an investigator. He had no interest in being even-handed. As historian John Brooks succinctly observed, "Pecora, three-quarters righteous tribune of the people, was one-quarter demagogic inquisitor."[49] Not every member of the Senate panel wanted to preside over an inquisition. Sen. Carter Glass (D-VA) was a vocal critic, persistently objecting to Pecora's tax questions. Glass was furious at the counsel for trying to pillory Morgan, and he repeatedly sought to shift the line of questioning. According to one journalistic observer, the audience was not amused, responding with an "angry murmur" when Glass made his celebrated "circus" comment, "as might a real circus audience if some cantankerous authority tried to interfere with the marvelous parade, headed by the greatest of all giants."[50]

No matter what he tried, Glass couldn't stop Pecora. The counsel had too much support, not least from the newly inaugurated president. Roosevelt regarded the Wall Street investigation as manna from heaven, just what he needed to help build the case for wholesale economic reform. By mid-March, he was an active spectator of the Pecora investigation, if only from a distance. He met repeatedly with Pecora and Banking Committee chair Duncan Fletcher (D-FL). In fact, it was FDR who suggested that the panel focus on Morgan in the first place. Pecora had all the political cover he might need.[51]

Leaders of the Banking Committee followed the president's lead, endorsing Pecora's tax crusade despite—or perhaps because of—the counsel's theatrical tactics. Pecora's finger pointing (often *literal* finger pointing) was fine theater and simply too good to resist. And Democrats hoped they could leverage popular outrage in support of Roosevelt's broader legislative agenda.

Morality, Legal Ethics, and Tax Avoidance

The Pecora investigation gave rise to a vigorous debate over the moral status of tax avoidance. The political world divided between those who believed legal tax avoidance was morally neutral, and those who considered it a moral failing. Pecora, of course, stood squarely on the latter side of this divide. "The country, in 1933, was in no mood for nice distinctions between tax 'evasion' and tax 'avoidance'," he later recalled. Tax avoidance, although technically legal, was simply unconscionable in times of national emergency. Pecora stopped short of any ringing moral indictment, but he clearly left the impression that Morgan and his partners had shirked their responsibilities. "Approved by the existing tax authorities or not," he wrote, "the public could not see the justice or equity of financial giants paying nothing, while Tom, Dick, and Harry scraped the bottom of their modest purses to meet their tax obligations to the Government."[52]

While Pecora refused to recognize moral distinctions between evasion and avoidance, others believed there was a world of difference. Carter Glass considered Morgan's tax avoidance a matter of good business. *Business Week* explained his position sympathetically: "He knew, as virtually everyone in banking circles who had given a moment's thought to it did, that if the Morgans had not written off enough losses to prevent income tax payments in the years just past, they were just foolish." Indeed, foolishness and stupidity were something of a touchstone for the Morgan defenders, and *Business Week* drove the point home: "Any individual who pays unnecessary taxes is merely stupid. Among all the charges and innuendoes that have been flung about, not one yet accuses the Morgan outfit of stupidity."[53]

Some experts actually questioned this assumption. Several court decisions in the early 1930s had tried to look beyond the letter of the law to determine whether a taxpayer was dealing with the government in good faith. But generally speaking, the tax bar recognized that legal avoidance, however unappealing, was not immoral. "As yet, taxpayers have not become philanthropists, dunces, or unerring individuals, and it is a fallacious rule of law which presumes that they might be," concluded one tax expert. "If Congress intended to tax them, tax them. If exemption or deduction is allowed, permit it."[54]

Morgan himself stressed his fealty to the law. "I want to make clear about it that I take great pains, and I have all my life, to pay the income taxes and other taxes I am called upon to pay by the various governments," he insisted. Moreover, he had always sought professional assistance in calculating his taxes, ensuring that he completed his returns accurately. "I get the best advice I can find out," he assured the Banking Committee, "that I do not underpay or overpay."[55]

To critics, that Morgan defense only broadened the locus of moral turpitude. In getting "the best advice" he could find, Morgan had turned to the tax bar, which was then in its relative infancy as a distinct—and lucrative—specialty within the legal profession. Lawyers, as well as certain high-end accountants, took a beating in the press. The *New Republic* bemoaned the role of high-priced tax advisers. Gaming the tax system only served to discredit the income tax as an institution, the magazine complained: "This is a genuine disservice to their country on the part of the Morgan partners—and of all the others who, though well able to pay, employ the most expensive brains in order to find out how not to." Pecora made the same point when looking back on the hearings. "So long as we have tax statutes," he wrote, "we will have keen-eyed lawyers and accountants seeking to circumvent them."[56]

For someone like Morgan, of course, professional tax advice was a necessity. The tax law was already complicated by 1933; many of its provisions were so obtuse as to essentially require professional interpretation. In fact, lawmakers had judged the income tax so complicated in 1926 that they had established a special panel, the Joint Committee on Internal Revenue Taxation (JCIRT), to develop plans for simplification.

But lawyers weren't simply filing returns. By 1933, they were earning most of their money with tax planning: sophisticated efforts to minimize the tax liability of well-heeled clients. And the tax law gave them room to work. "The law had holes through which any competent attorney could drive a team and a hayrack," *Business Week* observed. And Morgan's loss deductions were not some sort of inadvertent loophole. They were the predictable result of some very deliberate lawmaking.[57]

The Morgan debate hinged on deductions for capital losses. The inclusion of capital income in the income tax base was not a foregone conclusion when the income tax first appeared. Great Britain had exempted both gains and losses from its version of the levy. And including such periodic (as opposed to regular) income streams in the tax had made the American levy highly unstable. The steep drop in income tax revenues that accompanied the onset of the Great Depression was due, in no small part, to the decline in capital gains and the dramatic increase in capital losses.

The Revenue Act of 1932 had expressly permitted the deduction of capital losses from the sale or exchange of securities held less than two years, though only to the extent of capital gains; the losses could not be applied to regular income. The law permitted taxpayers to carry forward any disallowed losses to subsequent years, but again, the losses could be applied only to capital income.[58]

Wealthy taxpayers had long complained that Congress knew only too well what effect such provisions might have. Morgan, for one, indicated that he would have been more than pleased to exchange his loss write-offs for a corresponding removal of capital gains from the calculation of taxable income. "Be it said that wealthy men protested the capital gains and losses provisions of the income tax law back in the boom years," Business Week pointed out. "Nobody listened to them."[59]

Morgan critics dismissed such complaints about the law, insisting that tax avoidance, even when legal, was morally suspect. Moral responsibility trumped legal technicality, they insisted. Paul Y. Anderson, Pulitzer Prize–winning reporter for the St. Louis Post-Dispatch, made the point dramatically. "For them [Morgan and his partners] to seize upon the 'capital-losses' provision of the existing law for the purpose of withholding contributions to the support of the government under which they have prospered so greatly, was as natural as for a hog to snap up an ear of corn," he wrote.[60]

Anderson pointed out that he spurned loss deductions on his own returns. "It would have been legal, no doubt, but on the moral side it would have been a plain case of cheating the government," he said. Anderson objected to the common refrain, offered frequently by Morgan's defenders, that tax avoidance was a game for everyone:

We have our faults. Some of us lose more than we can afford at golf, bridge, or poker; some indulge in an extravagant passion for old furniture or rare editions; still others punish their lives unbearably with poor rye, bad Scotch, and worse gin; but it is manifestly unjust, if not libelous, to name us in the same breath with Morgan, Lamont, Stotesbury, Mitchell, and that gang.[61]

Franklin Roosevelt was notably silent when it came to the specifics of the Morgan tax revelations. His reticence might be explained by his own tax returns: in 1932, he had taken a capital loss deduction of his own.[62] But since his returns were not public, he had no reason to fear any disclosure of that deduction. And he seemed to content to let Pecora and the liberal press rage against Morgan's similar deductions.

Meanwhile, Morgan knew he had a public relations disaster on his hands. On June 9, he submitted a written statement to the Senate Banking Committee, seeking to clarify his tax position "because at first blush, there can be no doubt that many persons, failing to realize that during prosperous times we had paid heavy taxes upon our profits, felt it to be unjust that during the last 3 years we have paid no income taxes; again failing to realize that our losses had more than wiped out our taxable income." His explanation did little to salvage his reputation.[63]

The Morgan revelations prompted a call for tax reform. "The situation has been glaringly obvious and repeatedly pointed out," the *New Republic* declared. "Public resentment at the ease with which men of vast wealth and huge incomes completely evade the tax burden, in a time of depression, has put a force behind the effort to correct these indefensible flaws in our tax system." Allowing wealthy taxpayers to avoid taxes— legally or not—posed a threat to the income tax as a whole, the magazine went on to argue. "You cannot enforce painfully high income-tax rates on the moderately well off if the rich are not proportionately taxed." Failing to address problems with the income tax could only lend support to those people seeking its replacement with a national sales tax.[64]

Indeed, the Morgan disclosures contributed to a sense of crisis surrounding the income tax. Tax avoidance struck many critics as profoundly undemocratic. And by discrediting the income tax's claim to fairness, it raised doubts about the very foundation of national fiscal policy. Progressive tax supporters worried that the income tax was on its last legs, besieged by rich tax avoiders on the one hand, and by declining revenues on the other. If the tax was neither fair nor productive, then its future was bleak.

Some hoped the Morgan disclosures would revive support for public tax returns. Progressive legislators in both parties supported the idea. They believed that by shining light on the behavior of taxpayers, public returns might forestall evasion. Publicity might even shame wealthy taxpayers into forswearing aggressive tax avoidance, even when it was legal.

Almost a decade earlier, a coalition of rural and western lawmakers had managed to include a publicity requirement in the Revenue Act of 1924. The law required the public release of every income taxpayer's name, address, and tax payment; many newspapers published the information in long but well-read lists. The idea drew vociferous opposition, much of it from taxpayers, but also from the Republican political establishment. In 1926, Treasury secretary Andrew Mellon and his deputy Ogden Mills managed to get the provision repealed.[65]

The Morgan tax disclosures, however, gave new life to the publicity idea. Paul Y. Anderson in the *Nation* insisted that public returns could be a powerful force for good. The cries of unhappy taxpayers merely demonstrated the importance of this enforcement technique. "Is it any wonder that old Andy Mellon squalled like a panther at every suggestion that income-tax payments be made public?" Anderson asked. "Is it any wonder that Ogden Mills became purple over such attempts to 'pry into private affairs'? They knew where the cat was buried, and whose cat it was."[66]

The Political Response to Tax Avoidance

The Morgan revelations prompted quick action from Congress. Lawmakers modified the pending National Industrial Recovery Act (NIRA) to include several anti-loophole provisions. Even more important, they began work on a more comprehensive reform measure, the Revenue Act of 1934. Together, these laws eliminated numerous inequities in the tax law. At the same time, however, they created a few new ones. While closing a range of ostensible "loopholes," legislators removed several with genuine claim to fairness.

While Morgan was testifying before the Pecora committee, the NIRA bill was making its way through Congress. The legislation included $3.3 billion in public works spending, and lawmakers were absorbed in a debate over how to fund it. The money itself would come from new government bonds, but Roosevelt and most congressional leaders were committed to finding new revenue to pay interest and sinking fund requirements. Policymakers needed roughly $220 million to tide them over.[67]

At one point, congressional and administration leaders neared agreement on a "reemployment tax," a rebranded version of the manufacturers' excise tax defeated in 1932. Critics had a field day with the semantic gamesmanship. "The words 'reemployment tax' do not change the nature of the proposed levy," pointed out the *Washington Post* with evident glee (the paper had long supported a sales tax). The *New York Times* complained that the tax was renamed solely "to make it smell sweeter to the labor unions."[68] In fact, organized labor had grudgingly accepted the new levy. But rank and file Democrats remained cool to the idea. With revolt brewing, House and Senate leaders began to kick around alternatives, including a so-called breakfast table tax: a collection of excise levies on food items, including sugar, coffee, and tea. Such taxes, however, were unlikely to raise sufficient revenue, and they drew ample criticism for their regressive incidence.

Chastened by the chilly reception every tax idea seemed to encounter, Roosevelt passed the buck, instructing his budget director, Lewis Douglas, to present several revenue ideas to Congress without endorsing any of them.[69] Douglas, a fiscal conservative, outlined a variety of possibilities, including a general sales tax of 1.125 percent; an increase in the "normal" rates of the personal income tax; the inclusion of corporate dividends in the tax base for the normal income tax; and a collection of miscellaneous taxes, including levies on "breakfast table" goods, as well as telephone use, entertainment admissions, and gasoline. Notably, Douglas did not suggest higher surtax rates—a move that would have focused the increase on rich taxpayers.[70]

The Ways and Means Committee decided to raise normal rates. In their report, the committee pointed out that income tax exemptions had been left unchanged; the base was just as narrow as always. The committee also embraced Douglas's suggestion that dividends be taxed under the income tax normal rates. Stockholders could well afford the added burden. "The man with income from dividends is obviously a man with capital," the committee explained, "while the man with an equal income from salary may have no capital."[71]

As the NIRA bill came before the House for a final vote, Morgan was finishing his testimony before the Pecora committee. The outrage over tax avoidance spilled over into the NIRA debate, and lawmakers quickly added several anti-loophole provisions to the pending bill. Predictably, they took special aim at partnerships and capital loss provisions, taking their cue from Pecora's public statements. "So far," the Banking counsel told reporters, "we have shown at least that the Income Tax Law as it stands is not a tax on income when persons have large incomes and may offset their incomes with capital losses. A man of moderate income is not in a position to do any such thing, and to that extent the law is grossly inequitable."[72]

To Pecora and others, it was all a question of ability to pay. While capital loss deductions were economically reasonable, they seemed morally indefensible. Generally speaking, such losses were the exclusive province of wealthy taxpayers—people with ample ability to pay. In times of national emergency, such people had a responsibility to shoulder their fair share of the overall tax burden.

House lawmakers quickly added a new loss provision to the NIRA bill, limiting deductions for stock losses on securities held less than two years. Henceforth, taxpayers would only be able to apply their loss deductions against income earned in the same year; they were barred from carrying forward any excess loss to subsequent tax years. Effectively, the change disallowed many loss deductions entirely, since taxpayers often had far greater losses than gains, especially in the midst of an economic downturn. Carryovers were the only way to recoup many losses.

In the Senate, the Morgan disclosures prompted further changes to the NIRA bill. Finance Committee Chairman Pat Harrison (D-MS) was no liberal, but he objected to the Morgan loss deductions. His committee approved language barring partners from deducting their share of business losses from individual income. The final bill included both the House and Senate restrictions on loss deductions.[73]

Revenue Act of 1934

Ultimately, the NIRA tax debate was just a skirmish in the larger battle against tax avoidance. Liberal journals like the *New Republic* called on Roosevelt to take the lead. And once again, Paul Anderson, writing in the *Nation,* offered a dramatic suggestion. "The Morgan revelations have made it perfectly plain that what we really need is a capital levy, which would present the twin virtues of obtaining an ample revenue to finance all the government's undertakings and squeezing the fat cats who have studiously avoided their duty to the nation."[74]

A capital levy was not in the cards, but anti-loophole provisions certainly were. In June 1933, the Ways and Means Committee began studying ways to curb tax avoidance. Members created a special subcommittee to seek new revenue, principally through a reduction in loopholes and tax preferences. The resulting legislation would, indeed, raise considerable money by cracking down on tax avoidance. At the same time, however, it would eliminate several provisions designed to promote tax fairness, not hinder it. Eager to raise the tax burden on businesses and wealthy individuals, lawmakers turned out to be more interested in soaking the rich than they were in promoting fairness.

Standards of Tax Fairness

Tax fairness is a heterogeneous idea, encompassing a variety of ethical and moral standards for evaluating tax policy. In broad strokes, however, it comprises two major elements: horizontal and vertical equity.

Horizontal equity requires the equal treatment of equals; similarly situated taxpayers should pay similar amounts. In the context of an income tax, that generally means that two people with the same income—regardless of source—should get the same tax bill. This standard of tax fairness has historically enjoyed broad support across the political spectrum, although it has proven contentious around the subject of capital income generally and capital gains taxation in particular. While liberals have generally argued that capital income should be taxed the same as income from labor, some conservatives have insisted that it should be taxed more lightly, chiefly to encourage saving and investment.

Vertical equity has been altogether more contentious throughout the modern history of American taxation. Generally speaking, vertical equity concerns the tax treatment of nonequals. The liberal tradition in American political thought has long required that rich people be saddled with higher taxes than poor people. Of course, a 10 percent tax on someone making $10,000 annually will yield more than the same tax on a person earning $1,000. In that sense, a proportional tax, enacted at a flat rate, still serves the standard of vertical equity. But supporters of progressive taxation have generally argued that *rates*, as well as total payments, should rise with income. Ability to pay increases as people get richer, and the marginal sacrifice of the last dollar of income falls as income rises.[75]

The problem with progressive taxation, however, lies in those graduated rates. Historically, support for graduation has been evident across the political spectrum. But what degree of graduation? Consider, for instance, just the top rate on personal income. Should it be 25 percent? Fifty percent? Seventy percent? Ninety-four percent? Over the years, it's been all of those and many more. And neither economics nor politics can definitively tell us which one is the "right" rate. The same holds true for every other rate embedded in the tax system, as well as the entire rate and exemption structure itself. Reasonable people can disagree about the appropriate amount of graduation—or even the notion of graduation itself.

Sometimes, horizontal and vertical equity amount to the same thing. Assume, for example, that certain rich people are reducing their tax burden through the use of loopholes or sophisticated tax planning. These rich people will pay lower tax rates than other rich people, who have failed to organize their finances in a tax-advantaged fashion. This situation violates the principle of horizontal equity. At the same time, however, this situation also violates the principle of vertical equity, since tax avoidance produces a lower effective tax rate for a few lucky rich people, relieving them of some portion of their tax burden. In that case, the tax system will no longer be distributing its overall burden according to ability to pay. People with plenty of ability will be paying artificially low taxes.[76]

In their 1933–1934 campaign to curb tax avoidance, lawmakers struggled to define and apply standards of horizontal and vertical equity. And in the process, they sometimes privileged the latter over the former. The anti-loophole campaign was, in one sense, an exercise on behalf of horizontal equity; the Ways and Means subcommittee didn't believe that men like Morgan, who could exploit the partnership and loss provisions to reduce their personal tax liabilities, should pay less than someone without recourse to such tax preferences.

It soon became clear, however, that the 1934 revenue bill would be designed to raise taxes on the rich even when ostensible loopholes served the cause of fairness. In particular, partnerships would be denied equitable treatment of losses simply as a means to raise their tax bills. Lawmakers were more interested in extracting money from the rich than they were in making the system fair—at least to the extent that fairness could be measured by horizontal equity.

The Equity Compromise of 1934

In consultation with the Treasury Department, the Ways and Means loophole subcommittee set about crafting a report. Lovell H. Parker, chief investigator for the JCIRT, prepared a memorandum, designed to serve as a starting point, and he gave a copy to the Treasury, which responded with its own set of ideas.[77]

A native of Osterville, Massachusetts, Parker had received an engineering degree from the Massachusetts Institute of Technology. After graduation, he went to work as an appraisal engineer for the Pennsylvania Railroad, the New York state government, and the United States Shipping Board. In 1924, he signed on with a special Senate committee, headed by Sen. James Couzens (R-MI), investigating misdeeds at the BIR. Two years later, Couzens got Parker a job with the JCIRT, created that year to give Congress its own source of tax expertise. Later, Parker was named the panel's chief of staff, where he developed a reputation for solid expertise and a low handicap; a long-time member of the exclusive Burning Tree Golf Club in suburban Maryland, he was known to mix putting with policymaking.[78]

When originally established in 1926, the JCIRT was charged with finding ways to simplify the income tax system—then barely more then a decade old but already the source of innumerable complaints. Soon, however, the panel expanded its purview to include a wide variety of tax research. By the 1930s, it was an important, if not quite pivotal, player in the tax policy process. Treasury still enjoyed a substantial administrative advantage, employing a much larger technical staff.

In the middle of 1933, however, Treasury was at a low point in its influence. First, the president had made it clear that Congress should take the lead in tax matters. He was happy to let lawmakers take the heat when it came to the fiery issues of tax reform. A second factor, however, was even more important. The Treasury Department lacked a strong leader. FDR's first Secretary of the Treasury, William Woodin, served just nine months before he was replaced. Meanwhile, the department was operating with a staff of tax experts inherited from the Hoover administration. Not until January 1934, when Morgenthau took the department reigns, did the Roosevelt administration begin to develop its own source of ideologically sympathetic tax expertise.[79]

Congress jumped into the Treasury's administrative void, seizing on the tax-avoidance investigation as a means to advance the primacy of

Congress in the tax policy process. Congressional officials jealously guarded their prerogatives throughout the investigation, consulting with Treasury but ultimately rebuffing any substantive role for the department until the bill was fully drafted. If the White House was unprepared to carry the ball, Congress was more than willing.

In December 1934, the loophole subcommittee delivered its report, recommending a variety of major and minor changes.[80] Most were designed to eliminate narrow tax preferences, but others involved general policy revisions. Among the latter was a proposal to slash depletion and depreciation allowances by 25 percent. This arbitrary reduction, which was sure to encounter fierce resistance from business and extractive industries in particular, did not purport to close a loophole. In fact, the committee acknowledged that such deductions were entirely legitimate, designed to account for the declining value of depleted resources. But the panel was "impressed" by the extent which such allowances, especially when applied to mineral deposits, were used to reduce taxable income unreasonably.

The committee also proposed new restrictions on personal holding companies, the deductibility of partnership losses, and the tax treatment of corporate reorganizations. Finally, the panel suggested a new scheme for taxing capital gains that would adjust the rates according to the length of time an asset was held.

Treasury Secretary Henry Morgenthau congratulated lawmakers on this collection of tax changes. The revenue system depended upon a perception of fairness, he said: "If taxpayers become convinced that the provisions [of the tax law] are essentially unjust, or that numerous people are evading them by the use of various devices, our whole income-tax revenue system will be seriously injured." If, on the other hand, taxpayers generally believed the system to be fair, then it could function effectively, even when fiscal emergencies required lawmakers to impose heavy burdens.[81]

The president joined this chorus of pro-reform rhetoric. "We have been shocked," he told Congress in January, "by many notorious examples of injuries done our citizens by persons or groups who have been living off their neighbors by the use of methods either unethical or criminal." Roosevelt was still unwilling to join the tax debate with specific proposals, but he seemed content to cheer congressional efforts from the sidelines. He instructed Morgenthau to avoid making any significant recommendations of his own.[82]

Morgenthau's kind words notwithstanding, the Treasury had various problems with the subcommittee report. Administration officials warned Congress to avoid measures that violated canons of tax fairness or that might antagonize business unnecessarily. The law should be revised, Morgenthau contended, to eliminate loopholes and distribute the tax burden fairly. Further, tax provisions should not encourage distortions in economic behavior merely for the sake of minimizing taxes. But law-makers should not throw the baby out with the bathwater. Many of the changes recommended by the loophole committee would unfairly burden legitimate business operations, he said, discriminating in almost random fashion against certain activities and types of organizations. "The income tax should properly take a reasonable toll from the business transactions in the community," he declared. "It should not stop the traffic entirely."[83]

To some degree, Morgenthau's statement reflects the Roosevelt administration's early solicitude for business interests. In this early stage of the New Deal, Roosevelt and his advisers were eager to cooperate with industry, and the administration's tax stand reflected a genuine concern for the health of American business.

But another factor was at work as well, prompting Treasury to resist some of the more punitive aspects of the tax reform program offered up by House lawmakers. In general, the Treasury and its staff had tried to assume a disinterested posture in many revenue debates, seeking to defend the fisc against depredations from left and right alike. The department cherished its reputation as the guardian of good tax law, and the initial loophole report was filled with provisions that didn't merit that description. While Congress was clearly interested in punitive measures aimed at wealthy individuals and certain types of businesses, the Treasury sought to protect the overall functioning of the tax system.

Morgenthau welcomed the additional revenue promised by the committee report, and he saw virtue in the panel's effort to tighten tax provisions. But he was unwilling to accept a sacrifice in horizontal equity—not to mention standards of accurate accounting—for the sake of greater progressivity. For instance, the subcommittee's plan to reduce depreciation allowances was manifestly unfair, Morgenthau claimed. The committee, in fact, had struck a defensive tone in its report, insisting that "these amounts deducted from income do not represent cash outgo like wages, repairs, and similar expenses, but are annual reserves generally theoretically set aside to replace property and plant investments." In other words, no cash-flow hardship should follow from the deduction restrictions. But Morgenthau insisted that deductions for depreciation were "fundamentally the same in character as deductions for the cost of goods sold in the case of a merchant." Treasury opposed the arbitrary limitation of these deductions, citing the provision's "doubtful constitutionality" and "inherent unfairness."[84]

The Treasury was not simply playing the toady for business interests. Morgenthau suggested, for instance, that depletion allowances for minerals and other natural resources be completely eliminated, citing fairness concerns. "To exempt the income of mine owners or of any other class necessitates simply that the amount be made up by other taxpayers," he said. Abolishing depletion allowances was an explosive—and politically impossible—idea. But it represented the Treasury's best effort to protect the revenue system from unwarranted favors and special provisions.[85]

On the controversial subject of partnership losses, the Treasury challenged the pell-mell rush to punish all partnerships for the ostensible sins committed by J. P. Morgan and company. Partnership losses should certainly be deductible against other forms of personal income, Morgenthau asserted. "There can be little question as to the propriety of this arrangement, since the individual's capacity to pay the income tax is directly reduced by such losses," he said. If partnership gains were to remain taxable to the partner personally, then losses should be deductible as well, even when applied against other forms of income. "The losses now deductible are not fictitious or imaginary and do not represent either evasion or avoidance of the income tax law."[86]

These were odd sentiments for a Roosevelt crony. The president, after all, had cheered enthusiastically as Pecora vilified Morgan for his deduction of partnership losses. But Morgenthau spoke for the Treasury, and the Treasury's agenda—at least in this stage of the New Deal—was not yet permeated by such strong soak-the-rich tendencies.

The tax-avoidance subcommittee took special aim at what it called incorporated pocketbooks—personal holding companies. A popular tax-avoidance scheme, the idea was to establish a corporation and exchange personal income-producing property for stock in the new company. The income would then be subject to corporation income tax rates, but would escape personal income taxation so long as it was not distributed to the shareholders. The committee provided an example:

> Suppose a man has $1,000,000 annual income from taxable bonds. His tax under existing law will be $571,100. However, if he forms a holding company to take title to the bonds and to receive the income therefrom, the only tax paid will be a corporate tax of $137,500 as long as there is no distribution of dividends.[87]

The Treasury was sympathetic with the committee's effort to tighten the personal holding company provisions. But Morgenthau warned against several specific changes, arguing that most attempts to define affected companies were bound to be either too broad or too narrow. Such "over-specific legislation," he said, only served to complicate the tax law while also facilitating evasion. Morgenthau assured the committee that Treasury was working on a better, more nuanced solution.[88]

Ultimately, the Ways and Means Committee incorporated many of the Treasury's suggestions into its draft of the Revenue Act of 1934. Perhaps most notably, members removed their punitive restrictions on partnership losses. But the panel stuck to its guns on other issues, including several provisions that effectively lowered the tax burden on wage and salary income while raising the burden on investments.[89] The bill sailed through committee, and leaders moved it through the House itself without amendment. Ways and Means Chairman Robert L. Doughton (D-NC) gave the bill a strong endorsement. The income tax was no longer functioning as intended, he told his colleagues. Rich taxpayers were escaping the surtax rates through a variety of legal machinations. If the income tax was to remain a mainstay of federal finance, he declared, then "every citizen and every corporation should be compelled to bear a fair share of the tax." Apparently his colleagues in both parties were eager to agree, passing the bill by a vote of 390 to 7.[90]

The bill moved to the Senate, where administration officials continued their efforts to moderate its more punitive provisions. And carrying the ball for Morgenthau was a new player in the tax policy process: New York lawyer Roswell Magill.

Morgenthau's First Tax Expert

Then a Republican law professor at Columbia, Magill had served in Mellon's Treasury Department. Morgenthau asked him back, heeding the suggestions of friends who repeatedly cited Magill as a trustworthy and talented tax lawyer. It was an important personnel decision, imbuing the Treasury with a new source of administrative expertise. But it also put a conservative face on New Deal tax policy.

Magill's appointment in late November of 1933 came as a surprise to many observers. The post had been expected to go to Harold Groves of the University of Wisconsin, a noted liberal and champion of the La Follette approach to tax policy (named for Wisconsin progressive

Robert La Follette and marked by a preference for steep marginal income rates and relatively lower exemptions). Groves, however, had been named by Morgenthau's predecessor, and the acting secretary wanted "some one of my own choosing."[91]

Strikingly, Morgenthau claimed to have no knowledge of Magill's tax philosophy. Quite possibly, he was being disingenuous, but it was not out of character for Morgenthau to make ideology a secondary concern in hiring decisions. The new secretary valued personal loyalty above all else, and he sought "good character" in his subordinates, even at the expense of ideological compatibility. For Morgenthau, Magill possessed some signal virtues. First, he was well regarded by the secretary's friends. Even more important, he hailed from New York, where he served on the Columbia faculty with people familiar to the Roosevelt entourage. Indeed, Columbia had served as a breeding ground for FDR's tax advisers while he was governor, and Morgenthau had met many of them during his time in Albany. Magill was not the last Treasury tax official to venture south from Morningside Heights. Indeed, he would soon call on his former colleagues to help staff the department. Magill was the leading edge of a new tax bureaucracy in the Treasury.

Liberal critics complained that Magill was too conservative. His appointment, complained the *Nation,* more or less closed the door on substantive tax reform. "Magill has been engaged under Morgenthau principally in building traps for tax-dodgers and inventing plugs for holes in the tax laws rather than in devising the whole new system of taxes needed to supplant the present Old Deal holdover which places at least half the burden on consumption taxes," the magazine reported. And the editors were right—at least for the time being.[92]

Arriving at Treasury just as the Ways and Means loophole sub-committee was preparing its report, Magill got quickly up to speed. Morgenthau put him to work drafting an "independent study" meant to provide the secretary with his own source of information on tax avoidance. Simultaneously, Magill began organizing a major study of the nation's income tax system, with an eye toward comprehensive reform. This study would become, in fact, his major focus; over the next six months, it would also occupy most of the new staff he recruited to the department.[93]

For the time being, however, Magill prepared the administration's response to the Ways and Means loophole bill. He played a vital role in explaining the Treasury's position to skeptical lawmakers, in both the

House and the Senate. His stature in the tax community provided a counterweight to the Joint Committee's growing reservoir of expertise, helping boost the Treasury's credibility as it struggled to build its administrative capacity around tax research. Magill led the Treasury's effort to fend off radical change, with an eye toward crafting the department's own revenue bill the following year.

As the Revenue Act of 1934 arrived in the Senate, it found broad support in the Finance Committee. Magill figured prominently in the committee's hearings, meeting with senators in executive session to hammer out details. Indeed, the Treasury did not testify in public hearings, leaving such sessions to the business community. Finance Chairman Pat Harrison (D-MS) considered a few significant changes to the bill, but when all was said and done, the committee accepted most of the House language.[94]

On the Senate floor, progressives in both parties tried repeatedly to boost rates on incomes and estates, but the leadership was loath to cooperate. Harrison was in no mode to work with La Follette and Couzens, who were leading the charge for higher rates. None of the progressives, he told Morgenthau, had been loyal soldiers for the administration. Moreover, higher rates might impede recovery. Indeed, Harrison confided that he was inclined to reduce rates as soon as possible.[95]

Eventually, however, senators approved higher surtax rates on incomes under $32,000, as well as an "emergency" 10 percent surtax on total income tax liability. They also voted for a boost in estate and gift tax rates, as well as a provision making income tax returns open to public inspection. Later, in conference with the House, senators won most contested points. The final bill raised surtax rates on upper-income taxpayers, while also cutting effective rates in the lower brackets. Conferees watered down the publicity provision, requiring the release of only limited information from each return. The final bill also included higher estate rates, which now topped out at 60 percent. All told, the legislation was expected to raise $417 million in new revenue.[96]

But most important, the Revenue Act of 1934 did, in fact, close a variety of loopholes. Its restrictions on personal holding companies were particularly important—and controversial. The campaign against "incorporated pocketbooks" would soon provoke at an outcry among wealthy taxpayers, but for the time being, it seemed a popular measure. And while lawmakers heeded the Treasury's caution against undue restrictions on partnership losses, the act did tighten the law around such losses, limiting deductibility in ways the Treasury still considered unfair.[97] When all was said and done, the department's sober voice had managed to tame the more florid tendencies of congressional taxwriters. But not before tax avoidance had enjoyed a very prominent turn in the political spotlight.

Conclusion

Those looking for crystalline ideological clarity will not find it in early New Deal tax policy. During the 1932 campaign and subsequent presidential transition, Roosevelt flirted with any number of tax ideas, only to ignore all of them once in office. But Congress was far more active, if perhaps no less muddled when it came to tax ideas. Once the Pecora revelations threw the spotlight on tax avoidance, Congress responded with enthusiasm. The NIRA tax provisions and the Revenue Act of 1934 drew strength from a deep wellspring of political outrage (in Congress, and by most subjective accounts, among average Americans as well). The Democratic majority in both houses of Congress coalesced around the proposition that tax policy must be measured by a stricter standard than technical legality. As Ways and Means Chairman Doughton had observed, they wanted all taxpayers to pay their "fair share," whether or not the law demanded it.

In the hands of energized congressional leaders—including several with conservative sympathies, like Pat Harrison from the Senate Finance Committee—"fair share" took on a distinctly progressive edge. Lawmakers turned out to be less interested in scouring the tax law for inadvertent loopholes, and more concerned with simply raising the burden on rich taxpayers. Legislators targeted numerous "loopholes" that actually served ideals of horizontal equity and tax fairness. Hoping to raise the burden on rich taxpayers through whatever means might be available, they were prepared to sacrifice one form of fairness in pursuit of another. Lawmakers believed that the income tax was endangered by legal tax avoidance, especially among the rich. If the income tax were to remain a pillar of American federal finance, it had to be saved from the depredations of wealthy tax shirkers. Soon enough, Roosevelt would find a place for that argument on his New Deal tax agenda. But first he needed someone to write that agenda in the first place.

5

New Deal Economists and the Case for Saving the Poor

In the summer of 1934, Franklin Roosevelt's new Treasury secretary, Henry Morgenthau, recruited a staff of experts to help shape the New Deal's emerging tax agenda. This fiscal brain trust quickly delivered a sweeping program of progressive tax reform. The approach was ambitious and elaborate, including hundreds of revisions to dozens of federal levies. Broadly speaking, however, they offered three simple suggestions: tax income more broadly, estates more heavily, and consumption more lightly.

The Treasury economists believed this program was realistic, even given the budgetary strictures of a depression-wracked economy. They rejected every idea that might cost money. Even while calling for lighter consumption taxes, for instance, they acknowledged that such levies were a necessary evil for the forseeable future. The Treasury staff believed in progressive reform, but not at the expense of fiscal responsibility. Theirs was a balance between justice and expediency.

But expediency doesn't guarantee viability, at least in politics. Some of the economists' recommendations got a warm reception. In 1935, Congress agreed to raise income and estate taxes, much as the Treasury staff had suggested. But suggestions to broaden the income tax—specifically by extending it down the income scale into the middle class—proved to be a hard sell. And rollbacks in federal consumption taxes were simply too expensive to seriously contemplate, even in the abstract. Measured solely by the yardstick of legislation, then, the Treasury plan was a failure.

But lawmaking is not the only standard of success. The Treasury plan had a subtle but enduring influence on federal tax policy. It quickly became a touchstone for New Deal tax experts, as they spent the 1930s building a consensus for progressive tax reform. When World War II finally triggered a fiscal watershed, this consensus helped shape the nation's most enduring tax regime.

The Search for Expertise

After taking office in January 1934, Henry Morgenthau avoided most tax issues, letting congressional Democrats take the lead in a series of minor but contentious tax debates. That passive approach suited Morgenthau, who was trying to bring order out of chaos at the Treasury. The new secretary had inherited a confused and disorganized department. As *Fortune* magazine observed, "Morgenthau's task was to reconquer and subdue his province."[1]

Most of the Treasury's tax experts were holdovers from the Mellon regime, and they had little interest in crafting plans for progressive tax reform. Indeed, Morgenthau considered most of them worse than useless. "The Treasury," he told Marriner Eccles, "is an empty shelf."[2] If Morgenthau wanted to make his mark, he would have to assemble his own tax staff, including a stable of ideologically sympathetic advisers.[3] He began, however, with the surprising choice of Roswell Magill.

Magill was a distinguished tax lawyer, with broad support among both Democrats and Republicans. But he was widely considered a conservative, perhaps even a Republican. His appointment did little to reassure anxious liberals that the Roosevelt administration would champion the cause of progressive taxation.[4]

Magill was only the first of several appointments. Throughout the first half of 1934, Morgenthau added to his staff of experts, and by June, he was ready to move ahead. He began by asking several key aides, including Magill, to draft a New Deal revenue agenda. Three months later, they delivered the Viner Studies, a series of detailed tax reform proposals.

Morgenthau had recruited Jacob Viner in the summer of 1934, asking him to oversee studies on banking and taxation. Viner came to the department with a larger-than-life reputation. He was a demanding task master—"a strutting Talmudic Napoleon," in the words of one former student, with "big yellow teeth, the remains of a mop of red hair, and facial expressions alternating at express-train speed between joviality, challenge, and utter contempt."[5] But Viner was also one of the nation's leading economists. He is generally credited with helping establish the so-called Chicago School of economics, a tradition of study that placed a premium on free market incentives. But with a real, if limited, tolerance for government activism, Viner was not a comfortable fit in that neoclassical mold. Indeed, he resisted the label. "At no time was I consciously a member [of the Chicago School]," he later wrote, "and it is my vague impression that if there was such a school it did not recognize me as a member, or at least as a loyal and qualified member."[6]

Viner was not a follower of John Maynard Keynes—few economists were until later in the 1930s. But the Chicagoans' policy formulations often resembled those later associated with the famed British economist. In the early 1930s, Viner argued for a stimulative fiscal policy rooted in borrowing. The best way to fight the depression, he insisted, was to spend freely and tax lightly. Only by inflating prices could government stem the vicious downward economic spiral. In conjunction with several Chicago colleagues, Viner urged Roosevelt in late 1933 to limit the tax burden, writing the president with an appeal for deficit spending. The government should raise enough money to pay for normal expenditures, the group wrote, but emergency costs associated with the depression should be financed with debt. "In a deep depression," they declared, "the injury inflicted upon taxpayers by requiring them to defray the cost of every governmental activity by current taxation appears to be greater than can be justified." Balancing the budget, in other words, was best viewed as a multiyear project.[7]

The Chicago economists took pains to warn Roosevelt against a national sales tax, insisting that it would be regressive and deleterious to the nation's economic health. Offered amid growing speculation that the president-elect was about to propose a sales tax to help narrow the budget gap, such comments were politically charged—and perhaps well-timed. But the economists urged FDR to look elsewhere for new revenue. If the country needed money, then it should make better use of the income tax. In particular, lower exemptions would bring millions of new taxpayers into the system, making the income tax much more productive. By contrast, raising the tax rates paid by rich Americans, while politically appealing, was unlikely to produce much additional revenue, especially during a depression. This, in fact, was the fundamental dilemma of progressive income taxation: while the tax could produce enormous revenue, it was extremely sensitive to economic fluctuations, at least while it remained narrowly focused on the rich. Economists of the 1920s had made much the same point, as had Andrew Mellon during his numerous efforts to broaden the tax base.[8]

In his solo writing, Viner had expressed doubts about the progressive rate structure of the federal income tax, arguing that it functioned poorly whenever prices were in flux. During inflationary periods, taxpayers were thrust into higher brackets, despite the absence of real change in their capacity to pay. He was also on record in support of capital gains preferences, contending that such income should be taxed more lightly than wages and salaries. Clearly, Viner was no paragon of liberal taxation. But his opposition to a sales tax distinguished him from many conservative political leaders, and his support for deficit financing put him at odds with majorities in both parties.[9]

Viner resisted ideological pigeonholing. "I don't know whether I am a conservative, or a liberal, or a radical," he later explained to a colleague. "I aspire to being a blend—a judicious one, I hope—of all three." Generally speaking, he was committed to the efficacy of free markets but remained cognizant of their limitations. He was willing to consider government action to compensate for market failures and inefficiencies, including the overconcentration of wealth. But he did not support wholesale wealth redistribution, through the tax system or by any other means. He simply acknowledged that concentrations of wealth, along with other issues of distributive justice, posed a problem for free market societies.[10]

Viner's appointment—like Magill's in late 1933—reflected a conservative impulse in Morgenthau's Treasury. Other economists would have brought better progressive credentials to the table. Liberal voices, like those of the *Nation* magazine, would have been happier with someone like Harold Groves, a noted liberal among academic economists. But Viner won his job by virtue of his reputation and professional stature. "These people have been recommended to me as being intellectually honest," Morgenthau said of his new tax experts, "and that is all I have required." Morgenthau gave Viner and his assistants a broad mandate. "The lid is off and I have given these men carte blanche authority to approach these problems as they see fit," the secretary told reporters. Morgenthau wanted a fresh look at U.S. tax policy, free of preconceptions or political constraints. "Just because the Treasury always has been doing a certain thing in a certain way does not make it right," he explained.[11]

Viner delegated day-to-day management of the tax study to young but promising Carl Shoup. Shoup supervised a staff of seven more economists, collectively dubbed the "Sub-Brain Trust" by the *New York Times*. In addition, Viner called on a variety of short-term consultants, including some of the nation's leading economists. Ultimately, however, Shoup dominated the group, writing many volumes personally and serving as a careful steward for the work of all the others.[12]

Shoup was a veteran of Roosevelt tax policy, having served on the staff of the New York State Commission for the Revision of the Revenue Laws for two years during Roosevelt's term as governor. While independent, the revenue commission had loomed large in several fiery tax debates, including Roosevelt's dramatic proposal to hike state income taxes in 1931 and 1932. Shoup was never a Roosevelt confidant; he had been far too junior to attract the governor's attention. But his presence was emblematic of the role that New Yorkers would play in New Deal revenue policy. Morgenthau, of course, was the most prominent and powerful representative from the Empire State, at least when it came to taxes. But he, in turn, relied on Roswell Magill to handle the details. Magill then hired an army of lesser-known New Yorkers, including Shoup, Louis Shere, and Reavis Cox. Several more served as Treasury consultants, including Robert Murray Haig, coauthor, with Shoup, Cox, and Shere, of a major study on state-level sales taxation. All in all, it was a chummy bunch, with numerous professional ties, both to one another and to other members of the nation's tax community.[13]

Shoup was hard to characterize politically. He jealously guarded his reputation for even-handed analysis. He was, in fact, an economist's economist—deeply engaged in the scholarly debates of his profession and disinclined to sully himself with partisan entanglements. He was also enamored of his faculty position at Columbia, and while agreeing to join the Treasury for a limited engagement, he never considered a permanent move to government service.

As a scholar, Shoup had developed considerable expertise on sales taxes, having written his dissertation on French sales levies and coauthored a book with Haig on the sales tax in the American states. Despite, or perhaps because of, this expertise, Shoup was lukewarm toward most sales tax proposals. While careful to evaluate them in neutral fashion, he consistently resisted plans to expand sales taxation, especially at the federal level. Instead, he was a fan of income taxation, supporting its use at both the state and federal levels.[14]

Shoup's team at Treasury focused on four general issues: (1) administrative revision and simplification of the tax system, (2) the distribution of the tax burden, (3) the relationship between the federal, state, and local revenue systems, and (4) the use of taxation to stabilize the business cycle. This was a sweeping research agenda, but the group completed it in just three months. Recalling the effort many years later, Shoup described a feeling of excitement. The sense of possibility pervading Washington in the early years of the New Deal was just beginning to make its way into the tax arena. Having watched as other vehicles of economic reform got the lion's share of national attention, tax experts were finally getting their moment. They were determined to make the most of it.[15]

By and large, the Treasury group worked alone. Neither Shoup nor his colleagues relied on extensive help from congressional staff to prepare the studies, although relations with Capitol Hill were warm. The group enjoyed a particularly collegial relationship with the professional staff of the Joint Committee on Internal Revenue Taxation. Footnotes to the Viner Studies include numerous citations to JCIRT publications, almost all of them respectful if not uncritical. But Morgenthau was determined to develop his own source of expertise within the Treasury Department. Shoup and his colleagues tried to give him what he wanted, pursuing their tax studies independent of fiscal experts outside the Treasury, including those in Congress, other administration departments, or the private sector.

The Viner Recommendations

The Viner team delivered its final recommendations in September. "We find ourselves," Shoup reported happily, "in substantial agreement on the use that should be made of the various taxing instruments available."[16] The Viner Studies covered enormous ground, with volumes on everything from alcohol taxation to tobacco duties. But three topics got the most sustained attention: individual income taxes, estate taxes, and federal consumption taxes. The group also explored other topics in depth, including business income taxes, excess profits taxes, and the use of taxation to stem inflation. Some of these issues would prove politically potent, especially those concerning business taxes. But for the time being, the group recommended no dramatic reform for any of these areas, instead counseling further study and minor improvements to the existing structure.

The Viner Studies began with a stern warning about debt financing. "The situation calls for more than merely drifting with the tide of expenditure," Shoup warned in his summary memo. Debt was salutary—perhaps even necessary—when used to encourage recovery. But it should never become a substitute for long-term fiscal discipline. Debt redistributed the fiscal burden across time, saddling future generations with the cost of current expenditures. "Viewed narrowly as a matter of tax technique, hidden taxation of this type is the worst kind of tax," Shoup wrote. The distribution of its burden was almost impossible to predict, and it tended to penalize certain sectors of the economy more than others. In general, excessive debt financing could lead "with disquieting swiftness" to unjust distributions of the fiscal burden.[17]

Even more important, debt had a corrosive effect on the American polity. It encouraged taxpayers to expect more for less, fostering self-indulgence and weakening "tax morale": the willingness of people to impose taxes on themselves (through representative government) and to pay those taxes once they are imposed (either through self- or exogenous assessment). Once a nation got used to debt, Shoup contended, it quickly became a bad habit. Accordingly, Shoup and his colleagues were willing to accept any tax increase—even one they found objectionable for reasons of fairness or administrative practicality—if the only alternative were unrestrained debt.[18]

In fact, debt had already become a national habit, albeit of necessity. The country had been running a deficit since 1931, caught between plummeting tax revenue and rising relief expenditures. But the Viner team acknowledged that trying to balance the budget over the short term was unrealistic and unwise; debt financing might spark recovery, while fiscal austerity threatened to nip it in the bud. Many economic advisers in the Roosevelt administration believed deeply in the need for fiscal balance—not immediately, and not every year. But someday, they argued, the federal government should return to paying its bills. This strain of fiscal conservatism had a powerful appeal in the Treasury Department, especially in the secretary's office. The department's tax experts were equally committed to the goal of a balanced budget. Just not right away.[19]

Clearly, the tenets of fiscal Keynesianism had not yet established much of a foothold in the Treasury. While most of the department's economists held some vague sense that deficits were tolerable, and perhaps even desirable, in the depths of depression, they were by no means advocates of countercyclical tax policy. In retrospect, it can be hard to fathom their innate fiscal conservatism. If they understood that tax hikes could prolong the depression, then why didn't they question more vigorously the orthodoxy of balanced budgets? As economist Herbert Stein later pointed out, "there was not then in the country enough sophistication— or sophistry—to generate such questions."[20] The Viner economists, in fact, were acutely aware of their ignorance and technical limitation; the state of economic knowledge was too humble to support the creative, countercyclical use of the federal taxing power.

For similar reasons, the Viner group cautioned policymakers against social and economic engineering through the tax law. Taxes had always been employed for nonfiscal goals: tariffs had been used to regulate trade, not just to raise revenue, and sumptuary taxes had long been justified as a means to discourage consumption of socially suspect products. Other regulatory taxes were designed to protect narrow business interests, such as the punitive levy that butter manufacturers had managed to impose on oleomargarine to forestall competition. Nonfiscal taxation was not inherently evil, Shoup wrote, but it was dangerous territory. Poorly designed taxes could easily undermine the goals they intended to serve. Lawmakers trod this ground at considerable risk.[21]

Regulatory taxation was most ambitious when used to regulate the economy as a whole. "The tax system, so the argument runs, may be employed to eliminate business cycles," Shoup wrote, "or at least to lessen their severity, by penalizing 'over-saving' and encouraging consumption, by checking speculation, by favoring certain geographical or social classes at the expense of others, by encouraging business initiative, by discouraging 'unwise' business expansion, and so on."[22] While tempting, such tax activism was dangerous. No one understood taxes well enough to predict macroeconomic effects with any certainty. Moreover, existing economic data were not equal to the task.

Choosing just one example, the Viner group noted widespread interest in using taxes to discourage "excess" saving, especially among corporations. This argument would soon become a key justification for the undistributed profits tax (UPT), the most ambitious tax reform of the New Deal era. In fact, however, evidence for the oversaving hypothesis was thin, and proposed remedies were untested. Before embarking on this sort of macroeconomic experiment, policymakers would need more and better information. "There is a heavy burden of proof to be borne by those who would attempt to use the tax system to influence decidedly the major economic currents of the country," they concluded. And while all taxes necessarily had some nonfiscal effects, the system was best kept as neutral as possible.[23]

This sort of intellectual caution didn't sit well with many of the administration's most influential figures, including several who would play a vital role in shaping New Deal tax reform. The 1936 effort to enact a UPT would draw strength from this group of tax activists, most of whom were also champions of high-end progressivity. And while the careful economists of the Treasury tax staff would lend their support to the UPT campaign—as well as to other ventures in social taxation—they remained suspicious of such plans.

Individual Income Tax

The most important recommendations to come out of the Viner Studies concerned the individual income tax. The group called for a broader, steeper levy, urging policymakers to make better use of this fair and efficient revenue device. With an eye on the government's budget shortfall, the panel recommended higher rates for every bracket. More important, however, they urged a broad reduction in personal exemptions. By adding more people to the tax rolls, lower exemptions would make the income tax much more productive and reliable. Lower exemptions would also foster tax awareness, "increasing the number of direct taxpayers and thereby the number of persons having a conscious interest in government."[24]

The income tax had been a salutary addition to the nation's revenue system, according to Louis Shere, author of the Viner volume on distribution of the tax burden. "It is probably safe to conclude that before the enactment of the individual income tax law the Federal tax system was regressive, and thereafter it became progressive," he wrote. The Viner economists argued that future reforms should add to this progressivity. Higher rates, especially in the upper brackets, would certainly help. But lower exemptions were the key to progressive reform. When evaluating progressivity, Shere wrote, it was vital to assess the combined burden of direct taxes, like the income tax, and indirect levies, such as excises on consumer goods. Given the federal government's heavy reliance on consumption taxes, a broader income levy could still lead to greater progressivity, as long as new revenue from this progressive tax paid for cuts in more regressive levies.[25]

By and large, Democrats had traditionally opposed major expansions of the income tax base. Only in moments of national crisis, sparked either by war or depression, had they agreed to lower exemptions. During the Hoover administration, Mellon had repeatedly suggested exemption cuts, both to close revenue shortfalls and to help boost tax consciousness among lower-income groups. But most Democrats insisted that the tax should remain as narrow as possible. During the revenue-buoyant 1920s, party leaders had even championed increases in the already-high exemptions. In 1924, they managed to win passage for a major exemption hike, ignoring objections from Mellon and many Republican legislators. The Revenue Act of 1924 raised individual exemptions by 50 percent and married exemptions by 40 percent.[26]

The depression forced lawmakers to backtrack. In 1932, Congress returned exemptions to their 1924 level, urged on by Mellon and his successor, Ogden Mills. Even at this lower mark, however, exemptions remained high and the income tax quite narrowly focused on the rich. In 1932, Americans filed 3.89 million tax returns—up sharply from previous years but still representing just 3.1 percent of the total U.S. population.[27] In early 1933, president-elect Roosevelt had briefly considered further reductions to help shrink the deficit. A few party stalwarts swallowed hard and agreed to support the idea.[28] But most Democrats howled in protest. Politically speaking, lower exemptions were a Republican idea, and Democrats were not willing to embrace such a plan absent a major fiscal crisis.

Tax experts, however, were broadly sympathetic to the idea. Lower exemptions enjoyed bipartisan support among economists, especially when they were combined with a rollback in regressive consumption taxes. Legislators, of course, were fond of excise taxes on consumer goods; in general, they raised maximum revenue with minimum complaint. And as Jean Baptiste Colbert, finance minister to Louis XIV, is reputed to have said, "The art of taxation consists in so plucking the goose as to obtain the largest possible amount of feathers with the smallest possible amount of hissing."[29]

But economists, while acknowledging the importance of expedience, were far less inclined to use excises taxes for general revenue. As one economist noted in early 1935, "A readjustment that would base our entire tax program quite definitely on the principle of ability to pay rather than on convenience and opportunism would receive the commendation of practically every person whose opinions on the subject of taxation I have read."[30] For most economists, such a readjustment implied a two-part reform agenda, combining broader, more robust income taxes with a general reduction in consumption taxes.

In 1934, the Tax Policy League surveyed public finance professors at 52 of the nation's 100 largest universities, seeking their opinions on various tax policy issues. Unanimously, the respondents endorsed a graduated income tax. By contrast, only 12 percent supported a federal sales tax. Tobacco and gasoline excises won more support, but respondents believed that consumption taxes should remain a secondary source of federal revenue. The economists were not asked specifically about personal exemptions, but their overwhelming support for income taxation implied the possibility of a broader levy. In addition, the group supported higher taxes on "unearned" income from investments than on "earned" income from wages and salaries. Such preferential treatment was intended to benefit middle- and lower-income taxpayers, who presumably worked hard for their money. If the income tax were paid solely by the rich, there would have been no equity argument to justify such a preference. The earned income distinction only made sense as part of a broader income tax.[31]

The Viner Studies made a strong case for broader income taxes. Economist Roy Blakey of the University of Minnesota prepared the volume on personal income taxes. He was a solid liberal, having helped found the General Welfare Tax League, a research organization devoted to progressive taxation. Blakey's colleagues in that group included John R. Commons of the University of Wisconsin and Harold Groves of the university and the Wisconsin Tax Commission. For his own part, Blakey was probably best known for his annual summaries of federal tax legislation, published regularly by the *American Economic Review*. In them, he was a dependable champion of progressive income taxation.[32]

During prosperous years, Blakey argued, the income tax should be made to supply 50 percent to 75 percent of total federal revenue. During recessions, it could still provide 25 percent to 50 percent. But as currently structured, the tax could never meet these goals, at least not reliably. The depression had caused incomes to plummet, and revenue had dried up accordingly. High exemptions contributed to this problem. Since the income of a rich person tended to fall faster than the income of a poor person, the tax base shrunk more rapidly than overall national income. If the income tax were to be rescued from its depression-borne inconstancy, then it must be broadened, Blakey contended. He was not suggesting some sort of cosmetic extension of the income tax, a symbolic effort to assess small amounts against modest incomes, chiefly as a means of promoting tax awareness. Rather, Blakey wanted a genuine expansion of the tax base, one that made the income tax a meaningful part of life for millions of previously exempt Americans. Only by extending the tax well into the middle class could it become the nation's principal, and most reliable, revenue source.[33]

In the early years of the depression, Blakey observed, income tax revenues had slumped dramatically. Critics seized on the decline, using it to justify reduction, or even repeal, of the individual income tax. A vocal minority even suggested replacing it with a new federal sales tax. Such a turn of events would be disastrous, Blakey argued. The best thing about the income tax, he said, was its ability to offset more regressive taxes—those "which fall all too heavily on 'the forgotten man'." If saving the income tax meant asking that forgotten man to pay part of it, then it was still, on balance, a worthy progressive reform.[34]

In one long, convoluted sentence, Blakey invoked two distinct fairness arguments to justify the income tax: "It raises most of the taxes for ordinary and emergency purposes from the most prosperous businesses and the individuals who have the most ability and who profit most from the opportunities which society and governmental protection afford them." The first half of this statement rests on the ability-to-pay argument for progressive taxation. Taxes, Blakey was suggesting, should take account of the different economic circumstances of various taxpayers; those with the greatest resources should be asked to pay the most. Economists of Blakey's generation generally regarded ability to pay as the best benchmark for tax fairness. But the standard was also notoriously problematic: it was hard to define and easy to manipulate. On a practical level, it required policymakers to make a series of more or less arbitrary decisions about exemptions and rates. Political leaders could invoke "ability" standards to defend just about any tax reform they might choose, and experts struggled vainly to reconcile real-world tax issues with this nebulous ideal.[35]

For all its faults, however, ability to pay was a better standard than Blakey's second stab at defending the income tax. Raising revenue from people who "profit the most" from governmental services had once been a popular idea among economists. "Benefit" theories tried to distribute the tax burden according to the benefits that individual taxpayers received from the public sector. In the latter years of the 19th century, however, critics had begun to complain that such a standard was impractical; many benefits were simply not conducive to measurement. With the impact of most government services spread broadly and variously throughout the population, benefit was too vague to serve as a practical guide. As a result, benefit theories had given way to "ability" theories, at least among experts.[36]

In any case, Blakey remained committed to the fairness of an income tax. It was, he declared, a bulwark against the inherent injustice of a modern economy. Its adoption in 1913, moreover, had been a triumph for political and economic democracy. "The masses of people and their representatives have seen the phenomenal growth of industry, of cities, with their large corporations, trusts, incomes, and other numerous evidences of wealth," he wrote. The people would never abandon the income tax— "one for which they struggled hard and long and one which serves perhaps to mitigate rather than to exaggerate the harsh injustices of fortune and the even more irritating injustices of those who have controlled industry and government in the modern economic regime."[37]

Equity, however, was only part of Blakey case for income taxation. Expediency also figured prominently. The levy was a fine revenue tool, productive and resilient, in potential if not reality. In good years, it could yield large surpluses for the federal treasury. If allowed to accumulate, such surpluses might even carry the government through lean times, staving off economic turbulence by correcting for imbalances in the economy. "They may check the overextension of plant and unbalanced production that would follow unduly large profits and surpluses, and they may help to build up industrial and government insurance reserves that may steady purchasing power and decrease tax drains for relief purposes in bad times," he wrote.[38] These were attractive possibilities, especially as economists debated the possibility that business miscalculation, overinvestment, and underconsumption had been root causes of the depression. But such thinking also ran perilously close to the sort of macroeconomic regulatory taxation that the Viner economists had warned against in their general recommendations. In Blakey's case, however, it was simply too tempting a possibility to ignore.

When it came to specifics, Blakey urged that exemptions be dramatically reduced. Broadening the income tax would "lessen its narrow class, or undemocratic character"; millions of new taxpayers would join the system, diluting complaints that the levy was designed to "soak the rich." Policymakers should be bold. "It probably is not politically feasible to lower them as much as should be done," Blakey conceded, but major reductions were vital. Exemptions might reasonably be cut from $2,500 to $2,000 for married couples and heads of household. Even better, they could be slashed to $1,600. Individuals, meanwhile, should see their exemption fall from $1,000 to $800.[39] Contemporary estimates put the average family income in 1935–1936 at $1,622, with 20.9 percent of families making more than $2,000 annually.[40] Blakey's suggestion, then, implied a dramatic expansion of the income tax.

Lower exemptions were the centerpiece of Blakey's plans for income tax reform. Policymakers would continue to face "tremendous pressure" for regressive taxation, including a national sales tax. While a broader income tax would necessarily move the tax burden down the income scale (absent cuts in other, more regressive levies), it would be less onerous than likely alternatives. And lower exemptions were not solely a burden on those taxpayers drawn into the system for the first time. They also raised the effective rate for existing, higher-income taxpayers, since more of their income would now be subject to taxation.

While calling for lower exemptions, Blakey also suggested an increase in rates. It was important, he said, to raise them across the board, including the lowest brackets. Under the Revenue Act of 1934, the "normal" income tax was levied at 4 percent. (The normal rate applied to all income above the exemption level. In addition, many well-to-do taxpayers also paid a surtax according to a steeper progressive rate schedule.) By comparison, Great Britain imposed a normal rate of 22 percent. Blakey urged a modest move in the British direction. The bulk of personal income, he pointed out, was found in the middle and lower regions of the income scale. As a result, modest rate hikes could raise enormous revenue. Each increase of 1 percent, he predicted, would bring in roughly $50 million in depression years and perhaps $100 million in more prosperous times. Of course, increases in the normal rate would raise the burden on the lowest brackets, but this was no reason to hold back. Such increases, Blakey said, "may not be necessary in prosperous times, but, if large revenues from the income tax are absolutely essential in times like these in order to provide for emergency relief and also in order to avoid large general sales taxes which are regressive, it is necessary to call on these income classes."[41]

Higher rates, of course, would be unpopular—even more so when combined with lower exemptions. But lawmakers could not bend to the winds of popular opinion. "This revision should be within the bounds of political expediency but there should be no shrinking from a courageous tax policy for the maintenance of STRONG public credit even in the face of contemporary unpopularity," he declared. "Such taxes as these are not popular and never will be popular, but real statesmen must face realities and, if necessary leave popular acclaim to history."[42]

Such urgency notwithstanding, calls to broaden the income tax were not destined for quick success. Lower exemptions were not popular, particularly with most liberals. It would take the fiscal crisis of World War II to make them a reality. And even then, "real statesmen" would have to struggle hard for this version of low-end progressive reform.

Estate Taxes

To complement a broader, steeper income tax, the Viner team also endorsed a vigorous estate tax. Like the income tax, it was one of the best sources of federal revenue, they argued. It had the potential to be a revenue workhorse, helping policymakers close the federal budget gap. It was also easy to administer, hard to evade, and unlikely to cause much economic distortion. Perhaps most important, it served the cause of social justice, reducing inequality and preventing large concentrations of wealth.[43]

Henry F. Walradt, a veteran of New York state tax debates and a professor at Ohio State University, wrote the Viner memo on estate taxation. Walradt endorsed existing estate levies, including the basic tax enacted in 1926, as well as the special surtax approved in 1932. But he also recommended important changes to the tax, including a major reduction in the levy's exemption, as well as a significant hike in its rate schedule. Taken together, he predicted, these changes would make the tax fairer and more productive.

Walradt suggested a novel reduction in estate tax exemptions. In 1934, the exemption was $100,000 for the normal estate tax and $50,000 for the surtax. These figures should be replaced, he wrote, with a set of graduated exemptions scaled to the number and relationship of an estate's beneficiaries. The exemption for that portion of an estate left to a surviving wife, for instance, would be $15,000, while a surviving husband would be due $7,500. Exemptions for children would depend on age, ranging from as little as $300 for a 20-year-old to $3,500 for an infant. Since the estate tax was levied on the total deceased taxpayer's assets (not the individual shares due to the heirs, as would have been true under an inheritance tax), such piecemeal exemptions would be totaled to calculate the estate's overall exemption. In no case would the total exemption be allowed to exceed $50,000.[44]

The new exemption structure was designed to confer the greatest benefits on those most in need. Wives and young children were the first concern, while husbands and older children could be expected to fend for themselves to a greater degree. Meanwhile, the taxable estate should be subject to a new, steeper rate structure, with graduated rates increasing with the size of the estate. Rates for the normal tax would range from 1 percent to 25 percent on all amounts above the exemption. The surtax would take an additional 2 percent to 60 percent. These proposed rates were much higher than existing levies, reflecting the Walradt's desire to raise additional money from this attractive tax.

Walradt's most potent argument for the estate tax rested on its fairness. The levy would bring about "a more equitable distribution of wealth," he wrote. Inherited wealth conferred huge advantages on lucky heirs. Children born into poverty, by contrast, faced overwhelming hurdles. "So far as it is possible more nearly to equalize opportunities for all without sacrificing economic and social progress," Walradt wrote, "it is desirable to do so." Moreover, allowing wealth to travel freely between generations was often a burden on the recipients. Often, Walradt said, "those who are brought up 'in the lap of luxury' develop shiftless and wasteful habits." Everyone would be better off if such children were forced to pull their own weight.[45]

Walradt's analysis reflected common assumptions about the nature of work and wealth. It drew on a suspicion of inherited privilege, while paying indirect homage to the American myth of individualism and self-reliance. Many taxes were rooted in such moral assumptions; most fairness arguments were, on some fundamental level, rooted in cultural constructs of value and responsibility. Most economists of the late 20th century have recognized the inherently arbitrary nature of such commentary, and the discipline's literature has moved away from such moral musing. But economists of the 1930s were comfortable in the realm of tax fairness and social justice. Even economists in government service were prone to such commentary.

Walradt rejected arguments that the estate tax was inherently unfair. Opponents of the levy, he noted, tended to view the power to transmit property—in both life and death—as a natural right. But Walradt believed the doctrine of natural rights was discredited; prevailing opinion granted individuals living in a society only "such rights as that society sees fit to allow them," he wrote. The government had an obvious interest in regulating the transmission of wealth, for reasons of both revenue and social justice. People had no claim to any absolute right of property transmission, and the federal government was justified in setting any limits that the political process might produce.[46]

Furthermore, Walradt insisted that estate taxes did not "destroy capital," as some critics charged. According to this antitax argument, large accumulations of capital were necessary for economic growth. Estate taxes diminished this capital, and by extension, the material comforts enjoyed by Americans; a smaller, less productive economy would provide fewer benefits to the nation's citizens and residents. Adam Smith was perhaps the most famous exponent of this argument, writing in *The Wealth of Nations*:

> All taxes upon the transference of property of every kind, so far as they diminish the capital value of that property, tend to diminish the funds destined for the maintenance of productive labour. They are all more or less unthrifty taxes that increase the revenue of the sovereign, which seldom maintains any but unproductive labourers, at the expence of the capital of the people, which maintains none but productive.[47]

Such an argument was specious, Walradt insisted. Taxes had no direct bearing on the existing stock of capital. "There are just as many factories, etc., after the payment of such a tax as there were before," he wrote. And since capital was often held in the form of securities, selling such instruments to raise money for estate taxes merely shifted ownership, not the nature of capital itself.[48]

In fact, capital delivered to the government through the estate tax might be more useful after its transfer. "It is quite possible that the Government may spend it more productively than it would have been spent if left in the hands of the taxpayers," he wrote. "The point is that whether or not taxes 'use up' capital depends primarily not on the type of tax used but upon how the revenue is expended." Walradt was challenging those tax critics who insisted that economic growth was best spurred through private investment. He believed that growth depended on the quality of investment, whether made by individuals or their political representatives.[49]

Walradt's memo broke with more than a decade of official Treasury statements on the estate tax. Under Mellon, the department had repeatedly endorsed reduction and repeal of all death taxes. Mellon argued vociferously that estate taxes decreased the nation's productive output by diminishing the incentive to work. "After a man has become sufficiently civilized to provide for the reasonable requirements of living, the impetus to further effort at production is found largely in the desire to leave one's family well provided for," he wrote in his 1924 annual report to Congress. "A man will not seek to build up a large fortune just to have it taken away from his family at death."[50] Walradt, however, rejected Mellon's assumption. Individuals, he argued, were motivated by a slew of other factors, too, including a desire "to have the power of command, to have influence in the financial and commercial world, to have the satisfaction that comes from accomplishment, and just the love of 'playing the game'."[51]

Echoing the work of several prominent economists, most notably A. C. Pigou, Walradt insisted that such incentives were more than sufficient to ensure that rich men would keep their noses to the grindstone. In his influential 1920 study, "The Economics of Welfare," Pigou had argued that death taxes, while certainly creating some disincentive to capital formation, were probably less distorting than other popular levies, like the income tax. People had a tendency to discount future taxes as compared to present taxes, Pigou argued, especially when those taxes were levied after death. In the meantime, a drive for power and prestige would keep people toiling away. Or as economist Thomas Carver put it: "Accumulated capital becomes then one of the instruments of the game. So long as the player is left in possession of this instrument while he is one of the players, he is not likely to be discouraged from accumulation merely by the fact that the State, rather than his heirs, gets it after he is through with it."[52]

Walradt suggested that estate taxes might actually spur productivity, rather than hindering it. Aware that taxes would take a sizable bite from his estate, a rich man might work harder to amass an even larger pretax fortune. Similarly, presumptive heirs might "be more inclined to make something of themselves"; cognizant of the looming tax burden, they might work more assiduously, live more frugally, and save more aggressively.[53]

Death taxes, then, were particularly appealing to Walradt and his colleagues on the Viner team. They served standards of fairness by falling most heavily on the rich, and they did so without undue economic distortion. Estate taxes would never solve all the government's revenue problems; even optimistic projections kept them relegated to a secondary role in the federal tax system. But combined with steeper, broader income taxes, they could set the tax system on a more progressive footing.

Consumption Taxes

Consumption taxes were not popular with the Viner economists. Whether structured as excise, sales, or processing taxes, they were regressive and undesirable. But they were extremely popular with legislators, who depended on them to raise roughly 50 percent of total revenue. Given the nation's fiscal crisis, then, the Viner team had to walk a fine line. While calling for an eventual rollback in consumption taxes, they made room for their temporary role as emergency levies. It was a grudging concession, but one necessitated by economic realities.

In fiscal year 1934, excise taxes provided 45.8 percent of total federal revenue. When combined with the processing tax levied in the Agricultural Adjustment Act, consumption taxes were supplying roughly half of the government's annual receipts. By contrast, individual income taxes contributed just 14.2 percent, and corporate income taxes another 12.3 percent.[54] Given such facts, major cuts in consumption taxes were simply not realistic, at least over the short term. As the Viner economists concluded, they were a necessary, if distasteful, expedient.

Some consumption taxes, however, were less distasteful than others. The best were user fees, especially automotive taxes on gasoline and related products. These were the only excises worth keeping, argued Carl Shoup, who wrote the Viner study on excise taxes. Paid principally by drivers and roughly correlated with benefits derived from government-built roads, these taxes had some claim to fairness. "As 'user' taxes to finance the Federal highway program," Shoup wrote, "they are, in differing degrees and at certain rates, justifiable." Policymakers clearly agreed, making good use of them; in 1933, automotive taxes raised $174 million, of which $125 million came from the gasoline tax. But Shoup warned policymakers to avoid temptation; claims to fairness depended on the earmarking of associated revenue.[55]

While defensible, however, user fees were a distinctly secondary source of federal revenue. Other consumption taxes, most notably the excises on alcohol and tobacco, dwarfed the automotive levies. They were, in fact, pillars of the revenue system. In 1933, alcohol taxes had raised $43 million—almost $10 million more than estate and gift taxes. Tobacco brought in vastly more. Raising $402 million in 1933, its revenue eclipsed the $352 million brought in by the individual income tax.[56] This was big money, and it posed a dilemma for the Viner economists. Their proposed expansion of the income and estate taxes would not raise sufficient revenue to eliminate excise duties taxes. Even reducing them would be prohibitively expensive, especially in the current fiscal climate. How, then, to reconcile revenue needs with standards of tax fairness?

Fairness clearly demanded the elimination of most consumption taxes. "On the whole," wrote Carl Shoup, "they do not form a desirable part of a fiscal system in normal times."[57] Since World War I, most economists had endorsed cuts in excise taxation, arguing that such levies were regressive and economically inefficient. They fell heavily on the poor, while discriminating almost randomly among products and taxpayers.

But the depression had made selective excises more important, not less. Receipts from income and estate taxes had fallen precipitously along with the nation's economic fortunes. Many excises, by contrast, were less sensitive to economic conditions, depending on the elasticity of demand associated with the taxed product. During the depression, excise taxes had generally held up well. The growing importance of excise revenue, however, was not an automatic function of the sinking economy; it also reflected a conscious decision by federal lawmakers to lean more heavily on this reliable revenue tool. The Revenue Act of 1932 had imposed a slew of new excises, while raising rates on many that already existed.

In fact, economists shared this fondness for the familiar. The Viner economists seemed to conclude that if they had to have consumption taxes, they might as well be productive ones. Among tax professionals, it has long been received wisdom that an old tax is a good tax; novelty is no virtue, creating problems for both payers and collectors.[58] Taxes on tobacco and alcohol were among the most familiar revenue tools of American government. In some form, they had been levied for most of the nation's history. The early history of American nationhood placed consumption taxes front and center, from the revolutionary era through the Early Republic.[59]

Often, excise taxes had played the role of the villain in American history. They had a starring role in the Whiskey Rebellion of the 1790s.[60] George Washington's ride through the Pennsylvania frontier had silenced critics temporarily, but the taxation of alcohol, tobacco, and other consumer goods remained a subject of spirited debate for most of the nation's early history.[61]

But for all the controversy surrounding excise taxes, they had been a fixture of American taxation since at least the Civil War. Alcohol even remained a taxed product during Prohibition. Given this familiarity—not to mention enormous productivity—the Viner economists were unwilling to part ways completely with alcohol and tobacco taxes. Both, they acknowledged, would remain part of the revenue system for the foreseeable future.

Tobacco taxes were such a vital source of revenue that the Viner team devoted an entire volume to the subject. Columbia University economist Reavis Cox, author of the chapter, did not like the tobacco taxes. They were too steep, he wrote, and they discriminated among different tobacco products without rhyme or reason. But he acknowledged they were here to stay. "The fiscal situation necessitates high taxes," he conceded, "and the tobacco taxes are too reliable and too productive to be reduced at this critical juncture."[62] The Viner team urged lawmakers to avoid using tobacco taxes to raise additional revenue; "The tobacco taxes as a group should not be considered in the front rank if an appeal for additional revenue must be made," they advised in their summary. But faced with fiscal pressures, lawmakers could use the taxes to bring in more revenue.[63]

In his detailed study, Cox took pains to compare the relative burden imposed by tobacco and income taxes. In general, the tobacco taxes were far too heavy. At current rates, he noted, someone smoking a pack a day would pay $21.90 annually in federal cigarette taxes. That was the same amount that a single man earning $1,568 annually would pay in income taxes; a family of four could earn $3,868 before paying that much. With contemporary estimates putting the mean family income for 1935 at $1,631, tobacco taxes were clearly regressive. Paid at the same rate by every smoker, they imposed a much higher burden on the poor than the rich.[64]

Of course, tobacco levies might be justified as luxury taxes. Smoking was a choice, not a biological imperative. "Life can be sustained without the use of tobacco," Cox conceded. But he quickly dismissed the argument, pointing out that notions of "luxury" were socially determined, dependent on custom and the standard of living. Efforts to impose taxes on the basis of "luxury" status were necessarily arbitrary, unfair, and inconsistent. Moreover, if popular opinion and consumption patterns were any indication, tobacco did not seem to be much of a luxury. The inelasticity of demand for tobacco products suggested that many people considered them necessities. And if tobacco taxes were intended to be sumptuary duties, that was even more offensive, Cox declared: "Why the judgment of a few that tobacco is at best a waste and at worst pernicious should be permitted to outweigh the contrary judgment of the vast majority remains a mystery."[65]

If the tobacco taxes were bad, most other excises were indefensible. The Viner economists did not mince words, urging that such levies be eliminated as soon as possible. Excise taxes were an easy refuge for lazy political leaders. Absent political considerations, excise taxes would be reduced to "an almost insignificant role" in the tax system. Even during a depression, when revenue was scarce and alternative taxes unproductive, excise levies were properly consigned to a supporting role. More progressive levies could achieve any legitimate economic goal currently assigned to excise taxes. And to the extent that excises were intended to regulate business, rather than raise revenue, nontax mechanisms could do the same job better.[66]

In a detailed memo on "miscellaneous" taxes—a rubric the Viner team used to describe excises other than those on alcohol, tobacco, and automotive products—Carl Shoup outlined the nation's convoluted system of consumption taxes. In general, he explained, excises could be divided into four groups. The first were levied on items consumed almost exclusively by the rich: works of art, pleasure boats, club dues, jewelry, and the like. The second group taxed articles and services used by the middle class as well as by the wealthy, but almost never by the poor: things like cameras, the telegraph, telephone calls, firearms, phonographs, and radios. A third group focused on items used by a broad array of people, save the very poorest of the poor: candy, meat, chewing gum, public transportation, playing cards, and soft drinks, for instance. The last excises were imposed on necessities consumed by almost everyone: butter, candles, chicory, coal, coffee, cotton, flour, and other items of mass consumption.

In general, taxes in the first group yielded little revenue. Using projections for 1935, Shoup predicted that luxury duties would raise just under $207 million, or roughly 0.5 percent of total federal revenue. Excises on the poor and middle classes, by contrast, would bring in more than $1.8 billion. Lawmakers, Shoup concluded, were using excise taxes to reach taxpayers near the bottom of the income scale—people who were not currently earning enough to pay income taxes but who still had some taxpaying capacity. In other words, excise taxes were imposed because they were regressive, not despite that fact.[67]

Regressivity did not necessarily mean that all excises were inherently unfair, Shoup pointed out. When imposed on unnecessary or superfluous items of consumption, they were in some sense optional—people could choose to avoid them by shifting their consumption patterns away from taxed goods. To the extent that people did not change their consumption, it was an indication that they had some ability, or at least willingness, to pay. "Consider the tax on [entertainment] admissions," Shoup wrote. "Why are admissions taxed, and not salt? Obviously, one answers, because the latter is a necessity that even the poverty-stricken must have, whereas purchase of the former is evidence, if not of luxury, at least of a well-being that forms a basis for equitable taxation."[68]

But if ability to pay were the standard, Shoup complained, then other taxes were better suited to the task of raising revenue fairly. "Luxury" was famously hard to define and impossible to administer as a standard of tax policymaking. The entire effort was haphazard, producing a set of taxes with no internal and extrinsic logic. "The 'non-necessity' concept, logically applied, would involve a much wider range of taxes than exist at present," Shoup wrote. "If radios are taxed, ask the radio manufacturers, why not household oil burners, washing machines, electric waffle irons, fans, etc., also?"[69] Indeed, makers of taxed goods complained bitterly—and legitimately—that they were being singled out.

Consumers, too, suffered from the piecemeal approach to excise taxation. In trying to identify and codify the items of taxation, Congress often missed its intended target. Or they hit the target, but brought down a variety of similar goods as well. One ostensible luxury tax targeted "articles made of, or ornamented, mounted or fitted with, precious metals" that sold for $3 or more. In trying to tax jewelry, however, lawmakers had inadvertently taxed most fountain pens as well.[70]

Luxury, then, was an elusive concept, easy to grasp in general terms but extremely difficult to define with precision. And in fact, most excise taxes were only loosely based on the notion of luxury, if at all. Instead, lawmakers were often guided by a keen sense for political vulnerability. Industries with mediocre representation in Washington often found their goods saddled with taxes. Frequently, the tax legislative process degenerated into a mad scramble among manufacturers, with every business trying to shield itself from the tax system. When the going got rough, there was no "business community"; it was every industry for itself.[71]

Some excise taxes were designed to protect narrow business interests from competition. The oleomargarine tax was the most famous example. First imposed in 1886, it raised the price of margarine relative to butter. It originally taxed yellow margarine more heavily than white margarine, on the presumption that consumers might be fooled into thinking the item was, in fact, butter. Supporters defended the tax as a blow for consumer rights. In fact, however, it was a blight on the tax system, representing a triumph of special interests.[72]

Finally, Shoup outlined the myriad administrative problems that plagued excise taxes. Even when lawmakers managed to define items narrowly, they couldn't anticipate all the attendant complexities of trying to make the tax work. As a result, the Bureau of Internal Revenue fought an endless battle to bring order out of chaos, promulgating one regulation after another. The agency was forced to make delicate and dubious distinctions:

The toiletry tax did not apply to "permanent wave solutions," Shoup pointed out, but did apply to substances producing "finger waves" or "wave sets." "Fur" taxes applied to all kinds of fur, including mink, sable, and even sheepskin. Assuming, that is, that the sheepskin was dyed, and therefore more fur-like; regular old sheepskin was exempt. A clock included in a car was an "automobile accessory" instead of a clock and therefore taxable at 2 percent instead of 10 percent. But a clock built into a thermostat was, in fact, a clock and therefore taxable as such. A plain gold cross was taxable as jewelry—unless it was a crucifix, in which case it was not.

Such tortured interpretations were inevitable when trying to tax certain items and not others. Of course, similar problems surrounded income taxation, where definitions of income were notoriously subject to interpretation. But excise duties were also regressive, casting doubt on the entire enterprise. Why spend so much time trying to make an unfair tax somewhat less unfair?

General sales taxes, of course, avoided some of the problems inherent in the patchwork excise system. By taxing almost all items, they were at least consistent. But to the Viner team, that made them even more distasteful: they were consistently unfair. "A sales tax should not be used to replace any of the tax revenue now being received by the Federal Government," the team declared. "Even if revenue needs should force an increase in taxation, it would be preferable to rely first on increases in income and estate taxes, and possibly on some of the temporary excises, before levying a sales tax."[73]

While some excises could be dubiously defended as luxury taxes, a general sales levy lacked even that fig leaf of fairness. Luxuries were hard to define, but necessities were easier, and a sales tax would fall on many. Shoup evaluated several kinds of sales taxation, including a retail sales tax imposed directly on the consumer at the point of sale. He focused, however, on a manufacturers' tax. When levied at this earlier stage in the economic cycle, a sales tax involved fewer taxpayers and, consequently, fewer administrative problems. A manufacturers' sales tax, moreover, promised to raise substantial revenue. A 1 percent levy would yield between $240 million and $290 million annually. Its yield would also be fairly reliable, Shoup predicted. "To those in search of a 'stable' tax base, the manufacturers' sales tax offers far more than either the personal or corporation income tax," he wrote.[74]

But the sales tax was undesirable for any number of reasons. It would undermine relief efforts; "it is wasteful," Shoup complained, "for the Government to hand out relief payments with one hand and with the other take back part of the money through a tax on necessities." And while exemptions for food and clothing might ameliorate that problem, the tax would still be highly regressive. Second, the sales tax would be hidden from consumers; paid by manufacturers, who would then presumably pass it on in the form of higher prices, it would remain invisible to most Americans. Hidden taxes were bad taxes. They ran counter to ideals of a democratic society, and they made people careless about the cost and functions of government.

Finally, Shoup concluded, the sales tax might not be fully shifted to consumers, in which case its burden would fall on producers or merchants. Such incidence was unintended, and would presumably undermine the distributive—and regressive—intent of the tax in the first place. The degree of shifting would vary by industry, depending on elasticities, but it added an element of unpredictability. The tax seemed likely to hurt businesses that were operating at a loss, as well as those lacking adequate working capital. "Over the long run," Shoup concluded, "the tax would probably not halt any recovery that might otherwise occur, but the period of readjustment might be severe."[75]

Conclusion

As a whole, the Viner Studies provided a comprehensive, largely dispassionate assessment of the federal tax system. Prepared by some of the nation's leading tax experts, the memos were careful, closely reasoned documents. Many, many pages were filled with detailed analysis of highly technical issues, as befits a study of an arcane subject like taxation. But the studies were also animated by a lively commitment to progressive ideals. The economists recruited to Treasury proved to be strong supporters of a progressive federal tax system, and they were particularly fond of the individual income tax, a levy they regarded as the best overall tool for raising national revenue.

But the Viner Studies were not simply intellectual underpinning for Democratic party dogma. While the overwhelming majority of Democrats supported the income tax, most wanted a narrow version of the levy. For the Democratic majority, the income tax was best kept steep and narrow; it was established to exact a fair contribution from the rich, serving as a counterbalance to regressive but remunerative excise taxes on consumption. Democrats wanted to keep the income tax in this role.

The Viner economists challenged this view. The income tax would best serve the cause of progressive taxation if it were dramatically broadened, they argued. It should tax the middle class, not just the wealthy. And while rates on the rich should remain fairly steep, they were not a place to look for additional revenue. Raising rates on wealthy taxpayers promised to raise little revenue but cause substantial economic harm. The best reform would extend the tax downward into the heart of the middle class. This was not a popular message in Democratic circles, including the White House. President Roosevelt would soon propose a major tax bill, but this central recommendation of the Viner team was nowhere to be found in the new legislation. It would take a more serious national crisis to make the mass income tax a political reality.

6

New Deal Lawyers and the Case for Soaking the Rich

The Revenue Act of 1935, known to contemporaries as the Wealth Tax, marked an abrupt shift in New Deal tax policy. During his first two years in Washington, Franklin Roosevelt had avoided contentious tax issues. But in the summer of 1935, he changed course, asking Congress for steep new taxes on the rich, including higher income tax rates, a new inheritance levy, and a graduated tax on corporate profits. Compliant lawmakers gave FDR much of what he wanted, and the Wealth Tax opened a new chapter in the chronicle of New Deal economic reform.

Viewed by the numbers, the Wealth Tax was a modest achievement; it raised relatively little revenue and left the distributive burden of the tax system largely intact. But politically, the law was crucial. In the short term, it gave Roosevelt a much-needed victory, shielding him from critics on the left, especially Huey Long and other advocates of redistributive taxation. It also sharpened ideological cleavages, embittering Roosevelt's opponents and opening a new, more hostile era in New Deal–business relations. Conservatives understood that when Roosevelt declared war on the "unfair advantage of the few," wealth and capital were in for a rough ride.

But the Wealth Tax was most important for the ideological changes it brought to American tax policy. The act reflected Roosevelt's personal understanding of tax justice; rooted in a moral, and often moralistic, sense of personal responsibility, this brand of tax justice focused on the social obligations of the rich. To critics on the left, FDR's sense of fairness seemed to ignore the tax burdens shouldered by the poor. But soak-the-rich taxation did, in fact, reflect a concern for lower-income taxpayers. Advocates of high-end progressivity, including the president, believed that steep taxes on the rich could help justify necessary, if regressive, taxes on the poor.

Taxation as Social Policy

Late in 1934, FDR asked Treasury Secretary Henry Morgenthau for a brief memo on tax reform. Roosevelt wanted ideas on how the revenue system might be changed "to strengthen the economic structure and to conform more nearly to the social objectives of the new Administration."[1] The president was unhappy with the tax system, believing that it overburdened the poor and underburdened the rich. He understood that fiscal pressures made any sort of tax cut impossible; reducing taxes on the poor was simply not feasible. As an alternative, Roosevelt wanted to raise taxes on the rich, using progressive levies near the top of the income scale to balance regressive ones near the bottom.

On December 11, 1934, Morgenthau brought the president a memo by Herman Oliphant, the Treasury's general counsel.[2] At the time, Oliphant was Morgenthau's principal adviser on tax issues, orchestrating the New Deal's first substantive venture into revenue reform. He had come to Washington from academia, having taught law at the University of Chicago, Columbia, and Johns Hopkins. Initially, he assisted Morgenthau at the Farm Credit Administration, but in 1934 he followed his boss to Treasury, where he assumed broad new responsibilities for a range of contentious issues. Morgenthau trusted him implicitly, as he did most of his close advisers. As a result, Oliphant enjoyed considerable freedom in crafting the New Deal's tax agenda. To his friends, Oliphant was known for his enthusiasm. As one prominent journalist observed, he had "a talent for the old-fashioned, campmeeting type of moral indignation." His critics viewed him less charitably; *Fortune* magazine called him a "brilliant, if somewhat inexperienced and dogmatic, legal adviser." Brains Trust member Raymond Moley considered him something of an intellectual fraud, and a dangerous one at that.[3] Moley's scorn was predictable but misplaced. Love him or hate him, Oliphant was a force to be reckoned with. He was a distinguished member of the legal academy; with a specialty in commercial law, and he had developed a reputation as one of the nation's leading exponents of legal realism. Generally speaking, realists believed that the law was best studied using the empiricist and functional techniques of the social sciences. By rooting abstract legal issues in real-world conditions, rather than abstract premises and legal doctrine, realists believed they could connect legal issues to their social and economic environment. Many of the New Deal's most prominent advocates of regulation and economic reform hailed from this legal tradition, which drew on a sort of veblenite institutionalism.[4]

When it came revenue reform, legal realism led Oliphant to advocate bold new directions in the taxation of personal and corporate wealth. Tax policy, he insisted, could be made the vehicle for fundamental social reform, specifically targeting the accretion of economic power among a small group of companies and the people who ran them. This approach, which infused all of Oliphant's tax work at the Treasury, found favor with both Morgenthau and Roosevelt, who appreciated the general counsel's progressive zeal and creative policymaking.[5]

Old Taxes

In his December tax memo, Oliphant offered several innovative proposals to reduce the concentration of wealth and economic power. But he began his memo with a more pedestrian, if more pressing, issue. A slew of special emergency taxes, enacted in 1932 to compensate for slumping income tax receipts, was due to expire on June 30, 1935. Most were consumption taxes, including excises on lubricating oil, gasoline, brewer's wort, electric energy, and chewing gum, among many others. These were exactly the sort of consumption taxes that economists—especially those in the Treasury Department—wanted to eliminate.[6]

But if allowed to disappear, these taxes would take a lot of revenue with them: $378 million in fiscal year 1936.[7] With a huge deficit already looming for 1935 (it eventually reached $2.8 billion out of a total federal budget of $6.4 billion), such a loss was inconceivable. Administration officials worried that any reduction in revenue would imperil the president's relief and reform programs. The government needed more money, not less.[8]

Oliphant urged that the expiring taxes all be renewed. In fact, such renewal was never really in question: not in the administration and not on Capitol Hill. The revenue imperative was simply too compelling. The only salient question was whether additional taxes might be added to the bargain. Oliphant had a few in mind. He suggested a 2 cent tax on bank checks, as well as new levies on insurance premiums, light bulbs, cigarette rolling papers, and pool halls. Some of these taxes would raise considerable revenue, Oliphant predicted, especially the check tax and the insurance tax, each projected to bring in about $45 million. But Oliphant acknowledged that such revenue came at a price. Most of the taxes were regressive, he pointed out. "Except for those designed to reduce existing evasions," he wrote, "nearly all the foregoing taxes would tend to be shifted to consumers."[9]

That Oliphant, a tribune of liberal moral indignation, could endorse regressive taxes speaks volumes about the fiscal environment of late 1934. Tax cuts of any kind were simply out of the question. While new taxes on consumption were distasteful, they enjoyed broad, if grudging, support as a necessary fiscal expedient. Morgenthau, a well-established spokesman for balanced budgets, repeatedly urged FDR to minimize borrowing, even as he accepted the necessity of short-term deficits. And while Roosevelt was no fiscal conservative, he shared a predilection for limited red ink. Perhaps most important, congressional leaders were committed to shrinking the deficit. Given these realities, Oliphant knew that new taxes were unavoidable.[10]

The proto-Keynesians peppered throughout the administration were skeptical of the need to raise taxes. But they had scant support inside the Treasury, where Morgenthau enforced an atmosphere conducive to budget stringency. Marriner Eccles, the most ardent and articulate fan of deficit spending in the Roosevelt administration, had recently departed his Treasury post to head the Federal Reserve. With him went any vestige of countercyclical tax policy, at least in Treasury. The group of administration officials considered sympathetic to such a policy, which also included Mortimer Ezekiel, Henry Wallace, Harry Hopkins, and Jerome Frank, were not in good standing with Morgenthau.[11]

New Taxes

The real heart of Oliphant's memo did not concern the expiring taxes, nor even the handful of new consumption taxes that he appended to the list. Oliphant's plan for ambitious tax reform hinged on several new taxes aimed at wealthy individuals and large corporations. He warned FDR that his ideas would cause a political firestorm. "While the measures here proposed involve no radical attack upon the fundamental character of the capitalist system they may well be regarded otherwise at first in influential circles," he wrote.[12]

Taxing Wealth

Oliphant began with a proposal to raise death taxes. For years, the federal government had levied an estate tax; applied to the entire estate of a decedent, it was an important source of federal revenue, contributing $212 million in fiscal 1935, or roughly 5.9 percent of total receipts.[13] Now, Oliphant was suggesting that lawmakers impose an additional tax, popular in many states, on inheritances. The inheritance tax was levied on the distributive share of an estate as it passed to the beneficiary, not on the estate as a whole. Oliphant believed that a new federal inheritance tax, when levied in conjunction with the existing estate tax, would slow the growth of hereditary fortunes—something the estate tax had been unable to do by itself.[14]

Death taxes of all types were popular among liberals. In the Viner Studies of 1934, Treasury economist Henry Walradt had endorsed both estate and inheritance taxes, noting their propensity to fall most heavily on the rich. Both taxes raised substantial revenue while also serving as a vehicle for social reform. By discouraging large concentrations of wealth and economic power, they checked undemocratic tendencies in a free market economy.

Some tax experts preferred inheritance taxes to other forms of death taxation, arguing that they were more easily adapted to a taxpayer's particular ability to pay. Specifically, they could be readily graduated according to the size of the bequest. Someone receiving $100,000 from an estate of $500,000 presumably had greater ability to pay than someone else getting $50,000 from an estate of $5 million. Yet the latter bequest faced a heavier burden under the estate tax, since the size of the estate was larger. Oliphant believed that a graduated inheritance tax would ameliorate this inequity, while also raising additional money for the Treasury.[15]

Taxing Business

Oliphant's most dramatic recommendations targeted some of the nation's largest companies. He began by suggesting a new attack on holding companies, using a tax on intercorporate dividends to discourage their creation. Holding companies were business organizations whose principal assets were the stocks of other companies. They often produced nothing and sold nothing, instead making money from the dividends paid by companies they controlled. The key advantage of a holding company was the power it conferred on a small group of investors and managers. In the 1930s, many critics blamed holding companies for stock market woes, insisting that a small group of insiders could use the structure to manipulate stocks for their own advantage.

Lawmakers and federal regulators had been considering means to limit and regulate holding companies for several years. In March 1935, Roosevelt would ask Congress for tough new regulation of holding companies in the public utility industry, and lawmakers would respond with the Public Utility Holding Company Act. But Oliphant's proposal was much broader, designed to counter the growth of holding companies in every industry. It was, in fact, an assault on corporate consolidation of all types.

Oliphant developed a plan for taxing the dividends that one corporation paid to another. Under then-current law, dividends received by a corporation were not taxable to the recipient; only the company that earned the money in the first place paid any tax. Oliphant suggested that by taxing the money again when it passed to the holding company, an intercorporate dividend tax could make holding companies prohibitively expensive. Wall Street was sure to react poorly, driving down stock and bond prices for any company with large stock holdings in other corporations. But that was a small price to pay, Oliphant contended, considering the benefits of such a tax. "An inter-corporate dividend tax would operate powerfully to reduce existing complexities in corporate structure," he wrote. Such a levy would also "provide one effective element in a program for the breaking up of the larger business units that dominate our economic life."[16]

Oliphant coupled the intercorporate dividend tax with a plan for taxing companies according to the size of their profits. While the dividend tax would discourage holding companies, he explained, it might also prompt companies to avoid the new tax by simply merging with one another. The resulting businesses would be even bigger than their predecessors, frustrating the whole purpose of the dividend tax. To prevent such combinations, Oliphant suggested a graduated tax on corporate income, scaling the tax rate according to the size of the business. With larger companies paying steeper rates than smaller competitors, consolidation would again become too expensive.[17]

Finally, Oliphant recommended a tax on undistributed corporate earnings. Under existing law, earnings retained by a corporation were taxed only at the corporate level. Since they were never distributed in the form of dividends, they were never subject to the individual income tax. Critics like Oliphant argued that retained earnings were a principal means of tax avoidance; by letting money pile up within corporations, wealthy shareholders could shelter profits from the steep surtax rates of the individual income tax. Obviously, companies must be allowed to accumulate reasonable surpluses—enough to carry them through hard times or allow for investment and innovation. But excessive surpluses might well be taxed at something between 5 percent and 25 percent, depending on the amount of money involved.[18]

Taxing accumulated earnings would presumably induce companies to pay larger dividends. Not only would that raise money for the federal government by allowing the individual income tax to take its bite, but it would also diminish the accumulation of large, powerful, and often sterile corporate cash hoards. There was an element of proto-Keynesian thinking in this argument. Supporters of taxing undistributed profits often suggested that such a levy would curb excess saving by corporations, a phenomenon many believed responsible for the depression. Oliphant was sympathetic to such arguments, but his plan to tax retained earnings emphasized equity, not economic efficiency. "Existing surpluses are a major factor in the domination of American business by a relatively small group," he asserted. While getting rid of existing cash hoards would be difficult, requiring a capital levy of some sort, the government could at least prevent future accumulations.[19]

The Rise of Social Taxation

Taken as a whole, the Oliphant memo urged a striking departure from Roosevelt's existing tax policies. Using the federal tax system to regulate business and private wealth was hardly unprecedented; both the income tax and the estate tax had frank social goals, and virtually every tax was understood to have nonrevenue effects, whether deliberate or inadvertent. But economic reform through the tax law was not usually pursued in such straightforward terms. Oliphant was clearly sympathetic to those liberal voices that had been calling for "social taxation" since the beginning of the Roosevelt presidency.

The *New Republic,* for instance, had long urged boldness on the tax front. "If consciously used as an instrument of policy," the editors wrote, "the taxing power is capable of a far more beneficial effect on the general life than it has ever before had." Or as the *Nation* later explained: "Since a concrete policy of social taxation is by all odds the most important element of both reform and recovery, essential to the very survival of our economic system, we urge the Administration to lose no time in squaring off to this fundamental task."[20]

But Oliphant's embrace of social taxation meant breaking with some of his Treasury colleagues. Specifically, the Oliphant agenda departed from Treasury recommendations as outlined in the Viner Studies. Generally speaking, Treasury economists were wary of social taxation. "The use of taxes for other than revenue purposes is not necessarily an evil," they had explained in September 1934. "But in all such cases great care should be taken to consider all possible effects, some of which may be undesirable and contrary to the ultimate goal originally contemplated."[21] Oliphant's corporation taxes, plainly designed to regulate the structure of American business, were not the kind of taxes that these economists liked. Similarly, Treasury economists were disinclined to endorse a new inheritance tax, contenting themselves with revisions to the existing estate levy. Absent a compelling reason to experiment, they preferred to stick with taxes already on the books.

Brandeis and New Deal Tax Reform

So where did Oliphant get his ideas? Many seemed to come, albeit indirectly, from Supreme Court Justice Louis Brandeis. While he was never a member of the jurist's inner circle, Oliphant was sympathetic to Brandeis and his long-standing campaign against corporate consolidation. When it came time to draft the 1934 revenue plan, Oliphant turned to Brandeis and his chief acolyte, Felix Frankfurter, to chart a new course in federal tax policy.

As the nation's leading foe of corporate consolidation, Brandeis had argued long and hard for the dissolution of large corporations, trusts, and syndicates. He urged a return to smaller business units, with government enforcing limits on corporate size and power. He specifically urged Roosevelt to use the tax system as a means to regulate economic consolidation. Steep income and inheritance taxes would prevent the accumulation of large, sterile, and potentially dangerous fortunes. Even more important, taxes could be used to stave off corporate consolidation. Progressive levies on corporate income would discourage big companies and give a break to small ones. Similarly, a tax on intercorporate dividends would make holding companies economically inefficient, discouraging the creation of such pernicious entities. Brandeis had made such arguments repeatedly and consistently. He also relied on several key emissaries—including Frankfurter, Tommy Corcoran, and Benjamin Cohen—to carry his case to Roosevelt.[22]

In 1934, the Brandeis cohort within the administration had drafted a bill for special taxes on "tramp corporations": companies that set up shop in states where they did no substantive business, usually for tax reasons. Corcoran and Cohen also developed a bill for Sen. Burton K. Wheeler (D-MT) that would have replaced the existing flat-rate corporate income tax with a graduated levy. Generally speaking, the Brandeisians wanted to hobble shady or undesirable corporate practices by taxing them out of existence.[23]

When it came to taxes, however, Frankfurter was the most effective advocate of Brandeis's antimonopoly ideology. He used his close relationship with Roosevelt to carry the anti-bigness message directly to the White House. At the same time, he forged a valuable relationship with Henry Morgenthau. Morgenthau was deeply suspicious of Frankfurter, resenting his friendship with Roosevelt and his policy prescriptions. Oliphant gave Frankfurter—and Brandeis—a back door into the department's policy formulation. In late 1934, that point of entry proved highly effective.[24]

The early years of the New Deal had left Brandeis and Frankfurter disappointed on the tax front. But in November 1934, Frankfurter promised to take another run at the issue, urging FDR to adopt a more reformist approach to tax policy. The results came almost immediately. Working with Oliphant, Frankfurter helped craft the Treasury tax plan of December 1934, giving the document a distinctly Brandeisian flavor.[25]

While antimonopoly ideas were central to Oliphant's memo, they had only modest influence on the ultimate character of the 1935 tax legislation. In guiding his plan from inception to realization, Roosevelt retained much of the Brandeis-inspired rhetoric, warning of the danger inherent in economic consolidation. But while Brandeis and his minions took a broad view of taxation, seeking to make it an instrument of structural reform, Roosevelt increasingly framed his tax arguments in terms of fairness and morality. Specifically, he invoked ability-to-pay arguments, using them to justify steeper taxes on the rich, as well higher taxes on large corporations. Such rhetoric was not inconsistent with the Brandeis agenda; in many ways, it was complementary. But Roosevelt was more interested in using taxes as an instrument of social justice than he ever was in using them to regulate economic behavior. His was a more personal, less abstract, and sometimes more vindictive version of tax reform.

The guiding spirit of Roosevelt's 1935 tax message, especially as it evolved throughout the spring of 1935, is not to be found in the hallowed chambers of Justice Brandeis. Rather, the bill was a product of Treasury experts. Not, however, the experts who wrote the Viner Studies—those economists who completed numerous detailed reports on the federal tax system during the summer of 1934. Rather, the message found its roots among a different group of experts: the Treasury lawyers working for Herman Oliphant.

The Lawyers

Treasury economists were not the only administration experts working on tax reform in the mid-1930s; lawyers in the Bureau of Internal Revenue (BIR) were also hard at work, using different methods and reaching different conclusions. While Treasury economists focused on structural reform, the BIR lawyers, who reported to Oliphant through BIR General Counsel Robert H. Jackson, emphasized improvements in administration and enforcement. And while both groups were driven by a commitment to progressivity, they sometimes differed on how to serve that ideal.

Broadly speaking, the economists wanted to cut taxes on the poor while the lawyers wanted to raise taxes on the rich. The economists argued passionately for what might be called low-end progressivity: a reduction in regressive consumption taxes, paid for with new revenue from a much-broadened income tax. The economists opposed most excise levies and were visceral foes of a national sales tax. They believed a broader income tax, paid by the middle class as well as the rich, would allow the federal government to eliminate many taxes on the poor. The lawyers, meanwhile, were spokesmen for "high-end" progressivity, including steeper, more effective taxes on the nation's richest taxpayers. They stressed the dangers of tax avoidance, including its corrosive effect on both revenue and taxpayer morale.

Usually, the economists and the lawyers agreed on substantive tax issues. But their different emphases had a profound effect on the New

Deal tax agenda, especially in the mid-1930s. Over the long run, the economists would be vindicated; the fiscal watershed of World War II was built on their recommendations for a mass income tax. But high-end progressivity, with its emphasis on curbing tax avoidance and giving real teeth to steep statutory tax rates, also shaped the wartime tax regime.

In the mid-1930s, however, the lawyers dominated the policy process to the virtual exclusion of the economists. Enlisting President Roosevelt in their plans for steeply progressive taxation, they championed higher taxes—both statutory and effective—on rich individuals and large businesses.

Statutory rates are those enshrined in the letter of the law. Effective rates reflect the impact of the graduated rate structure, as well as various deductions and exemptions contained within the law. Effective rates are always lower than statutory rates, but aggressive tax avoidance can make them *much* lower. Advocates of high-end progressivity generally believed that loopholes were undermining the statutory rates, making a mockery of the progressive rate structure. The lawyers called for better tax enforcement among the rich and famous, as well as higher statutory rates on income and estates. On both counts, they found a willing audience in the White House, where such ideas resonated with presidential notions of social and economic justice.

By early 1935, several leading lawyers in the Roosevelt administration had established their position as spokesmen for high-end progressivity. Oliphant was the most prominent, and he tied his advocacy of higher rates to larger plans for economic and social reform. But another Treasury lawyer, BIR chief counsel Robert Jackson, who had fallen in with Roosevelt's western New York cronies during the 1920s, played an equally important, if somewhat less visible, role in shaping the 1935 revenue law. From his perch within the BIR, Jackson prepared detailed studies on tax avoidance. He sounded a clarion call for better tax enforcement, insisting that America's richest families were routinely gutting the income tax, through both legal avoidance and outright criminal evasion. When the wealthy shirked their fiscal responsibilities, Jackson insisted, it threatened the political legitimacy of the entire tax system. Cracking down on cheats and chiselers was the first order of business.

Jackson focused many of his studies on a handful of rich Americans, exploring the finances of Henry Ford, William Randolph Hearst, John W. Davis, and the duPonts. He vilified tax avoiders, adopting a prosecutorial style both in private and public. In fact, Jackson's most celebrated effort at character assassination was, in fact, a prosecution: the 1934 attempt to charge former Treasury Secretary Andrew Mellon with criminal tax evasion.

Early New Deal Interest in Tax Avoidance

Franklin Roosevelt began to consider tax avoidance early in his presidency. Four months after taking office, he received a letter from Felix Frankfurter, urging him to crack down on tax cheats. Curbing avoidance and evasion would serve the cause of progressive taxation, Frankfurter told the president, giving teeth to the graduated rate structure. "A very careful survey of existing revenue measures should be made in the interest of increasing the revenue," he insisted. It should be conducted by someone new to federal tax policymaking, someone with "an entirely fresh mind which has not become accustomed to glaring defects or wrongs in past legislation and administration made in the interest of the heavy taxpayer."[26]

Frankfurter insisted that the government was losing out on hundreds of millions of dollars every year, principally through shoddy tax enforcement. Avoidance was bad enough, but outright evasion was even more galling. To bolster his case, Frankfurter forwarded a letter from Judge William Green of the U.S. Court of Claims. Green, a former chairman of the House Ways and Means Committee, bemoaned the vast sums lost through poor enforcement. Frankfurter related similar comments from Supreme Court Justice Harlan Stone. "More money can be lost to the government in a single badly conducted case," Stone contended, "than [administration budget director Lewis] Douglas can save in a year."[27]

Roosevelt sympathized with such arguments, although largely for moral rather than economic reasons. As he would soon make clear, the president agreed on the need for stiff tax enforcement, especially when the targets were politically attractive. He thought of taxation in starkly moralistic terms. Robert Jackson later recalled the president's penchant for personalizing tax policy. Roosevelt "was inclined to think about economic matters in terms of rights and wrongs," he wrote. The president routinely attributed dark motives to his opponents, even when their actions could be explained in less sinister terms. Roosevelt thought of antitrust policy, for instance, as a means of "punishing a conspiracy, thinking of a conspiracy as a dark cellar operation in which evil men got together in masks and plotted to do something." Roosevelt brought exactly that frame of mind to tax policy, where he tended to demonize tax avoiders even when they stayed within the letter of the law.[28]

Roosevelt's fondness for vilification was most evident in the tax trial of Andrew Mellon. Since the early 1920s, the former Treasury secretary had been dogged by rumors of shady tax practices. Sen. James Couzens (R-MI) had pursued the matter while Mellon was still in office, only to find himself the target of a retaliatory investigation by the BIR. After Mellon left office in 1932, the rumors continued to fly, and in 1934, the Roosevelt Treasury charged Mellon with criminal tax evasion.[29]

For Democrats, Mellon represented everything that was bad about Republican fiscal policy. While at the Treasury, he had successfully engineered a major reduction in income tax rates, as well as substantial cuts in the estate tax and repeal of the gift tax. The depression had forced lawmakers to rescind some of these cuts; the Revenue Act of 1932 raised income and estate rates, while also imposing many new consumption taxes. Mellon endorsed some of these increases, but he was still regarded as a patrician apologist for America's wealthy elite. Not surprisingly, then, he was a popular target for partisan sniping. When the chance came to humble the mighty Mellon, Democrats jumped.

In March 1934, the Treasury and Justice accused Mellon of submitting fraudulent tax returns. The millionaire owed more than $3 million in back taxes and penalties, the administration contended, and should also be prosecuted for his crimes. Mellon struck back immediately: "The action which the Attorney General has taken in seeking to secure an indictment against me on the charge of income tax evasion is politics of the crudest sort," he told reporters. Government officials were conducting "a campaign of character wrecking and abuse," though he had "always been scrupulous to give the government the benefit of every doubt in making up my tax return."[30]

In May, a Pittsburgh grand jury refused to indict Mellon, and the administration found itself embarrassed and embattled. Journalists took up Mellon's complaint, suggesting that prosecutors were engaged in nothing more than political harassment.[31] Into this fray stepped Robert Jackson.

Jackson had been reluctant to join Roosevelt in Washington, rejecting Morgenthau's initial effort to recruit him as chief counsel for the BIR. Ultimately, however, he seems to have been swayed by Oliphant. A longtime Democrat and supporter of Roosevelt's progressive agenda, Jackson was predisposed to embrace Oliphant's version of tax activism. But he had little experience as a policymaker or politician, having honed his skills in the courtroom, not the backroom. Under Oliphant's tutelage, he would soon turn his liberal inclinations to the job of tax research, but first he had to resolve the Mellon case.

Following the grand jury embarrassment, Jackson was determined to vindicate the government's case. A successful civil trial, he believed, would prove Mellon's culpability in the tax charges. "If that could be established, it would save the Administration's face," Jackson later observed. "It was pretty much in need of being saved."[32]

Morgenthau gave Jackson a rousing pep talk. "I consider that Mr. Mellon is not on trial," the secretary declared, "but Democracy and the privileged rich and I want to see who will win."[33] Indeed, Morgenthau always took a hard line on enforcement; he was no more willing to coddle tax avoiders than the president was. And he was just as unwilling to recognize any moral distinction between legal and illegal methods of tax minimization.

Jackson was suitably enthusiastic, too, but he urged caution at several key points. Specifically, he recommended that the government not seek fraud penalties against Mellon, since fraud required a different and more demanding standard of proof. To win on fraud, Jackson would have to establish that Mellon had conducted his tax-avoidance transactions in bad faith. Absent fraud penalties, the burden would be on Mellon to prove that he did not owe back taxes. It was a tactical decision, Jackson later recalled, not a moral one.[34]

But Roosevelt overruled Jackson, giving personal assent to the fraud charge. After hearing the details of Mellon's tax avoidance, the president theatrically held his nose and directed the attorney general to take a hard line.[35] Roosevelt was clearly outraged by Mellon's tax avoidance, and not without some cause. While serving as Treasury secretary, Mellon had requested from the Bureau of Internal Revenue a memorandum on popular tax-avoidance techniques. Mellon later admitted that he had employed five of these techniques himself. During his tenure, moreover, leaks from the BIR suggested that Mellon's influence may have distorted enforcement efforts; in one instance, a tax return from the Standard Steel Car Company bore the handwritten warning from one BIR agent: "This is a Mellon company."[36]

The Mellon case dragged on for several years, with aggressive tactics on both sides. When it was finally settled by the Board of Tax Appeals, the recently deceased Mellon was again exonerated of any deliberate evasion. And while his estate was assessed more $480,000 in back taxes, the decision was broadly considered a vindication for the Republican icon. But the real importance of the Mellon case was the spotlight it threw on Roosevelt's attitude toward tax evasion. The president had been a vocal champion of the prosecution, as well as the civil case. He and Morgenthau monitored the Mellon trial, and remained avid spectators during the civil case. In fact, they were more than spectators, intervening at key moments to ensure that Mellon never escaped too easily. It was not simply a partisan persecution, although it had a certain element of political opportunism. Morgenthau and Roosevelt both believed that Mellon's tax avoidance was emblematic of a larger problem: immoral tax dodging—whether legal or illegal—by the nation's richest citizens.[37]

Roosevelt's fondness for vilification—and political meddling in tax enforcement—was again on display in September 1934, when the president told Morgenthau that William Randolph Hearst planned to attack the administration for its economic policies. Could the Treasury take a look at Hearst's personal tax returns, perhaps turning up something useful? Morgenthau was happy to comply. "I did subsequently look up his income tax and found that there was plenty there," Morgenthau later recalled in his diaries. He also found information on Hearst's mistress, actress Marion Davies. Morgenthau advised FDR to mount a preemptive attack on both. "If we stated something after he attacked us," Morgenthau advised, "he would say that we were doing it for revenge and spite."[38]

Legal Tax Avoidance among the Rich and Famous

Roosevelt's tendency to personalize tax issues took more substantive form in the hands of administration lawyers. Again, Robert Jackson played a key role. As BIR chief counsel, Jackson was pivotal in shaping the administration's first major foray into tax policy. He served as a key advocate for the president's tax plan during congressional debate over the Revenue Act of 1935. More important, he drafted the president's dramatic tax message of June 19, 1935, in which FDR outlined his plans for soak-the-rich taxation. But Jackson was not simply a lead lobbyist on tax issues: he was also a major architect of New Deal tax reform. In the summer of 1935, as Congress debated the president's tax plan, Jackson undertook a series of studies on tax avoidance and evasion designed to bolster the case for high-end progressivity. His stated goal was to save the income tax from the depredations of rich tax shirkers.

Jackson's memos on tax reform, while much briefer than the Viner Studies, had a larger short-term impact than those voluminous economic reports. Much of Jackson's work was highly technical, exploring administrative, interpretive, and constitutional issues of federal tax policy. Other memos, however, were overtly political, particularly those focused on tax avoidance among the nation's richest families. In several key memos, Jackson and his staff demonstrated that rich Americans were avoiding their fair share of the tax burden, sometimes through outright fraud, but more often through technically legal but morally dubious avoidance schemes. These memos were not abstract. Rather, they pried open the financial lives of America's super rich, using records only available to the nation's tax collectors. Jackson removed progressive taxation from the abstract realm of the economists and thrust it into the sumptuous homes of the American upper class.

Perhaps the most striking memo among Jackson's several that he wrote over the summer of 1935 was titled, simply, "Income and Income Taxes." He set out to evaluate the efficacy of the progressive tax system. "In general terms," he wrote, "the problem was to investigate into the ratio between what persons of large wealth have taken out of the social product and what they have contributed to the support of government in the way of income taxes." His conclusions were not happy ones, at least for anyone eager to see the rich pay their fair share.[39]

Wealthy taxpayers—or nonpayers, as was often the case—made frequent use of one particular avoidance vehicle: tax-exempt securities issued by state and local governments. For decades, Treasury officials had been calling for the elimination of this exemption. Mellon, in fact, had been a vigorous opponent of the loophole, insisting that it cost the government enormous sums in lost revenue while also distorting investment decisions. But lawmakers had been unwilling to attack this sacred cow of the financial system. Many questioned whether the Constitution even permitted the federal government to tax state securities, although most tax lawyers believed the Sixteenth Amendment provided ample authority. More to the point, tax-exempt bonds were a cherished prerogative of state and local politicians across the nation. Few members of Congress were inclined to pursue the issue.

But the Treasury kept trying, and Jackson's memo was another in a long series of official studies that criticized the exemption. It was, however, more pointed than many earlier efforts. The Viner Studies, for instance, had considered the issue in passing, concluding that the problem was real but not serious; the revenue loss was comparatively minor, concluded Roy Blakey, and the fairness issues exaggerated.[40] Jackson, however, took a different view, and he had numbers to bolster his case. To his mind, the tax avoidance made possible by state and local bonds was intolerable—a blight upon the nation's revenue system.

Jackson began by examining individual tax returns from people earning more than $1 million in annual gross income. This was a small group, numbering about 58. In several cases, Jackson pointed out, people in this group had very low taxable income, at least when compared to their huge tax-exempt income. Wall Street giant and outspoken New Deal critic E. F. Hutton, for instance, had reported $20,047 in net income for 1932, while his gross income, including returns from exempt securities, was more than $2.7 million. Vincent Astor had paid tax on just $101,150, a far cry from the $3.1 million he made overall. Mellon earned $3.5 million during his last year as Treasury secretary, but paid taxes on just $1.2 million. Perhaps most striking, John D. Rockefeller Jr. reported a taxable income of $5.2 million—no small sum except when compared with his total income of more than $22 million. Rockefeller alone had deprived the Treasury of more than $2 million in tax revenue. Altogether, the 58 taxpayers on Jackson's list paid $24.4 million in federal income tax during 1932; they saved another $11.8 million by investing in state and local bonds rather than other securities.[41]

This lost revenue wasn't small change, totaling almost 3 percent of total individual income tax collections for fiscal year 1934. Viewed another way, the loss was equal to more than two-thirds of the revenue raised through the excise tax on entertainment admissions—a quintessentially regressive tax on the nation's lower and middle classes.[42]

Jackson concluded that exempt securities were costing the government too much money. Even more important, they were giving rich people a convenient means by which to avoid the steep surtax rates on individual income. Jackson offered a few additional thoughts, including some only incidental to the exemption issue. The figures in his study indicated that wealth was highly concentrated, he pointed out. The 58 individuals represented just 30 families. One family alone—the duPonts—had five people on the list. Furthermore, most of the 30 families drew their wealth from single enterprises, including several new ones. "At least two of them are national retail merchandising enterprises," Jackson reported, "a more recent phenomenon in the United States." This was new money, "accounting for the lack of social position on the part of these families." Clearly, this was more than just a statistical sampling of the nation's rich families, with an eye toward closing the exempt securities loophole. Jackson was straying far afield to offer his thoughts on the evolving social order. It would not be the last time.[43]

Another section of the July 1935 memo explored the duPont family in special detail, seeking to illuminate how wealthy families used trusts and other legal devices to minimize their taxes. Rather than attempt a laborious survey of numerous taxpayers, Jackson focused on a single family, including not just blood relatives but also friends and colleagues. Investigation revealed that the duPonts had spread their considerable income over several family members. When the income was split this way, it could sometimes elude the steep rates near the top of the income tax.

Trusts were extremely efficient, allowing grantors to retain use of their money, even as they divided it among various beneficiaries for tax purposes. There was nothing illegal about this arrangement, at least on its surface. But Jackson clearly disapproved, rejecting the notion that the hundreds of duPont returns actually represented discrete taxpaying entities. In particular, Jackson noted with disapproval that substantial income was being reported by minor children in the family.[44]

Despairing at the prospect of trying to trace the entire duPont fortune, Jackson decided to focus further on "those who might be said to control the duPont enterprise": a short list of just seven individuals including five family members, one son-in-law, and John J. Raskob, a close family friend and business associate (as well as a prominent Roosevelt critic). This list, Jackson acknowledged, had been derived from *Fortune* magazine, which published a detailed three-part study of the duPont family in late 1934 and early 1935. According to *Fortune,* the most important member of the family was Pierre S. duPont, followed closely by his younger brothers, Irenee and Lammot.[45]

Having examined the tax history of the seven leading duPonts, Jackson concluded that the group had engaged in some fairly shady tax practices, "in some cases making them open to fraud charges." Overall, he concluded, "these seven persons have consistently avoided the full impact of the surtax system." Between 1928 and 1932, they had managed to avoid about 20 percent of their theoretical tax liability by relying on trusts, tax-exempt bonds, and losses claimed for "hobbies" such as farming or horse breeding.[46] Pierre S. duPont was the most aggressive avoider. While having no children of his own, he had created numerous entities to shield his income from taxation. Using five trusts, he had managed to save $1.3 million in taxes between 1928 and 1932. Irenee duPont, father of nine children, had also made good use of his progeny by dividing his income into small portions for the maintenance of his family. He had saved almost $1 million between 1928 and 1932. Lammot duPont, who also had nine children, had established trusts for all but the last, who was just one year old.[47]

John J. Raskob was not a duPont, but having once served as Pierre S. duPont's secretary, he was a key player in the operations of the family enterprise. Raskob, strikingly, had not created any trusts. "His tax history, however, is none the less checkered," Jackson noted. In particular, Raskob was under investigation by the BIR for a series of wash sales: transactions in which depreciated securities were sold to claim a loss deduction, followed by an almost immediate repurchase of identical stock. In Raskob's case, he was accused of colluding with Pierre S. duPont, as well as members of the Raskob family, to conduct wash sales that were difficult for tax authorities to identify.[48]

All in all, Jackson concluded, the seven leaders of the duPont family had paid $13.5 million in taxes between 1928 and 1932; they had avoided paying, chiefly through the use of trusts, another $3.4 million. In actuality, these numbers were probably conservative, Jackson added; if the Bureau had possessed better information on the family's tax-exempt securities and wash sales, the figure would have been substantially higher.[49]

The trust device had created a gross inequality in the tax system, Jackson argued. Rich taxpayers could escape steep surtaxes by putting their money into trusts and using the proceeds to support individual family members. Once segregated into smaller, bite-sized fortunes, the original mass of money was shielded from steep rates. Meanwhile, the wealthy donor typically maintained control of the donated assets, including voting rights for stock and the right to reclaim assets in the case of a beneficiary's death. "The wealthy man not only obtains exemption but suffers practically none of the disadvantages that might be expected to inhere in a segregation of assets," Jackson complained. Meanwhile, "the ordinary and less wealthy person is disallowed the ordinary expenses involved in caring for his wife and his children."[50]

Jackson's memo concluded with a remarkable section titled "Wealth by Reputation." Seeking to determine how much rich people were actually paying, Jackson assistant Samuel Klaus surveyed the finances of roughly 50 taxpayers for the years 1928 to 1934. The list was compiled in somewhat haphazard fashion. Initially, it included the officers and directors of major American companies, to which were added numerous taxpayers from well-known wealthy families. The list quickly became unmanageably large, and Klaus selected about 200 for his initial focus. Still overwhelmed, he further reduced that number by examining only those who had not been the subject of earlier investigations (such as those people grilled by the Pecora committee in its Wall Street trading investigation). The result was a list of 50 names.

The list included some random figures, added at the behest of Jackson and his associates in the Treasury. Charlie Chaplin, Douglas Fairbanks, and Mary Pickford stood in for the Hollywood crowd. Paul Cravath, John W. Davis, and Frank Hogan represented the legal community. Under the heading of "inherited or invested wealth," the list included more than 20 names, including the Astors, the Wanamakers, the Whitneys, the Goulds, the Fricks, and the Fords. Finally, a few people were added for no apparent reason other than their prominence, including car manufacturer Horace Dodge, brewer Adolphus Busch, and circus maestro John Ringling.

The "Wealth by Reputation" study revealed a steep decline in annual income among the super rich during the early years of the Great Depression. Income among the very rich always varies widely from year to year, depending on capital gains, stock dividends, and similar irregular events. But the famous wealthy of Jackson's study clearly suffered during the depression, at least compared to the heady days of the late 1920s. John D. Rockefeller went from an income at $37.8 million in 1928 to just $2.5 million in 1933. Doris Duke's income fell from $8 million to $215,000. Walter Chrysler saw his income plummet from $5.7 million to just $600,000. Of course, there was no genuine hardship in the group, but the depression had clearly taken a toll on the incomes of the rich and famous.[51]

Klaus concluded that rich taxpayers were getting plenty of professional assistance in preparing their returns and planning their tax avoidance—a safe bet, given the high stakes of tax avoidance among this income cohort. Transactions were so complex, he pointed out, that it seemed probable these taxpayers were engaging "hired and possibly, in some cases, full time tax men." Since lawyers and accountants were also signing returns for these wealthy taxpayers, it would be harder to prove fraud; with the taxpayer's "state of mind" not at issue, the fraud standard was much harder to reach.[52]

While Klaus was completing his study, Jackson was preparing his own memo, "Effectiveness of Income Tax Law in Higher and Lower Brackets." The tax law was not effective in the upper reaches of the income spectrum, Jackson concluded, at least not compared to its functioning in the lower brackets. Rates set forth in the statute were consistently undermined by sophisticated tax avoidance, and the government had compounded the problem by enforcing the law poorly. Predictably, Jackson fingered tax-exempt securities as the number one source of inequity. Such securities were owned principally by wealthy taxpayers, since the tax advantages outweighed their meager rates of pretax return. For people in lower brackets, the tax advantages were comparatively smaller, and hence not worth the sacrifice of a low interest rate. Exempt securities were threatening the vitality of progressive taxation, Jackson said. "By reason of this tax exemption shelter, the high bracket rates which have the appearance of being extremely severe are, in fact, moderated, and to a large extent, ineffective while the taxes in the small brackets are fully effective."[53]

Jackson also attacked the "hobby deductions" so prevalent among the rich. Titans of industry often reported their occupation as "farmer," allowing them to deduct maintenance costs for their large estates. Others reported their occupation as "racing," permitting them to take business deductions for their sporting interests. Smaller taxpayers could not generally avail themselves of such devices, if only because their hobbies could never remotely rise to the level of an occupation. The revenue costs of this sort of evasion were substantial but not enormous, Jackson said. More important was its inherent unfairness. "It is an unsportsmanlike advantage which certain large taxpayers have taken," Jackson wrote.[54]

Preventing tax avoidance among the rich—or even detecting it—was notoriously difficult, Jackson observed. "The evasion devices of the little fellow are often crude," he wrote, "based on curbstone or inexperienced advice, and accomplished only with the aid of his family or immediate employees." Tax avoidance among the rich was a grand enterprise, planned for years "by a clinic of able counselors with many corporations, banks, and individuals in full cooperation." The Bureau could readily track most penny ante avoidance. But the tax-avoidance transactions common among wealthy taxpayers were hard to unravel. Often, audits failed to uncover shady behavior. And when the Bureau did manage to identify tax avoidance among the rich, it was often inadvertent, with leads arising from other, less spectacular investigations. Catching wealthy tax avoiders, in other words, often depended on a healthy dose of dumb luck.[55]

Jackson's research found an eager audience in the White House. As he began his famous turn to the left in 1935, Roosevelt grew more interested in the tax shenanigans of his political enemies. Indeed, the president increasingly viewed tax policy in moralistic terms, denouncing tax avoidance as the moral equivalent of tax evasion. It was not a position shared completely by his legal advisers. Even Jackson took a consistently more measured approach. FDR, he later recalled, always understood that taxes were important, affecting the lives of every American, rich or poor. "But he viewed the taxation problem perhaps too exclusively as a social problem," Jackson observed, "and not sufficiently as one in economics."[56]

Roosevelt's 1935 tax message showed the unmistakable influence of Jackson's research, as well as his prosecutorial work on tax evasion. The president did view tax policy in moralistic terms, tarring tax avoiders with the same brush as tax evaders. More broadly, however, he believed that the tax laws themselves did not sufficiently constrain the rich or demand adequate sacrifice from them. As would soon become clear, Roosevelt hoped to use the 1935 revenue bill to correct that sorry state of affairs.

Drafting the Tax Message

Roosevelt reacted coolly to Oliphant's December 11 memo on tax reform, but Morgenthau kept his staff working on the subject. By January 7, Jackson had prepared the rough draft of a presidential message on tax reform; three days later, George Haas, chief of the Treasury's economic research staff, delivered a similar document. These drafts, which were soon combined, differed in only minor respects, both emphasizing the social utility of federal taxation and the importance of crafting a tax system with careful attention to the taxpayer's ability to pay. Both memos laid out the case for a new inheritance tax, giving pride of place to this ideologically charged idea. Indeed, Jackson and Haas emphasized the most controversial aspect of such a levy: the limit it might place on hereditary fortunes. Unchecked inheritance was a "menace to the very existence of the democratic form of government," they argued, "as offensive to this generation as the inheritance of political power was to the generation that formed our government."[57]

The Jackson-Haas draft also included a proposal to raise income taxes drastically on the nation's richest taxpayers—enough to "tax away for public purposes virtually all of any income in excess of an amount approximating one million dollars." Such an income was vast, far more than anyone could possibly require, they asserted. "It cannot be justified by any quantity or quality of public service."[58]

The Jackson-Haas draft went on to detail the Oliphant proposal for a graduated tax on corporate income, stressing the dangers of large business units. "Our economic and political stability is not increased by the growth and existence of such enormous business aggregations," the document stated. "Smaller business enterprises, which have always played a vital part in American economic life, have been placed at a growing disadvantage." Unfettered business consolidation served only to concentrate power in the hands of a small minority, often for the sole purpose of establishing monopoly control over an industry. To address these problems, a new tax on corporate income would replace the flat rate 13.5 percent corporate income tax then in operation. New rates might range from 10 percent for small companies to 20 percent for large ones. Such graduation would have salutary effects on American business, presumably limiting the size of companies by making big ones too expensive.[59]

Finally, Jackson and Haas outlined a new intercorporate dividend tax, arguing that it would help discourage complex corporate structures and challenge the concentration of economic power within a small minority. By making holding companies expensive, it would encourage greater transparency in corporate structure. "The looseness of our laws has lent itself to a pyramiding of control through holding company devices, by means of which a few individuals have been enabled, with a relatively small investment, to control huge enterprises representing the savings of many," they contended.[60]

Internal debate over the tax message continued, with Roosevelt taking his time developing the document. Meanwhile, the president told Congress that he had no plans for additional taxes. He warned lawmakers, however, that he would not ignore pernicious inequalities in wealth and opportunity. "We have not weeded out the over privileged and we have not effectively lifted up the underprivileged," he declared. The administration would do nothing to undermine the profit motive, but neither could it ignore "a clear mandate from the people, that Americans must forswear that conception of the acquisition of wealth which, through excessive profits, creates undue private power over private affairs and, to our misfortune, over public affairs as well."[61]

Clearly, Roosevelt was prepared to target big business, and corporate profits in particular. He worried about the injustice of inequality, but he also connected that injustice to the larger impact of concentrated wealth. FDR worried that unregulated, overconcentrated wealth was a source of social, political, and economic corruption. In his 1932 campaign speeches, he had railed against powerful economic interests and their cavalier attitude toward average Americans. If America were to avoid the rise of an economic oligarchy, as well as the economic stagnation that would accompany it, then government must regulate private power, he declared. As president, Roosevelt had continued to harbor deep suspicion about the motives and activities of America's economic elite.[62]

In late January, Roosevelt began to cast about for advice on the Treasury tax plan, which was then in its third revision. He showed the draft to some of his advisers, including Raymond Moley. Moley was aghast. He argued against the message "as a whole and in detail." He was particularly unhappy about the Brandeis-inspired attack on corporate bigness. "I opposed it as an attempt to put over dubious social reforms in the guise of tax legislation," he later recalled. "It was one thing, I said, to reform the tax system—which certainly needed overhauling—and another to try to stand the industrial and financial system on its head under that pretext." Moley blamed Oliphant, who he regarded as an intellectual charlatan full of "radical and half-baked ideas on social reform."[63]

At Roosevelt's request, Moley developed his own draft for a tax message, and he took pains to strike a much different tone than Jackson and Haas. While accepting the principal Treasury recommendations, he couched them in far different language. His section on the graduated corporate income tax, for instance, softened the Treasury's attack on big business. "This recommendation is not based upon any absolute idea that either bigness or smallness in business is good per se," Moley wrote. Rather, it was merely intended to account for differences in ability to pay, with large corporations better equipped to shoulder heavy taxes than their smaller competitors. More substantively, Moley proposed somewhat higher rates on small corporations and substantially lower rates on big ones. The tax was still graduated, but now the rates ranged from 10.75 percent to 16.75 percent.[64]

The Springtime of Roosevelt's Discontent

While his advisers debated the tax message, Roosevelt continued to stall. He wasn't ready to take the discussion public, instead biding his time and supervising the fine-tuning of his message. But pressure for action was mounting from both ends of the political spectrum.

Roosevelt's 1935 tax initiative is often explained as a response to Huey Long, and his famous "Thunder on the Left." In 1934 and 1935, Long was riding a wave of surging popularity, organizing a loose network of Share Our Wealth clubs around his proposals for radical social reform. Specifically, Long proposed a capital levy that would have limited personal fortunes to roughly $5 million; he later revised that number downward several times, eventually reaching $1.5 million. The resulting windfall in tax revenues would be used to provide a guaranteed minimum income of $2,000 to $3,000 for every American family, as well as old-age pensions and free higher education. Supposedly drawing his inspiration from the Freedman's Bureau and its "40 acres and mule," Long held out the prospect of a radical tax agenda hitched to the fortunes of average Americans.[65]

Long had considerable popular support; in 1935, his organization claimed to have 27,000 local clubs and more than 4.5 million members. These numbers were certainly inflated, and the organization was extremely decentralized, basically amounting to a mailing list. Its tax program, moreover, was little more than a farce. As historian Mark Leff has pointed out, even the total confiscation of every estate over $40,000 would not have yielded the $165 billion that Long promised to raise with his tax on millionaires. But Long's popularity was undeniable, and the persistent depression only served to heighten it. Meanwhile, Roosevelt's failure to turn the economy around had left him feeling vulnerable to critics on the left. Hugh Johnson, former director of the National Recovery Administration, attacked the Louisiana senator publicly and bitterly, while postmaster general James Farley counseled Roosevelt to co-opt some of Long's liberal support with a more progressive stance on economic issues. Democratic chieftains, including Roosevelt, grew increasingly concerned that Long would mount a third-party candidacy in the 1936 presidential election.[66]

Meanwhile, restive liberals in Congress stepped up their pressure on Roosevelt, especially around tax policy. A group of House progressives, dubbed the Mavericks, pressed for a host of liberal priorities, including steeper income and estate taxes. In the Senate, Burton Wheeler offered his Brandeis-inspired plan for a graduated corporate income tax, and George Norris endorsed sharp increases in the taxation of large estates. Robert La Follette, perhaps the most outspoken congressional advocate of serious income redistribution through the tax code, chastised the White House for ducking the issue. "The administration of President Roosevelt has thus far failed to meet the issue of taxation," he declared. "Progressives in Congress will make the best fight of which they are capable to meet the emergency by drastic increases in taxes levied upon wealth and income."[67]

Editorial opinion in liberal journals was equally harsh, with writers chastising Roosevelt for dropping the ball on tax reform. The *Nation* bemoaned the low profile assigned to revenue issues. "No serious attempt has been made to devise a system which finances the governments— Federal, State, and Local—for definite social purposes," the editors complained. "Since a concrete policy of social taxation is by all odds the most important element of both reform and recovery, essential to the very survival of our economic system, we urge the Administration to lose no time in squaring off to this fundamental task." The magazine called for an overall tax increase of $500 million, a huge number given that total federal revenue was just under $3 billion in FY 1934. New money, the editors argued, should come from higher estate taxes, as well as steeper individual and corporate income levies. Notably, the editors endorsed a broad expansion of the income tax, with lower exemptions that would extend it well into the middle class. Money from that more robust levy could then be used to reduce regressive consumption taxes.[68]

Editors at the *Nation* had drawn most of their ideas from the writing of Paul Studenski, advocate of sweeping tax reform. In his own article for the magazine, Studenski was explicit about the need for broader, not just steeper, taxes. "The required supplemental revenue cannot be obtained by additional impositions on the wealthy classes alone," he explained. Studenski suggested a 40 percent cut in the exemption for married couples, and roughly the same for minor children. He also endorsed a 37.5 percent reduction in the estate tax exemption, rate hikes of 1 percent to 10 percent for both the individual income tax and the estate tax, moderate increases in the taxation of corporate income, and an increase in tobacco taxes. This last was striking for its regressivity. Studenski did not elaborate on it, but he likely viewed the levy as a sumptuary tax—a status which gave the tax a reasonable claim to social equity. Taken as a whole, Studenski argued, his reforms would remake American society. "Of all the peaceful means of bringing about a new social state," he declared, "taxation is the most potent one. It should be used not merely as an expedient to raise revenue, but as a positive force for social reconstruction."[69]

The *New Republic* struck a similar note, arguing that tax reform had enormous potential. "Ultimately no single feature of the administration's economic policy will be more important than its taxation program," the editors wrote. "If consciously used as an instrument of policy, the taxing power is capable of a far more beneficial effect on the general life than it has ever before had." Every tax had social effects, they insisted, whether deliberate or incidental. Using them straightforwardly as a means of social control was simply a more honest way of approaching the issue. The magazine later contended that a tax on corporate profits was particularly attractive. In keeping with their editorial slant on behalf of centralized economic planning, the editors viewed a tax on profits as the best way to move investment decisions "from individual to social hands."[70]

Pressure from a disappointed left, coupled with a potential third party challenge from Huey Long or some other radical tribune, almost certainly prompted Roosevelt's new interest in tax policy during the first half of 1935. Just as important, however, was his growing alienation from the business community. Tax policy was proving to be a particular sore point for many business leaders, who were alarmed by the "Share Our Wealth" arguments about wealth redistribution, not to mention more high-minded calls for heavy taxation of corporate profits. Indeed, while liberals thought Roosevelt too timid on tax issues, conservatives suspected him of being far too bold, in his heart if not yet in his policies. The early part of 1935 brought an uptick in conservative criticism of Roosevelt's tax policy, despite the administration's failure to introduce any serious tax proposal during its first two years. Conservatives seemed to detect progressive stirrings in the White House attitude toward taxes, and they were quick to denounce them.

In a well publicized speech, Nicholas Murray Butler, president of Columbia University, insisted that inequality of income and wealth were not serious problems. In fact, he contended, both were widely distributed within the United States. John C. Cresswill, a columnist for the *Magazine of Wall Street*, reported in early 1934 that wealth redistribution was an unspoken tenet of the Roosevelt agenda. William Stayton, an organizer of the American Liberty League—a bipartisan group of Roosevelt foes with deep pockets and strong opinions—warned that FDR had every intention of redistributing wealth. And Bertrand Snell (R-NY), minority leader in the House of Representatives, insisted that the New Deal was designed to redistribute money from the thrifty to "those who have been and still are shiftless."[71]

David Lawrence, a well-known columnist, warned that wealth redistribution would prompt a revolt among conservatives. "If the tax collector bars the way and stands like the angel of death at the crossroads of human initiative and says: 'Thou shalt not earn aught but a small tithe, thou shalt give to the tax collector now and till the end of thy years,' would it be surprising to find that the so-called revolution of 1933 had resulted in a counterrevolution?" he asked. While confiscation of wealth might satisfy vengeful and retaliatory impulses, he argued, "it is the path of national suicide."[72]

Percy H. Johnston, president of Chemical Bank and Trust Company and a spokesman for the Merchants' Association of New York, told a nationwide radio audience that the country was struggling under an "overwhelming" tax burden. The root of the problem, he argued, was excessive spending. Overeager legislators had mortgaged the nation's future, running up huge bills and then raising taxes to pay for them. Business, industry, commerce, labor, and capital were all members of the national economic "team," he continued. "Business is the lead horse in this team, but if we pile tax after tax upon it until the load is beyond its power to carry and live then we shall not get started on the road to real economic recovery."[73]

Walter S. Landis, vice president of the American Cyanamid Company, complained that federal income taxes had lost their roots in "ability to pay" and shifted decisively into soak-the-rich territory. "Ignorance and misuse of the power to tax slowly are wrecking our economic structure, and the people who are hurt are the very ones the income and estate taxes were supposed to help—those who work for a living." He also attacked consumption taxes, taking special aim at levies that tried to disguise their identity. Excise taxes, AAA processing taxes, luxury taxes, and the like were all just renamed sales taxes, he declared. In fact, he contended, sales taxes were desirable, especially if they could be administered efficiently and fairly. But when hidden, and poorly enforced, they undermined their own worth.[74]

Mark Eisner, a professor of tax law at New York University and chairman of the New York State Board of Higher Education, assailed soak-the-rich theories of taxation. "There are many good people in this country who believe in our high taxation as the means of correcting economic disequilibrium," he said. In fact, however, efforts to redistribute wealth would be disastrous, costing the nation more in lost productivity than it could possibly gain through greater diffusion of wealth. "It is like a family depriving itself of sustenance in order to fatten a pig so that when it is slaughtered it will be a juicier morsel for the family to consume," he suggested. "The meal will not equal the deprivation suffered."[75]

Even a few of Roosevelt's supporters were unhappy with the state of federal taxation, worrying that fiscal burdens were slowing recovery. Samuel Untermyer, a devoted Democrat and supporter of the New Deal, insisted that the administration's taxation, when combined with steep state and local levies, had brought industry to its knees. Recovery was impossible, he insisted, until the nation revamped its jury-rigged but highly punitive system of income and estate taxes. "These many well-intentioned artificial devices, useful as they may be to bridge the chasm, are mere crutches," he stated. "They are helpful makeshifts to the lame man, but they do not teach him how to walk."[76]

Given Roosevelt's passive approach to tax policy during 1933 and 1934, these conservative criticisms seem surprising. In fact, however, Roosevelt had inherited a tax system that was already imposing heavy burdens on the nation; the Revenue Act of 1932 had been the largest tax increase in American history, and it spread its burden widely across the population with steep new rates for income taxpayers, as well as numerous new levies on consumption. But the more immediate source of conservative discontent was almost certainly the stepped-up discussion of numerous soak-the-rich tax schemes, especially Long's plan for a capital levy. "Share the wealth" debates were in the air throughout the latter half of 1934 and the early months of 1935. Conservatives understood that such ideas were getting serious consideration, even in the White House.

Conservative opposition had coalesced around the American Liberty League. Founded in August, 1934, its membership included many members of the economic oligarchy targeted by the Treasury's budding tax plan. Funded with duPont money, the league was notable for its Democratic contingent: John J. Raskob, John W. Davis, and Nathan Miller were all prominent members. Former presidential candidate and past New York governor Al Smith, who had broken decisively with Roosevelt, also served as a league spokesman.

The league prompted outrage and worry in Roosevelt's inner circle, and leading advisers mounted a vigorous counteroffensive, similar to their attack on Long. James Farley famously referred to the group as the "American Cellophane League": it was a duPont product, he quipped, and you could see right through it.[77]

Roosevelt was infuriated by the overt hostility of business and conservative leaders. Raymond Moley, writing long after he had abandoned Roosevelt for the conservative camp, remembered the president's genuine outrage. Hugh Johnson said Roosevelt had declared his intention to make business leaders return to him "on their hands and knees." The president even refused to send a message of greeting to the annual meeting of the U.S. Chamber of Commerce. Hostility on both sides, then, had mounted dramatically by May 1935. Moley later attributed the 1935 tax proposal to the twin influence of this hostility and Long's threat from the left. "It was at this point," Moley wrote, "that the two impulses—the impulse to strike back at his critics and the impulse to 'steal Long's thunder'—flowed together and crystallized."[78]

On May 27, the Supreme Court struck down key aspects of the National Industrial Recovery Act, effectively ending the NIRA and closing this vital chapter in Roosevelt's odyssey of economic reform. The decision left him even more interested in a Brandeis-inspired attack on big business, and administration tax officials stepped up their work on the tax message. By the middle of June, the group had settled on something close to a final draft, focusing on several key proposals: the intercorporate dividend tax, the corporate income tax scaled to size, and the new inheritance tax. Additionally, the president had made clear his interest in raising income tax rates on high-income individuals. No such proposal had been included in the original Treasury memo of December 11, 1934.[79]

In the final round of discussions, Roosevelt voiced misgivings about the intercorporate dividend tax, suggesting it be eliminated or at least downplayed in the final message. Treasury officials, especially Jackson and Oliphant, continued to fight for the idea, but even Frankfurter seemed willing to let it go. Apparently, he believed the attack on corporate bigness was best made through the newly graduated corporate income tax. Moley, of course, was strenuously opposed to the dividend tax, and he came close to convincing Roosevelt to drop it. Ultimately, it stayed in, but it was not a featured part of the president's message.

Roosevelt personally made the final round of changes, trying to give the message "greater clarity and less technicality," Jackson later recalled. FDR took the opportunity to declare unequivocally that new taxes were necessary, and that they should fall almost wholly on the rich. Consumption taxes that burdened the poor were not only unfair, the president told his tax advisers, but also economically unwise. It was spending, he said, not sterile saving that kept the economy going; taxes must not hinder purchasing by consumers.[80]

On the eve of sending his message to Congress, Roosevelt was feeling excited and vindictive. He understood the speech's potential impact, and he seemed to welcome the uproar it would cause. Reading a draft to Secretary of the Interior Harold Ickes, the president stopped at one point and remarked gleefully, "That is for Hearst." The breach between Roosevelt and the newspaper magnate was huge and growing bigger every day. Joseph Kennedy had tried repeatedly to reconcile the two, according to Ickes, but Roosevelt remained convinced that Hearst was the most vicious individual in American politics. Hearst reciprocated the feeling, decrying the 1935 tax proposals as "a betrayal of the American ideals of equality and justice," accusing the president, whom he called Stalin Delano Roosevelt, of developing a "soak the successful" tax program that was "essentially Communism."[81]

Moley was despondent at Roosevelt's happy anticipation of conservative outrage. He was particularly offended by FDR's evident joy in torturing conservative Democrats, who would be caught between party loyalty and their convictions. In reference to the conservative Democratic chair of the Senate Finance Committee, Roosevelt predicted, "Pat Harrison's going to have kittens on the spot."[82]

The Message

The message Roosevelt delivered to Congress on June 19, 1935, made a passionate case for steeply progressive taxation. When Roosevelt said, "Our revenue laws have operated in many ways to the unfair advantage of the few. They have done little to prevent an unjust concentration of wealth and economic power," he was warning that Americans would demand change. The president thus offered his controversial collection of reform proposals, including steeper income taxes on the super rich, a new inheritance levy, and a graduated tax on corporate earnings. "Social unrest and a deepening sense of unfairness are dangers to our national life which we must minimize by rigorous methods," he declared.[83]

The president did not seek a reduction in consumer taxes, a lightening of the burden on those least able to pay; revenue needs made such a cut impossible. Instead, he urged lawmakers to serve the cause of fairness by boosting the burden on those best able to pay. Heavier taxes on the rich were entirely justified, he argued, since the privileged few owed great debts to the less privileged masses. "Wealth in the modern world does not come merely from individual effort," he contended, "it results from a combination of individual effort and of the manifold uses to which the community puts that effort." Individuals had no absolute right to the fruits of their labor, because it was not solely their labor in the first place.

As a start, Roosevelt urged, lawmakers should enact a new inheritance tax to slow the growth of hereditary fortunes. "The transmission from generation to generation of vast fortunes by will, inheritance, or gift is not consistent with the ideals and sentiments of the American people," he said. Citing his Republican cousin for support, he quoted extensively from Theodore Roosevelt's 1907 call for estate taxation. The estate tax alone, however, was not equal to the task of limiting large fortunes. It required a supplement in the form of a new inheritance tax. In a sop to fiscal conservatives, including congressional leaders and a few within his own administration, Roosevelt suggested that money raised from a new inheritance tax could be earmarked for debt reduction rather than spending.

Congress should also raise income taxes on the very rich, Roosevelt said. These levies provided the most direct means of limiting the concentration of wealth. While declining to offer specific rate proposals, Roosevelt called on Congress to focus on the super rich: those making more than $1 million annually. The top bracket began at $1 million, he pointed out; above that point, the rates were essentially flat. "In other words," he explained, "while the rate for a man with a $6,000 income is double the rate for one with a $4,000 income, a man having a $5,000,000 annual income pays at the same rate as one whose income is $1,000,000." Additional graduation at the very top of the income scale seemed only reasonable.

Finally, Roosevelt offered his plan for a graduated corporate income tax. He was careful, however, not to frame his argument as a Brandeis-style attack on bigness. "The community has profited in those cases in which large-scale production has resulted in substantial economies and lower prices," he acknowledged. But size brought responsibility, including the duty to shoulder a larger share of the tax burden. Roosevelt invoked two distinct standards of tax justice: benefits received and ability to pay. To begin with, he said, large companies benefited from government services more than their smaller counterparts. As a result, they should pay more to support those services. Additionally, however, large corporations were also better able to shoulder large tax payments than were their smaller competitors. "The smaller corporations should not carry burdens beyond their powers; the vast concentrations of capital should be ready to carry burdens commensurate with their powers and their advantages," he said. The president suggested replacing the existing flat rate of 13.75 percent with a graduated schedule ranging from 10.75 percent to 16.75 percent. He declined to specify how the brackets should be drawn.

Roosevelt next offered his suggestion for an intercorporate dividend tax. But while Oliphant had given this idea pride of place in his original plan, it now appeared as an adjunct to the new graduated corporate tax. To prevent companies from simply breaking themselves into smaller, affiliated units, Roosevelt said, Congress should consider a dividend tax to discourage holding companies. This was a neat reversal of the original Oliphant plan, in which the corporate rate structure was cast in the supporting role and the dividend tax—and its controversial attack on holding companies—was made the principal reform. In fact, these two levies were closely linked, really two sides of the same coin. But the rhetorical shift was significant, demonstrating the waning influence of Brandeis and his disciples.

In closing, Roosevelt asked lawmakers for a constitutional amendment to allow federal taxation of state and local bonds, as well as reciprocal state taxability of federal bonds. He did not elaborate, and the idea seemed little more than an afterthought. Given the Treasury Department's fervent desire to eliminate this popular tax-avoidance technique, Roosevelt's terse treatment seems surprising. In fact, however, the recommendation was largely pro forma; while the idea enjoyed broad, bipartisan support, especially in the tax community, it had few champions on Capitol Hill. Determined to protect the finances of their various state governments, lawmakers were not inclined to enact such a major change, and Roosevelt wasted little capital on asking for the impossible.

Initial Reactions

Roosevelt had begun his tax message with a bit of disingenuous gratitude, thanking the congressional Joint Committee on Internal Revenue Taxation (JCIRT) for its help in studying the nation's tax problems. In fact, while the JCIRT had joined in a few important studies, including Roswell Magill's influential report on the British income tax, the panel had not been privy to the administration's development of the tax proposal.[84] The White House and Treasury had closely guarded the secrecy of their work, their proposals hammered out by a small group of close tax advisers. Members of Congress had been kept in the dark, and they were not happy about it.[85]

Congressional leaders reacted to Roosevelt's message with dutiful but distinctly muted enthusiasm. In the Senate, Pat Harrison had, indeed, had "kittens on the spot." A whole litter, according to his friends. Harrison was not a tax activist. He believed that the revenue system should be used principally, if not quite exclusively, to raise revenue. In this view, he had ample support from his colleagues, including Majority Leader Joe Robinson. Harrison cautioned that swift action on the president's tax plan was unlikely. "To deal with the tax question as suggested in the message," he said, "will take considerable thought and consideration." Raymond Moley later reported that Roosevelt's message had deeply wounded Harrison. "Those, like Pat Harrison, who felt that party loyalty compelled them to support it, bled inwardly," Moley wrote.[86]

In the House, Democratic lawmakers greeted the message with applause. The leadership was fairly agreeable, although like their Senate counterparts, they were irritated at Roosevelt's cavalier treatment of their treasured tax prerogatives. Ways and Means chair Robert L. Doughton (D-NC) viewed the plan with some suspicion. Like Harrison, he preferred to use taxes for revenue, not reform. But he was also highly attuned to fairness issues, having long been an ardent foe of federal sales taxation. And he was a genuine fiscal conservative, with a strong predilection for balanced budgets. As such, he was able to find in his heart some modicum of sympathy for the president's plan. He would certainly have preferred a more moderate version, one that raised more revenue without alienating moderates. But he quickly fell in line with the White House agenda.[87]

Outside the leadership, reactions to the Roosevelt message were predictable. Liberal Democrats and progressive Republicans were enthusiastic. Sen. George Norris declared that "the tax program suits me 100 percent both on the inheritance tax and the corporation tax." And Sen. Matthew Neely (D-WV) hailed the message as a blow for social equity. "It is the beginning of the end of plutocracy," he said, "and a lifesaver for democracy." Perhaps most important, Huey Long greeted the message with a loud "Amen," swaggering around the chamber, grinning, and pointing to his chest. At one point, observed a *New York Times* reporter, "Mr. Long stopped abruptly, grimaced, raised his eyes and almost waltzed."[88]

La Follette's Qualified Embrace

Sen. Robert La Follette dubbed Roosevelt's statement "a splendid message."[89] He urged swift action, seeking to attach the president's plan to pending tax legislation. Notably, La Follette also sought one very important amendment: a reduction in income tax exemptions. He believed such a change would raise substantial new revenue while also establishing the tax system on a more broadly progressive footing. From 1934 to 1939, La Follette would annually introduce this plan for reducing exemptions; he also endorsed higher rates, including application of the surtax in lower brackets. At times, he found significant support among his legislative colleagues, especially in the Senate. But he never managed to muster a solid constituency.

La Follette defended his plan as a necessary tool of federal finance. The traditional, narrow income tax, levied almost exclusively on the rich, had proven itself highly vulnerable to fluctuations in the economy. A broader tax would be less volatile, guaranteeing the federal government a more stable source of revenue. La Follette also insisted that his plan would strike a blow for social equity. The federal revenue system relied too heavily on excise taxes, straining the consumption of poor Americans and forcing them to shoulder too large a portion of the nation's tax burden. Revenue from a broader, progressive income tax—which by its very nature, would burden people more consistently according to their ability to pay—would allow for a reduction in more regressive taxes. La Follette's argument was virtually identical to the one offered by Treasury tax experts, and La Follette had considerable support within the tax community. But he had a hard time selling the idea to fellow liberals, especially among more traditionally minded Democrats. They were wed to the notion of steep but narrow income taxes. Support from conservatives, including many Republicans, kept La Follette's plan visible, but it was never viable, at least not politically. Even some of La Follette's erstwhile supporters among the Senate's progressive faction cooled to the proposal. Ultimately, broader income taxation was an idea whose time had not yet come.

Meanwhile, Republicans were predictably livid, complaining the president had outlined a plan for confiscatory taxation that would imperil recovery and do little to balance the budget. Sen. Arthur Vandenberg (D-MI) offered a stinging indictment, insisting that Roosevelt's ideas didn't even amount to a "a good soap-box formula." Rather, the message was a misguided effort to pander to the political left. In truth, Vandenberg said, it would not satisfy the more radical voices, but it would go a long way toward prolonging the depression.[90]

In the House, the few GOP voices that could be heard above the Democratic din were similarly outraged. Republican leader Bertrand Snell dismissed the message as just so much electioneering. "I think it was a fine stump speech," he said. "It looks like the president is trying to get the jump on Huey Long and the other share-the-wealth people."[91]

Press reaction to the tax message was mixed, but critics carried the day, even in typically liberal papers. Among the more reliably conservative papers, the plan fared predictably. The *New York Herald Tribune* complained that it was "composed of equal parts of politics and spite." The *Boston Herald* predicted it would "aggravate fear and uncertainty in the very quarters where the administration needs support in its re-employment efforts," meaning the wary business community. And the *Philadelphia Inquirer* complained that "the President without warning bears down upon the slowly reviving forces of returning prosperity with a tax program to lure hosannahs from the something-for-nothing followers of Huey Long, 'Doc' Townsend, Upton Sinclair, and the whole tribe of false prophets." Critical reporters had little patience with the attack on business consolidation, as manifest in the new graduated corporate tax and the intercorporate dividend levy. "It looks to some like an effort to drive business back to the horse and buggy stage by penalizing large units," wrote Raymond Clapper in the *Washington Post*.[92]

Liberal papers struck a less contentious note, but most viewed the president's message skeptically. The political motives behind FDR's statement were too obvious to ignore. Across the board, editorial writers explained the message as an attempt to co-opt some of Huey Long's support with a tepid version of the Kingfish's share-the-wealth plan. A few papers endorsed the general philosophy behind Roosevelt's plan. "The president applies up and down the line the most equitable of all principles of taxation," asserted the *New York World Telegram,* namely the principle that "taxes should be levied in proportion to the ability to pay and in proportion to the benefits received."[93] The *Philadelphia Record* dismissed complaints that the tax proposals would be unfair to wealthy taxpayers. "If this is soaking the rich, it's soaking them with a life preserver when they're near drowning."[94] But many more papers dismissed the message as a political ploy. The *New York Times* pointed out that revenue from Roosevelt's higher tax rates on millionaires would pay the government's bills for barely six hours.[95]

Legislative Rush

Opinions aside, lawmakers faced an immediate problem: what were they supposed to do with this message? Did the president want immediate action? The House had already begun work on a bill to extend expiring "emergency" taxes. While adding the president's plan to this vehicle was possible, it would require almost immediate action. More to the point, it would give Congress little time for the sort of careful consideration that Pat Harrison thought necessary.

Many congressional leaders were irritated that the president had delivered this message so late in the session. Ready to adjourn, they dreaded the prospect of remaining in the Capitol throughout Washington's long, hot summer. A *New York Times* reporter compared the prevailing mood among lawmakers to that of "a small schoolboy who has been detained after hours to get his lessons, including a lesson which had not been given until the time for the 3 o'clock bell was in sight and his mind was on a baseball game in the neighborhood sand lot."[96]

In the White House, staffers were uncertain what the president wanted. After delivering his message to Congress, the president left town to watch his son row in the Yale-Harvard crew races. People close to the president were initially convinced that the message was simply a statement of principle. Morgenthau called it "a campaign document," setting down ideas but not intended for immediate action. Nine days later, when it looked like the president might be serious about a bill, Morgenthau put the question to him point blank: did he want legislation during the current session? Strictly between the two, the president admitted he wasn't sure: "I am on an hourly basis and the situation changes almost momentarily." Meanwhile, lawmakers tried to accommodate the rushed schedule that Roosevelt seemed to expect. Senate progressives like La Follette and Norris, eager to ensure that Roosevelt's message did not become simply a symbolic statement of intent, urged that the plan be appended to the pending resolution that would have extended the expiring emergency taxes. But that resolution had to be passed in less than a week since the levies would expire on July 1. Would Congress agree to such a rushed timetable?[97]

When Roosevelt returned to Washington on June 24, he called lawmakers to his office and demanded swift action. Apparently emboldened by the support he had found among progressives, he was eager to move quickly. Harrison began drafting rate schedules and legislative language, gritting his teeth but obediently following orders from the White House. On the House side, Doughton did the same. But resistance from many quarters began to mount. Lawmakers split into numerous factions, and many saw hope for their ideas only in a slower legislative pace. Editorial writers around the country complained loud and long about the rush to enactment. Roosevelt soon backed off his demand for quick action, and by the beginning of July, Congress settled down to a slightly less frenzied pace, scheduling hearings but still planning to pass a bill in short order.

The Debate

Debate over the tax bill unfolded over the course of a long, hot summer. Indeed, complaints about the weather loomed large in most discussion of the legislation, perhaps serving to move things along more quickly. But the battle lines were clear. Roosevelt's message had alarmed many critics, including both liberals and conservatives. The latter proved more passionate, and many of the former eventually returned to the Democratic fold when they contemplated the intemperate comments of business and conservative spokesmen. In retrospect, however, what seems striking about the debate is the almost universal distaste for Roosevelt's plan, at least among opinion leaders. Politicians were more supportive, knowing a political winner when they saw one.

Important criticism came from the left. Many liberals complained that Roosevelt's plan did not go far enough. The *Nation* welcomed the advent of a vigorous debate on tax policy, but they criticized Roosevelt for sacrificing principle on the altar of expedience. The Roosevelt tax message failed to offer any important reforms, the magazine declared. Even the rich would not pay enough under this supposedly progressive plan. A taxpayer earning $25,000 annually would face an income tax bill of just $3,000—hardly enough to diminish concentrations of wealth. La Follette's plan for broader income taxation was much preferable, with new revenue used to eliminate regressive consumption taxes and pay for much-needed social programs.[98]

Similarly, the *New Republic* considered the message a half-baked version of genuine reform. It would not check the accumulation of great fortunes, nor would it hinder the growth of big business. Walter Lippmann also complained that by focusing tax hikes only on the rich, the plan fostered a sense of social irresponsibility, with one class voting to impose taxes on another. The plan would "diminish the evils of plutocracy by encouraging the evils of demagogy," he wrote.[99]

In the middle of July, the U.S. Chamber of Commerce opened a vigorous campaign against Roosevelt's tax plan. What the country needed was "not more taxes on income but more income to tax," the group declared. Using the tax system to work social change was dangerous and disingenuous. It distorted the democratic process and limited the possibility for free and honest debate. If the president wanted to confiscate wealth and regulate business, he should bring those issues to the country directly rather than disguising them as a revenue measure.[100]

In testimony before the Ways and Means Committee, Chamber spokesman Fred Clausen called on lawmakers to lower taxes, not raise them. While higher levies might be advisable in the future, especially if used to shrink the deficit and repay debt, they were unwise in the midst of an economic slump. Clausen stressed the unfairness of taxing wealth too heavily. "If through taxation or other governmental action there be confiscation—outright or near—of the economic rewards of enterprising and prudent citizens, injustice may result," Clausen said. Confiscation was antithetical to the ability-to-pay standard of tax equity, since it destroyed the very ability on which it depended.[101]

Another business witness, George Marklan of the Philadelphia Board of Trade, denounced tax hikes of all kinds, but especially those targeting the rich. "We are attempting to tax people who work, who create wealth and distribute wealth—we are attempting to tax them to support the incompetents and the ne'er-do-wells, and the will-nots, and it is time we stopped it."[102]

Business leaders, however, reserved their harshest criticism for the graduated corporate income tax. Clausen offered a compelling critique of the ability-to-pay argument as it applied to the corporate tax. Since the tax took no account of invested capital, it could not serve the standard of ability to pay. A company with $800 million in invested capital, he pointed out, might return 1 percent for an annual income of $8 million. Another company, with a capital investment of $600,000, might return 20 percent or $120,000. Clearly, the latter company had greater ability to pay, since its owners were making a killing. "Almost any form of a graduated corporate income tax ignores capital investment and therefore ignores every accepted principle of income taxation," Clausen said.[103]

NAM spokesman Robert Lund offered a distinct but similarly compelling critique of the graduated corporate tax. Companies, he pointed out, don't pay taxes, people do. The ability-to-pay standard was only sensible when applied to individuals. When used to justify graduated rate structures on corporate income, it yielded perverse results. Many large corporations had stockholders with small incomes, while some small businesses were owned by wealthy entrepreneurs; a graduated tax on corporate income would penalize the former and deliver a windfall to the latter. Lund also noted that a graduated tax would discourage corporate bigness but take no account of the social and economic benefits that often came with size. Modern business had brought prosperity and efficiency to the nation, he argued, and any misguided attempt to check corporate size would damage the nation's well-being. As structured, he warned, the graduated corporation tax "would tend to return us, industrially, past the horse-and-buggy stage to the monkey stage of economic evolution."[104]

Indeed, many conservative critics stressed the damage that the bill would do to recovery efforts. A spokesman for the Ohio Chambers of Commerce insisted that the bill "is not a redistribution of wealth; it is a redistribution of poverty." Enacting it would imperil the nation's economy and its traditional respect for property rights. Reaching new heights of hyperbolic oratory, he suggested that confiscatory taxation was better suited to the Soviet Union. "Perhaps some of the oily propagandists whispering around Washington think Russia is a better country to live in than the United States," he said. "If so, the seas are open to them."[105] Fred G. Clark, leader of the Crusaders, an anti-Prohibition group that subsequently became an outspoken source of anti–New Deal vitriol, declared the president's plan an economic menace. "Now it is again proposed to hold up business initiative by placing over the heads of business men a veritable sword of Damocles," he warned. The law as proposed would slow recovery and damage business confidence. It was, he concluded, best described as "soak-the-thrifty" legislation, targeting those Americans who did the most for the nation's economy. "We are arriving at that point in our national affairs where inflammatory demagogues and radical politicians are actually soaking the by poor by paralyzing capital," he asserted.[106]

The American Liberty League offered a host of criticisms, insisting that the bill was politically motivated, economically unwise, and fundamentally unfair. "It represents a gesture to satisfy radical agitation for a redistribution of wealth," the group said in a written statement. The administration was trying to use taxes as a means of social reform, but it couldn't even raise adequate revenue in the process. Worst of all, by penalizing wealth and business, the bill threatened to hamper recovery.[107]

Supporters of the tax message tended to focus on large-scale issues of social justice. In their eyes, steep new taxes on the nation's richest individuals and biggest corporations were only fair. Ability to pay was a touchstone for these advocates, although they tended, like Roosevelt, to focus on the great ability of rich taxpayers rather than the limited ability of poor ones. In other words, they were inclined to support soak-the-rich taxation, but they soft-pedaled the need for lighter taxes on the poor.

In testimony before the Ways and Means Committee, Sidney Goldstein of the Conference of American Rabbis praised the Roosevelt plan for its attempt to redistribute wealth. He hailed the effort to "democratize our economic organization and income," suggesting that the Chamber of Commerce and other business groups were simply trying to protect their privileged status. Such efforts were doomed to fail, he warned. "America cannot tolerate an economic autocracy together with a political democracy," he said. "We cannot survive politically free and economically enslaved."[108]

Sen. Edward P. Costigan (D-CO) hailed FDR's tax message as a major achievement for progressive reform. "In the judgment of progressive liberals," he said during a well publicized speech, "it instantly claimed and is fated to hold a foremost place among the remarkable state papers of our country." It was fair and balanced, fundamentally just and constructive. "Whether the President's plan be labeled 'Share-the-Wealth' or 'Share-the-Burden,' as alternatively described, it suffices for the average citizen that it promises wide economic justice and surer equality of opportunity under Government."[109]

Indeed, while many liberals were eager to attack the president for his timidity, a few stood firm in the defense of his courage. The tax message was a major departure from past practice, they argued. For the first time, social goals were being placed front and center in a revenue debate. Edgar J. Goodrich, former member of the U.S. Board of Tax Appeals, noted the insignificant revenue impact of the president's proposals but insisted they were nonetheless politically crucial: "The fundamental significance of the new proposals cannot be overstated." The law was destined to check bigness wherever it might be found, whether in business or personal wealth. It would "raise the parapets and narrow the exits in the tight wall around wealth built by taxation."[110]

Congressional Action

The first legislative draft of Roosevelt's message came from Pat Harrison, who cobbled together a rough version in the first few days after the president dropped his bombshell. Senate progressives were pushing hard for quick action, maneuvering to keep Congress in session as long as possible; La Follette tried to attach a version of the plan to the pending excise extension resolution, and Gerald Nye helped organize a petition asking for quick action on the measure. The progressives seemed intent not just on passing a tax bill, but on calling FDR's bluff. Concerned by talk that the president wasn't serious about getting a bill off the ground, they were determined to test his sincerity. Speaker of the House Joseph W. Byrns (D-TN) also called for quick action, dismissing the need for further study of the president's plan.[111]

Harrison's plan, which hewed closely to FDR's proposal, included an inheritance tax with a $300,000 exemption and rates ranging from 4 percent to 75 percent; the top bracket applied only to inheritances of more than $10 million. The draft also featured new surtax rates on incomes over $1 million; marginal rates ranged from 60 percent to 80 percent in this rarefied territory, with the top bracket kicking in at $10 million in annual income. Finally, Harrison's language included a new graduated rate structure for the corporate income tax, with rates ranging from 10.75 percent on incomes less than $2,000 to 16.75 percent on incomes over $20 million. Taken together, this package was initially predicted to raise about $340 million annually; later projections put this figure lower. In any case, the yield was much smaller than liberals had hoped to see. Senate progressives, for instance, had been seeking at least $1 billion in annual revenue.[112]

But the president had made clear his intention to keep these taxes narrowly focused on the very rich. The *New York Times* reported that just 46 people made more than $1 million in 1934, giving the new surtax rates a narrow base. The inheritance tax, with its $300,000 exemption, wasn't much better. While Harrison wanted to reduce the exemption to $100,000, Roosevelt insisted on the higher figure, despite complaints from his own Treasury experts. "Our boys say that that is what killed the revenue," Morgenthau told his boss. Roosevelt was unconcerned. "We will have to step it up steeper on the bigger boys," he responded.[113]

In the House, many Democrats wanted the new income surtax rates to kick in well below $1 million. The Treasury was reportedly sympathetic.[114] When the House finally passed the bill, it included higher rates beginning at just $50,000. The House bill also included new graduated rates for the corporate income tax, but the range of graduation was quite narrow: 13.25 percent on the first $15,000 of net income and 14.25 percent on the remainder. Finally, representatives approved a new inheritance tax, just as Roosevelt had requested, with rates reaching 75 percent.

In the Senate, Harrison tried hard to craft a bill that would please the White House, including steeper graduation in the corporate tax rates. But he lost a key battle when the Finance Committee rejected the inheritance tax, choosing instead to raise existing estate tax rates. Ultimately, the Finance bill raised surtax rates on incomes over $1 million; added an extra 1.25 percent to the top rate of the newly graduated corporate income tax, bringing it to 15.5 percent; increased rates for the federal estate tax; and imposed an intercorporate dividend tax along the lines Roosevelt had requested.

The final bill passed by both houses represented a compromise for all parties, including the president. It raised individual income surtax rates on incomes over $50,000—a far lower threshold than Roosevelt had suggested but still high. Contemporary estimates put the mean family income for 1935 at $1,631.[115] The top rate jumped from 59 percent on incomes over $1 million to 75 percent on incomes over $500,000. This was a far cry from what Roosevelt had suggested; the president had sought to introduce graduation at the very top of the income scale, but lawmakers had pushed it much lower. The change reflected congressional worries about revenue adequacy, however, not fairness. By lowering the threshold—making rates steeper for the very rich, not just the super rich—lawmakers were able to substantially increase the revenue yield from the bill.

Lawmakers agreed to a graduated rate structure for the corporate income tax: four brackets beginning at 12.5 percent for incomes over $2,000 and reaching 15 percent for those in excess of $40,000. The estate tax exemption was cut from $50,000 to $40,000, while the top rate increased to 70 percent from 50 percent. Finally, the bill included a new intercorporate dividend tax, although companies were allowed to deduct 90 percent of their income from dividends. The remaining net income was taxed at graduated rates ranging from 20 percent on everything less than $2,000 to 60 percent for everything over $1 million.

Conclusion

What had Roosevelt achieved? Not much, according to his critics.

The law did not raise much money. Projections suggested it would bring federal coffers about $250 million annually, representing an overall tax increase of about 14 percent. That was substantial but far below what budget balancers had hoped to achieve. The law also failed to seriously redistribute either wealth or income. Targeted very narrowly at the nation's richest taxpayers, it couldn't make a serious dent in the concentration of wealth. The new top rate for the income tax, for instance, applied to precisely one taxpayer for the first three years after the bill passed: John D. Rockefeller Jr. Such rifleshot legislation was a poor substitute for serious efforts to redress inequality. "A tax completely to effect wealth-sharing must do more than skim the top," pointed out one analyst. It must also reach down through the income scale to collect money from the vast majority of Americans.[116]

The tax debate also strained Roosevelt's relationship with lawmakers. It was particularly damaging to his relationship with conservative members of this own party. Harrison and Doughton were irritated at FDR's effort to ram the tax bill through with little concern for their legislative prerogatives. They and like-minded Democrats, including a large group of southerners, were also uncomfortable with "social taxation" aimed more at reform than revenue. Raymond Moley later suggested that the 1935 tax debate marked a turning point for the Democrats: the beginning of a deep split between the party's urban, progressive, reformist wing and its more traditional southern branch. While perhaps overstated, that analysis had some truth to it. Roosevelt would soon begin to lose his hold over congressional taxwriters; Doughton and Harrison would increasingly exercise their autonomy in revenue debates.[117]

But Roosevelt's tax law did seem to be a political winner. The president had lost several key points, including his proposal for an inheritance tax. And the new corporate income tax was graduated more narrowly than Roosevelt had originally proposed. But FDR's tax initiative was never really about the details of his proposal. It was, in fact, about the rhetoric surrounding it. Roosevelt wanted to make a statement about fairness and economic justice.

Huey Long's "thunder on the left" was certainly the proximate cause for Roosevelt's new tax activism; the president hoped to steal a march on Long and his fellow populist tribunes, Dr. Francis Townsend and Father Charles E. Coughlin. FDR also sought to silence the criticism of more moderate liberals, who complained loudly that New Deal tax policies were tepid and inadequate. In the latter goal, he did not succeed. Many liberals considered the 1935 law thin gruel indeed. But FDR did seem to recapture some of his progressive momentum from Long and company. It was a political triumph, if not an economic watershed.

But the most important, and enduring, aspect of 1935 tax debate was the new prominence it gave to heavy progressive taxation. It sharpened ideological cleavages, embittering conservatives even as it pleased most progressives. The 1935 tax message was certainly an exercise in political expedience. But Roosevelt believed deeply in progressive tax reform, especially at the high end of the income scale. Robert Jackson had demonstrated rampant tax avoidance among the rich, and Roosevelt was eager to combat such social irresponsibility. Like Jackson, he believed that rampant tax avoidance was undermining the federal income tax, diluting its redistributive effect by undermining its graduated rates. New taxes on wealth and business were a defensive measure, if only a symbolic one, designed to protect the system against the depredations of wealthy tax avoiders.

7

Profits, Preferences, and Tax Avoidance

For two years in the mid-1930s, taxation found a place near the top of the New Deal agenda. In 1936 and 1937, Franklin Roosevelt advanced two seemingly disparate tax proposals, the first designed to overhaul the taxation of corporate profits, the second to close loopholes in the personal income tax. In substance, the undistributed profits tax of 1936 and the anti-loophole campaign of 1937 were entirely distinct, addressing different problems and targeting different taxpayers.

But the proposals shared a common ideological lineage. Both reflected a commitment to high-end progressivity—the notion that higher taxes on the rich could balance unpalatable but necessary levies on the poor. And while neither worked lasting change on the federal revenue system, both affirmed the moral touchstone of New Deal taxation: the conviction that all Americans, and rich Americans in particular, should pay their fair share.

Financing Social Security

Before kicking off his campaign to revamp corporate taxation, Roosevelt engineered a tax innovation that would prove central to the New Deal tax regime: the Social Security payroll tax.

The central question in the history of Social Security finance can be posed as a puzzle: why did Franklin Delano Roosevelt, progressive hero, choose a regressive levy to finance his most enduring contribution to the American welfare state?[1] To some degree, this question is misguided. As Mark Leff has pointed out, it presumes that Roosevelt was always and everywhere opposed to regressive taxation. If that were the case, then the payroll tax would stand out as an aberration from the New Deal norm. But as we have seen, FDR's antipathy toward regressive taxation was not complete. True, he didn't much care for taxes that burdened the poor, and he dearly loved progressive levies on the rich. But he was willing to tolerate regressive taxes when they proved necessary or expedient.[2]

Still, the question remains: why did Roosevelt insist on using payroll taxes as the *sole* funding mechanism for Social Security? He certainly had options. Most other countries offering public pensions combined payroll taxes with contributions from general revenues. As historian William Leuchtenburg observed, "In no other welfare system in the world did the state shirk all responsibility for old-age indigency and insist that funds be taken out of the current earnings of workers."[3]

Meanwhile, domestic champions of old-age insurance—people like Francis Townsend, a physician activist who mobilized a vocal constituency to support his plan for generous public pensions funded by a national sales tax—were hardly agreed on the desirability of a payroll levy. Neither, for that matter, were political leaders at the state level, where contributory taxes were not used to finance pensions.

More important, many of Roosevelt's own advisers were disinclined to rely exclusively on payroll taxes, or even to insist that retirement pensions pay for themselves. Harry Hopkins and Rexford Tugwell, both close to the president, were united in opposing the tax on fairness grounds. The Treasury Department, meanwhile, worried that a payroll tax would shrink aggregate purchasing power at a time when "underconsumption" was already getting blame for causing the Great Depression.

Indeed, early Social Security proposals, including those prepared by FDR's handpicked advisers, did not rely exclusively on the payroll tax to fund pensions. Instead they made room for contributions from general revenue. Roosevelt quickly nixed this idea, insisting that the program be entirely self-financing and contributory. He sent his advisers back to the drawing board, and they reluctantly drew up a new version of the program hewing closely to the president's restrictive guidelines.

Economic or Political Genius?

So why the intransigence from the White House? Two explanations seem most plausible: fiscal conservatism and political genius.

Generally speaking, "fiscal responsibility" always ranked near the top of FDR's list of political priorities, right after "end the depression" and "reform American society." For most of the 1930s, items 1 and 2 sucked all the air from most policy debates, suffocating budget concerns in the process. But FDR's commitment to a distinctive strain of fiscal conservatism did survive the spending and regulatory onslaught of the early New Deal. Kept alive by the support of Treasury Secretary Henry Morgenthau, it surfaced at odd but crucial moments.[4]

One such moment occurred during the Social Security debate. Roosevelt was genuinely committed to the notion that old-age pensions be self-supporting. As he said in 1937, "as regards social insurance of all kinds, if I have anything to say about it, it will always be contributed, both on the part of the employer and the employee, on a sound actuarial basis. It means no money out of the Treasury."[5]

Indeed, it meant money into the Treasury, since workers would begin paying payroll taxes immediately, while benefits would not begin for several years. These revenues would diminish the size of the federal deficit and limit the amount of borrowing necessary to fund government operations. This revenue potential was feared by many economists, who worried that the tax would be deflationary. But for Roosevelt the would-be fiscal conservative (and actual fiscal spendthrift), smaller deficits would be a welcome change.

Of course, the economists were right—payroll taxes *were* deflationary. And when the recession of 1937–1938 plunged the nation back into the economic abyss, many critics fingered Social Security taxes as the leading culprit. Under pressure from Congress, the administration agreed in 1939 to delay a scheduled increase in the payroll tax, while also accelerating some benefits. These changes weakened the program's long-term viability, dispensing with the notion of self-contained financing and accepting (implicitly, at least) the need for eventual contributions from general revenues.

Nevertheless, Roosevelt was genuine in his commitment to keeping the program solvent—and limited. By insisting, at least initially, that it be self-financed, he hoped to check the congressional impulse toward unrestrained spending. Absent such a constraint, he worried that lawmakers would simply spend the country into oblivion. The payroll tax was certainly designed to be a money machine, financing a grand, enduring social program. But it was also meant to serve as a check on that program, ensuring that new spending came with a certain amount of pocketbook pain.[6]

If the payroll tax quickly lost its claim to fiscal conservatism, it retained its political justification as a bulwark for social democracy. From the start, Roosevelt was committed to the insurance model of old-age pensions, in which payroll taxes were akin to premiums and pensions were an "earned" benefit of having paid those premiums.

Roosevelt was deeply attached to this conceptual scheme, and he used it repeatedly to defend the payroll tax specifically and Social Security more generally. Payroll taxes, he insisted, would protect the program from its enemies. He famously declared to Luther Gulick, a critic of the payroll tax:

> I guess you're right on the economics, but those taxes were never a problem of economics. They are politics all the way through. We put those payroll contributions there so as to give the contributors a legal, moral, and political right to collect their pensions and their unemployment benefits. With those taxes in there, no damn politician can ever scrap my social security program.[7]

This quotation has been trotted out many times and by many people to explain the distinctive funding scheme established for Social Security. But the statement is not without its problems, at least as a piece of historical evidence. Leff has pointed out that the quotation comes from the recollection of an associate, recorded some six years after FDR decided on a payroll tax. By then the payroll tax had already come under attack, with lawmakers seeking (successfully) to limit and delay scheduled increases. Roosevelt, then, might actually have been trying to protect the tax from its critics by draping it in the popularity of the associated program, even though the quotation seems to make precisely the opposite link. In any case, Roosevelt was speaking with the benefit of hindsight.[8]

Nonetheless, the decision to use a payroll tax was clearly a functional masterstroke, whether it was deliberate, inadvertent, or otherwise.

The Revenue Act of 1936

The bruising battle over the Revenue Act of 1935 had left most policymakers eager for a respite from contentious tax debates. And Roosevelt seemed ready to oblige. The administration's tax agenda was "based upon a broad and just social and economic purpose," he told newspaper publisher Roy Howard. But the reform program was now substantially complete. "The 'breathing spell' of which you speak is here," Roosevelt assured Howard, "very decidedly so."[9]

In a similar vein, FDR told Congress to ignore "gloomy and erroneous predictions" about the need for another tax hike. "It is clear to me," he said in September, "that the Federal Government under provisions of present tax schedules will not need new taxes or increased rates in existing taxes to meet the expense of its necessary annual operations and to retire its public debt." On January 3, 1936, he went even further, predicting that economic growth would produce more than enough revenue from existing tax laws.[10]

Eager to smooth ruffled feathers, Roosevelt even tried to diminish his recent victory on the tax front. The Revenue Act of 1935 had raised taxes for only a handful of taxpayers, he said. And even this wealthy minority had gotten off with "slight increases." Looking forward, revenue would come from old taxes, not new ones. "The great bulk of increased Government income," he said, "results from increased earning power and profits throughout the Nation and not from the new taxes imposed by the Revenue Act of 1935".[11]

Roosevelt, however, was well aware that events were conspiring to darken this rosy picture. Lawmakers were poised to approve an expensive soldier's bonus over the president's strong objection. And the Supreme Court was on the verge of striking down the processing tax enacted as part of the Agricultural Adjustment Act (AAA). Either development alone would worsen the budget outlook; together, they promised to unleash a full-scale fiscal crisis.

Three days after Roosevelt delivered his budget message, the Supreme Court invalidated the AAA, including its processing tax. The decision opened a $500 million hole in the budget. A few weeks later, Congress made things worse, overriding FDR's veto of the soldiers' bonus. In the current fiscal year, the accelerated bonus would cost the government $120 million. To Roosevelt's mind, both these events vitiated his pledge to avoid a tax hike. But he remained committed to the letter, if not the spirit, of his promise. The administration, he told reporters, was seeking "replacement" taxes, not "new" ones.[12]

Roosevelt's search for replacement revenue would soon lead him to the undistributed profits tax. Revenue needs were clearly the driving force.[13] But the UPT was more than just a budgetary expedient. Rooted in broad social and economic goals, it was also a daring venture in social taxation. Advocates insisted that it would reshape American society, checking the concentration of wealth and promoting economic democracy. At the same time, it would serve the cause of tax justice, forcing rich Americans to pay their fair share of the nation's tax bill.

Taxing Business Profits

Business income is hard to tax. Or at least hard to tax well. Since the inception of the income tax, business levies have been the subject of endless debate, legislation, and litigation.[14] Problems are myriad, and solutions elusive. Some of the most persistent complaints have focused on the treatment of different business structures, including corporations, partnerships, and sole proprietorships. Each type of business organization is treated differently by the tax system, making for complexity, inequity—and no small degree of acrimony.

While often arcane, arguments over business taxation are not strictly technical. Often, they are bound up with larger debates about the nature of American capitalism. Lawmakers have repeatedly tried to use business taxes as a means of corporate regulation, enacting levies to control the size, structure, and behavior of business entities. Many of these efforts have been futile, and regulatory goals have sometimes run counter to the revenue function of corporate taxation: a tax that successfully regulates often fails to raise much money. But that hasn't kept lawmakers from trying to use taxation an instrument of large-scale economic control.

In the early 1930s, tax experts and administration policymakers brought a variety of perspectives to the knotty problem of business taxation. They shared a recognition that existing taxes were unfair and possibly unwise. But their analyses and solutions differed significantly. Inside the Roosevelt administration, at least three distinct strains of thought eventually converged on the subject of business taxation. Together, they gave rise to the undistributed profits tax.

Treasury Experts on Business Taxation

Most tax experts of the 1930s—including lawyers, economists, and accountants—took a somewhat jaundiced view of the corporate income tax. They recognized its inconsistent application of theoretical principles. Most were willing to grant that corporate taxes were justified as a revenue expedient, and many were eager to defend their theoretical fairness. But almost all experts were troubled by the many inequities and inefficiencies plaguing such levies. While slow to suggest remedies, they recognized the need for change.[15]

In 1934, Carl Shoup, assisting with the Viner Studies, was charged with assessing the state of federal business taxation. Shoup was a charter member of the expert policy community taking shape around New Deal taxation, and he was widely regarded as a rising star within his profession. And as he surveyed the landscape of corporate taxation, he was not pleased.

"Shot through with complex technical factors," Shoup complained, federal business taxes were burdened with numerous failings. Discrepancies in the treatment of income, especially among different types of business organizations, posed a particularly knotty problem. And congressional efforts of the early 1930s to crack down on loopholes had actually made matters worse.[16]

In charting the rise of the modern corporate income tax, legal historians have emphasized the importance of "entity theory." During the late 19th century, lawmakers had begun to treat the corporation as a separate legal entity, distinct from its shareholders and subject to its own range of taxes.[17] In 1909, this view had helped justify a new excise tax on corporate income.[18] Four years later, it bolstered the case for a general corporate income tax. But if entity theory had certain advantages, it also posed a number of problems. Specifically, it gave rise to significant disparities in the treatment of business income.[19]

Businesses, explained Shoup, were generally organized in one of three ways: as sole proprietorships, partnerships, or corporations. Under existing law, sole proprietors merged their business income with the rest of their personal income to calculate liability under the personal income tax; the business itself was not taxed. Similarly, partners combined their share of the full partnership's income with other sources of personal income; again, the business entity itself was not taxed. Notably, the law required partners to pay tax on their share of partnership income, even if that income were retained within the partnership; reinvested earnings offered partners no tax advantage.

Finally, corporations were required to pay an income tax at the business level, reflecting their status as independent entities. Income distributed to shareholders in the form of dividends was then taxed again under the individual surtax rates.[20] Corporate income retained within the business—and not distributed to shareholders—was free from individual income tax rates, until the company declared a dividend.[21]

These different arrangements made for serious inequities. Corporate income was taxed twice, first at the corporate level when it was earned and a second time at the shareholder level when it was paid out in dividends. This was arguably fair, assuming that entity theory could, in fact, justify the separate taxation of corporations apart from their shareholders. But in that case, the treatment of retained earnings was manifestly *un*fair. Shareholders could avoid the second round of taxation as long as corporations opted to retain income within the business.[22] Since many shareholders were rich, this meant that undistributed corporate income was sheltered from the high marginal rates of the individual income tax. Partnerships gave their members no similar advantage, creating a worrisome disparity in the treatment of business income.

As Shoup pointed out, the effort to distinguish between the business as a unit and its investors was rife with difficulties. In fact, he concluded, it violated norms of horizontal equity. Investors in similar circumstances, except for the mere legal form of their businesses, were treated differently. Such disparities were unjust, he insisted, since standards of fairness were rightfully applied to people, not artificial legal entities. "To 'burden' 'the corporation' or 'the partnership' as such is impossible," Shoup wrote. "Such bodies can feel no burden. It is to the persons behind the organizations that one must look."[23]

Shoup recommended a variety of changes to equalize the burden on business owners. Most immediately, he proposed to eliminate several inequities plaguing partnership owners. Restrictions on the deductibility of partnership losses, included in the Revenue Acts of 1933 and 1934, had created serious problems. These restrictions, enacted in the wake of J. P. Morgan's admission that he and several of his partners had paid no federal taxes during the dark days of the early Depression, were manifestly unfair. The laws severely restricted partnership owners' ability to claim losses against other forms of income, while requiring them to include partnership gains in their income totals. This arrangement left partners at a disadvantage relative to owners of corporations or sole proprietorships. Such restrictions should be eliminated immediately, Shoup wrote: "This step is so obviously desirable in the interests of equity, even apart from the particular point raised here, that is should be taken as soon as possible."[24]

Retained profits were another major problem. For Shoup, the answer seemed inescapable. "There seems to be no other way to lessen inequality of treatment in this matter," he wrote, "short of stripping aside entirely the corporate veil and subjecting the individual shareholder to both normal tax and surtax on his share of the corporation earnings, whether distributed or not—just as income from a partnership is now, in general, treated." In other words, policymakers might eliminate the pernicious influence of entity theory by taxing all business income only once, at the shareholder level.[25]

It was a compelling argument, but not one that Shoup was in fact prepared to endorse. Having stepped to the brink, he backed off. From an equity standpoint, he pointed out, it was unclear whether shareholders really got much benefit from retained earnings. Treasury experts thought the bonus might be more theoretical than real. And even if such benefits were substantial, the inequity was hard to measure. While attractive in theory, then, any tax remedy to the problem of retained earnings was problematic in practice. Ultimately, the ever-cautious Shoup—who remained at heart a careful intellectual, wary of broad generalizations and rash recommendations—declined to endorse a UPT.

The Brains Trust on Business Taxes

If Shoup was lukewarm about the UPT, other members of the Roosevelt administration were not. Presidential advisers had been pondering the tax even before FDR's victory in 1932. In a celebrated campaign memo— featuring the first recorded use of the "New Deal" moniker—Raymond Moley, Adolf Berle, and several colleagues suggested a tax on undistributed corporate profits, chiefly as a means to regulate the business cycle.[26] Companies, they argued, had traditionally distributed earnings by paying dividends to shareholders. Increasingly, however, many were choosing to retain their profits, "hoarding" cash in company coffers. According to Moley and Berle, these retained profits had contributed to the depression by disrupting the natural flow of supply and demand. In particular, retained profits had encouraged companies to overinvest in productive capacity.

To correct this tendency, Moley and Berle suggested that companies be taxed on some share of their undistributed earnings. An undistributed profits tax could be levied on companies that failed to distribute a reasonable percentage of their annual profits. If made steep enough, the rates would force companies to disgorge their annual profits (though not their existing surpluses).

This was a dramatic proposal but not entirely novel. An early version of the UPT had been implicit in the Civil War income tax, which taxed shareholders not only on dividends but on their share of a corporation's undivided profits.[27] In the early 20th century, lawmakers had revived this idea, adapting it to reflect the advent of a corporate income tax. During World War I, Treasury adviser Thomas S. Adams—a leading light of the economics profession with admirers in both political parties—had recommended the UPT as a matter of fairness. "The undivided profits of a corporation should be taxed at the rates which would apply if such profits were distributed to the shareholders," he wrote in 1918. In 1920, Woodrow Wilson's secretary of the Treasury had also proposed a new tax on undivided profits. The Joint Committee on Internal Revenue Taxation, while eschewing a decisive stand, supported some version of the tax in the late 1920s. Meanwhile, the tax system already included a weak version of the UPT, although exemptions and exceptions had rendered it a dead letter.[28]

The Moley-Berle version of the UPT differed substantially from these previous incarnations. While most earlier plans had been rooted in a desire to redress inequity, the Brains Trusters wanted to change the world. They believed the UPT could rationalize a dysfunctional free market, correcting structural deficiencies in the organization of American capital.

Advocates of large-scale economic planning, like Rexford Tugwell, were among the most vocal proponents of taxing corporate reserves. Properly designed, a tax on retained earnings, Tugwell maintained, would prevent corporate managers from investing too heavily in productive capacity. Like many of his contemporaries, Tugwell believed that overinvestment was a principal cause of the Great Depression. With easy access to investment capital—in the form of retained earnings—managers had made foolish investments. A tax on undistributed profits would prevent companies from expanding recklessly during prosperous years. If designed with a steep, almost punitive rate structure, a UPT would force companies to part with their precious cash. Managers still intent on expansion would then be forced to seek funds in the open, and presumably more rational, capital market.[29]

Many of Tugwell's colleagues in the academy and liberal intelligentsia believed that companies were sitting on huge piles of cash. The Treasury Department estimated that from 1923 to 1929, corporations had retained more than 45 percent of their total earnings.[30] Some observers believed this propensity to retain earnings reflected the growing divide between ownership and management.[31] In a 1932 study of corporate structure, Berle and Gardiner Means had stressed the size and importance of this gap. By 1930, they pointed out, most of the nation's largest companies were controlled by managers, not owners or their direct representatives.[32] And these managers had their own interests and imperatives. Many were inclined to invest corporate income, even when prudence dictated otherwise. "Officers of a billion dollar corporation certainly enjoy higher incomes and greater social prestige, even if the rate of return on invested capital is lower, than officers of smaller corporations that are very prosperous," observed one economist.[33]

In their New Deal memo, Moley and Berle embraced Tugwell's theory of excess investment. At the same time, they offered a proto-Keynesian case for the UPT. By forcing money out of corporate coffers and into the economy at large, they predicted, a tax on undivided profits would "liberate a tremendous amount of purchasing power." Excess saving was a drag on the economy, and steep taxation on corporate reserves would turn sterile accumulations to more productive use. Since inadequate demand had conspired with excessive supply to create the depression, the distribution of corporate profits might help turn the economy around.[34]

The UPT quickly disappeared into the volatile policy process of the early New Deal. But some of the reformist arguments offered in the New Deal memo would reappear in the mid-1930s, as another group of policymakers adopted the UPT as their pet project.

High-End Progressivity and the UPT

For senior officials in the Treasury Department, revenue needs were a constant worry. The Supreme Court's abolition of the AAA processing tax raised a serious problem, and tax experts working for Henry Morgenthau cast about for ways to close the budget gap. What, they wondered, should replace this highly productive consumption tax?

Not, to be sure, another consumption tax. Since its inception, the processing tax had been derided as a "breakfast table" levy, boosting the price of common foodstuffs. Treasury experts had scorned it for being deeply regressive. In the Viner Studies of 1934, Reavis Cox had described the processing levy as "a sort of sales tax, with all the shortcomings of such taxes intensified by the fact that these are basic necessities consumed in large quantities by the very poor." But Cox and his colleagues declined to recommend alternatives. The regressive burden of the AAA was rooted in its system of crop restriction, not its funding mechanism. Replacing the processing tax with a more progressive levy would make little difference. "Crop control would continue to take from the consumer a charge which is regressive in its incidence," Cox wrote. "If, now, an additional tax were imposed on some base unrelated to the commodity in question, it would mean merely a new burden upon whatever taxpayers were selected for the purpose, not a relief for those who are paying what is in effect a tax in the form of increased prices."[35] Of course, a new burden on someone else—particularly the rich—was not entirely unappealing, at least for advocates of high-end progressivity. Even as consumers continued to suffer, steep taxes on the rich might ease their pain. And once the Supreme Court had thrown out the processing tax, even Treasury experts urged a search for less regressive replacements.

But why choose the UPT? If revenue were the sole determinant of tax policy, then other taxes could have raised the same money with less fuss. The rise of the UPT can be explained by the actions of one person: Herman Oliphant, the administration's leading champion of social taxation.

Oliphant had long favored a tax on undistributed corporate income. In 1935, he had asked Roosevelt to consider the UPT, arguing that corporate surpluses were a "major factor in the domination of American business by a relatively small group." Oliphant worried incessantly about the power of big business, and his tax proposals were often designed to humble large companies. He was something of an antitruster, sympathetic to the ideas of Justice Louis Brandeis and eager to disperse concentrations of economic power. He was not among the first rank of New Deal Brandeisians, which included Felix Frankfurter, Tommy Corcoran, and others. But Oliphant believed tax policy could be used to discourage monopoly and stem the concentration of wealth. Artfully employed, he contended, taxes could remake American society.

Oliphant's suspicion of concentrated economic power extended to individuals as well as to organizations. He worried that a handful of wealthy, well-connected oligarchs was dominating the economy. This concern had led him to champion steep new taxes on wealth and income; the progressive emphasis of the 1935 revenue act bore the hallmark of Oliphant's soak-the-rich ideology. In 1936, he built on this success by arguing that the UPT would tame not just large companies, but the men who ran them. By forcing the corporate elite to cede control over profits, the UPT would promote economic democracy.[36]

In 1935, Raymond Moley had convinced Roosevelt to table Oliphant's plan for a UPT. Since writing the New Deal memo in 1932, Moley had soured on the levy. By early 1935, he was warning Roosevelt that such a tax would penalize thrift, hamper recovery, and destroy business confidence. Roosevelt agreed to sideline the proposal, but his revenue message retained an oblique warning about the danger of retained profits.[37]

In 1936, Oliphant revived his plan, and this time he had a revenue crunch to aid his cause. Moley had since parted ways with Roosevelt, and Oliphant quickly lined up support from several other presidential advisers. Jacob Viner agreed that the UPT would promote equity among shareholders. The tax, according to Viner, would strip corporate directors of their unfettered power over corporate profits, giving the small investor a chance to "determine what is done with his money." Similarly, Columbia law professor Roswell Magill, another Morgenthau confidant, stressed the fairness of a UPT. Corporate profits, he said, should be taxed under the progressive rate structure of the personal income tax. Sheltering that income through the device of retained earnings was a blow to vertical equity. Magill also believed the tax would be relatively uncontroversial, raising additional revenue "with the least possible wailing."[38]

One key Roosevelt adviser was not enthusiastic: Henry Morgenthau. The Treasury secretary was inclined to oppose the new tax, worried that its introduction—especially when coupled with repeal of existing corporate taxes—would threaten the stability of federal revenue. He also seemed to understand that the tax would prove highly controversial. And on this point, even Oliphant agreed. "If we have to fight," Oliphant told his boss, "we might as well fight the people who are our enemies anyway."[39]

Oliphant's pugnacity presaged a looming battle. While he supported the UPT for its potential to reform the economy—he was, after all, a committed social taxer—Oliphant now cast the tax principally in terms of fairness. The levy, he argued both publicly and privately, was a means to prevent wholesale tax avoidance among the nation's very rich. His argument depended on the presumption that all taxes were ultimately borne by people, not companies. "When all is said, taxes come out of the pockets of individuals," he told the Senate Finance Committee. And some of these individuals were not paying their fair share. The injustice of the current tax structure "makes no other form of taxation at this juncture possible of defense," he said.[40]

Making a Selective Case for the UPT

Against his better judgment, Henry Morgenthau recommended the UPT to Roosevelt in February 1936. FDR did not wait long to approve the idea, and he consulted few of his advisers before sending the plan to Congress on March 3.[41] "I invite your attention," he told lawmakers in a special budget message, "to a form of tax which would accomplish an important tax reform, remove two major inequalities in our tax system, and stop 'leaks' in present surtaxes." Notably, he did not describe the UPT as a vehicle for fundamental economic reform. He was silent on its potential to curb corporate overinvestment, discourage monopoly, or boost consumer purchasing power. Such arguments—while popular with the Brains Trust, Oliphant, and many private-sector advocates of the UPT—were secondary in the political debate of 1936. The official party line, established by FDR and echoed by his lieutenants, placed the emphasis on equity. The UPT would stem tax avoidance, eliminate the penalty on noncorporate businesses, and—not incidentally—raise some much-needed cash for the Treasury.[42]

Roosevelt hit all the requisite high notes in his case for the UPT. Retained earnings, he contended, were a dangerous source of tax avoidance. The loophole offered enormous benefits to the rich, who could shelter much of their income from the steep marginal rates of the individual income tax. At the same time, retained earnings were of no use to the investor of modest means. Shareholders who didn't need access to their money could let it pile up happily in corporate coffers, but anyone waiting for a dividend check to pay the rent was out of luck.

"The evil has been a growing one," Roosevelt declared. This nefarious method of tax evasion—he frequently conflated legal avoidance with illicit evasion—took a huge bite out of federal revenue. In 1936, Roosevelt said, corporations would retain $4.5 billion in profits, depriving the Treasury of $1.3 billion in tax revenue.

FDR asked Congress to repeal all existing corporation taxes, including the regular corporate income tax. These outmoded levies should be replaced by a robust version of the UPT, he told lawmakers. The president did not remark on irony of this request; less than a year earlier, he had championed a major reform of the corporate income tax, including the introduction of graduated rates, declaring it a great victory for the standard of ability to pay. This inconsistency would not escape business leaders as they turned their sights on the UPT.

When Congress sat down to consider Roosevelt's plan, Henry Morgenthau was noticeably absent from the hearing room. Some observers took it as a sign of disapproval; others suggested that he was protesting his own marginalization during the administration's development of the tax.[43] Officially, however, the secretary was sidelined by illness. BIR commissioner Guy Helvering took his place before the House Ways and Means Committee.

In defending the UPT, Helvering stressed the campaign against tax avoidance. "The fundamental objective of this proposal," he explained, "is to increase the Federal revenues by plugging up a major source of tax avoidance and tax evasion now existing, and thereby greatly to increase the fairness and balance of the Federal income-tax structure as a whole."[44] Any hike in income tax rates was futile as long as tax avoidance continued to undermine the rate structure. Helvering stressed that rich Americans would bear most of the increased tax burden that would flow from the UPT. More than 71 percent of the increase in taxable income would be received by individuals making more than $25,000 annually; some 45 percent would go to those making more than $100,000.[45]

Helvering went out of his way to assure the committee that the UPT was not designed to interfere with internal corporate decisions. Corporations were free to retain as much of their earnings as they might desire. But the UPT would ensure that such decisions did not "unreasonably and inequitably" deprive the federal government of necessary revenue.[46] In fact, Helvering said, existing law intruded much more onerously on private-sector prerogatives. Discriminating between businesses solely on the basis of their organizational structure encouraged corporations and discouraged partnerships.

Throughout the spring of 1936, administration officials echoed FDR's message, trumpeting the UPT as a blow for tax fairness, not a tool for economic reform. In a speech before the Young Democratic Club of New York, Robert H. Jackson, recently installed as the assistant attorney general for the Justice Department's tax division, acknowledged some of the broader goals behind the tax. Existing levies encouraged monopoly, he warned; corporations hoarded their cash, using it for acquisitions, not dividends. In 1933, more than 53 percent of corporate property was owned by just 618 companies, he said. Five percent of corporations owned fully 85 percent of total corporate wealth. And in 1932, more than 50 percent of total net corporate income had gone to just 201 companies, representing three-tenths of 1 percent of the number of corporations reporting some net income. This sort of economic consolidation was dangerous, Jackson contended.[47]

But taking his cue from the White House, Jackson focused his argument on fairness. Retained earnings were a source of manifest injustice, he said; rich stockholders used them to avoid steep surtaxes, while poor shareholders were left to muddle through. "How many [Americans] lost homes for want of a dividend to help meet interest?" he asked pathetically. These small shareholders deserved a voice in the disposition of corporate profits. Jackson ended with the obligatory nod to fascism on the march: "The distress caused by this policy of regimenting all stockholders and making them goose-step to the tune of tax avoiding management can not be fully known."[48]

The Outcry

Goose-stepping managers were not amused. Roswell Magill had predicted that business would accept the UPT with minimal "wailing," but by mid-March, he was proven quite sadly wrong. The business community, speaking with almost a single voice, denounced the president's plan as an abomination. Sympathetic voices in the press joined the chorus of complaint.

A search began to identify the culprit. Critics insisted that this hairbrained idea must have originated among the New Deal's notorious Brains Trust. Many fingers pointed to Rexford Tugwell, and even some Democrats fretted that FDR was under the sway of his egg-headed advisers.[49] Herman Oliphant insisted, disingenuously, that none of the usual suspects deserved credit. While declining to identify the plan's chief sponsor (and minimizing his own role), Oliphant cast the UPT as simply another tax reform emerging from the Treasury's faceless but highly professional bureaucracy.[50]

Opponents offered four principal objections to the UPT, at least one of which ultimately proved compelling even within the Roosevelt administration.

The Risk to Government Revenue

In hearings before House and Senate committees, a string of witnesses warned that Roosevelt was gambling big money. "Gentlemen, there is just one thing definitely known about the proposed bill," declared M. L. Seidman of the New York Board of Trade, "It will abandon an assured revenue totaling $1,132,000,000, in exchange for something which is highly speculative and entirely conjectural in its revenue-producing possibilities." The fisc required stability, he warned, especially in the face of economic uncertainty. "At a time like the present, when the need for revenue is so great, when we are spending so much more than we are taking in, when business is recuperating from the worst depression in our history, and when industry is so sensitive to every disturbing influence, how can we possibly afford to gamble such a vast sum of known public revenue for what is so much an adventure in the wilderness?" [51]

Even those who welcomed the campaign against tax avoidance were unhappy with the president's plan to scrap existing taxes. As the *Times* observed, it was akin to "burning the ship to make sure of catching the rats."[52] One witness after another urged Congress to slow down. Passing such sweeping reform in the midst of a presidential election was almost certainly ill-advised. Business needed its "breathing spell." As noted tax expert George May of Price Waterhouse pointed out, "continuity in taxation is a consideration of great importance."[53]

The Risk to Business Confidence and Recovery

Many opponents insisted the UPT would deal a severe blow to business. Companies needed reserves to make necessary investments. Perhaps even more important, they needed a cushion to survive periodic downturns. Deprived of adequate cash, companies would be deeply vulnerable. "The unfortunate effects of such a policy upon the stability of business corporations," declared Fred R. Fairchild of the Manufacturers' Association of Connecticut, "upon the prosperity of future profitable business, upon the confidence with which those who direct the destiny of American business shall view the future, and so upon the rate at which the American people shall escape from economic depression, would appear well nigh obvious."[54]

Americans in all walks of life would suffer, predicted G. L. Walters of the Illinois Manufacturing Association: "We believe that if this proposal were enacted it would adversely affect every one of the tens of millions of citizens in this country who are dependent upon the financial soundness of business corporations." Forced to survive with almost no margin for error, companies would be forced to lay off workers at the first sign of trouble.[55]

An economist with the National Association of Manufacturers pointed out Roosevelt's inconsistent approach to corporate taxation. The Revenue Act of 1935 had introduced a graduated tax on corporate income, which the president had defended as a blow for fairness generally and "ability to pay" specifically. Now, the president was asking Congress to strike this same tax from the books. Were prior claims to fairness spurious?[56] "The advocacy of one new tax policy one year, and the advocacy of another new tax policy less than a year later, which contemplates abandonment of the tax policies of the previous year, is not exactly the way to promote business confidence in stability of Government policy," he said, "And at least a reasonable amount of such confidence is really necessary to sound business recovery and reemployment."[57]

Fundamentally, the UPT threatened the very foundation of American prosperity. Franklin W. Fort, president of the Lincoln Bank of East Orange, New Jersey, considered the tax a plague on private enterprise. "The fundamental defect of this whole plan, gentlemen, is that it is essentially contrary to the basis of any capitalistic society," he said. Economic growth depends on thrift, he said, and the UPT would destroy that moral foundation. "No system of private property has any other base," he warned, "and none can endure if that base is destroyed."[58]

The Risk to Small Business

Many supporters of the UPT, including Herman Oliphant, believed that it would help protect small businesses from the depredations of overcapitalized competitors. But witnesses before Congress hammered home exactly the opposite message. Established companies with large surpluses could afford to distribute profits under the new tax; they could still fall back on their existing fat bank accounts. New companies would be deprived of adequate investment capital, leaving them unable to challenge their established competitors.[59]

Indeed, many large corporations could escape taxes entirely, as long they agreed to pay out all the profits in dividends. In a letter to Morgenthau, Sen. Harry Byrd (D-VA) suggested that of the 600 companies with income over $1 million, 138 would pay no taxes under the UPT. Fully half would have seen their taxes drop by at least 50 percent.[60]

G. L. Walters drove home the infant corporation argument with a suitable metaphor: "I believe that if you inquire you will find that most of the business and industrial corporations that today form the backbone of its [sic] business and industrial structure, first became established and grew out of their swaddling clothes, not on a diet of security issues and loans, but on a diet of savings from net earnings."[61]

Administration officials vehemently denied that small business would suffer, pointing out that the proposed rate schedules allowed more flexibility to small corporations in the amount of profits they might choose to retain. But Republicans pressed hard on this issue, eager to exploit their advantage. Rep. Harold Knutson (R-MN) pointed out that big companies had been conspicuously absent from the hearings. "General Motors was not here; Standard Oil was not here; none of the big ones have been here," he said.[62]

The Threat to Managerial Prerogatives

Business leaders were deeply offended by the UPT. The tax, they complained, was an affront to their integrity. "Businessmen cannot support a bill which has for its thesis the assumption that taxes on incomes of commercial and industrial corporations are being generally evaded or avoided," declared Chamber of Commerce spokesman Fred Clausen. Even more serious, however, was the bill's attack on the prerogatives of modern management. "The plan would tend to provide substitution of public control for private management in important fiscal operations of business," Clausen said. Managerial decisions would be dictated by government tax rules, not prevailing business conditions.[63]

"Government would just as well take away from all those who have the responsibility of driving automobiles their control over the brakes, the clutch, the throttle, or the steering wheel," complained G. L. Walters.[64]

Witnesses did not mince words. Their anger was sincere and their language heated. Images of fascism and dictatorship, so often invoked by FDR opponents against elements of the New Deal, peppered the hearings. "It is a further step toward government regulation and regimentation of business corporations," declared Noel Sargent of NAM.[65] T. J. Priestley Jr., president of his own small printing company, was even more blunt. The UPT, he declared, was a tool for "malicious regimentation, so that the profits honestly made by a corporation may not be spent or divided in the best manner by the directors, but must be subject to Government dictation."[66]

Congress Enacts

The Ways and Means Committee followed most of Roosevelt's suggestions in approving the UPT. Rates for the new tax were graduated to encourage distribution of annual profits—the larger the percentage of profits retained by the firm, the higher the rate of tax. Small companies were treated more leniently than large ones; the latter faced rates as high as 42.5 percent, while the former topped out at 29.5 percent. Democrats defended the bill as a blow for justice and equality. The panel—and subsequently the full House of Representatives—agreed to repeal substantially all existing corporate taxes, including the income tax. Treasury experts predicted that the bill would raise as much as $1.3 billion in additional revenue; with distributed corporate profits taxed at the high rates of the individual income tax, money would fairly cascade into the Treasury.[67]

Roosevelt's proposal had a much harder time in the Senate, where conservative southern Democrats made their objections plain. Led by Sens. Harry Byrd (D-VA) and Josiah Bailey (D-NC), the Finance Committee set out to gut the bill. After a rehash of the House hearings, the committee approved a much weaker version of the undistributed profits tax. In its report, the panel pointed out that the new tax was "untried" and "uncertain."[68] Members endorsed many of the business attacks on the House bill, arguing that it would penalize young corporations that needed retained profits to expand, hurt small corporations more than large ones that already enjoyed substantial reserves, retard economic growth and business expansion, impair business confidence, and inject lawmakers into a domain of corporate decisionmaking best left to managers.[69]

The panel, and subsequently the full Senate, declined to repeal the existing corporate income tax, instead raising its rates by 3 percent. In addition, the panel approved a modest tax of 7 percent on undistributed profits.

Meanwhile, Morgenthau was losing his nerve. Still worried that the repeal of existing corporate taxes was too risky, he now complained to his subordinates that the UPT might hinder the growth of small businesses. Despite impassioned pleas from several members of his staff, including Oliphant and Viner, the secretary continued to waver. His administrative assistant, Cy Upham, endorsed his concerns. Noting the vehement protests evident at congressional hearings, Upham observed that "the whole world can't be wrong." Morgenthau was ready to cave, and several days later informed his staff that he was prepared to accept the Senate bill.[70]

Morgenthau, however, was still being outmaneuvered on the UPT. Much to the secretary's chagrin, Marriner Eccles approached Roosevelt with a plan for a slightly modified UPT. The Federal Reserve chairman believed the tax would boost consumer purchasing power; distributed earnings would not molder uselessly in corporate coffers. Eccles argued, however, that the UPT should apply only to large corporations, and he endorsed retention of the existing corporate income tax as a revenue expedient.[71] Roosevelt tried to sell this compromise to the Finance Committee as members prepared to vote on the UPT, but the committee ultimately charted its own course.

As the UPT went to the conference committee, the outlines of a final compromise were quickly emerging. Morgenthau sided with the Senate, urging retention of the corporate income tax. Senate negotiators, however, agreed to boost UPT rates; in the final bill, they ranged from 7 percent to 27 percent depending on the percentage of profits retained by the corporation, as well as its size. Corporate income taxes climbed, too, and the levy retained the graduated rate structure first introduced in 1935.[72]

The Demise of the UPT

On January 11, 1939, Herman Oliphant dropped dead of a massive heart attack. Six months later, his cherished UPT followed him to the grave. Opponents of the tax had never thrown in the towel. Before the ink was even dry on the Revenue Act of 1936, the battle for repeal was in full swing. Soon enough, UPT foes would carry the day.

Why did business leaders resist the UPT so ferociously? Having defeated the administration's robust version of the tax, they might have been expected to tone down their campaign against it. Money provides some of the answer. Even the watered-down version of the tax represented a progressive shift in the country's tax burden. Wealthy shareholders would soon see their tax burden rise substantially, as the UPT induced companies to distribute a larger share of their 1937 income.[73] For corporate managers, the UPT also promised to complicate investment decisions, eliminating the easiest source of corporate financing. The tax, in other words, had real and sometimes expensive ramifications for corporate managers and the shareholders to whom they ostensibly reported.

But opposition to the UPT also included an ideological element. Business leaders understood the UPT all too well. Spokesmen for the Roosevelt administration insisted that the tax was an instrument for revenue and fairness. But business leaders understood that it was also a means of corporate regulation. The UPT represented a major foray by government into the domain of business decisionmaking. Corporate leaders cherished their prerogative to determine dividend policy. And while the federal government had several times threatened to intervene in such decisions over the course of the 20th century, the tax act of 1936 represented the first serious effort to regulate corporate investment. As legal historian Steven A. Bank has argued, the UPT violated norms of business-government relations, and corporate America was in no mood to accept the change. Even a weak version of the UPT had important implications for business and government.[74]

The UPT also suffered from tepid support among tax experts. In general, most endorsed the fairness and even the theoretical efficiency of such a tax. But the UPT, especially as enacted, was not the sort of levy they had in mind. Ultimately, business critics who insisted that the tax was poorly conceived may have had a point.[75] In 1938, a committee of the National Tax Association criticized the levy, not so much in theory as in execution. As Carl Shoup and the Treasury staff had concluded in 1934, so this independent group of tax experts maintained four years later: taxing undistributed profits was an interesting but problematic idea. The committee did not see fit to endorse the concept, and they certainly had few kind words for the legislative compromise that emerged in 1936. As the UPT came under sustained attack, most tax experts were unwilling to defend it with much vigor.[76]

Business opposition and expert skepticism were both important to the demise of the UPT. But ultimately, the tax fell prey to the president's plunging political fortunes. Roosevelt and his minions continued to defend the tax as a blow for fairness and tax equity. But in 1938, Congress voted to gut the UPT, reducing it to purely symbolic status. Even this was too much for critics, and lawmakers abolished it completely in 1939. Buffeted by the recession of 1937 and the Court-packing fiasco, Roosevelt had precious little political capital to spend defending his tax. In fact, tax policy in the late 1930s was a rearguard action for the administration. Champions of high-end progressivity would have just one more chance to make their case before World War II changed the landscape of federal taxation.

The Revenue Act of 1937

Tax avoidance has a murky moral status. In the United States, where deep and persistent strains of suspicion surround the governmental power to tax, avoidance enjoys a certain claim to legitimacy. As Judge Learned Hand, one of the nation's most esteemed jurists, put it, "Any one may so arrange his affairs that his taxes shall be as low as possible; he is not bound to choose that pattern which will best pay the Treasury; there is not even a patriotic duty to increase one's taxes."[77]

Tax evasion, by contrast, is roundly condemned; willful, often criminal violations of the tax laws are broadly considered immoral. But the distinction between avoidance and evasion, while generally clear in legal terms, is murkier in the political arena.[78] Since the inception of the modern U.S. income tax in 1913, political leaders have regularly denounced legal tax minimization, often conflating such avoidance with evasion. As Franklin Roosevelt framed the issue in 1937, "If Congress passes the [tax] act in good faith and then somebody comes along and through the aid of high-priced lawyers discovers some . . . new loophole, is that the moral thing to do or not, even if it is a legal thing? That is the big question."[79]

In the spring of 1937, Roosevelt set out to answer that question. Loopholes—a popular if imprecise term—are provisions of the tax law that grant preferential treatment to certain kinds of income or taxpayers. Some loopholes are inadvertent artifacts of the legislative process; errors and omissions plague the drafters of every revenue act, and skillful lawyers are quick to exploit them. Other loopholes are deliberate, inserted to benefit specific taxpayers or encourage certain activities.

Roosevelt believed deeply that most loopholes were immoral. In fact, he considered the distinction between avoidance and evasion little more than a legal technicality. "The President," noted one observer in 1937, "appears unwilling to distinguish between the moralities of tax evasion and those of tax avoidance." Both betrayed a reluctance to shoulder the burdens of citizenship. Roosevelt's Treasury secretary, Henry Morgenthau Jr., crystallized the president's view when he warned that if taxes were the price of civilized society, then "too many citizens want the civilization at a discount."[80]

Two issues prompted Roosevelt to launch his attack on loopholes. First, his New Deal coalition was losing political momentum in early 1937, and the president was eager for a new issue to energize his supporters. In particular, his effort to restructure the Supreme Court had proven extremely damaging. And while the economy was just beginning its slide into resurgent depression, the political fallout from this decline was already evident. Second, the administration was confronting a $600 million shortfall in Treasury receipts. Treasury analysis of the shortfall suggested that tax avoidance was partially to blame. In Roosevelt's view, an attack on tax loopholes might solve both problems.[81]

Treasury Secretary Morgenthau shared the president's indignation over tax avoidance. In the summer of 1936, he had written FDR to suggest a comprehensive study of tax avoidance, with an eye toward general revision of the revenue laws. And he was convinced that tax evasion was responsible for much of the budget shortfall. He prodded his staff to find the link, telling Treasury Undersecretary Roswell Magill that the president "wants to say flatly that our estimates and our methods of estimating were correct, but the citizens—that's the word he used—found a trick way of finding loopholes."[82]

Roosevelt longed to put a human face on tax avoidance. He asked the Treasury Department for a memo that not only outlined egregious avoidance schemes, but also identified the taxpayers using them. "The time has come when we have to fight back, and the only way to fight back is to begin to name names of these very wealthy individuals who have found means of avoiding their taxes both at home and abroad," he told Morgenthau.[83]

Treasury officials resisted Roosevelt's plan for vilification, but Morgenthau, ever the faithful lieutenant, pressed his case. "The question," he told Treasury staff, "is whether we are going to have a Fascist government in this country or a government of the people,"

> whether rich men are going to be able to defy Government and refuse to bear their burdens. Are we going to make progress in liberal government or is it going to take a revolution finally to settle the question? The rich are getting richer in this country and the poor poorer. In France they settled this problem by successive revolutions. If it had not been for the revolutions, a few men would own all France today.[84]

Treasury staff went to work on a study of tax avoidance and evasion. Ultimately, Undersecretary Roswell Magill produced two versions of the same memo, one featuring the names of prominent tax avoiders, the other describing them in only general terms. Both offered a stunning indictment of tax avoidance, lumping legal loopholes with various illegal schemes for evading taxes.

The Magill memo, which Morgenthau delivered over his own signature, assured the president that vigorous enforcement and remedial legislation had already closed many loopholes. "But we still have too many cases of what I may call moral fraud," Morgenthau warned, "that is, the defeat of taxes through doubtful legal devices which have no real business utility, and to which a downright honest man would not resort to reduce his taxes."[85]

The Treasury memo described a variety of avoidance devices. Domestic and foreign holding companies were particularly popular, with taxpayers using them to manage personal assets, including houses, yachts, and race horses. George Westinghouse Jr., for instance, had established a $3 million holding company in the Bahamas. To make things hard for the BIR, he also moved his home address "from one small hamlet to another every year." In fact, Westinghouse had a number of neighbors in his island haunts, at least according to official records; most suspect holding companies were incorporated in the Bahamas, although Newfoundland and Panama were also popular. These arrangements were often legal, at least barely. But a few seemed to cross the line into fraud.[86]

Many taxpayers found it convenient to incorporate their yachts and country estates, presumably to allow for upkeep deductions as a cost of doing "business." The recently deceased Alfred I. du Pont had saved $59,000 using this technique, and several other taxpayers named in the memo saved between $15,000 and $40,000. Wilhelmina du Pont Ross had done the best, saving $80,000 on her taxes while also paying her husband a salary for managing her estate.[87]

The du Ponts appeared regularly throughout the avoidance memo. In 1935, BIR counsel Robert Jackson had prepared a detailed analysis of the families' tax avoidance, focusing on the use of multiple trusts. Apparently, the family was still at it. The revenue reforms enacted in 1935 and 1936 had done little to close such loopholes. Earlier efforts to reign in holding companies, including the tax reform bill passed in 1934, had been similarly ineffectual.

Morgenthau did not confine his criticism to legally suspect loopholes. In fact, he reserved his most damning criticism for well-established provisions of the tax law. Percentage depletion drew much of his ire. "This is perhaps the best example of legalized theft from the United States Treasury which the revenue laws still permit," he complained. Similarly, he denounced the ability of married couples to divide income between husbands and wives, especially in community property states. "This is another legalized fraud on the revenue," he told the president. Morgenthau even criticized the purchase of tax-exempt state and local bonds by wealthy taxpayers. While this loophole had drawn the ire of Treasury officials for decades, it was vigorously defended by numerous members of Congress. Many advocates insisted that such tax exemptions were deeply enshrined in the constitutional structure of American federalism.[88]

Morgenthau reserved special scorn for the tax lawyers who made avoidance possible. "One of the most disheartening facts disclosed by our investigation," Morgenthau continued, "is that lawyers of high standing at the bar are advising their clients to utilize devious tax-avoidance devices, and they are actively using them themselves." The secretary offered a roster of malefactors, including several prominent New York and Washington law firms. In later congressional testimony, he would complain that these lawyers had developed "what might be called the sporting theory of tax administration."[89]

"Legalized avoidance or evasion by the so-called leaders of the business community is not only demoralizing to the revenues," Morgenthau concluded in his memo, "it is demoralizing to those who practice it as well." Like the president, Morgenthau conflated avoidance and evasion. His was a "hate the sinner" approach to tax minimization, although most of his solutions involved legislative attacks on the "sin" itself.

Roosevelt was delighted with Morgenthau's memo. Eager to vilify a few tax malefactors, he took his case to Congress. Efforts at tax avoidance and evasion had become "so widespread and so amazing, both in their boldness and their ingenuity, that further action without delay seems imperative," he told legislators. Some efforts were legal, Roosevelt conceded, and others arguably so. Nonetheless, "all are alike in that they represent a determined effort on the part of those who use them to dodge the payment of taxes which Congress based on ability to pay. All are alike in that failure to pay results in shifting the tax load to the shoulders of others less able to pay, and in mulcting the Treasury of the Government's just due."[90]

Roosevelt joined Morgenthau in condemning tax lawyers. "It is also a matter of deep regret to know that lawyers of high standing at the Bar not only have advised and are advising their clients to utilize tax-avoidance devices, but are actively using these devices in their own personal affairs," he said. Congress must take decisive action to eliminate these "evil practices." The time had come to banish from the bar any sense that "it is all right to do it if you can get away with it."[91]

At Roosevelt's urging, Congress had established a Joint Committee on Tax Evasion and Avoidance. The panel soon began hearings on the tax shenanigans of prominent taxpayers. And while FDR had refrained from naming names (after much pleading from his staff and the Justice Department), the hearing room brought identities to light. Among the targets were several members of the du Pont family, actor Charles Loughton, newspaper publisher Robert Scripps, top executives for U.S. Steel and General Motors, and violinist Fritz Kreisler. This last tax dodger had organized a corporation to manage his career, the company paying him a salary but retaining most of the earnings. Treasury estimated that he had saved $30,000 over three years.[92]

In his testimony before the committee, Morgenthau again returned to his criticism of the tax bar and accounting professionals. The BIR had just 2,800 field agents dedicated to the income tax. In their efforts to enforce the tax laws, these agents faced a relative army of private-sector tax professionals, including more than 45,000 lawyers and accountants. "The contest is, of course, unequal," Morgenthau lamented. Lured by huge salaries, the Bureau's best agents were quick to depart for private firms. "The government then becomes a training school for many of its opponents," he said. Numerous editorial writers responded with mock sympathy, pointing out that lawmakers could eliminate this problem if they stopped enacting such complicated revenue measures.[93]

Roosevelt received plaudits from various quarters. Felix Frankfurter, a longtime champion of stepped-up tax enforcement, wrote to congratulate the president. William Allen White applauded the president's willingness to confront the power of entrenched wealth. The *Nation* endorsed any effort to spread the tax burden more equitably and cited the Roosevelt administration for its continuing commitment to the standard of ability to pay.[94]

But skeptics and administration critics weren't all convinced by Roosevelt's rhetoric. Many suggested that FDR was using the tax-avoidance issue to distract the country from his political floundering. And some used the occasion to lambaste the administration for its larger approach to tax policy. If Roosevelt insisted on trying to soak the rich, argued the *New York Times* and the *Wall Street Journal,* then avoidance was both inevitable and defensible. The president's tendency to conflate evasion and avoidance, moreover, was ridiculous.[95]

J. P. Morgan was the most celebrated critic of the president's position, dismissing his message as a misguided, moralistic crusade. "Taxing is a legal question pure and simple," he declared. "Anyone has the right to do anything as long as the law does not say it is wrong. I object strenuously to treating income tax evasion as a moral issue. If the Government objects to tax evaders it should change the law."[96] Of course, changing the law was exactly what the president wanted to do, but he certainly enjoyed vilifying a few rich taxpayers along the way. And he was delighted to have the politically clumsy Morgan defending tax avoidance; he was just the sort of enemy Roosevelt loved to engage.

But Morgan had his defenders. Conservative leaders echoed his complaint that taxpayers were unfairly maligned when they simply followed the letter of the law. Even some of the president's supporters had misgivings. Randolph Paul, who later counseled the president on tax matters during World War II, observed that "taxpayers are not the keepers of the Congressional conscience." Defending Morgan's remarks, he offered his own quotation from Learned Hand:

> Over and over again courts have said that there is nothing sinister in so arranging one's affairs as to keep taxes as low as possible. Everybody does so rich or poor and all do right, for nobody owes any public duty to pay more than the law demands: taxes are enforced extractions, not voluntary contributions. To demand more in the name of morals is mere cant.[97]

From a legal perspective, Hand's argument was indisputable, and tax experts generally dismissed Roosevelt's elevated sense of morality.[98] But politically, "mere cant" remained a potent force. Roosevelt was able to muster impressive support for his anti-loophole campaign.

The Joint Committee issued a report in August recommending legislation to close several loopholes, including those derived from personal holding companies, incorporated hobbies, artificial losses and deductions, multiple trusts, and foreign holding companies. But the panel delayed action on the more serious forms of legal tax minimization: depletion allowances and the treatment of community property. Properly speaking, these were not forms of tax avoidance at all, since both were deliberate provisions of the tax law. Lawmakers agreed to study both issues, but few expected any sort of imminent action. Meanwhile, the Ways and Means Committee drafted a bill embodying the Joint Committee recommendations. It passed the House and Senate with minimal debate.[99]

Conclusion

When it came to New Deal tax policy in the mid-1930s, tax avoidance was the tie that binds. The Revenue Acts of 1936 and 1937 both focused on tax minimization, most of it licit. In 1936, avoidance was the leading rationale for corporate tax reform, although UPT advocates had much grander goals. In 1937, avoidance was front and center in the tax debate, giving the policy process a deeply moralistic quality.

Roosevelt himself was a pivotal figure in shaping both laws, seizing on the political resonance of tax avoidance and playing an active role in shaping the debate. Revenue shortfalls helped spur him to action, but his principal motives were political and ideological. He clearly believed that a vigorous attack on tax avoidance—driven home by a rhetoric of social justice and public morality—would bolster his political fortunes. But Roosevelt also had a sincere commitment to tax fairness, with an emphasis on equitable distribution of the tax burden. Advisers noted his genuine enthusiasm whenever discussions turned to tax avoidance, and he seemed particularly eager to expose what he considered the antisocial behavior of the nation's wealthy tax cheats. This Roosevelt, sometimes driven by a desire to demonize and vilify, was not always an appealing figure. It is the same Roosevelt who, in 1934, urged his Treasury secretary to scour Hearst's tax returns for something useful. But for better or worse, this was the real Roosevelt. And he managed to make his moralistic case with convincing results, at least through the mid-1930s.

8

The Fall and Rise of Progressive Reform

W orld War II gave birth to the modern American fiscal state. In the face of national crisis, lawmakers strengthened the sinews of federal finance, establishing a powerful, flexible, and durable tax regime. The revenue structure emerging from the wartime crucible included three principal components: a broad-based personal income tax, steep new taxes on corporate profits, and a sweeping array of excise levies.

Two imperatives drove wartime reform: the need for revenue and the fear of inflation. Early in the war, a bipartisan coalition emerged to support steep new defense taxes. Franklin Roosevelt and congressional leaders cooperated to raise old taxes and impose new ones. Inflation worries bolstered their resolve; desperate to slow a surge in prices, they used taxes to limit consumer purchasing. In the process, they made taxation a vital component of macroeconomic policy. The "fiscal revolution" was a product of wartime finance.[1]

Necessity, then, was the mother of fiscal invention. But wartime exigencies can't explain the shape and course of tax reform. Lawmakers had a range of weapons in their fiscal arsenal, and choosing among them was a political process. Ideology and institutional dynamics were pivotal, as were electoral pressures and partisan rivalry. The wartime revenue regime grew out of a vibrant, often heated debate over fairness and efficiency. Franklin Roosevelt and his Treasury asked lawmakers for steeply progressive tax reforms, even as they endorsed a range of taxes on low- and middle-income Americans. Congress responded with a watered-down version of the president's agenda, raising less money for the Treasury and granting more favors to well-heeled taxpayers.

The result was a victory, albeit qualified, for the administration's progressive agenda. More specifically, it represented a vindication for the Treasury program of low-end progressivity, first articulated in 1934 but unable to gain traction until 1940. Success came despite a groundswell of congressional resistance. Restive since the late 1930s, taxwriters on Capitol Hill made life difficult for administration officials throughout the war. But Roosevelt's leadership, and Treasury expertise, carried the day, at least for a few years. While the revenue laws enacted between 1940 and 1942 required painful compromises, they bore the unmistakable imprint of Roosevelt's progressive ideology.

This chapter focuses on the wartime changes to the taxation of American business, with a special emphasis on excess profits taxation. Personal taxation—including the individual income tax and various consumption levies—are the subject of chapter 8.

The Ebb Tide of New Deal Tax Reform

The late 1930s were frustrating years for members of the Roosevelt administration. Treasury tax officials were no exception. Advocates of high-end progressivity, including Herman Oliphant and Robert Jackson, watched helplessly as lawmakers ravaged their most cherished reforms. The UPT succumbed to a determined campaign for repeal. The Treasury, meanwhile, adopted a new, more conciliatory stance toward the business community. Eager to boost business confidence in the face of renewed depression, Henry Morgenthau unveiled an "appeasement" campaign stressing cooperation, not confrontation. But rhetoric alone couldn't heal the rift between business and the New Deal. It would a national crisis to change the tenor of debate.

In mid-1937, the economy began a steep decline into renewed depression. The downturn was prompted, at least in part, by Roosevelt's renewed commitment to fiscal austerity. The president had succumbed to Morgenthau's arguments for "sound" finance, calling for budget stringency throughout the government. The nation watched as expenditures declined and tax receipts rose. At the same time, the Federal Reserve tightened the supply of credit, and soon enough, a resurgent depression had appeared.[2]

Morgenthau continued to argue to budget discipline, and he had support from some of his department economists. They believed that business required a demonstration of fiscal responsibility, especially after a decade of deficits. Outside the administration, critics were having a field day, with many blaming the president's tax policies—and the UPT in particular—for the recent downturn. Business leaders were solidly arrayed against the UPT, and lawmakers on Capitol Hill were giving serious thought to repeal. Even some administration figures urged reform, including Agriculture Secretary Henry Wallace, Reconstruction Finance Corporation Chairman Jesse Jones, and even Marriner Eccles.[3]

A Ways and Means subcommittee, headed by Rep. Fred Vinson (D-KY), drew up plans to revamp the tax. Emphasizing the need to encourage business and promote prosperity, lawmakers proposed to retain the UPT while draining it of substance. The full committee agreed, reporting a bill that gutted the tax even while paying homage to its intent. The measure raised the UPT exemption to $25,000, leaving it a narrow burden for the nation's largest companies. It also cut rates dramatically. Republican members of the committee were not satisfied, renewing their claim that Democrats were saddling business with unfair and oppressive taxes. On the House floor, a group of disaffected Democrats raised their voice in agreement, targeting a special provision aimed at closely held corporations. Democratic leaders were forced to retreat, giving the bill an even more probusiness cast. And as a parting shot, the House approved a range of dubious excise taxes, including imposts on pork and liquor. The bill passed by a vote of 293 to 97.[4]

Senators were even more eager to strike down the UPT, and the Finance Committee proposed its complete elimination. Majority Leader Alben Barkley (D-KY) urged his colleagues to retain some vestige of the tax, as did Sen. Robert La Follette (R-WI), who made an impassioned appeal for taxing retained profits. But Finance Committee Chairman Pat Harrison (D-MS) derided the UPT as a "beautiful theory" that had proven far less attractive in operation than it had in prospect. The repeal measure sailed through the Senate with scarcely a whisper of serious protest, passing on a voice vote with no objections.[5]

As the conference committee began trying to reconcile the House and Senate bills, Roosevelt sent a controversial letter to Ways and Means Chairman Robert L. Doughton (D-NC). Insisting that "important principles of fairness" were at stake, FDR urged Doughton to retain some version of the UPT. "Otherwise," he declared, "we grant a definite incentive to the avoidance of personal income tax payments through methods which are legal, but which are contrary to the spirit of the principle that every citizen should pay taxes in accordance with his means." FDR's letter irritated lawmakers, even Doughton, who was sympathetic to the president's cause. But Roosevelt had managed to stave off total defeat; lawmakers agreed to retain a modest version of the levy.[6]

Roosevelt let the bill become law without his signature, but not before voicing his disappointment. "For a great many years," he told the audience at a West Virginia high school graduation, "the Nation as a whole has accepted the principle that taxes ought to be paid by individuals and families in accordance with their capacity to pay." In general, this principle required a graduated tax on income, including any gains from investment. The UPT had been designed to protect this ideal, slowing the piecemeal erosion of progressive rates through the device of retained corporate profits. Roosevelt acknowledged that the UPT was not perfect; some companies, especially small ones, had been hurt by its unintended consequences. But that was an argument for reform, not repeal. Roosevelt paid lip service to the notion that tax policy should encourage business activity. But he complained loud and long that the 1938 revenue law sacrificed fairness on the altar of business confidence. As passed, he declared, it "abandons the accepted principle of progressive taxation at a point which is very important in our economic life."[7]

The gutting of the UPT was the most important tax defeat of Roosevelt's presidency to that point. Throughout 1939, he continued to defend the tax, expounding on its fairness and calling for its retention, even in symbolic form.[8] But Congress soon put the final nail in the UPT's coffin, repealing the last vestige of this fiscal innovation in the Revenue Act of 1939.

Roosevelt was disheartened. If anything, however, defeat seemed to bolster his commitment to progressive taxation. The West Virginia disquisition on fairness marked one of the high points in his presidential rhetoric on tax reform. As Roosevelt approached the turbulent years of World War II, he showed every sign of defending his belief in progressive taxation.

Business Appeasement

In the meantime, however, Roosevelt did a little pandering. The late 1930s were marked by a renewed commitment, rhetorical if not substantive, to business-government cooperation. With senior officials sounding a conciliatory note, the administration's progressive tax agenda receded into obscurity. In particular, the high-end progressivity that infused New Deal tax reforms in the mid-1930s was dead in the water, besieged by critics in both parties. Even some Treasury experts were starting to worry that business taxes had become a drag on the economy.[9]

Roosevelt's political fortunes were tumbling by the middle of 1937. The resurgent depression was a key factor, but so, too, was the president's ill-fated scheme to restructure the Supreme Court, as well as his attempted electoral purge in the congressional elections of 1938. Together, these events undermined his already waning influence on Capitol Hill.

By 1937, conservative opposition to the New Deal was gathering coherence and confidence. It was a bipartisan phenomenon, enlisting southern and rural Democrats, as well as the president's Republican opponents. The president's stock was particularly low among congressional tax-writers, many of whom were conservative southern Democrats. Sen. Harry Byrd used his seat on the Finance Committee to frustrate FDR's tax agenda; as a prominent coauthor of the Conservative Manifesto—which included tax cuts in its wish list for conservative reform—he was a persistent thorn in Roosevelt's side. Finance Chairman Pat Harrison (D-MS) was only marginally less disaffected from the New Deal. And he was certainly disinclined to support any White House initiative for progressive tax reform.[10]

Fretting inside his Treasury office, Henry Morgenthau decided to change course. If the administration were to avoid wholesale defeat on tax policy—as well as a slew of other economic issues—then opponents had to be mollified. As early as 1937, he had dispatched assistants to meet with business leaders, soliciting their opinions on controversial tax issues.[11] But by 1938, this modest effort at conciliation had become a matter of quasi-official administration policy. With Roosevelt's blessing, Morgenthau unveiled a campaign to assuage business fears. With an eye on international events, observers in the press immediately tagged the campaign with a provocative label: the Treasury, they reported, was pursuing a policy of "business appeasement."

Designed to quiet the nerves of anxious business leaders, the effort was more rhetorical than substantive. Leading officials—including Morgenthau and Commerce Secretary Harry Hopkins—called publicly for cooperation between business and government. Recovery, they stressed, was a goal shared by everyone. Even Roosevelt joined the chorus. "Amid the voices which now seek to divide group from group, occupation from occupation, section from section," he declared, "thinking Americans must insist on common effort in a common endeavor and a common faith in each other."[12]

Morgenthau embraced the business appeasement campaign with gusto. While a sometime-champion of soak-the-rich taxation, he had a natural conservative bent. Business leaders tended to view him more charitably than other administration figures, and in a series of speeches, Morgenthau tried to build on his reputation for policy moderation. The secretary emphasized his commitment to a business-friendly fiscal environment. "The business man should understand that the Administration wants him to go ahead," Morgenthau told reporters in February 1939, "and legislation should be of such a nature that it will not be a deterrent, so the business man can make a profit."[13]

Morgenthau also championed the appointment of a new undersecretary of the Treasury to replace Roswell Magill, who had announced his return to the private sector. John W. Hanes, a leading financier with impeccable business credentials, joined the Treasury to head the pro-business campaign. He was an unlikely spokesman for the New Deal, having spent his entire career on Wall Street. But as a governor of the New York Stock Exchange, he had developed a reputation as a reformer, and Roosevelt named him to the Securities and Exchange Commission in 1937. The next year he moved to Treasury, where he assumed principal responsibility for the tax program. Hanes was no expert in fiscal matters, and as a replacement for Roswell Magill, he left the Treasury's store of tax expertise much depleted. But Hanes brought something else to his new post: a sterling reputation among the New Deal's most bitter enemies.

If business appeasement was the job, then Johnny Hanes was just the man to get it done. His mandate was clear. "In recent weeks," observed the *New York Times,* "he has been recognized as the contact man between the administration and business and the chief mover in the effort to bring them together." Hanes took his mission seriously—perhaps too much so. But he radiated the requisite charm, charity, and goodwill. "In spite of an extreme view here and there," he wrote in an opinion piece for the *New York Times,* "I feel that out of the confusion of tongues in America there is emerging a new spirit of reasonableness, fair play, and honorable compromise, the same spirit that characterized the men who in 1787 gave us the charter of our liberty and the checks and balances of our national life."[14]

Hanes was committed to broad-ranging tax reform, with an eye toward pleasing business leaders. He invited comments from the general public, either in writing or in person; the Treasury received about a thousand letters and held roughly 80 conferences. Working with the Ways and Means committee, Hanes also began work on a new revenue program designed to please business leaders, even as it continued to raise substantial revenue. Taxes, Hanes declared, must be designed to promote free enterprise, encourage recovery, protect the fisc, and distribute fiscal burdens equitably.[15] It seems fair to say that he planned to address those goals in precisely that order. While fairness was not absent from the New Deal tax agenda of 1938 and 1939, it played a much-diminished role.

For 18 months, Hanes served gamely as Roosevelt's ambassador to the business community. Conservative pundits hailed him as the "man to watch," and his conservative friends on Wall Street seemed cheered by his presence in the very heart of the lion's den. But Hanes had his detractors, especially in Treasury. While the press took to calling him a tax expert, he was anything but. Economists in the Treasury's new Division of Tax Research considered him a rank, if well-intentioned, amateur. Having worked for a technician like Magill, they considered Hanes a feeble replacement.[16]

Meanwhile, doubts about business appeasement were starting to grow. Roosevelt had never embraced the effort enthusiastically, and by late 1939, the program was losing steam. In December, Hanes beat a hasty retreat to Wall Street. Roosevelt and Morgenthau issued grateful statements, their tender sentiments only slightly less saccharine than those offered coming from the business press. In fact, though, Hanes had been squeezed out of the New Deal, caught between its liberal stalwarts and a growing sense that New Deal–business relations were beyond repair. In any case, Hanes had always been a poor fit for the Roosevelt administration; he was simply too conservative. Soon enough, he made that fact abundantly clear. Six months after leaving the administration, he endorsed Wendell Willkie for president. "Hanes was always consistent," observed his successor at Treasury, Randolph Paul. "In and out of office he was for business appeasement first, last, and all the time."[17]

As Hanes shook the New Deal dust from the soles of his feet, the business appeasement campaign left town with him. Events had conspired to render it moot, as European warfare changed the nature of debate in Washington. Even while Hanes was reaching out to business leaders with the promise of lower taxes, Treasury experts were starting to plan for heavy defense taxation. Driven by a growing demand for revenue and a deepening fear of inflation, administration officials began to sketch the outlines of a new tax regime.

The Bureaucratic Infrastructure of Tax Policymaking

Many historians have chronicled the rise of Keynesian economics, including its inroads among Washington policymakers during the mid- to late 1930s.[18] Franklin Roosevelt's well-documented embrace of countercyclical spending in 1938—replete with a secretive train ride to Georgia and the intervention of private-sector policy entrepreneur Beardsley Ruml—tell part of the story. But the taxing side of the fiscal equation has received less attention that the spending element. Perhaps it's the timing, for the spending came first. But the macroeconomic importance of tax policy, while vaguely understood for decades, took on new prominence in the late 1930s. The run-up to war prompted serious thinking among federal tax officials, who realized quickly that taxes would play a vital role in managing the wartime economy. That realization did not require any specifically Keynesian insight; the "old economics" of the pre-Keynes era made room for an active tax program in emergencies. But Keynesianism underscored the importance of countercyclical taxation, opening the door to more active regulation of the economy.[19]

First, however, both Treasury and Congress needed to expand their stores of fiscal expertise. Officials were driven by their new appreciation for tax policy. Taxes, they understood by the late 1930s, weren't just for revenue anymore. Properly managed, they could also be a powerful tool for regulating the economy. To help chart this new course, officials beefed up their capacities for research and analysis. Treasury, long accustomed to dominating the field, maintained its ascendancy when it came to expertise. But increasingly, congressional staff would challenge their Treasury colleagues.

Treasury Experts

In 1938, the Treasury restructured its research staff. The Division of Tax Research replaced a more diffuse program organized by the Division of Research and Statistics. Reporting to the department's undersecretary, the new division was blessed with additional staff and growing influence. Morgenthau named Roy Blough, an economist who first came to the Treasury as a special adviser in 1937, to head the division; his first choice, Carl Shoup, had declined the job to return to his teaching post at Columbia.[20]

Blough, born in Pittsburgh in 1901, graduated from Manchester College, then the University of Wisconsin. After teaching at several colleges, he made his way to Washington during the early years of the Great Depression, as much for job security as anything else. By the mid-1930s, he had joined Shoup as a regular adviser to the Treasury. Blough was a skilled technician, with generally liberal political views. In contrast to Shoup, however, he was well attuned to the political realities of tax reform. While Shoup jealously guarded his academic credibility (and employment), Blough was comfortable in the public sector. After serving in the tax division throughout World War II, he would go on to other high-profile economic posts, including a stint on Harry Truman's Council of Economic Advisers. In all his official work, Blough displayed a keen appreciation for the constraints of real-world policymaking. And while he remained a careful economist, his heart seemed to lie in politics. Indeed, his most lasting contribution to tax scholarship was a study of the tax policy process, published just after he left the Truman administration.[21]

As director of the new research division, Blough took the lead in developing the administration's tax agenda. He and his staff were expected to craft original proposals, analyze plans emerging from Congress, and prepare detailed statistical publications. They were also explicitly directed to cooperate with congressional experts. For the most part, their work with the Joint Committee on Internal Revenue Taxation (JCIRT) was productive and collegial.[22]

All across the federal government, research assumed new importance in the 1930s, but nowhere was the trend more obvious than in Treasury. Tax policy put a huge premium on expertise, demanding specific technical skills including some not common among trained economists. Consequently, Treasury was forced to create some of its expertise in-house, expanding its support for economic research on tax issues. The need to coordinate efforts with congressional tax experts also underscored the need for a separate tax division; if Treasury experts were to maintain their central role in the tax policy process, they would need strong ties to their legislative counterparts.[23]

The creation of a separate tax staff signaled the maturing of modern fiscal policy. As one Treasury memo later noted, "The setting up of a separate organization to carry on tax research was both an expression of the growing recognition of research as an essential staff service in Government and a reflection of the growing importance of intelligent and informed tax policy to the effective functioning of the American economy." During the war, policymakers increasingly recognized that taxation was an integral part of managing the economy. The well-publicized use of taxes to restrain inflation and profiteering "led to a broader recognition and understanding of the economic role of taxation." The essential function of tax analysis did not change during this period, but its importance was more widely understood.[24]

The new tax division gave the administration a distinct advantage in the often contentious process of tax policymaking. The new division "stood the Treasury and the Government in very good stead," recalled the Treasury's administrative history. Specifically, the new stable of experts endowed the Treasury with unmatched expertise.[25]

Revenue Revision Studies

During its first several years, the tax research division focused primarily on peacetime tax problems, including fundamental reform of the federal tax system. In fact, the division itself was an outgrowth of the sweeping reform studies undertaken in 1937. Supervised by George Haas, these studies were roughly analogous to the Viner Studies of 1934. But while the Viner Studies had been permeated by a sense of immediate crisis, the 1937 research program took a broader, more contemplative view of the tax system. Nonetheless, the conclusions of 1937 looked much like those of 1934: Treasury economists urged broader reliance on the income tax and a much-diminished dependence on consumption levies. They also endorsed the UPT, while urging a certain amount of caution when it came to the overall tax burden on business.

Haas and his colleagues agreed on the broad outlines of what constituted good tax policy. Most important, they declared, taxes must raise adequate revenue. But adequacy had to be balanced against fairness and efficiency. Levies that violated norms of social justice or impeded economic growth had no legitimate place in the federal revenue system. And finally, any good tax system had to strive for administrative efficiency. Adequate and fair taxes that couldn't be collected were of no value to anyone.[26] These standards for good policy were notoriously incompatible. Administrative simplicity was often at odds with equity, and equity was frequently the enemy of efficiency. "Every tax system inevitably represents a compromise among these several aims," Haas acknowledged. And the compromises emerging from the revenue revision studies were predictable.

The Treasury's tax experts asked for greater reliance on the individual income tax, recommending both higher rates and lower exemptions. "The history of the Federal Income Tax since 1913 is the history of the extension of the ability to pay principle and progressiveness in taxation," they declared. Economic and political principles demanded that this process continue, with the tax assuming an ever-larger role in the revenue system. By increasing rates in every bracket—topping out at 75 percent for the richest taxpayers—the department's proposed revisions would "enable a more scientific distribution of the aggregate Federal tax burden." Specifically, it would raise the burden substantially on the middle brackets, which the authors believed to be substantially undertaxed.[27]

While the cut in exemptions would raise additional revenue, Haas and his colleagues endorsed it as a revenue-neutral reform. Lower exemptions should be coupled with a rollback in consumption taxes to achieve a more equitable revenue system. "The recommendation," he noted, "is primarily prompted by the desirability of obtaining substitute revenue from the low income classes in a more equitable manner than is possible through the miscellaneous excise taxes." Smaller exemptions would make lower- and middle-income Americans more acutely aware of governmental efficiency—always a good thing in a democracy. But to preserve equity, the lower exemptions could be ameliorated by granting a larger credit for earned income.[28]

The 1937 studies suggested that all existing corporation taxes should be repealed; the levies "are believed to be relatively high as well as defective," the authors declared. A new tax, scaled to income, would raise adequate revenue in a more practical, efficient, and equitable manner. Notably, the Treasury experts also endorsed an undistributed profits tax, although they proposed a variety of revisions to improve its fairness and efficiency. In general, however, the Treasury experts did not support any substantial increase in the burden of corporate taxation; cognizant of the recent economic downturn, they counseled moderation.[29]

On the subject of excise taxation, the studies acknowledged that consumption duties had a long history in the federal revenue system. But they suffered from numerous flaws. "Generally speaking, excise taxes other than those imposed for regulatory purposes are less desirable than progressive direct taxes and, so far as possible, should be replaced by a system of direct taxes," Haas wrote. Replacement, of course, was not possible across the board, if only because direct taxes were ill-suited for people near the bottom of the income distribution. Income taxes on the poor were administratively burdensome and economically inefficient. In general terms, they cost more to collect than they raised in additional revenue. Excise taxes might be reasonable for taxing this population.

Moreover, broad-based excise taxes were a dependable source of revenue. In a tight fiscal climate, such stable taxes were not easily abandoned. Haas and his staff concluded that excise taxes should have a continuing role in the revenue system, and not just at the bottom of the income scale; they also approved of several aimed at well-to-do taxpayers. But some excise taxes weren't even good revenue raisers; the study recommended repeal for 23 minor taxes.[30]

The tax revision studies of 1937 provided an outline for desirable federal taxation. They were not, however, the only plan circulating through the Treasury. When he asked the research staff to undertake their comprehensive assessment of the tax system, Undersecretary Roswell Magill had also given a similar charge to a pair of outside consultants: Carl Shoup and Roy Blough. In a relatively brief memo, Shoup and Blough endorsed most of the Treasury conclusions. Most important, they embraced the notion that income taxes should take a larger role and consumption taxes a smaller one. But they favored a steeper surtax schedule for the individual income tax, even at the cost of some efficiency loss. "To the present writers," they stated, "it seems most important to make the income tax a tax that will appeal to the community's sense of justice, even at the cost of having a higher rate scale."[31]

The Tax Research Division and its various prewar studies would play a central role in shaping the wartime tax regime. Many of their peacetime conclusions would fall prey to the wartime exigencies; plans for excise reductions were wholly off the table. But arguments for a broad-based individual income tax would prove central to the wartime debate, offering lawmakers and administration officials the foundation for emergency finance.[32]

Congressional Experts

While the Treasury was expanding its research function, so, too, was Congress. Since 1937, lawmakers had become more assertive in the tax policy process, resisting administration leadership and charting an independent course. Generally speaking, lawmakers were more sympathetic to business complaints about high taxation, especially after the recession of 1937. And the war only made matters worse for Roosevelt, Morgenthau, and their advisers. If lawmakers were stubborn in the late 1930s, they were downright ornery during the war. Roosevelt and his advisers had to fight tooth and nail for their tax proposals, battling Democrats and well as Republicans.

In this struggle between the executive and legislative branches, experts were central. Congress understood the power of technical information, and taxwriters on the Finance and Ways and Means committees moved to expand their own store of specialized knowledge. The JCIRT had been in existence since 1927, charged with developing congressional expertise on taxation. But in the decade and half since its creation, the panel had never seriously challenged Treasury dominance. While it remained in this supporting role throughout the war, the JCIRT's influence grew steadily.

Colin Stam was JCIRT staff director, and he figured prominently in every tax debate of World War II. Stam was a big man, both physically and politically. His imposing stature, bald head, and careless clothing were a fixture on Capitol Hill; one senator compared him to an unmade bed. While not exactly humorless, he had few interests outside the arcane world of federal taxation. A nonsmoking, nondrinking, lifelong bachelor, Stam lived with two sisters and a dog. Indeed, his canine companion figured prominently in his public persona. "As far as most acquaintances knew, his main recreation was walking his dog in Chevy Chase," reported the *New York Times*. Lobbyists eager to meet with Stam were known to loiter along his favorite route, intercepting dog and taxwriter for impromptu consultation.[33]

Stam was widely considered a conservative force in the tax policy process. He was no retrograde advocate of regressivity, but neither was he a fan of soak-the-rich taxation. After graduating from Washington College and Georgetown University, he started his tax career at the BIR. In 1927, he signed on with the fledgling joint committee and soon took the lead in a mammoth project to codify the internal revenue laws. In 1938, Stam was named to head the committee staff, his appointment coincident with Roosevelt's declining fortunes on Capitol Hill. Under Stam's guidance, the JCIRT would increasingly challenge Treasury expertise, empowering wartime taxwriters as they resisted administration blandishments and bullying.[34]

Stam headed a small but growing staff. In sheer size, the Treasury overwhelmed the JCIRT, but congressional experts were well positioned to shape the nation's tax laws. Increasingly, members of Ways and Means and Finance turned to their own advisers for estimates, projections, and proposals. In fact, envious lawmakers on other committees used the JCIRT as a model for their own efforts to develop a homegrown source of topical expertise.[35]

Taxing Business in Total War

The tax regime that emerged from World War II was the handiwork of both Congress and the administration. While most tax measures of the 1930s had been formatively shaped by Roosevelt and his Treasury, lawmakers flexed their legislative muscle during the war years. Without doubt, wartime reform would have looked different had either side had a free hand. But forced to work together, Congress and the administration managed to craft a remarkably durable compromise.

Business taxation was the subject of early, if fleeting, agreement. As policymakers began searching for ways to finance new defense spending, almost everyone agreed that businesses would foot much of the bill. But vigorous arguments soon emerged over the details, particularly when lawmakers began crafting a new excess profits tax.

After England and France declared war on Germany in September 1939, Franklin Roosevelt turned his attention almost immediately to revenue reform. Specifically, he took a renewed interest in war and excess profits taxation. Early in his presidency, Roosevelt had declared his support for such levies, especially when applied to large defense manufacturers. "The time has come," he declared in 1934, "to take the profit out of war."[36]

In fact, the time had come, and gone, and come again. The excess profits tax of World War I, which proved enormously effective as a revenue tool, was explicitly designed with moral considerations in mind. Political leaders had defended the tax not simply as a revenue device, but as a tool for ensuring fairness and social equity. The tax died a speedy death in the early 1920s, done in by its political opponents as well as its own complexity and burdensome operation. But politicians of all stripes continued to pay lip service to the steep taxation of wartime profits. Presidents Harding, Coolidge, and Hoover had all endorsed the principle, and Harding even featured it in his 1921 inaugural address:

> I can vision the ideal republic, where every man and woman is called under the flag for assignment to duty for whatever service, military or civic, the individual is best fitted; where we may call to universal service every plant, agency, or facility, all in the sublime sacrifice for country, and not one penny of war profit shall inure to the benefit of private individual, corporation, or combination, but all above the normal shall flow into the defense chest of the Nation. There is something inherently wrong, something out of accord with the ideals of representative democracy, when one portion of our citizenship turns its activities to private gain amid defensive war while another is fighting, sacrificing, or dying for national preservation.[37]

In 1928, both the Republican and Democratic presidential platforms had endorsed steep war taxes on corporate profits. And in 1931, a Republican secretary of war, Patrick J. Hurley, proposed a special wartime tax of 95 percent on excess profits.[38]

Roosevelt's sudden interest in war profits taxation was surely sparked by the Nye Committee, a congressional panel making headlines at the time with its investigation of war profiteering during World War I. An article on munitions makers published earlier in the year by *Fortune* magazine had ignited a firestorm of protest, and the Nye Committee, chaired by Senate progressive Gerald Nye (R-ND), had fanned the flames with a series of lurid hearings. Roosevelt made the most of the opportunity, appointing a special committee to investigate the issue. Its members included former National Recovery Administration chief Hugh Johnson, Treasury Secretary Henry Morgenthau, and financier extraordinaire Bernard Baruch, the last an acknowledged expert on the excess profits tax. Meanwhile, Congress soon responded to the Nye Committee with the Vinson-Trammell Act of 1934, which limited the profit margin on most major military contracts to 10 or 12 percent. The Merchant Marine Act of 1936 imposed similar limits on profits from the construction of civilian vessels.[39]

While war profits taxation enjoyed broad support, some observers worried that the issue was being exploited by the enemies of private enterprise. If the profit could be taken out of war, wondered the *Wall Street Journal*, could it also be removed from depression or any other sort of national emergency?[40] Administration critics suspected Roosevelt of using the war profit debate to intensify his attack on corporate America. The timing of his interest, coming just as the New Deal entered its most ideologically charged phase, only added to the suspicion.

But Roosevelt's interest in the taxation of war profits was by most accounts sincere, as events would soon demonstrate. He believed deeply that no one should profit from national misfortune. And while he abjured most tax issues in their early stage of his presidency, FDR took the lead on this issue. Later in the decade, when Europe took the decisive plunge into full-scale war, Roosevelt again seized the initiative. Worried that his Treasury Department would resist steep taxes on excess profits—this was, after all, the era of business appeasement—FDR sought outside help. He turned to a New York City tax lawyer of considerable renown: Randolph Evernghim Paul.

Randolph Paul was a giant of the tax bar. His career had started modestly; after graduating from New York Law School in 1913, he took a job as telephone operator for a large New York law firm. In 1918, however, he accepted a job working for George E. Holmes, a noted specialist in tax law. Paul applied himself to the same subject, and over the next two decades, he rose to prominence as one of the nation's leading tax attorneys.

In 1922 Paul organized his own firm, Lynn, Paul & Havens. In 1938 he joined Lord, Day & Lord. That same year, he also declined to join the Treasury as assistant secretary for tax policy. For the time being, Paul preferred to remain in private practice, where his well-heeled clientele gave him a lucrative practice; over the course of his career, he served a range of prominent individuals and corporations, including Henry Ford, the Standard Oil Co. of California, and General Motors.

Paul's sterling reputation among the nation's economic elite did not translate into conservative politics. In fact, he was an ardent champion of progressive taxation generally and the income tax in particular. He opposed most broad consumption taxes, including a national sales tax. And while he recognized the revenue necessity of certain excise levies, he was committed to a reform program that would ultimately replace them with money from a broader income tax.

Paul brought to his official duties a broad and flexible view of taxation. He was an early convert to Keynesian theory, though like most of his contemporaries, he was slow to recognize his intellectual debt to the British economist. Paul believed that taxes in the modern world must necessarily serve many purposes. "We must discard old notions that taxation is for revenue only," he observed after joining the Treasury officially in 1941. "We must use taxation as an instrument of inflation control. We must recognize its function of distributing the economic burden of the war in a fair and equitable manner." Taxes, in other words, were about more than just revenue. Properly employed, they also were a powerful instrument of social and economic control.[41]

When he asked Paul to prepare a series of memos on excess profits taxation, Roosevelt was presumably counting on Paul's flexible and pragmatic approach to fiscal policymaking. Paul obliged the president with a pair of secret reports, delivered to the White House after a series of clandestine meetings. Morgenthau was outraged when he discovered this invasion of his policy domain, although he initially blamed his subordinate John Hanes. But FDR had organized the Paul intrusion all on his own.[42]

Paul appeared on the Washington scene just as Herman Oliphant departed it. Paul and Oliphant were very different, in both style and substance, but they shared a faith in progressive taxation. Paul was not quite so smitten with soak-the-rich taxation as his predecessor. Roosevelt's new tax expert, however, did embrace the essential bargain of high-end progressivity: regressive consumption taxes could be morally and economically justified, at least during emergencies, if they were balanced by steep taxes on individual and corporate income. This inclination endeared Paul to the president, and he would soon become the principal architect of administration tax policy.

Paul's early memos on excess profits taxation had no immediate effect, but as war raged through Europe, the issue remained a subject of lively debate. German victories in the spring of 1940 prompted a renewed interest in defense spending, and on May 16, Roosevelt asked Congress to approve $1.2 billion in national defense spending. Congressional leaders met privately with Morgenthau and announced in late May that they would sponsor a version of the administration's request. The panel agreed to support additional federal borrowing of up to $3 billion, as well as new taxes raising $600 million to $700 million annually; the new revenue would be used to retire the defense loans over a five-year period.[43]

Before Congress could act, Roosevelt upped the ante. On May 30, he asked for an additional $1.3 billion, again slated for defense. Congress agreed to this request, too, eventually giving the nod to various tax hikes, both permanent and temporary. Lawmakers did not, however, propose an excess profits tax, despite Roosevelt's support for the idea.[44] Democratic members of the Ways and Means Committee insisted that they would not permit "the creation of new war millionaires or the further substantial enrichment of already wealthy persons." But they declined to rush a profits tax into law. Such a complex levy would have to wait for subsequent legislation.[45]

Republicans raised some mild objections, railing against New Deal spending even as they accepted the gist of the Democratic bill. GOP members of Ways and Means warned that a national sales tax was almost certain to follow in due course, although they blamed this necessity on Democratic profligacy, not military necessity. The first Revenue Act of 1940—there would soon be a second—passed the House by a vote of 396 to 6. The Senate followed suit, 75 to 5. On June 25, Roosevelt signed it into law.[46] The act was projected to raise roughly $1 billion annually, chiefly through new corporate and individual income taxes. Congressional leaders, meanwhile, had declared their intent to craft a new excess profits tax. Most observers expected another bill in short order.[47]

As Congress focused on the first 1940 tax law, Randolph Paul returned to the administration as a special tax adviser. Again, he set to work on excess profits taxation, but now he was joined by the Treasury research staff. While hard at work with his new colleagues, Paul was interrupted on July 1 by the assistant secretary for tax policy, John L. Sullivan (who had replaced John Hanes to head up tax policy). According to wire reports, Sullivan said, the president had just asked Congress for an excess profits tax. Unwilling to wait for his experts, FDR had crafted his own call for a "steeply graduated" tax on both individuals and corporations. "We are asking even our humblest citizens to contribute their mite," Roosevelt declared. "It is our duty to see that the burden is equitably distributed according to ability to pay so that a few do not gain from the sacrifices of the many."[48]

Roosevelt's 89-word message was admirably terse, but it still managed to create problems for the Treasury experts. The president had asked for a tax on individuals, which none of them believed wise. Paul soon convinced FDR to back off that idea, especially given the high surtax rates currently applied under the personal income tax. The president also agreed to endorse a provision allowing corporations to accelerate the depreciation of new facilities constructed for defense production—an important concession to business interests and their congressional allies.[49]

The bill that made its way through Congress as the Second Revenue Act of 1940 was extraordinarily complex, and even its advocates were willing to concede its shortcomings. Supporters of the bill, acknowledged Rep. Wesley Disney (D-OK), were "somewhat in the attitude of the sign which was placed over a piano in a dance hall in Dodge City in the roaring days, that stated, 'Don't shoot the piano player, he is doing the best he can.' "[50] The bill was complicated, but so was business. "Our taxes must follow the intricacies of business and not attempt to bend business to the pattern of simplicity we should all like to see in taxation," observed Robert Doughton.[51]

Much of the bill's complexity grew out of one issue: Which profits were, in fact, excess? What portion of a company's income should be regarded as a product of the defense emergency rather than normal operations? Congress and the White House disagreed vehemently on this issue, which had enormous implications for the nature and operation of the excess profits tax.

Treasury experts proposed a tax that would define excess profits in relation to a "normal" percentage return on invested capital. This normal return might be arbitrarily fixed by government officials, or it might be derived from the prewar returns enjoyed by a taxpaying company. Many, but not all, tax experts preferred this method. In their well-regarded 1937 study, economists for the Twentieth Century Fund, including the ubiquitous Carl Shoup, had endorsed the invested capital method. So, too, had Alfred Buehler, a noted expert on corporate taxation.[52]

By contrast, congressional leaders—prodded by Colin Stam from the JCIRT—endorsed the "average-earnings" method of measuring excess profits. Under this scheme, earnings during the taxable year that exceeded the average earnings during a three-year, prewar base period would be subject to the new tax. Advocates of this technique for measuring profits had their own stable of experts eager to back them up.[53]

Eventually, the House and Senate agreed to let taxpayers choose their preferred method, subject to certain rate penalties for those choosing the prewar profits technique. It was a business-friendly decision. Companies with big profits in the averaging period could choose the prewar earnings method and keep making big profits during the war. Corporations making small profits in the averaging years could choose the invested capital method and preserve their shot at a good return. Meanwhile, a large exemption left most companies entirely exempt.[54]

The Second Revenue Act of 1940 raised the normal income tax rate for corporations to 24 percent for all companies earning more than $25,000 in net income. Excess profits were taxed at rates ranging from 25 percent to 50 percent, depending on income. In computing the new tax, companies were granted a flat $5,000 exemption, plus a credit computed by one of the two methods described above. The bill also retained the accelerated amortization first proposed by the White House, although it notably deprived the government of any role in the postwar disposition of these facilities.

Just days after Congress completed work on the Second Revenue Act of 1940, Henry Morgenthau gave lawmakers a scare when he made the casual observation that any business should be satisfied with a 6 percent return on invested capital. To wary ears, this sounded like a trial balloon for a 100 percent rate above that amount. Treasury officials soon backed off this statement, and Morgenthau later claimed it was a slip of the tongue. But in fact, rates would approach that level within just a couple of years. In 1941, lawmakers raised the excess profits rates across the board, establishing a range from 35 percent to 60 percent. They also tightened available deductions to further boost revenues.[55]

In 1942, lawmakers abandoned the graduated rate structure for the excess profits tax, imposing a flat 90 percent rate. In 1943, the rate climbed again to 95 percent, although the exemption grew dramatically as well from $5,000 to $10,000. Such hikes were further offset by a range of relief provisions, enacted at several points during the war. Designed to ease inequities and encourage certain types of business activities, these provisions brought forth a deluge of refund claims from almost ten thousand corporations. Ultimately, such claims cost the government about $388 million. Various other provisions also softened the blow to corporate treasuries. Caps on the total amount of income that might be collected from a corporation (80 percent of total profit) and a 10 percent postwar refund on taxes paid (which gave the tax an element of compulsory lending) reduced the effective rate to as little as 72 percent. Still steep, but not quite so draconian as the statutory rates might suggest.[56]

Throughout the war, Treasury officials continued to argue for the invested capital method. In May 1941, the assistant Treasury secretary for tax policy complained to Congress that the existing pair of methodologies had allowed one company with $70 million in war orders to pay no excess profits tax whatsoever. Clearly, he declared, the tax was failing in its stated purpose. Roosevelt himself joined the argument, calling for more stringent standards; companies must be forced to share the burden of national emergency. "Excessive profits undermine unity and should be recaptured," he declared in his January 1942 budget message. "The fact that a corporation had large profits before the defense program started is no reason to exempt them now."[57]

But Congress stood firm, insisting on the two-method system. Some observers believed that this congressional preference reflected postwar intentions; an invested capital standard could have been converted to peacetime use, but the average earnings technique was clearly a wartime device. Similar arguments had surrounded the excess profits tax of World War I. But this time, most observers expected the excess profits tax to be a short-term addition to the tax system. Even those who favored peacetime use of the levy were skeptical of its long-term political viability. In 1942, Congress made explicit its intention to abandon the tax once peace returned.[58]

Excess profits taxes were not the only business levies imposed during the war, although they were certainly the most important. Congress repeatedly raised regular corporation income taxes. The First Revenue Act of 1940 raised rates, introducing three brackets of 15 percent, 17 percent, and 19 percent. The top rate applied to corporations with more than $25,000 in net income, and a special 10 percent defense surtax raised the effective rate even higher. In 1941, lawmakers raised the normal corporate rate from 24 percent to 31 percent and introduced a new surtax of 6 percent on net income under $25,000 and 7 percent on amounts over that threshold. Effectively, rates topped out at 24 percent for large companies, while those with smaller incomes paid 15 percent to 19 percent. In 1942, rates went higher still. The revenue from this tax was substantial, ranging from $3.7 billion in fiscal 1941 to $4.5 billion in 1943. But the tax raised far less than the levy on excess profits, which ranged from a $3.4 billion in 1941 to $11.4 billion in 1943.[59]

Despite its various shortcomings, the excess profits tax enjoyed grudging acceptance throughout the war. As early as 1940, political observers noted the broad support such taxes enjoyed. Calls for a profit tax "were representative of a widespread determination that the misfortunes of war should not be taken advantage of to create a lot of millionaires," reported Roy Blakey.[60] The tax was a political necessity, bolstering fairness at a critical point in the nation's political and fiscal history. "It was an answer to those who sought insurance that none would profit from the nation's misfortune," wrote Harold Groves. "It was demanded as a monetary counterpart to the sacrifice being made by persons who entered the armed forces." Its essential fairness, as well as its productivity, silenced many critics. "The profits tax, as a war measure," Groves concluded, "stems from some sound roots in the soils of expediency and principle."[61]

The Roosevelt administration insisted on the need for steep business taxes throughout the war. "There can be no fair quarrel with the imposition upon corporations of a substantial proportion of the increased load of taxation required by our national peril," declared Morgenthau in 1942. "We are fighting for the maintenance of the very system of free enterprise which makes corporate profits possible." The nation could not afford to focus on the bottom line. Profits, while important and legitimate, were a distinctly secondary concern. The nation, Morgenthau intoned, "must rise above the profit motive." Building on FDR's longstanding support for excess profits taxation, Morgenthau urged that this tax, and not the regular corporate income tax, become the principal vehicle for taxing business.[62]

Economists raised questions about the incidence of corporate taxation, suggesting that its burden might shift backward to workers in the form of lower wages or forward to consumers in the form of higher prices. This was a vigorous topic of debate throughout the war, much as it had been before. By the late 1940s, however, economists were beginning to agree that the incidence was distributed among various groups, including labor, consumers, and the owners of capital. Still, corporate income taxes enjoyed a reputation for progressivity. Most economists believed they fell principally where they were placed: on business.[63]

In many ways, the debate over the excess profits tax was remarkably subdued. Even business leaders tended to accept the principle, if not always the reality, of the levy. "To the best of my knowledge, no business executive opposes the principle of an excess profits tax which seeks to return to government exorbitant profits arising directly or indirectly from the war effort," wrote tax lawyer George Douglas. Leaders of the private sector had numerous complaints about the tax in operation, and Congress worked diligently throughout the war to ameliorate some of the more egregious problems. But the excess profits tax enjoyed remarkable, if not always enthusiastic, support from most quarters. Even the NAM endorsed a 90 percent levy in 1942.[64]

Still, business was restive under the steep burden. Randolph Paul complained that an initial burst of business patriotism faded dramatically over the course of the war. And certainly, business leaders were vocal in their support for moving more of the tax burden onto individuals rather than businesses. Often, they used inflation to bolster their case, cloaking their quest for lower taxes in the mantle of macroeconomic responsibility. But it was abundantly clear to most observers that business groups were principally interested in limiting their own tax burden.

As the war continued, even some supporters of steep business taxation wondered how heavy such taxes could become before they wreaked havoc with the economy. "Just how far can we go in preventing excess profits and excess wages without checking production vital for defense," asked Roy Blakey, "without increasing the ultimate cost in money and lives, and perhaps without losing the war?"[65] In the years to come, lawmakers would repeatedly ask themselves that same question.

9

The Creation of
the Mass Income Tax

The broad-based, individual income tax was the defining character-istic of the World War II tax regime. Fashioned jointly by Congress and the Roosevelt administration, it was a testament to compromise and cooperation. But the transformation of the income tax—its conversion from a "class tax" to a "mass tax"—was never a foregone conclusion. Many politicians and opinion leaders preferred a national sales tax, insisting that it would raise much-needed revenue while also curbing inflation. Even some members of the Roosevelt administration agreed.

But Franklin Roosevelt rejected the sales tax. The levy, he declared, was inefficient, unnecessary, and—most of all—unfair. In its search for revenue, Congress should look first to wealth and big business. And when it came time to tax Americans of modest means, the income tax was better suited to the task. Roosevelt was willing to tolerate a range of narrow consumption taxes, especially on luxuries. But he refused to consider a flat sales tax on personal consumption. That sort of levy, he complained, would spare the rich and soak the poor.

Roosevelt's vigorous leadership derailed the drive for sales taxation. Lawmakers turned, instead, to the individual income tax, pushing it deep into the middle class. By war's end, more than 90 percent of American workers filed annual returns. Fully 60 percent found they owed money to Uncle Sam, giving this rich man's tax a newly democratic cast. At the same time, lawmakers acceded to Roosevelt's demand that the personal income tax remain steeply progressive. Marginal rates soared above 90 percent for the nation's wealthiest taxpayers, while effective rates peaked at almost 60 percent.[1] These changes made the income tax a fiscal workhorse, the principal source of federal revenue. It would retain that distinction for the rest of the 20th century.

Inflation

The transformation of the individual income tax was driven by revenue imperatives. The exemption cuts enacted between 1940 and 1943 were designed to raise money. Lots of it. Very quickly.

But unlike business taxation, the income tax was also designed to fight inflation.[2] By early 1941, Henry Morgenthau was deeply concerned by the prospect of rising prices. At his behest, Treasury tax experts had begun debating the best means to check the price spiral. They quickly agreed on the importance of slowing consumer demand. Specifically, they suggested a range of taxes designed to drain consumers of their purchasing power.[3]

As the department's tax experts later recalled in a fit of self-congratulation, "The record shows that the Treasury in the autumn of 1941 was practically alone, among responsible groups in the executive and legislative branches, in urging special anti-inflationary taxes."[4] In part, the administration's slow start on wartime fiscal policy can be explained by Roosevelt's reluctance to consider the issue. He did not share the Treasury's inflation concern through the early years of the defense program. Convinced that the economy had room to absorb new government spending, he assured Congress that the sky was not, in fact, falling in. "I am opposed," Roosevelt declared in January 1941, "to a tax policy which restricts general consumption as long as unused capacity is available and as long as idle labor can be employed." The president had spent recent years defending the role of consumption in a prosperous economy, and he was not inclined to change his tune. Others in the administration, as well as many outside experts, agreed with the president's complacent outlook.[5]

Soon enough, events forced Roosevelt to hop aboard the anti-inflation bandwagon. Prices rose steadily throughout 1941, and by early 1942, a sense of crisis gripped policymakers. "Inflation was no longer something that might hit sometime in the nebulous future," recalled Treasury General Counsel Randolph Paul. "It had gained a tight hold on the national economy." In September, Leon Henderson, chief of the Office of Price

Administration, reported a 17 percent price hike over the previous year. In December, he predicted another 20 percent rise within four months. Retail prices were already increasing at 1.5 percent a month.[6]

As Treasury inflation hawks were quick to point out, massive defense spending almost guaranteed a price spike. Wages would grow as production increased and labor supplies dwindled. Demand for consumer goods would rise in tandem, as newly flush workers found money burning holes in their pockets. Meanwhile, defense production would crowd out civilian goods, leaving shelves bare and consumers agitated. The result? A vicious spiral of rising prices, as growing incomes chased a shrinking supply of available goods. Inventories might hold things in check for a while, but soon enough, shortages would be common. The outlook was sobering.[7]

As the federal government assumed a true war footing, the anti-inflation campaign developed rapidly and dramatically.[8] Its most famous components, including price controls and rationing, were falling into place during 1941; by early 1942, such price curbs were well established. But tax experts believed that price controls were insufficient. Only by draining consumers of their new purchasing power could the nation avoid a ruinous price rise. Tax revenues had been going up for several years, thanks to a growing national income. Steeper surtaxes imposed in 1940 and 1941 had further increased receipts. But existing taxes were inadequate to the herculean task of checking inflation. "Increased income lay smoldering in millions of pockets," wrote Randolph Paul. "It was an explosive factor in the economy."[9]

Taxing Consumption

Consumption taxes were a proven revenue tool, and many observers believed that they were the best weapon against inflation. And since many were already on the books, they enjoyed a certain degree of popular acceptance. For most of the nation's history, taxes on consumption had been the principal source of federal revenue, whether levied through the tariff or various excise duties. Even after the introduction of the income tax, consumption taxes remained a key source of revenue, propping up the federal tax system when income tax receipts fell precipitously during the Great Depression. It was only natural, then, that policymakers would look to consumption taxes as a key component of the wartime revenue regime.

But which kind? While some policymakers, including those in the Treasury, wanted higher excise taxes, others called for a national sales tax.

Excise Taxes

In the spring of 1941, Assistant Treasury Secretary John L. Sullivan asked Congress for more than $1 billion in new consumption tax revenue, chiefly from various excises on consumer goods. Sullivan—after replacing the Republican stalking horse John W. Hanes in January 1940—acknowledged that most excises "fail to meet the test of equity." But Secretary Morgenthau was determined to finance two-thirds of the war with taxes, not borrowing. That ambitious goal demanded a flexible, powerful, and heterogeneous tax system. Consumption taxes were reliable and productive, making them an indispensable part of the wartime regime.[10]

Sullivan pointed out that Treasury had eschewed new taxes on necessities. Instead, the department's experts had recommended levies on luxury items, including several that were broadly popular among all income groups. Candy, chewing gum, and soft drinks might not meet the traditional definition of luxury, but they were certainly nonnecessities. As such, they could be taxed more heavily without unduly burdening low-income Americans.

All the same, Sullivan also urged lawmakers to balance new consumption taxes with a range of more progressive levies. "The importance of increasing our reliance on ability-to-pay taxes cannot be overstressed," he told lawmakers. Excise taxes should be just one component of a larger, more progressive tax system.

The Joint Committee on Internal Revenue Taxation (JCIRT) responded to the Treasury plan with an even longer list of proposed consumption taxes. Chief of Staff Colin Stam told lawmakers that ability-to-pay taxes were already bearing too much of the burden. A quick look at receipts revealed plenty of room for higher consumption taxes, he insisted. "It may be desirable," he told the Ways and Means Committee, "to shift a portion of the proposed increased tax burden from the ability to the consumption group." He added 14 excise hikes to the Treasury's list, including levies on coffee, cocoa, sugar, and other common foodstuffs. At the request of unnamed Ways and Means members, Stam also outlined a manufacturers' excise tax, much like the one considered in 1932.[11]

The Revenue Act of 1941 ultimately included some $846 million in new excise taxes. Lawmakers imposed new taxes and raised old ones. Some were specifically aimed at goods that competed with war production, including refrigerators and automobiles. Others fell on luxury items like jewelry, furs, and toiletries. A few quasi-luxuries also made the list, such as playing cards, safe deposit boxes, radios, and club dues. (Some items in this latter collection, such as safe deposit boxes, were also considered vaguely progressive, since taxing them was thought to burden affluent taxpayers.)

Alcohol taxes, as well as those on tobacco, always seemed to get an easy ride when it came to fairness debates; their status as "sin taxes" insulated them from many attacks on their equity. In 1941, lawmakers raised existing taxes on wine and distilled spirits, but not those on tobacco. Finally, even churches were asked to bear some of the new tax burden, albeit indirectly; entertainment programs offered by schools, churches, and scientific societies, once free from the admissions tax, were now made taxable.[12]

In 1942, The Treasury recommended $1.3 billion in further excise hikes, including new or higher taxes on liquor, gasoline, cigarettes, soft drinks, candy, and chewing gum. As always, the Treasury acknowledged that such taxes were regressive. But they had a few redeeming qualities, Morgenthau noted in his testimony. Several, such as the tax on gas, were levied on scarce items; these were designed as much to curb consumption as they were to raise revenue. Others fell on items that were widely consumed but clearly unnecessary: candy and chewing gum met this standard, for instance. Because demand was fairly inelastic for most of these items, the taxes would cause minimal disruption. "Needed revenue will thus be obtained, consumer purchasing power will be tapped, the producers will not be injured, and the consumers will not be taxed on the necessities of life," he said.[13] After the usual wrangling, Congress approved the Revenue Act of 1942 with more than $650 million in new excise revenue, including a major hike in liquor and tobacco taxes.[14]

In 1943, another round of excise increases continued the upward march. Morgenthau recommended $2.5 billion in new revenue from consumption taxes, targeting most of the same levies from the year before. He also offered the same rationale. Congress agreed to just $1 billion in new excise revenue, disappointing the administration with such a relatively paltry sum. In 1943, Congress raised another $1 billion from the same source.

Over the course of war, excise taxes boosted the government's bottom line quite handsomely. Consumption revenue climbed from $2.5 billion in fiscal 1941 to $6.2 billion in 1945. At the same time, however, the excise yield declined relative to other revenue streams. Producing more than 29 percent of federal revenue in fiscal 1941, excises provided just 13 percent in 1945. Newer, more productive taxes had eclipsed these venerable revenue tools.[15]

Sales Taxes

Excise levies were the most obvious means of taxing consumption, but they were not the only one. During every wartime debate over excise taxes, a controversial alternative loomed in the background: the general sales tax. Many policymakers preferred a sales tax imposed on either manufacturers or retailers. At various points in the early years of the defense program, it seemed that such a tax was destined for the books. In the spring of 1942, unhappy Treasury officials—who urgently resisted sales taxation at every turn—were resigned. Congress was simply too enamored of the idea. Newspapers were filled with speculation about when, rather than if, the sales tax would find its way into law.

Ultimately, however, President Roosevelt deflated the drive for sales taxation by taking a firm and very public stand against it. With strong support from organized labor and compelling case from his Treasury experts, FDR ensured that income taxes would become the principal levy for taxing average Americans.

In 1940, Republican members of the Ways and Means Committee had offered a grumpy prediction that sales taxes were the wave of the future. Given the New Deal's history of profligate spending, only a broad-based tax on consumption could save the country from bankruptcy, they said.[16] Over the next year, such suggestions became commonplace, and many champions of the tax believed they had victory in sight.

Advocates insisted that a sales tax would raise new money while also discouraging consumption; since these were the twin imperatives of wartime finance, what could be better suited to the task? The *Washington Post* and the *Wall Street Journal* regularly endorsed the idea, and even the *New York Times* expressed interest. While most fans of the sales tax acknowledged its regressive burden, they stressed its revenue yield and its contribution to the war on inflation.

But the Treasury was unconvinced. While the Division of Tax Research prepared several plans for a national sales tax, all were prompted by congressional requests. The division's leadership and staff were firmly and unalterably opposed to the idea. In their view, numerous alternatives were preferable, including targeted excises and a much broader income tax. Assistant Secretary Sullivan made that point emphatically during hearings on the 1941 bill. Sales taxes, he said, violated the standard of ability to pay, and on a much broader scale than selected excise duties. Just as important, the administrative cost and economic dislocation associated with a sales tax were both prohibitive. Better, he concluded, to avoid such fiscal experimentation and stick with taxes known to work.[17]

Not every member of the Ways and Means Committee accepted Sullivan's argument. Indeed, even some Democrats were toying with the idea of a sales tax. At least one took the opportunity to needle the assistant secretary. "I notice," observed Rep. Wesley Disney (D-OK), "that when you refer to taxes that you like on the list they are excise taxes, but those you frown on, they are sales taxes."[18]

The pressing need for revenue seemed to weaken the resolve of many sales tax opponents. Sen. Josiah Bailey (D-NC), opening the door just a crack, told reporters that he would endorse a general sales tax "only as a last resort." Senate Majority Leader Alben Barkley (D-KY) mused that a sales tax might be unavoidable. Even Ways and Means Chairman Robert L. Doughton (D-NC) predicted in 1940 that a sales tax was in the offing. Doughton, who had made a name for himself by leading a rebellion against the sales tax in 1932, told colleagues to expect one in 1941.[19]

Meanwhile, most business leaders kept up a steady drumbeat for the sales tax. In testimony before Congress, they repeatedly endorsed the tax as a vital revenue tool and efficient weapon against inflation. They also stressed the inequities of targeted excises. Narrow levies burdened unlucky items while leaving others unscathed. Often as not, decisions about what to tax were driven by political considerations, not any broader sense of fairness; well connected industries could avoid new taxes while less favored ones could not. The NAM encouraged lawmakers to explore the possibility of a general sales tax; their timid endorsement of the idea in 1941 stressed the need for revenue and the inadequacy of existing levies. The New York Chamber of Commerce offered a similar proposal with a similar lack of enthusiasm; the explosive potential inherent in such ideas seemed to breed caution in these and other business groups.[20]

Popular attitudes toward sales taxation were hard to gauge, but opinion polls seemed to indicate substantial support. A survey sponsored by NAM in January 1941 found 32 percent of respondents in favor of the idea. A year later, the Gallup polling organization found support among 47 percent of respondents. And in 1943, Gallup reported that fully 54 percent of Americans preferred a new sales tax to higher income levies.[21]

Congress initially resisted plans for a sales tax but by 1942, the campaign for some sort of broad-based consumption tax had reached a fever pitch. As Congress prepared to tackle the most sweeping revenue bill in the nation's history, business groups bombarded Capitol Hill with calls for a retail sales tax. Gone was the hesitancy of a year earlier. Advocates were now eager to declare their support for a new consumption tax. Most urged that it be substituted for further hikes in personal income taxes. Others justified the innovation as a replacement for the motley collection of excise taxes. Petitions and letters piled up in congressional offices, and pro-sales-tax spokesmen jammed the witness tables at committee hearings. Advocates insisted that a modest sales tax would raise enormous revenue. NAM predicted than an 8 percent tax would produce at least $4.4 billion annually. The National Retail Dry Goods Association called for a retail sales levy, pointing out that such a position was pretty noble for a bunch of storeowners.[22]

Congress seemed to be listening. Throughout the spring of 1942, press reports indicated growing support for some sort of sales tax. House and Senate leaders seemed open to the idea, while the two taxwriting committees were reported to be well along in their planning for such a tax.[23] Talk of a sales tax grew so agitated that some observers managed to convince themselves that the White House was behind it all. "A Federal sales tax is in the works," predicted *Time* magazine. "The entire body of New Deal thinking, which long opposed sales taxes as a burden on the poor, has switched completely."[24]

In fact, the Roosevelt administration was still adamantly opposed to the sales tax. From the Oval Office to the Treasury, no administration official wanted anything to do with it. Together, political leaders and technical officials marshaled a powerful campaign to discredit the idea.

Treasury experts had long insisted that general sales taxes were unfair, unnecessary, and unworkable.[25] The first quality was the most damning. When levied on consumer goods, a sales tax burdened necessities and luxuries alike. Excise taxes were easier to target at appropriate goods, ameliorating the regressive quality inherent in consumption taxation more generally. "The conflict between the Administration's declared policy of avoiding regressive taxes and the imposition of consumption taxes can be minimized by the use of taxes on specific commodities selected with this objective in view," explained one Treasury expert in

1941. "By fitting the selective tax structure to the peculiar characteristics of individual commodities, regressivity can be kept to a minimum."[26]

On April 14, 1942, Roosevelt asked the Treasury to prepare some talking points on the sales tax, with an eye toward deflecting the proposal. Roy Blough obliged him with a memo, "Evils of the Sales Tax," that stressed its inequities while also scoring the levy for its administrative burden.[27]

And while sales taxes promised to raise more revenue than selective excises, they were far less productive than many advocates suggested. "The sales tax advocates were romantics about the amount of revenue the tax would yield," remembered Randolph Paul. While ostensibly levied on all consumer expenditures, the tax actually drew from a much smaller base. Out of more than $80 billion in total annual spending during the war, Paul estimated, roughly $30 billion went to services, which were considered untaxable. An exemption for food reduced the base even further, to $30 billion. To raise $5 billion in revenue, then, lawmakers would have had to approve a tax of 17 percent—far more than even the levy's champions would support.[28]

The sales tax had a complicated relationship to inflation. Many of the levy's most ardent opponents insisted that it would raise prices dramatically. In a January 1942 speech to the General Federation of Women's Clubs, Assistant Treasury Secretary Sullivan predicted that a sales tax would undermine the anti-inflation campaign. By raising prices, it would induce a demand for higher wages. That in turn would lead to even higher prices. "I have talked to you at such length about the sales tax," he told the assembled crowd, "because I look upon it as the start of a vicious spiral of rising prices. I know that you, who are leaders of your communities, can warn every household in the country against this threat."[29]

Organized labor also opposed the sales tax, repeatedly and emphatically. In 1942, Congress of Industrial Organizations president Philip Murray denounced the idea as "shocking," calling instead for a modest expansion of the income tax and steep additional levies on wealth and business income. Murray stated his feelings in bold terms. "In peacetime a sales tax is vicious enough," he declared, "but in wartime, when we are trying to assure our war workers of sufficient funds to maintain themselves, the proposed sales tax levy would be the equivalent of a military defeat."[30]

Morgenthau spoke out passionately against the sales tax, insisting that it was an idea whose time would never come. It failed any number of tests:

> The general sales tax falls on scarce and plentiful commodities alike. It strikes at necessaries and luxuries alike. As compared with the taxes proposed in this program, it bears disproportionately on the low-income groups whose incomes are

almost wholly spent on consumer goods. It is, therefore, regressive and encroaches harmfully upon the standard of living. It increases prices and makes price control more difficult. It stimulates demands for higher wages and adds to the parity prices of agricultural products. It is not, as many suppose, easily collected; on the contrary, its collection would require much additional administrative machinery at a time when manpower is limited.[31]

But still, the pressure for sales taxation continued to grow. JCIRT experts offered several plans, and under duress, the Treasury delivered one as well. At least two Democrats on the Ways and Means Committee were sold on the idea. On the Senate Finance Committee, Sens. Arthur Vandenberg and Harry Byrd mounted a bipartisan campaign for the idea. The committee chairman reported that more than half its members were sympathetic.[32]

But Franklin Roosevelt never wavered. At various points in 1940 and 1941, he had seemed to leave the door open, just a crack. War exigencies, he suggested, made it prudent to leave all options on the table. But his refusal to disavow the idea was misleading; when the time came to declare his position, Roosevelt came out firmly against the sales tax in all its forms. Time and again, when asked by reporters to reconsider his position, the president stood firm.[33]

Administration officials were not optimistic about their ability to stop the sales tax drive. In the spring of 1942, internal memoranda from the tax research division took some sort of sales tax as a given.[34] But in fact, presidential opposition, combined with pressure from labor groups, had tipped the balance of political opinion away from the sales tax. It was a near thing, especially in the Senate Finance Committee, where the idea had real momentum. Randolph Paul later remarked that the absence of a sales tax from the Revenue Act of 1942 was one of the most striking aspects of the law. When forced to make a choice, lawmakers had lined up with the president, choosing to focus on income, not consumption taxes. It was a fateful decision, shaping the federal revenue system—and the American economy—for decades to come.[35]

"Morgenthau's Morning Glory"

While Roosevelt ultimately won his battle over sales taxation, the fight was long and hard. Congress was in a contrary mood, and administration ideas were often rejected out of hand. *Time* magazine captured the atmosphere when it described a Treasury appearance before the Finance Committee in 1942. "Henry Morgenthau and his tax experts marched up Capitol Hill and marched right down again," the magazine reported. "They came up to propose a new tax program; for all political purposes they were almost kicked downhill."[36]

Time was describing the ignoble fate of the most innovative tax proposal to come out of the wartime Treasury: a progressive spendings tax. Conceived to bridge the gap between advocates of sales and income taxation, the idea went precisely nowhere. Lawmakers dismissed it immediately, and the tax made scarcely a ripple in its own time, slipping beneath the turbulent waters of a busy legislative season.

But the spendings tax was important for several reasons. First, it demonstrated the administration's commitment to tax fairness, even when it came to taxing consumption. Second, its swift preparation reflected the Treasury's formidable capacity for research and legislative drafting—usually an advantage but in this case a distinct liability. Third, the tax, and its swift demise, underscored the growing rift between Congress and the administration.

Morgenthau offered his plan for the spendings tax on September 3, 1942, while Congress was well into its work on the huge revenue bill ultimately passed in October. His motives were twofold. First, he faced an urgent need for money. Expenditures for fiscal 1942 were expected to exceed $80 billion, while revenue projections for the 1942 act were running at only $24 billion. Second, Treasury officials were still seeking new ways to control inflation. "The Treasury," Morgenthau asserted, "is seeking in these proposals to attack the problem at its roots and to attack it drastically."[37]

The spendings tax was designed to supplement, not replace, the individual income tax. In fact, Treasury suggested that the two taxes could be administered jointly, with taxpayers filing a combined return and sending in a single payment. Individuals would calculate their total spending indirectly, subtracting savings from the total amount of available funds (including current income and reductions in capital). Savings were broadly defined to include debt repayment, life insurance premiums, purchases of capital assets, gifts and contributions, tax payments, and increases in bank balances.

Using this base, the spendings tax would then be imposed in two parts: a flat rate tax of 10 percent to be refunded after the war, and a progressive surtax. The refundable portion, which would have applied to all individuals already paying the income tax, assessed a flat tax on all spending; the proposal made no provision for any deductions, nor did it exempt any minimum level of spending. Because it was refundable, this portion of the tax amounted to a compulsory noninterest loan from the taxpayer to the government. The surtax, by contrast, was to be imposed at progressive rates ranging from 10 percent to 75 percent. All expenditures in excess of certain exemption levels would be subject to the tax. Treasury left open the possibility that various "extraordinary expenditures" might be made deductible.[38]

The Treasury proposal drew on earlier studies of spendings taxation, including proposals by economists Thomas S. Adams and Irving Fisher, not to mention a proposal by arch-Republican Ogden Mills (drafted, in large part, by Adams). Unlike some of these earlier proposals, however, the Treasury version was never conceived as a replacement for the income tax. Rather, it was viewed as a temporary device for achieving pragmatic, not theoretical, goals.[39]

Treasury officials developed the spendings tax with a close eye on its alternatives, principally a further increase in income tax rates or the enactment of a general sales tax. The spendings tax enjoyed several advantages over the former, according to Treasury studies. First, it would more effectively curtail consumer spending, making it a better weapon for fighting inflation. Second, its progressive rate structure, if sufficiently steep, might permit fairly close regulation of individual spending levels. Third, the spendings tax was thought to be more politically palatable than further extension of the income tax; because individuals had considerable discretion in determining their spending patterns, they could largely determine their own tax liability, making the spendings tax less onerous than income levies.[40]

Treasury officials also believed the spendings tax enjoyed several important advantages over a general sales tax. First, it allowed for a much more efficient means of granting personal exemptions. Second, it would be less inflationary than a sales tax. Third, it would not upset wartime price controls, then in their early stages and already under considerable strain. Sales taxes, by contrast, were thought to involve such problems, given their tendency to raise the cost of production. Finally, sales taxes were considered more administratively burdensome, demanding an entirely new collection structure, while the spendings tax would piggyback on the income tax.[41]

But what appealed most strongly to advocates of the spendings tax was its element of choice. The tax, noted Randolph Paul, would have "left the taxpayer substantial latitude and freedom." People who wanted to spend lavishly were free to do so—they would simply have to pay the price in extra taxes. If, on the other hand, an individual wanted to minimize his tax burden, then he could adjust his consumption accordingly. "Thus to a considerable extent," Paul concluded, "he would have been his own tax assessor."[42]

Following Morgenthau's brief presentation to the Finance Committee, Paul stepped in to provide the details for skeptical lawmakers. He was careful to stress the dual objectives of the new levy. "The spendings tax," he said, "will raise very substantial amounts of revenue, and will accordingly be valuable in financing the war. Even more important, it would fight inflation by reducing consumer purchasing power and providing a strong incentive to save." Paul acknowledged that the spendings tax involved new administrative burdens. He maintained, however, that its compatibility with the income tax made these burdens manageable. Moreover, he warned, "in time of war, administrative difficulties cannot be allowed to stand in the way of measures vital to the Nation's welfare."[43]

The Finance Committee was unimpressed. Members complained that the tax was too complicated, and panel members seemed miffed that Treasury would present such a big idea so late in the game. The JCIRT, moreover, had almost no role in drafting the plan, further alienating lawmakers. Treasury had developed the proposal quickly and privately—a testament to the department's administrative capacity. But with Congress increasingly jealous of its legislative prerogatives, the Treasury's impressive feat was, perhaps, just a bit *too* impressive.

The Finance Committee voted the proposal down immediately. Few outside the Treasury lamented its defeat. It had only a handful of supporters on Capitol Hill, and even the administration seemed rather lukewarm toward the idea; Roosevelt invested exactly zero political capital in it. The tax died quickly and permanently. Perhaps the best epitaph was offered by Robert C. Albright of the *Washington Post*. The spendings tax, he quipped, was "Morgenthau's morning glory. It opened Tuesday morning and it folded before noon."[44]

Taxing Income

The transformation of the individual income tax—including the expansion of its base and the increase in its rates—unfolded over several years. Lawmakers slashed exemptions repeatedly, bringing millions of new taxpayers into the system. [45] At the same time, they raised rates across the board. For many political leaders, including President Roosevelt, this was the vital moral tradeoff behind wartime taxation. New taxes on the poor and middle class had to be balanced by steep new levies on the rich. This bargain worked itself out in debates over the relative importance of consumption and income taxes. But it also shaped the structure of the income tax itself, producing a tax both broad and steep.

Once again, revenue needs were the driving force. But the levy was not simply a product of exigency and expediency. It was also the realization of thoughtful design and careful planning. The mass income tax, while deficient in any number of ways, represented a triumph for its longtime advocates in the Treasury Department.

Prewar Plans

By early 1940, defense costs were beginning their steep spiral into the stratosphere. As they debated the best means of raising money, lawmakers did not begin with a blank slate; for at least two years, Treasury officials had been pondering new revenue tools. Originally, they had been looking for ways to shrink the peacetime budget deficit. But when European developments made war more likely, Treasury officials immediately began sketching the outlines of a revenue program for national defense.

In late 1937, Treasury Undersecretary Roswell Magill asked his tax staff for a program to raise at least $500 million in new revenue. Carl Shoup delivered a brief outline, recommending higher estate taxes as well as steeper surtaxes on personal income. Notably, Shoup did not suggest higher rates on the rich. Increases in the upper brackets, he warned, might discourage investment—a sobering prospect as the nation struggled through its resurgent depression of the late 1930s. In fact, Shoup endorsed a cut for the top brackets, principally to reduce disincentives to work and investment. Lost revenue, as well as any additional revenue, should come from the lower and lower-middle brackets of the income tax. Most of these taxpayers could afford to make a larger contribution, and relative to the rich, they were substantially undertaxed.[46]

Some of Shoup's colleagues objected to this plan. George Haas, director of the soon-to-be-reorganized Division of Research and Statistics, urged that that rate hikes be spread throughout the income scale. Focusing on the lower brackets might protect the incentive to invest, but it would demand "too great a sacrifice in equity." Haas was willing to consider lower exemptions, which almost all Treasury economists had endorsed since the early 1930s. But his preference was for broad-brush rate hikes in every bracket.[47]

In 1939, the new head of tax research, Roy Blough, revisited the issue of new revenue. Like Shoup, his friend and colleague, Blough concluded that estate and income taxes were the best options. But Blough put special emphasis on the personal income tax, which had the capacity to raise enormous revenue in short order. The key, Blough said, was to make the tax broader. "The exemptions which we grant are not only substantially above the average income of people all over the country," he pointed out, "but are also substantially above what the agencies who have studied the matter consider to be a minimum budget for efficiency." Blough acknowledged that lower exemptions would be politically unpopular. But careful timing, he suggested, might delay political repercussions until after the 1940 elections.[48]

Generally speaking, Blough was a fan of broad-based income taxes with a relatively steep rate schedule. Attuned to political imperatives, he believed that high—though not punitive—rates on the rich were necessary to justify more moderate taxes on the poor and middle class. As he and Carl Shoup had pointed out in 1937, "it seems most important to make the income tax a tax that will appeal to the community's sense of justice, even at the cost of having a higher rate scale." Both Blough and Shoup had argued in 1937 that exemptions should be slashed dramatically: $1,000 for couples, $500 for individuals, and $200 for dependents. (At the time, statutory exemptions were $2,500 for couples, $1,000 for individuals, and $400 for dependents.) But they also insisted that new taxpayers in the bottom brackets pay very low rates, perhaps around 4 percent. And existing taxes currently paid by this group, most notably excise levies, should be reduced in tandem with the income tax exemptions.[49]

This program, of course, was consistent with Treasury recommendations made throughout the 1930s: it encapsulated the program of low-end progressivity. The Viner Studies had made similar suggestions in 1934, as had the revenue revision studies of 1937. But throughout the depression decade, these proposals were dead in the water. Congress had no interest in broadening the income tax, and the senior administration officials were correspondingly cool to the idea. "I personally doubt whether we can get this thing through called broadening the tax base," Morgenthau told his staff in 1938. "And I think before we do that we've got to get the fellows in my class, and that's the fellows in that big middle group."[50]

By 1939, however, Roosevelt and Morgenthau had warmed to the idea. FDR even ventured to endorse in publicly, if tepidly. The income tax should be extended "a little bit," he told reporters in June. "It wouldn't bring in much revenue, but it does give added responsibility of citizenship." Andrew Mellon couldn't have said it better.[51]

In fact, the exemption cuts then under discussion in the Treasury *would* have raised substantial revenue. But Roosevelt was eager to soft pedal the issue, if only to give Congress some room to maneuver. Observers expected the exemption cut to unleash a firestorm of protest, despite broad support among the nation's editorial writers. Roosevelt told reporters not to expect much once the idea made it to Capitol Hill.[52]

Prospects were actually better than Roosevelt knew. By the time Congress met to consider the first Revenue Act of 1940, soaring defense costs had changed the political landscape. Congress began debating a variety of tax options, including a broad-based sales tax. But the individual income tax quickly emerged as the most likely source of new money. Support for lower exemptions seemed to cut across the political spectrum; even many liberals embraced the idea.

Revenue was almost always offered as the principal justification for lower exemptions. But as the war became a reality for Americans, the notion of sacrifice also emerged as a principal justification.[53] "A part of the sacrifice means the payment of more money in taxes," Roosevelt warned in 1941.[54] Advocates of broad-based taxation insisted that everyone should share the burden of mobilization. The income tax was perhaps the nation's most famous tax, and one deeply rooted in notions of social justice. And its annual filing requirement—while not yet the ritual it would become in the latter half of the 20th century—still made a connection between the taxpayer and his government. Such a connection was absent from most consumption taxes, making the income tax a better vehicle for the expression of shared sacrifice.

Notions of sacrifice were also tied up with tax visibility. Tax experts had long contended that people should be aware of the taxes they paid. Such awareness encouraged scrutiny of public affairs and left taxpayers more attuned to the costs of democratic governance. Indeed, visibility was the foundation of the "citizenship" arguments offered by Roosevelt, Mellon, and others on behalf of broader income taxation. During the war, visibility was tied explicitly to the notion of sacrifice. As the president of the American Farm Bureau Federation suggested in 1941, "I believe the American people would support a readjustment of the income tax rates and exemptions so that every gainfully employed person would pay some tax for defense and would know that he is paying such tax."[55]

Popular opinion seemed to bolster the notion that Americans would embrace income taxes to pay for the war. Polls showed considerable support for lower exemptions, at least when framed as an emergency measure. One survey even found broad support for cutting exemptions to the federal poverty level. At the same time, however, opinion polls showed substantial tolerance for a general sales tax, leaving policymakers with ambiguous signals when it came time to choose.[56]

Amid the drive for lower exemptions, one important dissenting voice came from labor leaders. In 1939 and 1940, labor organizations objected to most plans for a broader income tax, insisting that new revenue should come from business and wealthy individuals. After the United States entered the war, labor leaders retreated somewhat from this position, but they still urged relatively small exemption cuts. Well after most liberals had abandoned the traditional conception of the income tax as a rich man's burden, labor retained a preference for steep but narrow individual taxes.[57]

Wartime Revenue Acts

In the first six months of 1940, German armies swept across Northern Europe, prompting Roosevelt to send Congress a series of military spending requests, each bigger than the last. On May 16, the president asked for $1.2 billion; on May 30, he asked for another $1.3 billion. As lawmakers cast about for ways to pay those bills, the Treasury urged a cut in income tax exemptions. "I am convinced that the public is willing and ready to accept the personal sacrifices of paying the additional taxes that are necessary to provide the country with adequate national defense," Morgenthau told Congress. In fact, unsolicited contributions had been arriving at Treasury for weeks, with Americans volunteering amounts from 10 cents to $500.[58]

The First Revenue Act of 1940 cut exemptions by a fifth; individuals were taxed on income over $800, rather than $1,000, while couples paid on anything over $2,000, rather then $2,500. Lawmakers expected the cut to create 2 million new taxpayers and to raise about $75 million.

Treasury acknowledged that the lower threshold for returns would raise enforcement costs; each return cost between 50 cents and $1.56 to process, depending on its complexity. But officials believed that lower exemptions would also boost compliance among those already liable under the higher exemptions. Jolted into awareness by the new exemption cuts, taxpayers previously on the margin of taxability would probably pay up, offsetting the $8 million in new administrative costs.[59]

The 1940 law also raised surtax rates across the board. The biggest hikes were in the lower and lower-middle brackets, just as Shoup and Blough had suggested in the late 1930s. Taxpayers earning between $6,000 and $100,000 also saw major increases. The rate hikes were expected to raise $177 million. Finally, the law imposed a special 10 percent "defense surtax" on almost every existing internal revenue levy. This "supertax" was slated to expire in five years, while the exemption cuts and regular rate hikes were permanent.[60]

The income tax revisions of the 1940 bill were surprisingly uncontroversial. Almost no one objected to the exemption cuts or the rate hikes. To be sure, business groups warned that steep surtaxes diminished the incentive to work, and labor groups complained about any broadening of the tax base. But most people swallowed hard and accepted the heavier taxes with minimal complaint.

In 1941, things got more contentious. House lawmakers recommended another round of rate hikes. They did not, however, propose a further cut in exemptions. In April, Treasury officials had testified that exemptions were already low enough; individuals earning as little as $17 a week were paying the income tax. Republicans had needled the Roosevelt administration on this point, asking if civilians were sacrificing as much as military personnel. But Assistant Secretary Sullivan defended existing exemptions as a matter of fairness and practicality.[61]

The president, however, had other ideas. On July 31, he wrote Robert Doughton to endorse new, lower exemptions: $750 for individuals and $1,500 for couples. While revenue needs certainly prompted FDR's request, he again offered a moral, not an economic, argument for the broader tax. "I am convinced that the overwhelming majority of our citizens want to contribute something directly to our defense and that most of them would rather do it with their eyes open than do it through a general sales tax or through a multiplication of what we have known as 'nuisance taxes'."[62]

Irritated by the president's interference, Doughton rejected the request. But the Senate was more compliant, especially after Morgenthau caught up with Roosevelt's recommendation. Echoing his boss, the secretary predicted that Americans would welcome a broader tax. "It would enable them to feel that they were participating personally and directly in the defense program," he said. The Senate agreed, lowering exemptions to Roosevelt's specifications. House lawmakers accepted the move, and experts predicted that 5 million new returns would arrive at the Treasury the next year. More than 2 million would show taxable income. The 1941 revenue act also hiked rates across the board; they now topped out at 77 percent on incomes over $5 million.[63]

In March 1942, Morgenthau offered Congress a blueprint for tax hikes on an even larger, unprecedented scale. "Our task is more than the raising of a huge amount of new revenue," he told lawmakers. "It is to make the tax program an instrument of victory." Congress agreed, crafting a dramatic and far-reaching bill. Roosevelt later called the Revenue Act of 1942 "the greatest tax bill in American history," and the description may still be apt more than 60 years later. This sweeping measure is often credited with the creation of the modern U.S. tax regime. While it shares that distinction with several other pieces of wartime legislation, it was certainly the most important tax law of the war.

Initially, Morgenthau declined to recommend further exemption cuts, insisting that Americans making less than $15 a week were already heavily burdened (especially given the range of wartime excise taxes). Moreover, people exempt from the income tax were not a threat to price stability: "Their buying habits are governed strictly by the need of maintaining nutrition and health." The secretary did, however, suggest a series of rate hikes for the income tax, ranging from less than 0.5 percent in the bottom bracket to more than 16 percent in the middle and upper reaches of the levy.[64]

Roosevelt's newfound ardor for civic sacrifice and tax visibility, however, was not yet exhausted. On May 6, Morgenthau reluctantly suggested that exemptions be cut to $600 for individuals, $1,200 for couples, and $300 for dependents. The reductions would raise about $1 billion in new revenue and add about 7 million taxpayers to the rolls. Inflation worries lay behind some of these changes. "Prices were surging against their controls with the force of an angry sea," recalled Randolph Paul.[65] Leon Henderson told lawmakers that steep new taxes were absolutely vital if the country were to avoid ruinous inflation in the next year. Treasury experts agreed, urging Morgenthau to demand huge new hikes.[66]

But then Roosevelt caught his experts by surprise, yet again. In April, he proposed an apparently draconian measure to cap personal income.

"In time of this great national danger," he declared on April 27, "when all excess income should go to win the war, no American citizen ought to have a net income, after he has paid his taxes, of more than $25,000 a year."[67] The suggestion caused a brief firestorm of protest in the press, but it soon disappeared from serious discussion. Nonetheless, it demonstrated the president's commitment to steep taxes on the rich. Roosevelt was still a fan of high-end progressivity, especially after wartime imperatives forced heavy taxes on the poor.[68]

The Victory Tax

As House and Senate lawmakers debated Treasury recommendations in 1942, they put their own stamp on the revenue bill. Perhaps their most important contribution was the Victory Tax, a short-lived income levy that nonetheless played a key role in the development of the modern tax regime.[69]

Lawmakers conceived of the Victory Tax principally as a revenue device, but its legislative odyssey hinged on its role in fighting inflation. The tax, according to its champions, would bolster the regular income levy by taxing Americans near the bottom of the income scale. Levied as a flat 5 percent tax on "Victory Tax net income," it allowed an exemption of just $624. While regular income tax exemptions were also headed down in 1942, the Victory Tax allowed fewer deductions from gross income, making it effective at much lower incomes. According to contemporary estimates, the tax would fall on 13 million new taxpayers.[70]

The Victory Tax was most notable, however, for an innovation it brought to the federal tax system: withholding. The tax was deducted directly from both salaries and wages, ensuring that taxpayers would remain current with their obligations. Current collection gave Treasury quick access to new revenue. It also helped restrain inflation by reducing discretionary income before it ever reached a consumer's pocket.

A second innovation, even more fleeting than the Victory Tax itself, was compulsory lending. The Treasury had been studying this means of inflation control for months, and the corporate excess profits tax actually included a refundable component similar to a compulsory loan. In general, compulsory loans were taxes collected during the war that were slated for repayment—either with or without interest—once peace returned. The Victory Tax provided for a partial rebate of its 5 percent levy, effectively reducing the rate for most taxpayers to 3.75 percent for single persons and 3 percent for married couples.[71] Treasury decided in 1944, however, that taxpayers should take the credit currently, thereby obviating a need for postwar refunds—and ending the experiment in compulsory lending before it even began.

In general, Treasury was never a fan of the Victory Tax, complaining that it was complicated and regressive.[72] But Congress liked the tax, largely because it raised a lot of money. And while the tax was regressive, it was consistent with a growing congressional fondness for shifting elements of the tax burden down the income scale. Rates for the personal income tax were already very high, reaching 82 percent in the 1942 bill. The excess profits tax was now levied at a flat 90 percent. There was, of course, still room for new taxes on the rich and corporate taxpayers. But lawmakers believed that taxes at the bottom of the income scale were a better choice. Not only would they raise important revenue, but they would also help thwart inflation.[73]

Other Provisions of the 1942 Bill

The Victory Tax was only one of several objectionable features that lawmakers forced on the Roosevelt administration during preparation of the Revenue Act of 1942. In January, barely a month after the attack on Pearl Harbor, Roosevelt had asked for $50 billion to $60 billion in defense spending. By October, he had revised the figure upward to $76 billion. In March, Morgenthau asked Congress for $7.6 billion in new revenue to help support this massive spending request; later requests pushed the figure to almost $15 billion. Ultimately, however, Congress agreed to provide just under $7 billion: less than the March request and far less than the administration had been seeking in the months since.

The act cut exemptions to $1,200, $500, and $350 for couples, individuals, and dependents, respectively. The "normal" tax increased from 4 percent to 6 percent, and surtaxes went up in every bracket. The first surtax rate more than doubled from 6 percent to 13 percent. But at the peak of the income scale, the changes were even more dramatic. The top rate climbed from 77 percent to 82 percent. Even more important, however, the brackets were readjusted to make this top rate applicable to a much larger percentage of national income. Under the 1941 law, the top rate kicked in at $5 million in annual income. But in 1942, the new higher rate started at just $200,000. A single taxpayer earning $1 million would see her tax climb from $655,139 to $809,995 (after accounting for the Victory

Tax). A married couple with the same income would see a similar hike. Clearly, rich Americans were being asked to pay handsomely.[74]

Taken as a whole, the Revenue Act of 1942 was most notable for its emphasis on broad-based but very progressive income taxation. The law did not include a new national sales tax, despite strong support among lawmakers for such a levy. Instead, Roosevelt won the battle to make personal income taxes the foundation of wartime finance.

The Plan That Slogans Built

In 1943, Congress passed the Current Tax Payment Act, requiring taxpayers to stay current on their tax liability through a vast new withholding system applied to wages and salaries. The law represented a victory of sorts for the Treasury Department, where tax officials had been promoting current collection for years. Success, however, was a near thing, and it came at a steep price. Administration officials were forced to accept a tax forgiveness plan—championed by one of America's leading businessmen—that gave a windfall to rich taxpayers.

By 1943, withholding was already an old idea. During the Civil War, Congress had incorporated withholding into the fledgling—and fleeting—federal income tax. Later, during the early years of the 20th century, Congress again turned to withholding as it tried to craft a permanent federal income tax. (Withholding provisions were soon dropped from law, however, when administrative difficulties started to emerge.)

Policymakers of the World War II era had even more recent precedent for the advantages of withholding. In the years just before the United States entered the war, official Washington watched approvingly as new Social Security taxes were collected directly from wages and salaries. In impressive fashion, and without the use of computers, the Bureau of Old-Age Benefits managed to process over 312 million wage reports by mid-1940, posting more than 99 percent of them to 50 million employee accounts.[75]

Faced, then, with World War II's staggering revenue demands, tax officials saw withholding as a vital component of the new, vastly expanded federal income tax. Despite opposition from the BIR (whose leaders never seemed to encounter an innovation they actually liked) Treasury officials began agitating for the reintroduction of withholding. The idea, they insisted, was administratively feasible and economically crucial.[76]

Treasury officials believed that withholding was necessary if the federal income tax were to function effectively as a mass tax. Before wartime revenue needs forced Congress to add millions of new taxpayers to the tax rolls, the income tax could be administered without withholding. But with millions of new taxpayers, the system needed some mechanism of current collection, and withholding seemed the most promising. "The 39 million individual taxpayers required to pay income taxes of almost $10 billion for 1942 under the present law must be afforded a way of meeting their tax obligations with a maximum of convenience and a minimum of hardship," Randolph Paul told Congress.[77]

Officials had already begun a massive public relations campaign to advise new taxpayers of their fiscal responsibilities. In a multimedia campaign featuring posters, radio announcements, popular songs, and even a Donald Duck cartoon, Treasury drove home the filing requirements established by the new income tax laws. Officials stressed that millions of previously exempt Americans were now required to file annual returns.[78]

Treasury also argued that withholding would aid in the wartime battle against inflation. Withholding would withdraw more purchasing power more quickly from the economy, helping restrain the upward pressure on prices. Indeed, withholding could help transform the federal income tax into a potent tool for managing the nation's economy, allowing officials to regulate fiscal stimuli with enormous new flexibility.[79]

In November 1941, Morgenthau had presented a withholding plan to the House Ways and Means Committee, suggesting that new taxes should be collected at the source from wages, salaries, interest, and dividends. A wary committee deferred his idea. The following March, Morgenthau tried again, and this time, lawmakers were more receptive. Ignoring protests from the commissioner of Internal Revenue—who insisted that the innovation would be expensive and labor intensive—legislators added withholding to the House version of the 1942 revenue bill. Senators were not yet ready, however, and the provision was dropped from the final bill.

But withholding wasn't dead yet. The final version of the Revenue Act of 1942 had included withholding for the new Victory Tax. With that foot in the door, Treasury continued pressing the idea, arguing that Congress should extend this technique to the regular income tax. Roosevelt, too, lobbied for collection at the source, suggesting repeatedly in early 1943 that the income tax be put on a "pay-as-you-go" basis, a change that more or less required a withholding mechanism.[80] Such a system would keep taxpayers current, Roosevelt said, instead of allowing them to pay their taxes the year after they had incurred their tax liabilities.

Despite their rejection in 1942, current collection and withholding enjoyed considerable support on Capitol Hill. The BIR remained intransigent, complaining to Congress that withholding would be administratively burdensome and fundamentally unworkable given wartime personnel shortages. Randolph Paul, Treasury's general counsel and point man on tax matters, greeted the commissioner's statements unhappily. "It would be a masterpiece of understatement," he later wrote, "to say that these pronouncements, never submitted in advance by the Commissioner to the Treasury, were extremely embarrassing."[81]

Despite his best efforts, BIR commissioner Guy Helvering was unable to derail the drive for withholding. Only one serious obstacle remained: transition. Simply dropping withholding into the existing system would have required taxpayers to spend at least one year making "double" income tax payments. Under existing law, every taxpayer was expected to save enough money over the course of the year to cover his liability when it came due early in the next calendar year. If pay-as-you-go withholding were superimposed upon this system, then taxpayers would be further required to make simultaneous payments on their current liability.

Some observers saw nothing wrong with doubling up on tax payments during the transition year. The result was not really "double" taxation, they contended, since the lump sum payment and the current payments applied to income received during different years. If taxpayers had been vigilant in their saving, they should have had enough money to pay the past year's liability, leaving them enough room in their paycheck for payments on the current year.

In fact, however, many taxpayers did not set aside enough money for their tax payments, making double payments a problematic cash-flow reality. Consequently, almost all policymakers agreed that some sort of transition relief would be necessary. Among the various possibilities floated by lawmakers and lobbyists, most involved the forgiveness of some or all tax liability for the year preceding the introduction of withholding.

Treasury tax officials acknowledged the transition problem, and they set to work on a solution. They refused to consider any blanket forgiveness of 1942 tax liability, arguing that it would disproportionately benefit the nation's richest taxpayers.[82] Similarly, they opposed "doubling up" since it, too, would favor rich taxpayers with savings adequate to pay additional taxes without hardship. Partial forgiveness or postponement of 1942 taxes were the only viable alternatives.

As Treasury officials mulled the options, a powerful challenge emerged from the private sector. For several years, Beardsley Ruml, chairman of the New York Federal Reserve Bank and treasurer of R. H. Macy and Company, had been campaigning for current collection, calling it a "simple" change of tax basis from the past year's income to the current one. Effectively, Ruml was calling for a full year's tax forgiveness. Ruml pointed out that the Treasury would see no reduction in cash flow. "As far as the Treasury and income were concerned, things would move along just the same as time moves on under daylight saving," Ruml contended.[83]

Taxpayers immediately embraced the "Ruml plan." Popular speculation began to grow in late 1942 that Congress would pass legislation relieving all taxpayers of the need to pay their 1942 taxes. Treasury officials worried that people would be unprepared for the grim reality. House and Senate leaders issued a public statement reminding citizens that payment was still expected by March 15, covering at least the first quarterly installment of tax against 1942 income.

Meanwhile, Roosevelt rejected the Ruml plan out of hand: "I cannot acquiesce in the elimination of a whole year's tax burden on the upper-income groups during a war period when I must call for an increase in taxes and savings from the mass of our people," he declared. Treasury officials echoed Roosevelt's point, arguing that forgiveness "would bestow the greatest benefit on those best able to pay and the smallest benefit on those least able to pay."[84]

Congress and the administration agreed that resolution of the withholding issue was vital to the nation's economic health. Treasury officials restated their support for current collection, stressing the administrative need for such a system. But they also stressed their opposition to a full year's tax forgiveness. While acknowledging that revenue flows would be uninterrupted, they insisted that forgiveness was unfair. In its stead, they proposed a scheme of deferred payments, under which taxpayers would be required to pay at least a large percentage of their 1942 tax liabilities but would be allowed several years in which to do so.

Ruml weighed in against the Treasury plan, arguing that the government could forgive a full year's taxes without unduly burdening itself. The asset loss incurred by tax forgiveness would only be evident when examining the Treasury's position on Judgment Day. At that point, millions of

Americans would die owing the government money. "These would be bad debts in any case," Ruml observed wryly, so the government had nothing to lose.[85] While Ruml's original plan did not include provisions for withholding, he now added it to the list of reasons for supporting his plan. Collection at source, he declared, was fully consistent with his forgiveness plan.

The House Ways and Means Committee rejected the bulk of Ruml's argument, with Democratic members insisting that forgiveness was little more than a windfall for the rich. The full House, however, was more sympathetic, and the Ruml plan continued to surface in floor votes. The final bill emerging from the House embodied a modified forgiveness plan directing most benefits to taxpayers in the first income bracket.

The Senate Finance Committee, for its part, adopted the Ruml plan and its full-year forgiveness. Supporters and opponents of the Ruml plan raised the rhetoric to a fever pitch. Questions of sacrifice took center stage, with opponents of forgiveness arguing that Congress should not be delivering a windfall to rich Americans in the midst of national emergency. Sen. Homer T. Bone (D-WA) made the point emphatically:

> If I could abate any of the blood and tears and agony of the boys dying on the battlefields, if I could abate one little bit of the horror facing young men marching under the American flag into this world conflict, I would abate the horror coming to them, rather than abate a year's taxes for us who stay at home. I wish I could vote to abate blindness and insanity and vote away the blasting of boys' lives by shells on the battle fronts. But we cannot do that. All we can do is abate the tax on some fellow's income. The whole thing represents a grotesque twist of logic. It is a sort of madness.[86]

Such sentiment notwithstanding, a majority of the Senate remained persuaded of the Ruml plan's virtues. The bill went to conference with the forgiveness measures intact.

As the conference began, House and Senate leaders remained firmly at odds, the former digging in their heels against "excessive" forgiveness. Additionally, the issue had taken a distinctly partisan tone, with Republicans generally favoring the Ruml plan and Democrats denouncing it. Roosevelt wrote congressional leaders to emphasize his strong support for pay-as-you-go legislation and renew his strenuous objection to full-year forgiveness. Excessive forgiveness, he asserted, "would result in a highly inequitable distribution of the cost of the war and in an unjust and discriminatory enrichment of thousands of taxpayers in the upper-income groups."[87]

In fact, Roosevelt was well aware of those taxpayers who stood to benefit. In March, he had asked Treasury to draw up a list of taxpayers likely to reap the greatest benefits; "no names, of course," he added. The Treasury responded with a memo listing the 100 largest federal taxpayers—by name—along with their projected savings under the Ruml plan. The memo read like a roster of Roosevelt's staunchest opponents, although it also included a variety of celebrities and even the odd Democrat.[88]

After lengthy delay, the conference deadlock ended when Robert Doughton changed his vote, allowing a compromise bill to emerge. The final version of the bill included a substantial tax forgiveness—less than Ruml had sought, but considerably more than Treasury wanted. The Current Tax Payment Act of 1943 provided for current payment of all individual income tax liabilities and the cancellation of 75 percent of one year's existing taxes (the lower of either the 1942 or 1943 tax liability). Unforgiven liabilities were payable in two installments, one on March 15, 1944, and the other on March 15, 1945.

The introduction of withholding and the debate over the Ruml plan are significant for two reasons. First, they reveal the extent to which Roosevelt and his administration were willing to fight for tax fairness. The president and his tax specialists consistently opposed complete forgiveness, complaining that it would provide a windfall to the nation's wealthy. FDR's request for a list of rich taxpayers was consistent with his long-standing tendency to personalize abstract issues of tax justice. He always viewed tax issues in terms of winners and losers, and more often than not, he was willing to identify them. (Although in this case, discretion seems to have won out.)

Second, withholding changed the income tax forever. It made the levy more responsive and flexible, both reflecting and facilitating its conversion into a powerful tool of macroeconomic regulation. Moreover, as one legal historian has pointed out, it helped create a taxpaying culture, getting Americans comfortable with regular deductions from their paychecks. No small feat in an era when such deductions were all but unknown.[89]

Conclusion

In his noted study of federal taxation, political scientist John Witte describes the income tax revisions of World War II as "a series of incremental adjustments to existing policies."[90] Perhaps. But that's like telling the man at the end of a gangplank that his next step is just like any other: some increments are more important than others. The exemption cuts of World War II totaled just $500 for individuals, but they transformed the nature of the American state and society. Similarly, the rate changes, while often simply a matter of adjusting numbers in a table, were enormously important to the taxpayers who suddenly found themselves with marginal tax rates over 90 percent.

In many vital respects, the wartime tax regime broke with the history of New Deal revenue reform. Almost overnight, the income tax had "changed its morning coat for overalls."[91] Millions of middle-class Americans—long familiar with federal excise taxes but unaccustomed to paying direct levies—joined the tax rolls for the first time.

But if this change marked a departure from Democratic orthodoxy and its soak-the-rich ideology, it marked a victory for a different sort of progressive tax reform. The mass income tax of World War II represented a compromise between the New Deal's competing visions of progressive tax reform. On the one hand, its high rates reflected the traditional Democratic penchant for soaking the rich. This vision of progressive reform had found its purest expression in the great New Deal tax reforms of the mid-1930s, and its most energetic champions among the New Deal lawyers who guided tax policy during those years.

At the same time, the broad base of wartime income taxation derived from a second strand of New Deal thinking that emphasized the redistributional possibilities of a mass-based income tax. During the 1930s, Treasury economists had advanced proposals for such an income tax, arguing that it could be used to finance a rollback in regressive excise taxes. Neither element of this proposal was viable during the depression, as politics doomed the broader income tax and revenue needs quieted calls for excise tax reform. The war resolved political obstacles to broad-based income taxation, but revenue needs still precluded excise cuts. The creation of a mass income tax, however, paved the way for postwar reforms that *would* include such cuts.

10

Consolidation of the Wartime Regime

T he fiscal watershed of World War II was complete by the middle of 1944. Its capstone, the Revenue Act of 1943, was marked by tremendous acrimony, culminating in a veto battle between the White House and Congress. Indeed, the struggle over tax policy in late 1943 and early 1944 brought an end to the Roosevelt tax agenda. After years of restive complaint, lawmakers moved decisively to reject presidential leadership. In doing so, they marked the end of the old regime and the beginning of a new one. Congress would dominate this new era, taking the lead on most tax issues for at least the next forty years.

Even as the veto battle marked the end of Roosevelt's personal ascendancy in the fiscal realm, it also signaled the durability of the New Deal tax regime. The 1943 argument over loopholes revealed a policymaking dynamic that would support the regime—and the personal income tax in particular—for decades to come. Loopholes were the lynchpin of this dynamic, fastening taxpayers to their tax system and securing its political viability. But the regime also drew sustenance from the New Deal's political reconstruction of tax fairness, including a heavy emphasis on taxing the rich.

"Relief Not for the Needy but for the Greedy"

In late 1943, Henry Morgenthau asked Congress for another tax increase to provide $10.4 billion in new war funding. That figure included $6.5 billion from the individual income tax, $400 million in estate and gift taxes, $1 billion in new corporate taxes, and $2.5 billion in excise tax increases.[1] Morgenthau justified the hikes by underscoring the danger of inflation. "Nothing in the economic field can interfere with the war effort as much as an uncontrolled rise in prices," he told the House Ways and Means Committee. "An inflationary price rise is a source of grave social injustice," he said, as well as economic turmoil.[2]

Congressional taxwriters didn't want to hear such language, and they gave Morgenthau's package a chilly reception. Lawmakers fell on the plans "like Caesar's assassins," recalled one observer.[3] Increases for income and estate taxes took much of the heat, but so, too, did Morgenthau's suggestion that Congress repeal the Victory Tax, chiefly as a simplification measure. Repeal would have removed 9 million low-income taxpayers from the rolls, but congressional leaders found little to like in that prospect—or any other aspect of the administration's plan. "Almost before the Secretary had finished reading his prepared statement," reported *Time* magazine, "the U.S. Treasury's design for extracting another $10,500,000,000.00 from the U.S. pocketbook was mackerel-dead."[4]

Various administration officials echoed Morgenthau's call for higher taxes. Federal Reserve Chairman Marriner Eccles asked for even bigger numbers: $13.8 billion, including $4 billion in taxes that would be refundable after the war. Ways and Means Chairman Robert L. Doughton (D-NC) dismissed the higher figure out of hand. "Amazing, fantastic, and visionary. I don't like it at all. If possible, it is worse than the Treasury program," he declared.[5]

Ways and Means went to work on its own bill, which the House passed on November 24. The legislation bore little resemblance to the Treasury plan. Committee members argued that the need for new taxes had been diminished by revenue already in the pipeline. Coupled with promised reductions in nonmilitary sending, existing taxes would be nearly adequate. As for inflation, the panel declared that it could be controlled through discretionary spending cuts, effective price controls, rationing, and wage limits. Higher taxes were unnecessary.[6]

The Ways and Means Committee specifically opposed corporate tax increases. "It is vitally important that our corporations be kept in sound financial condition so that they may be able to convert to peacetime production and provide employment for men leaving the armed forces after the war," the lawmakers declared. In fact, complaints about corporate tax burdens were on the upswing by 1943, and by 1944, cuts seemed almost inevitable.[7]

New revenue in the Ways and Means bill came from several sources, including repeal of the earned income credit and a new minimum levy for the Victory Tax. Both provisions targeted low-income taxpayers. Excises provided another $1.2 billion, with much of the revenue coming from a 50 percent liquor tax hike—yet another blow to Americans of modest means. The bill reduced the invested-capital credit for large corporations, but increased the exemption for the excess profits tax from $5,000 to $10,000. Rates for the excess profits tax went from 90 to 95 percent. Postal rate hikes added a little more money, bringing the bill's total to about $2 billion—less than a fifth of the administration's request.

The House bill had its own problems in the public arena, eliciting a cool response from both Roosevelt and the press. Editorials across the country denounced the bill as inadequate. Meanwhile, Morgenthau tried to make up lost ground by working closely with the Senate Finance Committee. While eager to placate conservatives uneasy with the administration's penchant for heavy estate and income taxes, the secretary urged lawmakers to go easy on the little guy, too. The bill coming from the House already drew more than 50 percent of its revenue from people making less than $5,000, he pointed out.

Senators were unmoved. People earning less than $5,000 might be paying half the new taxes, but they also received four-fifths of the nation's income, critics pointed out. If the administration was serious about fighting inflation, then low- and middle-income Americans would have to shoulder a bigger share of the tax burden. "The principal Congressional objection to the Treasury plan," reported the *New York Times,* "has centered on the Administration's apparent unwillingness to increase taxes on low incomes."[8]

The Finance Committee endorsed the general approach of the House bill and opposed most additional increases. The panel tinkered with the Victory Tax and put off a long-planned increase in the Social Security payroll tax. The Senate passed the Finance bill, and the legislation emerging from a House-Senate conference closely resembled the preferences of the upper house. Congress sent the bill to the president in February 1944. And on February 22, Roosevelt vetoed it.

In explaining the veto, FDR cited its inadequate revenue yield. But the most serious flaw, he insisted, was its tendency to compromise sound tax policy for the sake of political expedience. Riddled with numerous loopholes and giveaways, the law was a travesty. "In this respect," the president complained, "it is not a tax bill but a tax relief bill providing relief not for the needy but for the greedy."[9]

To begin with, Roosevelt objected to the elimination of planned increases in the Social Security tax, a move that ensured a substantial drop in anticipated revenue. But he particularly scored a variety of provisions offering "indefensible special privileges to favored groups." Those privileges set a bad precedent, even threatening the viability of the tax system. By degrading fairness, they undermined the political consensus so fundamental to wartime tax policy.[10]

Roosevelt noted that some of his advisers wanted him to sign the bill, arguing that having asked for a loaf of bread, he should be content with a small piece of crust. "I might have done so if I had not noted that the small piece of crust contained so many extraneous and inedible materials," Roosevelt said.

The president went on to criticize Congress for enacting complex tax laws, indicting lawmakers for complexities plaguing the Victory Tax. "The Nation will readily understand that it is not the fault of the Treasury Department that the income taxpayers are flooded with forms to fill out which are so complex that even Certified Public Accountants cannot interpret them. No, it is squarely the fault of the Congress of the United States in using language in drafting the law which not even a dictionary or a thesaurus can make clear." Taxpayers need simplification, Roosevelt stressed. "These taxpayers, now engaged in an effort to win the greatest war this Nation has ever faced, are not in a mood to study higher mathematics."[11]

Roosevelt's caustic veto message enraged legislators. Doughton declared his intention to seek an immediate override, and 19 of his committee's 25 members signed a public letter denouncing the Treasury's original plan. Finance Committee Chairman Walter George (D-GA) warned that the nation needed tax reduction. Policymakers, he said, should not "cut down the tree in order to get the fruit." Most important, however, was the reaction of Senate Majority Leader Alben Barkley (D-KY). The day after the veto, he resigned his leadership post in protest. The veto, he declared on the Senate floor, was "a calculated and deliberate assault upon the legislative integrity of every member of Congress." Congress had a simple choice, he said: override the veto or surrender the legislature's role in the tax policy process.[12]

Roosevelt tried to calm things down, asking Barkley to rethink his decision. He also pointed out that Barkley had seen large sections of the veto message before it was released, making the senator's public display of surprise something of a surprise in itself. But Barkley followed through with his resignation, only to have his Senate colleagues immediately reelect him to the same post. The charade made headlines, underscoring Roosevelt's predicament.[13] Within a week of FDR's veto, Congress easily mustered the votes for an override.

As enacted, the 1943 revenue act failed to satisfy the twin imperatives of World War II tax policy: raising revenue and controlling inflation.[14] It succeeded, however, in allowing legislators to duck the responsibilities of wartime policymaking, and it even made room for a few special favors.

In vetoing the 1943 revenue bill, Roosevelt made history: it was the first veto of a tax bill in America. Ironically, this display of presidential power served to underscore the administration's growing weakness when it came to tax policy. Congress summarily dispatched the president's objections, establishing its primacy in the tax process. Lawmakers actually seemed to welcome the veto, since it gave them a chance to flex their muscles. As political observer Samuel Lubell later pointed out, Congress was "less concerned with the merits of its tax position than with showing Roosevelt who was boss."[15]

The Revenue Act of 1943 was a sign of things to come. The congressional penchant for handing out tax preferences would soon become a hallmark of postwar tax legislation. And while presidents of both parties— as well as a few key legislators—would continue to fight for the fisc, it was a sisyphean struggle. The modern income tax would be riddled with loopholes. Indeed, the steep progressive rate structure made this almost inevitable, raising the stakes for almost all taxpayers and making every tax preference more valuable.[16]

The Importance of Wartime Taxation

The 1943 revenue act was the last important tax law of the war. As the end of hostilities drew near, the tax system looked radically different than its prewar predecessor. Not only had the total amount of federal revenue increased more than sevenfold, but the composition of receipts had changed dramatically. Corporation taxes had grown substantially, their share of the total jumping from 18.3 percent in fiscal year 1940 to 35.4 percent in 1945; the excess profits tax accounted for most of this increase. Even more striking, the individual income tax, which provided just 13.6 percent of total revenue in 1940, ended the war supplying roughly 40 percent. Meanwhile, excise taxes, long a staple of American public finance, had declined dramatically from 30.2 percent to just 13.9 percent.[17]

Contemporary observers believed that steep wartime taxes had helped secure the nation's economic future. Most obviously, they had paid for a large share of the war's cost. During the last two years of fighting, tax receipts covered more than half of war expenditures. At the same time, they represented roughly half the nation's total domestic product. Such numbers described a massive transformation of the economy, but at the same time, they seemed to herald a bright economic future.

Which is not to say that policymakers were sanguine about the prospect of reconversion. Indeed, they fretted endlessly about postwar recession, inflation, and any number of other unpalatable possibilities. But wartime taxation was not the source of their fears. And in many respects, they recognized that the emergency fiscal regime had allowed the nation to escape ruinous inflation and a crushing war-borne debt.[18]

Success in the battle against inflation was most striking. In fact, the war opened a new chapter in the history of American fiscal policy, inaugurating the era of modern Keynesianism and granting tax policy a central role in macroeconomic regulation. As Herbert Stein has pointed out, stimulatory fiscal policy in the 1930s generally focused on spending; efforts to fight the depression rarely involved tax reductions, in part because Roosevelt believed such cuts to disproportionately benefit the rich. Just as important, most economists believed that rich taxpayers were disproportionately inclined to save; any increase in their after-tax income was unlikely to make its way back into the economy through increased spending.[19]

The war had changed this narrow view of fiscal policy, demonstrating that taxation could have an important effect on prices. By war's end, policymakers recognized that taxes had an important regulatory role to play, checking inflation when times were good and promoting prosperity when things looked bleak. Keynesian, countercyclical fiscal policy now had room for taxes. And the mass income tax—defined by its heavy focus on the middle class and its flexible system of current collection through withholding—suited the tax system to an active role in managing the economy; policymakers could raise and lower consumer demand with relative ease, at least when compared to the prewar period.[20]

Postwar Tax Reduction

As World War II drew to a close, American political leaders of almost every stripe agreed that taxes were too high. The Individual Income Tax Act of 1944 had taken the first tentative steps toward postwar tax reduction by simplifying the individual tax, especially for low-income taxpayers.[21] The next year, the Revenue Act of 1945 took more decisive action, slashing tax liabilities for calendar year 1946 by some $5.9 billion, or roughly 13 percent of total federal revenue. The act repealed the corporate excess profits tax and reduced income tax rates for both individuals and businesses. Lawmakers left most excise taxes at their wartime peaks, but they agreed to postpone a scheduled increase in the Social Security payroll tax.[22]

Contemporary observers regarded the 1945 act as a quick and dirty affair, designed to cut taxes swiftly while avoiding controversial issues. For instance, the law did not resolve long-standing questions about the taxation of corporate income. Tax experts had hoped to sort out, once and for all, whether profits should be taxed at both the entity and the shareholder levels. Some even longed to revisit the notion of an undistributed profits tax, chiefly as a means to curtail tax avoidance. But as it happened, the generosity of the 1945 law pushed those issues to the bottom of the tax agenda. Having already handed out a range of probusiness tax cuts, lawmakers were loath to consider further reform.[23]

For individuals, the 1945 act did not seem likely to preclude further relief. Carl Shoup urged lawmakers to give special attention to taxes on the rich. Extremely high rates had encouraged a proliferation of loopholes, which in turn allowed lawmakers to sidestep nettlesome questions of distributional equity. It was a dangerous game, Shoup warned: "equity issues cannot be consistently ignored without shaking the morale of those who are disadvantaged and rotting the morale of those who are favored, with incalculable consequences for the long-term future of the whole tax system."[24]

The Campaign for Tax Cuts

The Revenue Act of 1945 was the largest single tax cut enacted between 1940 and 1968.[25] By comparison, the Revenue Act of 1948 was almost 30 percent smaller when measured as a share of gross domestic product. When gauged by degree of controversy, however, the 1948 tax cut outstripped the 1945 law by a wide margin. In the three years between the two bills, bipartisan comity on tax reduction evaporated. Republicans reclaimed their heritage as inveterate tax cutters, and President Harry Truman pledged his troth to the ideal of a balanced budget.

It's not that Truman opposed further tax cuts in the wake of the 1945 law. Indeed, he considered the reductions almost inevitable, given the conversion from a wartime to a peacetime economy. But he differed fundamentally with many lawmakers on Capitol Hill when it came to the timing of cuts. Truman insisted that taxes should be cut after spending had been reduced, not before. As he later recalled in his memoirs, "There is nothing sacred about the pay-as-you-go idea so far as I am concerned except that it represents the soundest principle of financing that I know."[26]

By spring 1946 Truman had staked out his position. Stressing the need to control inflation, he laid claim to the mantle of fiscal probity. "It is the aim of our fiscal policy to balance the budget for 1947 and to retire national debt in boom times such as these," he said when releasing his budget projections. "In our present fight against inflation, fiscal policy has a vital role to play. A continuation of our present policy, which is to maintain the existing tax structure for the present, and to avoid nonessential expenditures, is the best fiscal contribution we can make to economic stability."[27] A projected deficit of $1.9 billion in fiscal 1947 bolstered Truman's argument.

Republicans tried to turn Truman's fiscal responsibility to their own advantage. By summer 1946 they had seized on the president's pledge to retain existing tax levels and made it a cornerstone of their campaign to win control of Congress. In July the ranking minority member of the House Ways and Means Committee, Rep. Harold Knutson, promised to cut income taxes by 20 percent if Republicans won control of the House. Congress could pay for it with a 50 percent reduction in spending, he said, and GOP appropriators backed him up.[28]

If Truman was intimidated by those promises, he showed no sign of it in public. Indeed, just a few days after Republicans declared their intention to seek sweeping tax cuts, Truman warned that tax increases might be in the offing. Rising prices threatened to unleash an inflationary spiral, he told Congress in a special message. If spending restraint and other anti-inflation measures proved insufficient, then tax increases might be unavoidable. "Such a tax program would, I realize, be unpalatable at a time when we are doing our utmost to increase production," the president conceded, "but if it is the only alternative to the ravages of inflation, we would have no choice."[29]

Democrats running for reelection were aghast. Senate Finance Committee Chair Walter George (D-GA) dismissed Truman's suggestion. "I do not think the suggestion that taxes can be raised in this period is a realistic evaluation of our present position and I think the President and the Treasury Department must know that," he said.[30]

The tax issue seemed tailor-made for the aspiring GOP majority. In polls conducted throughout the campaign, voters increasingly identified Republicans as the party of tax reduction. In both January and June, 36 percent of respondents said Republicans would do a better job of cutting taxes, as opposed to 31 percent who trusted Democrats to watch the purse strings.[31] After Knutson introduced his proposal for across-the-board rate cuts, Republican support climbed to 42 percent and Democratic support fell to 24 percent.[32]

When voters went to the polls on November 5, they gave Republicans the victory they wanted, returning them to majority status for the first time in 13 years. As Truman's daughter later recalled: "My father awoke aboard his special train, en route to Washington and discovered that he had a bad cold and a Republican Congress."[33] A leading member of Truman's own party, Sen. J. William Fulbright (D-AR), urged the president to resign.[34]

Democrats lost 111 seats in the House and 24 in the Senate. Truman's critics pinned the blame on the president's plummeting popularity. Labor unrest was probably the most pressing issue of the campaign, with Truman antagonizing organized labor by threatening to draft striking railroad workers into the army. Rising prices also fed popular discontent with the president.

Taxes also fueled the Republican victory. Truman had firmly established himself as a fiscal killjoy. Asked in late November who they trusted to ease their tax burden, 18 percent of respondents cast their lot with the president; 48 percent pinned their hopes on Gov. Thomas Dewey of New York, the leading contender for the 1948 Republican nomination.[35]

Republican Reductions

Flush with victory, Republicans set about securing a tax cut in 1947. They insisted that revenue reductions were the only effective means of curtailing the size of government. "The President's real reason for retaining the taxes is obviously to have more money to spend," argued Sen. Robert Taft (R-OH). "The best reason to reduce taxes is to reduce our ideas of the number of dollars which Government can properly spend in a year, and thereby reduce the present inflated ideas of the proper scope of bureaucratic activity."[36] Knutson, meanwhile, indulged a penchant for colorful hyperbole. Progressive taxation in the New Deal mode posed a threat to American society, he contended: "For years, we Republicans have been warning that short-haired women and long-haired men of alien minds in the administrative branch of government were trying to wreck the American way of life and install a hybrid oligarchy at Washington through confiscatory taxation."[37]

Still, Truman held his ground. He acknowledged that current burdens were unsustainable. "I recognize, frankly, that the present burden of taxation on our people is too heavy to be considered as permanent," he said, "and at a proper time I will support tax reduction and tax readjustment designed to reduce the burden and to adjust that burden to the needs of a peacetime economy."[38] But the time for tax reduction had not arrived, he maintained. Tax cuts in 1947 were likely to boost inflation and threaten prosperity.

Democrats kept up a drumbeat of complaints about the bill's fairness, insisting that rich taxpayers would reap too much of the benefit. In March, organized labor extended that complaint into a critique of the current tax system, which the group argued was too generous to the well-off. "Because the wealthy can hire expensive lawyers to reduce their tax bills, the taxes on workers are kept high to make up for the lost revenue," the Congress of Industrial Organizations (CIO) contended.[39] Someone making $236,000 a year would pay less proportionately that a man making $45 week, according to a CIO study. When the National Association of Manufacturers complained that such numbers were misleading, the CIO challenged NAM to support laws "closing the loopholes which allow wealthy individuals to evade paying their fair share of the tax bill."[40]

In response to complaints that their tax cuts were unfair, Republicans in the House revised their plan to give them a more progressive cast; reductions ranged from a high of 30 percent (on incomes under $1,000) down to 20 percent (for anyone making more than $1,400). The Senate went even further, scaling the cut back to 15 percent for high-income taxpayers. Liberals, eager to shift an even larger share of the tax relief toward the lower regions of the income tax scale, argued for an exemption increase. But Republicans prevailed and sent a rate cut bill to the president.[41]

Truman vetoed the bill, insisting that it provided "the wrong kind of tax reduction, at the wrong time." He reiterated his inflation concerns and dismissed the notion that any sort of economic stimulus was necessary to ensure prosperity. The nation's immediate economic priority should be debt reduction, he insisted.

Truman reserved some of his most impassioned language for a "fundamental objection" to the bill's fairness. "An adjustment of the tax system should provide fair and equitable relief for individuals from the present tax burden, but the reductions proposed in H.R. 1 are neither fair nor equitable," he declared. "H.R. 1 reduces taxes in the high income brackets to a grossly disproportionate extent as compared to the reduction in the low income brackets. A good tax reduction bill would give a greater proportion of relief to the low income group."[42] This complaint was steeped in Democratic traditions of tax fairness, including New Deal revenue policy.

The House sustained the veto, but only by two votes. The Republican majority in both Houses quickly agreed on a new bill substantially identical to the vetoed legislation. Once again Truman vetoed the legislation, and this time the House overrode him. But now the Senate sustained the veto, if only barely.

In January 1948, against a backdrop of still-steep wartime taxes, officials projected a budget surplus of $6.8 billion. Knutson put together a new bill, featuring a more progressive distribution of benefits than his previous efforts. It would raise the individual exemption from $500 to $600 and add new exemptions for the elderly and the blind. And even with all those bells and whistles, it was still projected to cost just $6.5 billion—less than the expected surplus.

The House embraced the plan, with Ways and Means ranking minority member Robert Doughton adding his crucial support. The bill passed the chamber by a 297 to 120 vote. In the Senate, the Finance Committee scaled back the rate cuts, and the bill sailed to passage on a vote of 78 to 11, with 30 Democrats joining the majority. Once again, Truman vetoed the tax cut, but this time, both houses of Congress overrode him.

1948 Campaign

As Truman and his GOP antagonists headed into a new campaign season, both tried to make hay of the tax struggle. Republicans called for still more cuts, underscoring their opposition to big government and high taxes. And they had reason to think that voters would respond well; in a July 1948 Roper poll, 69 percent of respondents rejected the suggestion that Congress had cut taxes too much.[43] And fully 57 percent of those polled in March 1948 believed they were still paying too much.[44]

But Republicans had not managed to identify themselves clearly as the party of tax reduction. In March 1948 only 37 percent of those polled thought Republicans would steer a different course on tax policy than Democrats, while 27 percent thought the parties would pursue similar policies.[45] Broad Democratic support for the GOP tax bill had muddied the waters, diluting the GOP's leverage on the issue. And while almost 70 percent of those polled wanted additional tax cuts,[46] they also insisted that future relief favor the poor over the rich.[47] Those sentiments were perhaps the most important legacy of New Deal tax debates. And they did not bode well for the Republican tax agenda, which still featured a preference for lower rates on upper-income taxpayers.

Voters also indicated a strong willingness to pay additional taxes for a strong military. Fully 72 percent were willing to pay more if the money would be used to send military aid to European countries threatened by the brewing Cold War.[48] And 69 percent were even willing to pay new taxes in support of public diplomacy, as the United States set out to make its case against the Soviet Union with an aggressive public relations campaign.[49]

Indeed, the 1948 election revealed a remarkable tolerance for high taxes, as long as spending was focused on things that people cared about. Americans had not embraced the Republican critique of big government. GOP efforts to scale back the New Deal state merely served to antagonize many voters. As William Leuchtenburg wrote of the Republican majority in the 80th Congress, "they veered so sharply to the right that they alienated one segment of the electorate after another."[50]

In fact, Truman later claimed that the 1946 election had been a godsend for him and his party. "The luckiest thing that ever happened to me was the Eightieth Congress," he recalled.[51] It gave him a foil for his 1948 reelection bid, in which he branded the legislative majority as the "do-nothing Congress." He went on to defeat Dewey's bid for the White

House, and Democrats won large majorities in both the House and the Senate. So much for realignment.

The 1946 election seemed to breathe new life into the New Deal. By giving voters a taste of limited government, it gave them an appreciation of big government. It was a lesson not lost on some Republicans, who quickly came to terms with the broad outlines of the New Deal revenue regime. While Republicans—and many voters—continued to express their distaste for heavy taxes, they just as regularly displayed a willingness to swallow hard and pay them.

Fighting Loopholes

High taxes can be reduced in many ways. The most ambitious method (and to economists, the most appealing) is through wholesale cuts, especially of marginal rates. But taxes can also be reduced at the retail level, by establishing preferences and loopholes that relieve certain taxpayers from part of their overall tax burden. Retail tax reduction has probably been a fixture of revenue policy for millennia. But the modern income tax is particularly suitable for this sort of policy approach, since its high marginal rates and broad base made loopholes valuable—and perhaps even necessary.

But loopholes violate standards of horizontal equity, allowing taxpayers with similar incomes to sometimes pay vastly disparate tax rates. They also violate notions of vertical equity by reducing effective tax rates beneath what they "should" be (assuming that statutory rates are not adopted with the effect of loopholes figured into the mix—a big assumption). As a result, loopholes have always been an easy whipping boy for politicians looking to score political points around taxation. No one understood their utility better than Franklin Roosevelt.

But the sustained New Deal campaign against tax avoidance, chronicled in earlier chapters, also reflected a powerful conviction among Democrats that loopholes posed a threat to the integrity of the tax system. Since revenue realities had forced the expansion of many taxes that burdened the lower and middle class, high rates on wealthy taxpayers were politically vital to the overall fairness of the tax regime. As a result, they could not be tolerated, even if other kinds of loopholes—including the expensive ones targeting the middle class, like preferential treatment for employer health benefits and home mortgage interest—were vital to the political durability of the tax regime. In 1950, the Truman administration renewed the New Deal attack on loopholes benefitting the well-to-do. Officials framed their attacks in the resonant rhetoric of past battles against special privilege, insisting that preferences allowed well-connected taxpayers to escape "their fair share" of the fiscal burden.

With a nod to the still-powerful appetite for tax reduction, Truman asked Congress to reduce a variety of regressive excise taxes. But to pay for these cuts, he said, they should also move quickly to close a variety of loopholes. "We should reduce excises only to the extent that the loss in revenue can be recouped by eliminating the tax loopholes which now permit some groups to escape their fair share of taxation," he insisted while lunging for the moral highground of fiscal responsibility. "The continued escape of privileged groups from taxation violates the fundamental democratic principle of fair treatment for all, and undermines public confidence in the tax system."[52]

Truman met with no grand success in his anti-loophole initiative. As other scholars have made clear, tax preferences were an integral part of the New Deal tax regime, embedded in the combination of its broad base and steep progressive rate structure.[53] But *fighting* loopholes, as opposed to actually eliminating them, remained a touchstone of Democratic politics—and tax politics more generally—throughout the postwar decades.

11

The Durability of Reform

Why did the New Deal tax regime last so long? A close look at its origins suggests two answers: exigency and equity.

Necessity drives policy, at least when it comes to tax. Over the decades, whole forests have been sacrificed to publish high-minded studies on tax reform. And that intellectual spadework has been important—when events have conspired to make it relevant. But the iron law of tax politics remains immutable: reform happens when it must, not when it should.

The modern tax regime—like every tax regime in American history— emerged as a response to crisis.[1] Or two crises, to be precise. The first was the Great Depression. In the early 1930s, revenues fell and deficits rose. By the end of the decade, economists would be arguing that red ink was just the ticket for recovery. But through the mid-1930s, most policy- makers considered large deficits alarming, not alluring. Fiscal "sound- ness," they insisted, was a prerequisite for recovery.

Such traditional thinking was common even among New Dealers. Franklin Roosevelt was himself a fiscal conservative, in impulse if not in action. Treasury Secretary Henry Morgenthau was even more convinced that red ink was the enemy of recovery. Most striking, many New Deal economists—and especially its tax experts—believed that higher taxes were probably unavoidable, even if deeply unpalatable.

As a result, many of the New Deal's signature tax reforms were driven by a quest for revenue. And by the late 1930s, the prospect of war spurred an even more determined search. Long before the attack on Pearl Harbor, it was clear that the nation's existing taxes weren't up to the task of war finance. Indeed, tax experts spent much of the late 1930s and 1940s pondering how to pay for preparedness. Ultimately, policymakers settled on sweeping changes to the individual income tax, as well as dramatic hikes in corporate taxes. (While economists argued then, as now, about the incidence of corporate taxes, most policymakers assumed that much of the ultimate burden fell on relatively wealthy shareholders, not on labor or consumers.) Not only would such levies raise money (and thereby limit borrowing), but they would also curb inflation.

Wartime taxation proved reasonably effective. It was not, perhaps, all that it might have been: Roosevelt administration officials complained regularly that Congress was taxing too little and borrowing too much. But by most accounts, the fiscal system did what it needed to do.

And after the war, it kept doing its job. The income tax proved highly flexible and effective in the postwar years, raising revenue as needed while also allowing for the sort of legislative tinkering that makes tax systems politically sustainable. It was not perfect, to be sure. And the postwar decades were peppered with episodes of important, if not exactly earth-shattering, tax reform. But the fundamentals of the tax system remained intact. Lawmakers left them alone because no crisis forced their collective hand. Indeed, the midcentury tax system—with the broad-based income tax at its center—proved well-suited to its postwar environment (not to mention a few subsequent wars, including the conflicts in Korea and Vietnam). Exigency, or the lack of it, provides part of the explanation for the durability of the New Deal tax regime. But ideas played a crucial role, too. The postwar regime embodied a distinctive vision of tax fairness that proved highly resonant and flexible.

In several respects, the wartime tax regime broke with the history of New Deal revenue reform. The broad-based income tax forced millions of middle-class Americans onto the tax rolls for the first time; though no strangers to indirect federal taxes on consumption, they were unaccustomed to direct taxes. This rich man's tax took on a newly democratic cast.

Roosevelt and his senior advisers had resisted this idea throughout the 1930s, ignoring the recommendations of their own Treasury experts. The president had paid lip service to the idea as early as 1935, when he told newspaper mogul Roy Howard that "sound arguments" could be advanced for a broad-based tax. And by 1939, he had begun to ponder the possibility of a much broader tax. But Roosevelt's political career had been built on steep and narrow income taxes, buttressed by a range of supplementary levies on estates and consumer goods. Breaking free of this mindset was no easy task.

The war, however, changed everything. Suddenly, the careful, consistent arguments of Treasury economists had a chance to see the light of day. Soak-the-rich advocates of high-end progressivity—once so dominant in New Deal policymaking—were diverted into wartime responsibilities. More important, their tax agenda was inadequate for wartime finance. High-end progressivity was never a big moneymaker; it was designed principally to boost fairness, not revenue. By contrast, low-end progressivity had always been about raising money; Treasury experts had recommended a broader base for the income tax principally because it would raise enough revenue to allow for a rollback in consumption taxes. The buoyant revenue of a mass income tax soon emerged as the principal foundation of wartime finance. Indeed, it was the only viable alternative to a national sales tax.

High-end progressivity did not disappear, it just ceased to be the guiding force of administration reform. During the war, high- and low-end progressivity would share the stage, the latter raising money and the former boosting fairness. These two versions of progressive taxation had never been mutually exclusive. In many respects, they were always complementary. Their respective advocates differed over timing and emphasis, but they shared a commitment to tax fairness, with a particular emphasis on ability to pay. When the war arrived, it demanded both kinds of progressivity; the emergency revenue regime needed steep taxes on the rich *and* new taxes on the low and middle classes. Indeed, this was the essential political bargain of wartime finance.

The most important progressive triumph in wartime tax policy was the defeat of the sales tax. Roosevelt himself was central to this effort. Once or twice in his career, he had seemed to flirt with the idea of broad-based consumption taxes, most notably during the months leading up to his first inauguration. But Roosevelt was a consistent opponent of general sales taxation, from his days as governor in New York through his final hour as president. It's possible to exaggerate his personal role in defeating the sales tax movement of 1941 and 1942, but not by much. Without a doubt, FDR's personal antipathy toward a sales tax exceeded that of even his most liberal tax advisers. While they were focused on the pressing need for revenue—and willing to accept many compromises in trying to meet that need—Roosevelt remained steadfast in his conviction that other taxes could pay the nation's bills.

In fact, at almost every turn, Roosevelt sought to defend the ideals of progressive taxation throughout the war. He supported steep levies on corporate excess profits and personal income. He opposed efforts to ease the burden on rich taxpayers and lucky corporations, including the tax forgiveness plan advanced by Beardsley Ruml and the various loopholes of the 1943 revenue act. As he declared in 1942, "Progressive taxes are the backbone of the Federal tax system."[2] In defending that proposition, even in the midst of national crisis, Roosevelt brought a vital element of continuity to his presidential tax policies. The New Deal tax agenda, while vastly altered by the war, did not disappear. And the wartime tax regime did not represent a defeat for progressive standards of tax justice.

The Future

Inertia notwithstanding, even a path-dependent policy process is not immune to change. The history of American taxation has been marked by at least four watersheds: moments when exigency, ideas, and institutions have combined to prompt fundamental reform. Wars have usually been the catalyst, but economic crises have figured prominently, too. Necessity, in other words, has always driven policy.

Have we reached another moment of necessity? Will the economic crisis that began in 2008 open the door to radical tax reform? Obviously, it remains to be seen. But what does seem likely is that that many of the political dynamics surrounding tax policy in the Great Depression are likely to find new salience in the years ahead. Issues of vertical equity are more prominent on the political tax agenda than they have been in decades. At the same time, long-term fiscal challenges suggest the need for more than simple fine-tuning of the nation's revenue structure. This combination of politics and necessity makes fundamental reform seem possible—maybe even probable.

Will Americans shake off the political legacy that has long made consumption taxes politically untenable at the federal level? Will they join the rest of the world in using a value-added tax to finance social spending? If so, they might find inspiration in the history of Roosevelt-era tax reform. New Dealers used their least progressive tax to finance their most enduring progressive program, Social Security. And ultimately, they accepted a vast expansion of the income tax to the middle class, despite a long tradition of keeping that levy confined to the nation's upper crust. These changes were possible because New Dealers couched necessary but unpleasant tax reform in terms of progressive fairness. In particular, they melded notions of vertical and horizontal equity into an enduring ideology of shared sacrifice: the simple but powerful notion that everyone should pay their fair share. That's a lesson that might prove relevant again.

Notes

Chapter 1

1. Compania de Tabacos v. Collector, 275 U.S. 87, 100 (1927).

2. For a fine and underappreciated history of these revolts, see David T. Beito, *Taxpayers in Revolt: Tax Resistance during the Great Depression* (Chapel Hill: University of North Carolina Press, 1989).

3. On the Tea Party, see Benjamin Woods Labaree, ed., *The Boston Tea Party,* Northeastern Classics (Boston: Northeastern University Press, 1979), 1:58; and Benjamin L. Carp, *Defiance of the Patriots: The Boston Tea Party and the Making of America* (New Haven, CT: Yale University Press, 2010). For an emphasis on the Tea Party's antimonopoly (as opposed to antitax) origins, see Arthur Meier Schlesinger, "The Uprising against the East India Company," *Political Science Quarterly* 32, no. 1 (1917). For analysis of the Revolution's role in popular memory and contemporary politics, see Jill Lepore, *The Whites of Their Eyes: The Tea Party's Revolution and the Battle over American History* (Princeton, NJ: Princeton University Press, 2010).

4. "Santelli's Tea Party," CNBC, 19 February 2009, http://video.cnbc.com/gallery/ ?video=1039849853.

5. W. Elliot Brownlee, "Reflections on the History of Taxation," in *Funding the Modern American State, 1941–1995: The Rise and Fall of the Era of Easy Finance,* ed. W. Elliot Brownlee (Washington, DC: Woodrow Wilson Center Press, 1996), 5.

6. W. Elliot Brownlee, "Tax Regimes, National Crisis, and State-Building in America," in *Funding the Modern American State, 1941–1995: The Rise and Fall of the Era of Easy Finance,* ed. W. Elliot Brownlee (Washington, DC: Woodrow Wilson Center Press, 1996), 37.

7. In surveys, Americans often confess ignorance about fiscal terminology; in 2003, for instance, 56 percent said they weren't sure what "progressive taxes" actually

were. "Americans' Views on Taxes" survey, February 2003, accessed 25 April 2011 from iPOLL Databank, http://www.ropercenter.uconn.edu/data_access/ipoll/ipoll.html.

8. "True Patriot Survey," August 2008, accessed 25 April 2011 from iPOLL Databank, http://www.ropercenter.uconn.edu/data_access/ipoll/ipoll.html.

9. Franklin D. Roosevelt, "Message to Congress on Tax Revision," 19 June 1935, American Presidency Project, http://www.presidency.ucsb.edu/ws/index.php?pid=15088.

10. Cordell Hull and Andrew Henry Thomas Berding, *The Memoirs of Cordell Hull* (New York: Macmillan, 1948), 1:58.

11. Joel Slemrod and Jon M. Bakija, *Taxing Ourselves: A Citizen's Guide to the Debate over Taxes*, 4th ed. (Cambridge, MA: MIT Press, 2008), 16.

12. "Americans' Views on Taxes."

13. W. Elliot Brownlee, *Federal Taxation in America: A Short History*, 2nd ed. (Washington, DC: Woodrow Wilson Center Press, 2004), 57.

14. "An Unnecessary Amendment," *New York Times*, 8 July 1909.

15. Brownlee, *Federal Taxation in America*, 63.

16. Percentages derived from data in "Table Ea748-757. Federal Income Tax Returns—Individual: 1913–1943" and "Table Ae1-28. Households, by Race and Sex of Householder and Household Type: 1850–1990," in *Historical Statistics of the United States*, ed. Susan B. Carter et al. (New York: Cambridge University Press, 2006). Millennial Edition online, http://hsus.cambridge.org/HSUSWeb/HSUSEntryServlet.

17. "Table Ea594-608. Federal Government Internal Tax Revenue, by Source: 1863–1940," in Carter et al., *Historical Statistics*.

18. Ibid.

19. Stanley S. Surrey and William Clements Warren, *Federal Income Taxation, Cases and Materials*, 1953 ed. (Brooklyn: Foundation Press, 1953), 15.

20. U.S. Department of the Treasury, Internal Revenue Service, "Personal Exemptions and Individual Income Tax Rates, 1913–2002," *Statistics of Income Bulletin* (2002).

21. Office of Management and Budget, *Historical Tables, Budget of the U.S. Government, Fiscal Year 2013* (Washington, DC: U.S. Government Printing Office, 2012), 30.

22. Ibid., 32.

23. The best treatment of New Deal tax policy is Mark Hugh Leff, *The Limits of Symbolic Reform: The New Deal and Taxation, 1933–1939* (New York: Cambridge University Press, 1984). While Leff's analysis suffers from its failure to consider tax policy during World War II, it remains far and away the best treatment of Roosevelt-era taxation.

Useful, if not particularly extensive, discussion of tax issues can be found in several general works on the New Deal, including many older ones. Among the best are Arthur Meier Schlesinger, *The Politics of Upheaval* (Boston: Houghton Mifflin, 1960); Schlesinger, ed., *The Crisis of the Old Order, 1919–1933*, Age of Roosevelt 1 (Boston: Houghton Mifflin, 2003) and *The Coming of the New Deal* (Boston: Houghton Mifflin, 1988); William Edward Leuchtenburg, *Franklin D. Roosevelt and the New Deal, 1932–1940* (New York: Harper & Row, 1963); Frank Burt Freidel, *Franklin D. Roosevelt: Launching the New Deal*, 1st ed. (Boston: Little, Brown, 1973); James T. Patterson, *Congressional Conservatism and the New Deal: The Growth of the Conservative Coalition in Congress, 1933–1939* (Lexington: University of Kentucky Press, 1967); and David M. Kennedy, *Freedom from Fear: The*

American People in Depression and War, 1929–1945 (New York: Oxford University Press, 1999).

24. In a series of books and articles, W. Elliot Brownlee has outlined a "democratic-institutionalist" model for studying tax history that I largely adopt in this study. See, for example, "Reflections on the History of Taxation," 3–36.

Brownlee's model explains the policy process as a function of four variables: politics, bureaucratic capacity, historical contingency, and ideas. On political dynamics, he incorporates the contributions made by "pluralist" theories of policy formulation, which stress the role of interest groups in the crafting of federal taxation. See, for example, John F. Witte, *The Politics and Development of the Federal Income Tax* (Madison: University of Wisconsin Press, 1985); Carolyn Webber and Aaron B. Wildavsky, *A History of Taxation and Expenditure in the Western World* (New York: Simon & Schuster, 1986); and Sven Steinmo, *Taxation and Democracy: Swedish, British, and American Approaches to Financing the Modern State* (New Haven, CT: Yale University Press, 1993).

On the vital and often independent role of government institutions and the experts they employ, see (among a vast number of other examples) Daniel P. Carpenter, *The Forging of Bureaucratic Autonomy: Reputations, Networks, and Policy Innovation in Executive Agencies, 1862–1928*, Princeton Studies in American Politics (Princeton, NJ: Princeton University Press, 2001); John W. Kingdon, *Agendas, Alternatives, and Public Policies,* 2nd ed. (New York: HarperCollins College Publishers, 1995); Ronald Frederick King, *Money, Time, and Politics: Investment Tax Subsidies and American Democracy* (New Haven, CT: Yale University Press, 1993); Julian E. Zelizer, *Taxing America: Wilbur D. Mills, Congress, and the State, 1945–1975* (New York: Cambridge University Press, 1998); Ajay K. Mehrotra, "Envisioning the Modern American Fiscal State: Progressive-Era Economists and the Intellectual Foundations of the U.S. Income Tax," *UCLA Law Review* 52, no. 6 (2005); Steven A. Bank, "Entity Theory as Myth in the Origins of the Corporate Income Tax," *William & Mary Law Review* 447(2001); Bank, "Corporate Managers, Agency Costs, and the Rise of Double Taxation," *William & Mary Law Review* 44, no. 167 (2002); Bank, "Rethinking Double Taxation's Role in Dividend Policy: A Historical Approach," *Tax Law Review* 56 (2003); and Carolyn C. Jones, "Mass-Based Income Taxation: Creating a Taxpaying Culture, 1940–1952," in *Funding the Modern American State, 1941–1995: The Rise and Fall of the Era of Easy Finance,* ed. W. Elliot Brownlee (Washington, DC: Woodrow Wilson Center Press, 1996).

On the pivotal role to historical contingency—and crises in particular—see Alan T. Peacock and Jack Wiseman, *The Growth of Public Expenditure in the United Kingdom* (Princeton, NJ: Princeton University Press, 1961); Robert Higgs, *Crisis and Leviathan: Critical Episodes in the Growth of American Government* (New York: Oxford University Press, 1987); Higgs, "Crisis, Bigger Government, and Ideological Change: Two Hypotheses on the Ratchet Phenomenon," *Explorations in Economic History* 22, no. 1 (1987); Charles Tilly, *Coercion, Capital, and European States, AD 990–1992,* rev. pbk. ed., Studies in Social Discontinuity (Cambridge, MA: Blackwell, 1992); Margaret Levi, *Of Rule and Revenue* (Berkeley: University of California Press, 1988); and Karen A. Rasler and William R. Thompson, "War Making and State Making: Governmental Expenditures, Tax Revenues, and Global Wars," *American Political Science Review* 79, no. 2 (1985).

On the role of ideas, the literature on social learning is especially valuable. Excellent examples can be found in two essay collections: Mary O. Furner and Barry Supple, eds., *The State and Economic Knowledge: The American and British Experiences* (Washington, DC: Woodrow Wilson Center Press, 1990) and Michael James Lacey and Mary O. Furner, eds., *The State and Social Investigation in Britain and the United States* (Washington, DC: Woodrow Wilson Center Press, 1993). For interesting work on the role of economists in the development of the New Deal, see William J. Barber, *Designs within Disorder: Franklin D. Roosevelt, the Economists, and the Shaping of American Economic Policy, 1933–1945*, Historical Perspectives on Modern Economics (New York: Cambridge University Press, 1996); and Michael A. Bernstein, *A Perilous Progress: Economists and Public Purpose in Twentieth-Century America* (Princeton, NJ: Princeton University Press, 2001).

25. Office of Management and Budget, *Historical Tables*, 32.

26. Mark Leff makes this point the centerpiece of his argument in *The Limits of Symbolic Reform*.

27. On the importance of policy communities to taxation, see Zelizer, *Taxing America*.

28. On the New Deal Order, see Steve Fraser and Gary Gerstle, *The Rise and Fall of the New Deal Order, 1930–1980* (Princeton, NJ: Princeton University Press, 1989). On the nature of the postwar tax regime generally, see W. Elliot Brownlee, *Funding the Modern American State, 1941–1995: The Rise and Fall of the Era of Easy Finance* (Washington, DC: Woodrow Wilson Center Press, 1996). Essays in this collection of special relevance include those by C. Eugene Steuerle, Herbert Stein, and W. Elliot Brownlee.

29. Tax Policy Center, "Historical Effective Federal Tax Rates for All Households," 4 April 2011, http://www.taxpolicycenter.org/taxfacts/displayafact.cfm?Docid=456.

30. On the tax-based origins of the Republican revival, see Isaac William Martin, *The Permanent Tax Revolt: How the Property Tax Transformed American Politics* (Stanford, CA: Stanford University Press, 2008); and Thomas Byrne Edsall and Mary D. Edsall, *Chain Reaction: The Impact of Race, Rights, and Taxes on American Politics* (New York: Norton, 1991).

Chapter 2

1. Between 1924 and 1925, the number of returns fell from 7,369,788 to 4,171,051. See "Table Ea748-757. Federal Income Tax Returns—Individual: 1913–1943," in Carter et al., *Historical Statistics*.

2. Marginal rates apply to a taxpayer's last and next dollar of income. Effective tax rates express the average rate of tax paid on *all* dollars of income. In a progressive tax system, effective rates are generally lower than marginal rates. For top rates, see U.S. Department of the Treasury, Internal Revenue Service, "Personal Exemptions and Individual Income Tax." For figures on the top 1 percent of households, see W. Elliot Brownlee, "Historical Perspective on U.S. Tax Policy toward the Rich," in *Does Atlas Shrug?*, ed. Joel B. Slemrod (New York and Cambridge: Russell Sage Foundation and Harvard University Press, 2000), 45. Until 1954, the income tax included both "normal" and "surtax" rates. The normal tax applied to all income over a basic exemption. The surtax applied to incomes above a higher threshold. The surtax provided most of the progressivity in the income tax rate structure, with normal tax rates hovering in the single digits.

3. The Mellon witticism is widely attributed to Sen. George Norris. See, for example, Randolph E. Paul, *Taxation in the United States* (Boston: Little, Brown, 1954), 125.

4. Andrew W. Mellon, *Taxation: The People's Business* (New York: Macmillan, 1924), 12. See also Witte, *Politics and Development*, 89.

5. Mellon, *Taxation,* 16.

6. Mellon repeatedly sought to eliminate the tax-free status of state and local bonds, but Congress just as consistently refused. On problems associated with tax-exempt bonds, see U.S. Department of the Treasury, *Annual Report of the Secretary of the Treasury on the State of the Finances for the Fiscal Year Ended June 30, 1931* (Washington, DC: Government Printing Office, 1932), 14; Gene Smiley and Richard H. Keehn, "Federal Personal Income Tax Policy in the 1920s," *Journal of Economic History* 55, no. 2 (1995): 287–303; and Brownlee, *Federal Taxation in America,* 74–76.

7. Paul, *Taxation in the United States,* 125.

8. For a succinct explanation of depletion allowances, see Joseph J. Cordes, Robert D. Ebel, and Jane G. Gravelle, eds., *The Encyclopedia of Taxation and Tax Policy* (Washington, DC: Urban Institute Press, 1999), 73. On the political utility of granting such tax breaks, see Brownlee, *Federal Taxation in America,* 73–75. See also Ronald King, "From Redistributive to Hegemonic Logic: The Transformation of American Tax Politics, 1894–1963," *Politics and Society* (1983): 1–52.

9. US. Senate and Select Committee on Investigation of the Bureau of Internal Revenue, "Investigation of Bureau of Internal Revenue," (Washington, DC: Government Printing Office, 1926), 7–8.

10. For a detailed discussion of the Senate report, see Joseph J. Thorndike, "Reforming the Internal Revenue Service: A Comparative History," *Administrative Law Review* 53, no. 2 (2001): 747–52.

11. Brownlee, "Historical Perspective," 49.

12. U.S. Department of the Treasury, *Annual Report of the Secretary of the Treasury on the State of the Finances for the Fiscal Year Ended June 30, 1921* (Washington, DC: Government Printing Office, 1922), 25.

13. Mellon, *Taxation,* 56–57.

14. On Mellon as a corporate liberal, see Brownlee, *Federal Taxation in America,* 75–77.

15. "Table Ea594-608. Federal Government Internal Tax Revenue, by Source: 1863–1940," in Carter et al., *Historical Statistics.*

16. Ajay K. Mehrotra, "Creating the Modern American Fiscal State: The Political Economy of United States Tax Policy, 1880–1930" (PhD diss., University of Chicago, 2003), 60–66.

17. For rates and exemptions, see U.S. Department of the Treasury, Internal Revenue Service, "Personal Exemptions."
On World War I taxation generally, see Mehrotra, "Creating the Modern American Fiscal State"; W. Elliot Brownlee, "Wilson and Financing the Modern State: The Revenue Act of 1916," *Proceedings of the American Philosophical Society* 129, no. 2 (1985); Brownlee, "Economists and the Formation of the Modern Tax System in the United States: The World War I Crisis," in *The State and Economic Knowledge: The American and British Experiences,* ed. Mary O. Furner and Barry Supple (Washington, DC: Woodrow Wilson Center Press, 1990); and Brownlee, "Social Investigation and Political Learning in the Financing of World War I," in *The State and Social Investigation in Britain and the United States,* ed. Michael James Lacey and Mary O. Furner (Washington, DC: Woodrow Wilson Center Press, 1993).

18. Brownlee, *Federal Taxation in America,* 65.

19. Josiah Stamp emphasized this distinction between war and excess profits in his survey of global profits taxes: "The Taxation of Excess Profits Abroad," *Economic Journal* 27, no. 105 (1917).

20. Brownlee, *Federal Taxation in America,* 58–61.

21. Mehrotra, "Creating the Modern American Fiscal State," 497–504; Sidney Ratner, *Taxation and Democracy in America* (New York: John Wiley, 1967), 365.

22. Woodrow Wilson, "7th Annual Message," 2 December 1919, American Presidency Project, http://www.presidency.ucsb.edu/ws/?pid=29560.

23. On the climate of opinion favoring tax reduction, see Smiley and Keehn, "Federal Personal Income Tax Policy," 287.

24. Roy G. Blakey and Gladys Blakey, *The Federal Income Tax* (New York: Longmans Green, 1940), 191.

25. "Business Favors Profit Tax Repeal," *Washington Post,* 27 February 1921; "Hit Excess Profits Tax," *New York Times,* 4 March 1921; "Tax League Favors Trial of Sales Tax," *New York Times,* 4 April 1921; "Proposes to Tax Undivided Earnings," *New York Times,* 3 January 1921; "Appeal to Fordney," *New York Times,* 19 August 1921.

26. "Survey Finds Nation Favors New Sales Tax," *Wall Street Journal,* 4 April 1921.

27. "Economic League Backs Income Tax," *New York Times,* 12 February 1921.

28. "Proceedings of the National Industrial Tax Conference, 1920," quoted in Blakey and Blakey, *Federal Income Tax,* 191–92.

29. U.S. Department of the Treasury, *Annual Report for 1921,* 21–22.

30. Ibid., 7–8. For a detailed description of the Mellon proposal, see Roy G. Blakey, "The Revenue Act of 1921," *American Economic Review* 12, no. 1 (1922).

31. On the farm bloc, see David Brady, Richard Brody, and David Epstein, "Heterogeneous Parties and Political Organization: The U.S. Senate, 1880–1920," *Legislative Studies Quarterly* 14, no. 2 (1989).

32. For contemporary comment on Adams's influence, see Blakey, "Revenue Act of 1921," 90, 105. For his initial support of the tax, see Thomas S. Adams, "Federal Taxes upon Income and Excess Profits," *American Economic Review* 8, no. 1 (1918); and "Principles of Excess Profits Taxation," *Annals of the American Academy of Political and Social Science* (1918). For his later opposition, see "Should the Excess Profits Tax Be Repealed?," *Quarterly Journal of Economics* 35, no. 3 (1921). See also Ratner, *Taxation and Democracy in America,* 409–10. On Adams's concern with administrative problems in taxation, see Brownlee, "Economists and the Formation of the Modern Tax System," 408.

33. E. R. A. Seligman, "Federal Taxes upon Income and Excess Profits—Discussion," *American Economic Review* 8, no. 1 (1918), 42–45; E. R. A. Seligman, "The War Revenue Act," *Political Science Quarterly* 33, no. 1 (1918), 24–31. Ajay Mehrotra has sought to rescue Seligman's reputation as a progressive; see "Creating the Modern American Fiscal State," ch. 2. For the more traditional view of Seligman as a moderate conservative, see Brownlee, *Federal Taxation in America,* 52; and Dorothy Ross, *The Origins of American Social Science* (New York: Cambridge University Press, 1991), 189–94.

34. Robert Murray Haig, "British Experience with Excess Profits Taxation," in "Papers and Proceedings of the Thirty-Second Annual Meeting of the American Economic Association," supplement, *American Economic Review* 10, no. 1 (1920), 14.

35. David Friday et al., "The Excess Profits Tax—Discussion," in "Papers and Proceedings of the Thirty-Second Annual Meeting of the American Economic Association": 19–22.

36. U.S. Department of the Treasury, *Annual Report of the Secretary of the Treasury on the State of the Finances for the Fiscal Year Ended June 30, 1919* (Washington, DC: Government Printing Office, 1920), 23.

37. Revenue Bill of 1921, H.R. Rep. No. 67-350, pts. 2, 4 (1921).

38. Ratner, *Taxation and Democracy in America*, 406–10.

39. "Opposes Sales Tax," *New York Times*, 19 May 1921.

40. "Farmers Fight Tax Repeal," *Washington Post*, 12 February 1921.

41. On labor attitudes toward the Mellon plan, see "Federation of Labor Raps Tax Revision Bill Rates," *Washington Post*, 20 August 1921; "Labor Will Fight against Sales Tax," *New York Times*, 12 May 1921; "Pleads with Labor on Tax," *New York Times*, 23 May 1921; "Labor Denounces Fordney Tax Bill," *New York Times*, 20 August 1921.

42. The act raised the regular corporate income tax rate from 10 percent to 12.5 percent. According to one contemporary estimate, the revenue lost from repealing the excess profits tax would amount to $450 million, while the new corporate income tax hike would raise just under $134 million. The law also lowered the top marginal income tax rate on individuals to 50 percent—a dramatic reduction from wartime highs but far less than Mellon had requested; established a top rate of 12.5 percent on capital gains from assets held more than two years; and increased the exemption for heads of families and for dependents. For details on the law, see Blakey, "Revenue Act of 1921," 76–77; Ratner, *Taxation and Democracy in America*, 402–12.

43. Ratner, *Taxation and Democracy in America*, 406–07; Blakey, "Revenue Act of 1921," 77, 80.

44. U.S. Department of the Treasury, *Annual Report for 1921*, 23–24. For similar arguments, see *Annual Report of the Secretary of the Treasury on the State of the Finances for the Fiscal Year Ended June 30, 1924* (Washington, DC: Government Printing Office, 1925), 11–13.

45. "Coolidge Assails but Signs Tax Bill as Better Than Existing War-Time Law; Will Seek Revision in Next Congress," *New York Times*, 3 June 1924; "Text of the President's Statement Criticizing Provisions of Tax Law," *New York Times*, 3 June 1924.

46. Andrew Mellon, "Statement to the House Ways and Means Committee," reprinted in U.S. Department of the Treasury, *Annual Report of the Secretary of the Treasury on the State of the Finances for the Fiscal Year Ended June 30, 1925* (Washington, DC: Government Printing Office, 1926), 351–52.

47. *Revenue Revision of 1925: Hearings Before the Committee on Ways and Means*, 69th Cong. 478 (1925).

48. "Back Quick Payment of the Public Debt," *New York Times*, 31 October 1925.

49. Roy G. Blakey, "The Revenue Act of 1926," *American Economic Review* 16, no. 3 (1926): 415.

50. 69 Cong. Rec. 3668 (1st sess. ed. 1926).

51. Blakey, "Revenue Act of 1921."

52. For Mellon's general argument on the futility of high marginal tax rates—and the greater revenue productivity of lower rates—see Mellon, *Taxation*, 69–89. Quotation

from Paul, *Taxation in the United States,* 132–33. See also Roy G. Blakey, "The Revenue Act of 1924," *American Economic Review* 14, no. 3 (1924): 477. On the importance Mellon and other policymakers attached to this tax-avoidance argument, see Smiley and Keehn, "Federal Personal Income Tax Policy."

53. Bascom N. Timmons, *Garner of Texas: A Personal History* (New York: Harper & Brothers, 1948), 104.

54. 68 Cong. Rec. 2439 (1st sess. ed. 1924).

55. Ibid.

56. Income data for periods before the middle of the 20th century are problematic, but one reasonable estimate puts the annual average earnings for U.S. workers across all industries (including farm labor) at $1,303 in 1924. See "Table Ba4320-4334. Annual Earnings in Selected Industries and Occupations: 1890–1926," in Carter et al., *Historical Statistics.*

57. Timmons, *Garner of Texas,* 106.

58. Blakey, "Revenue Act of 1924," 479–80; Paul, *Taxation in the United States,* 134–35; Ratner, *Taxation and Democracy in America,* 416–18; Blakey and Blakey, *Federal Income Tax,* 246–50.

59. U.S. Department of the Treasury, *Annual Report for 1925,* 4–5.

60. Ibid., 6.

61. *Revenue Revision of 1925,* 2.

62. "Tax Clubs—A New Factor in Tax Revision," *Literary Digest,* 21 November 1925, 68.

63. Rep. James A. Frear (R-WI), quoted in Blakey, "Revenue Act of 1926," 406.

64. Exemptions for single taxpayers increased from $1,000 to $1,500; married couples and heads of household saw their exemptions rise from $2,500 to $3,500.

65. "The Fight over the Little Fellows Tax," *Literary Digest,* 31 October 1925, 10–11.

66. Blakey, "Revenue Act of 1926," 410.

67. Revenue Bill of 1926, H.R. 1, 69th Cong. (1925), 35–36. On the burden of automobile taxes, see James W. Follin, "Taxation of Motor Vehicles in the United States," *Annals of the American Academy of Political and Social Science* (1924).

68. Revenue Bill of 1926, 14, 28–29.

69. Revenue Revision of 1925, 68 Cong. (2nd sess. 19 October–3 November 1925), 87, 106, 18.

70. Ibid., 142.

71. "The Text of Governor Roosevelt's Speech to 30,000 in Pittsburgh Baseball Park," *New York Times,* 20 October 1932.

72. Paul, *Taxation in the United States,* 142.

73. Jordan A. Schwarz, *The Interregnum of Despair: Hoover, Congress, and the Depression* (Urbana, IL: University of Chicago Press, 1970), 107–08.

74. On the arguments for budget balance—at least over a period of years, if not annually—see Herbert Stein, "Pre-revolutionary Fiscal Policy: The Regime of Herbert Hoover," *Journal of Law and Economics* 9 (1966).

75. On the history of balanced budgets as an ideological and political phenomenon, including a discussion of the Mellon-era budget debates, see James D. Savage, *Balanced Budgets and American Politics* (Ithaca, NY: Cornell University Press, 1988), 121–97. On the importance of budget balance even among Democrats, see Julian E. Zelizer, "The Forgotten Legacy of the New Deal: Fiscal Conservatism and the Roosevelt Administration, 1933–1938," *Presidential Studies Quarterly* 30, no. 2 (2000).

76. Schwarz, *Interregnum of Despair,* 111.

77. Ogden L. Mills, "The Spendings Tax," in *Proceedings of the Fourteenth Annual Conference on Taxation under the Auspices of the National Tax Association,* September 12–16, 1921 (New York: National Tax Association, 1922), 331. For a description of the 1921 Mills plan, see Steven A. Bank, "The Progressive Consumption Tax Revisited," *Michigan Law Review* 101 (2003).

78. On Adams's support for a progressive spendings tax, see Brownlee, "Economists and the Formation of the Modern Tax System," 431.

79. Herbert Hoover, "Annual Message to the Congress on the State of the Union," 8 December 1931, American Presidency Project, http://www.presidency.ucsb.edu/ws/ ?pid=22933#axzz1UehnLNDp; Schwarz, *Interregnum of Despair,* 112–14.

80. *Revenue Revision of 1932: Hearings Before the Committee on Ways and Means,* 76th Cong. 2 (1932).

81. Ibid., 3.

82. Ibid., 4.

83. Schwarz, *Interregnum of Despair,* 113–14; U.S. Department of the Treasury, *Annual Report of the Secretary of the Treasury on the State of the Finances for the Fiscal Year Ended June 30, 1932* (Washington, DC: Government Printing Office, 1933), 28; Roy G. Blakey, "The Revenue Act of 1932," *American Economic Review* (1932), 629.

84. U.S. Department of the Treasury, *Annual Report for 1932,* 29.

85. Ibid., 30–31. President Hoover was apparently willing to accept even higher rates for the estate tax. In fact, he was far less critical of the levy than Andrew Mellon had been throughout the 1920s, endorsing its fairness; Walter Lambert, "New Deal Revenue Acts" (PhD diss., University of Texas, 1970), 19.

86. U.S. Department of the Treasury, *Annual Report for 1932,* 30–31.

87. *Revenue Revision of 1932,* 167, 216, 123–24. One farm group support for lower exemptions, see "Blaine Again Blocks Finance Bill Action," *New York Times,* 17 January 1932; and "Higher Income Tax Favored by Grange," *Washington Post,* 17 January 1932.

88. *Revenue Revision of 1932,* 15.

89. Ibid., 55–60.

90. Ibid., 75–76.

91. Ibid., 206.

92. Ibid., 19. On the Hoover preference for wide-use nonnecessity taxes, see Leff, *Limits of Symbolic Reform,* 21.

93. *Revenue Revision of 1932,* 19.

94. Ibid., 24.

95. Leff, *Limits of Symbolic Reform,* 21–25; Lambert, "New Deal Revenue Acts," 22.

96. Attributed to Sen. Russell Long (D-LA), chairman of the Senate Finance Committee in a later era.

97. *Revenue Revision of 1932,* 181, 891, 906, 1194.

98. Ibid., 664, 66–67.

99. Ibid., 137, 206–09.

100. Ibid., 239–62.

101. Hearst editorial reprinted from 13 March 1932 newspapers in *Public Finance Pamphlets,* vol. 1 (Charlottesville: University of Virginia Library). On Hearst and Garner, see Schwarz, *Interregnum of Despair,* 115.

102. Lambert, "New Deal Revenue Acts," 28–29; Committee on Ways and Means, Revenue Bill of 1932, H.R. Rep. No 76-708, at 8–10 (1932).

103. Ibid., 9.

104. Ibid., 5.

105. Lambert, "New Deal Revenue Acts," 31; Schwarz, *Interregnum of Despair:* 116–17.

106. Lambert, "New Deal Revenue Acts," 31. Hoover insisted in his memoirs that the idea originated with the Ways and Means leadership; *The Memoirs of Herbert Hoover: The Great Depression, 1929–1941* (New York: Macmillan, 1952), 137.

107. Schwarz, *Interregnum of Despair,* 116, 118, 134; Lambert, "New Deal Revenue Acts," 37–38.

108. Quoted in Schwarz, *Interregnum of Despair,* 129.

109. For a detailed analysis of the sales tax fight on the House floor, see Jordan A. Schwarz, "John Nance Garner and the Sales Tax Rebellion of 1932," *Journal of Southern History* (1964): 162–80.

110. Schwarz, *Interregnum of Despair,* 135–37.

111. Ibid., 140.

112. Blakey, "Revenue Act of 1932," 620–21.

113. Committee on Finance, Revenue Bill of 1932, S. Rep. No. 76-665, at 7 (1932).

114. Schwarz, *Interregnum of Despair,* 121.

Chapter 3

1. For a useful summary of farm problems during the 1920s, as well as later New Deal efforts to resolve them, see Anthony J. Badger, *The New Deal* (Basingstoke, UK: Macmillan Education, 1989), 14–18, 147–89; Richard S. Kirkendall, "The New Deal and Agriculture," in *The New Deal: The National Level,* ed. John Braeman, Robert Hamlett Bremner, and David Brody (Columbus: Ohio State University Press, 1975).

2. Frank Burt Freidel, *Franklin D. Roosevelt: The Triumph* (Boston: Little, Brown, 1956), 35–37.

3. Ralph Theodore Compton, *Fiscal Problems of Rural Decline,* Special Report of the State Tax Commission, no. 2 (Albany: J. B. Lyon, 1929), 18–19.

4. Robert Murray Haig, "Taking the Burden from Real Estate," *Bulletin of the National Tax Association* 18, no. 2 (1932): 35.

5. Herbert Hoover and William Starr Myers, *The State Papers and Other Public Writings of Herbert Hoover,* vol. 2 (New York: Kraus Reprint, 1970), 169–75.

6. For summaries of the various committee recommendations, see New York State Commission for the Revision of the Tax Laws, *Preliminary Report Submitted February 15, 1931* (Albany: J. B. Lyon, 1931), 19–21.

7. "State Tax Changes Urged by Realtors," *New York Times,* 5 February 1928, 164.

8. "Roads, Good and Bad," *New York Times,* 14 September 1928, 20. See also "State Roads Built by Tax on Gasoline," *New York Times,* 6 October 1928, 33.

9. "Striking at the Root," *Wall Street Journal,* 20 November 1928, 1.

10. For a roster of the panel's membership, see "Farm Experts Offer Plan to Roosevelt on Rural Tax Relief," *New York Times,* 25 November 1928, 1.

11. Franklin D. Roosevelt, *Public Papers of Franklin D. Roosevelt, Forty-Eighth Governor of the State of New York, 1929* (Albany: J. B. Lyon, 1930), 689; John Morton Blum, *From the Morgenthau Diaries* (Boston: Houghton Mifflin, 1959–1969), 1–34; Bernard Bellush, *Franklin D. Roosevelt as Governor of New York* (New York: Columbia University Press, 1955), 78.

12. Quoted in Bellush, *Franklin D. Roosevelt as Governor,* 79.

13. "Farm Experts Offer Plan to Roosevelt on Rural Tax Relief," *New York Times,* 25 November 1928, 1; and Freidel, *Franklin D. Roosevelt: The Triumph,* 37–38.

14. "State Republicans Plan Land Tax Cuts," *New York Times,* 1 January 1929, 1.

15. "Gasoline Tax Urged in State Farm Aid," *New York Times,* 17 January 1929, 1.

16. Bellush, *Franklin D. Roosevelt as Governor,* 81. See also Compton, *Fiscal Problems of Rural Decline,* 179.

17. "Gasoline Tax Urged in State Farm Aid"; Roosevelt, *Public Papers of Franklin D. Roosevelt,* 477; Bellush, *Franklin D. Roosevelt as Governor,* 80–81; Freidel, *Franklin D. Roosevelt: The Triumph,* 37–38; Blum, *From the Morgenthau Diaries,* 16; Finla G. Crawford, "The Legislative Session of 1929 in New York State," *American Political Science Review* 23, no. 4 (1929).

18. Compton, *Fiscal Problems of Rural Decline,* 79.

19. "Roosevelt Urges Farm 'Square Deal'," *New York Times,* 16 February 1929, 1.

20. Roosevelt, *Public Papers of Franklin D. Roosevelt,* 688; Leff, *Limits of Symbolic Reform,* 54–55. Roosevelt quoted in Freidel, *Franklin D. Roosevelt: The Triumph,* 7, 39. See also, W. A. Warn, "Roosevelt Insists on Gasoline Tax in Tax Relief Plan," *New York Times,*1 February 1929, 1; "Roosevelt Tells of Farm Aid Plans," *New York Times,* 2 February 1929, 1.

21. "Tax Plan of Gov. Roosevelt," *Wall Street Journal,* 21 February 1929, 3. Graves had already endorsed the gas tax the previous year. See "Tells Farm Group Tax Cut is Distant," *New York Times,* 9 November 1928, 50; Freidel, *Franklin D. Roosevelt: The Triumph,* 8–39. See also F. G. Crawford, "Gas Tax Has Covered Country in Ten Years," *New York Times,* 10 March 1929, 162.

22. Roosevelt, *Public Papers of Franklin D. Roosevelt,* 140–41, 495–96.

23. Ibid. See also W. A. Warn, "Albany War Looms over Budget Cuts," *New York Times*, 10 February 1929, 1.

24. Freidel, *Franklin D. Roosevelt: The Triumph*, 39. See, also Groves, "Recent State Income Taxation."

25. Compton, *Fiscal Problems of Rural Decline*, 21.

26. E. R. A. Seligman, "The General Property Tax," *Political Science Quarterly* 5, no. 1 (1890): 62.

27. New York State Commission for the Revision of the Tax Laws, *Preliminary Report of the New York State Commission for the Revision of the Tax Laws* (Albany: New York State, February 15, 1931), 66. See, especially, the comments of Robert Murray Haig on page 88.

28. "Asserts Gasoline Tax is Generally Popular," *New York Times*, 3 March 1929, 20.

29. M. Slade Kendrick, "Public Expenditure: A Neglected Consideration in Tax Incidence Theory," *American Economic Review* 20, no. 2 (1930).

30. Freidel, *Franklin D. Roosevelt: The Triumph*, 9; "Roosevelt Urges Farm 'Square Deal'," 1.

31. "For 3-Cent Gasoline Tax," *New York Times*, 28 February 1929, 10.

32. "Roosevelt Urges Farm 'Square Deal'."

33. See, for example, "Dairymen Favor Gasoline Tax," *New York Times*, 13 December 1928, 7; "Real Estate Boards Approve Gasoline Tax," *New York Times*, 9 February 1929, 31.

34. "To Oppose Gasoline Tax," *New York Times*, 13 December 1928, 23; "Auto Men Protest Gasoline Tax Plan," *New York Times*, 6 March 1929, 22; "Gives Its Reasons for Opposing the Gas Tax," *New York Times*, 17 March 1929, XX18; "Auto Dealers to Act on Gas Tax Monday," *New York Times*, 30 March 1929, 2; "Gasoline Tax Unfair, Auto Men Declare," *New York Times*, 23 March 1929, 7. Taxi drivers also opposed the tax: "Plans Taxicab Parade to Albany as Protest," *New York Times*, 11 March 1929, 11; "Taxi Men Oppose a Gasoline Tax," *New York Times*, 13 March 1929, 4.

35. "The New State Tax," *New York Times*, 10 April 1929, 22.

36. "Painless Taxation," *Wall Street Journal*, 29 March 1929, 1.

37. Roosevelt, *Public Papers of Franklin D. Roosevelt*, 689; Freidel, *Franklin D. Roosevelt: The Triumph*, 8; Bellush, *Franklin D. Roosevelt as Governor*, 83. For an overview of the gas tax in operation, see M. Slade Kendrick, "The Collection of Taxes by the State Government and the Division of These Revenues with Units of Local Government, with Emphasis on New York," *Journal of Political Economy* 39, no. 1 (1931).

38. Bellush, *Franklin D. Roosevelt as Governor*, 79; Crawford, "Legislative Session," 917.

39. "Roosevelt for 20 Per Cent Income Tax Cut, Contingent on the 2-Cent Gasoline Levy," *New York Times*, 7 February 1929, 1.

40. "Roosevelt Appeals to People to Back His Taxation Plan," *New York Times*, 8 March 1929, 1.

41. Freidel, *Franklin D. Roosevelt: The Triumph*, 55. See also "Albany War Looms over Budget Cuts," 1.

42. "Republicans Lean to 25% Cut in Tax on Earned Incomes," *New York Times,* 11 March 1929, 1.

43. Roosevelt, *Public Papers of Franklin D. Roosevelt,* 141.

44. Crawford, "Legislative Session," 918.

45. "Jerry-built" comment from Freidel, *Franklin D. Roosevelt: The Triumph,* 3. "Will Ask Revision of State Tax Plan," *New York Times,* 5 March 1930, 16; "Governor Demands Reform of Tax Laws," *New York Times,* 6 March 1930, 5; "$10,000,000 Waste in State Taxes Seen," *New York Times,* 18 August 1930, 19.

46. W. A. Warn, "Roosevelt Objects to Mastick's Plan for State Pensions," *New York Times,* 24 February 1930, 1.

47. *The National Cyclopedia of American Biography, Being the History of the United States as Illustrated in the Lives of the Founders, Builders, and Defenders of the Republic, and of the Men and Women Who Are Doing the Work and Moulding the Thought of the Present Time,* vol. 56 (New York: J. T. White, 1892), 254. See also, "Tax Commission," *Wall Street Journal,* 7 March 1930, 3.

48. "State Tax Reform," *New York Times,* 2 August 1930, 12. The commission included Seabury C. Mastick, chairman; Charles R. White, vice chairman; Albert G. Preston, secretary; G. William Magly; Walter L. Pratt; Harlan W. Rippey; Edwin R. A. Seligman; Jesse Isidor Straus; and J. Frank Zoller. For the comment on real estate interests, see Haig, "Taking the Burden from Real Estate," 36.

49. Staff members included Robert Murray Haig, Beulah Bailey, Arthur R. Burnstan, Philip H. Cornick, R. Parker Eastwood, Audrey Davies, Don L. Essex, Stanley Feitler, Luther Gulick, E. S. Lawler, E. H. Mereness, Arnold Miles, Paul R. Mort, Mabel Newcomer, Louis Shere, Carl S. Shoup, Alfred D. Simpson, Edwin H. Spengler, G. F. Warren, and Morton D. Weiss.

50. For Haig's generous assessment of the 1918 law, see Robert Murray Haig, "Revenue Act of 1918," *Political Science Quarterly* 34, no. 3 (1919).

51. *The National Cyclopedia of American Biography, Being the History of the United States as Illustrated in the Lives of the Founders, Builders, and Defenders of the Republic, and of the Men and Women Who Are Doing the Work and Moulding the Thought of the Present Time,* vol. 54 (New York: J. T. White, 1892), 265–66.

52. Haig's much-quoted wording is more concise: "Income is the money value of the net accretion to one's economic power between two points of time." Economists often describe this as the accretion concept of income. See Robert Murray Haig, "The Concept of Income—Economic and Legal Aspects," in *The Federal Income Tax,* ed. Robert M. Haig (New York: Columbia University Press, 1921), reprinted in *Readings in the Economics of Taxation,* ed. Richard M. Musgrave and Carl S. Shoup (New York: Richard D. Irwin, 1959), 54–76.

53. Robert M. Haig, "Simplification of the Federal Income Tax—Discussion," *American Economic Review* 18, no. 1 (1928): 120–21. The Haig-Simons definition has become a sort of gold standard for income taxation. See J. A. Kay, "Tax Policy: A Survey," *Economic Journal* 100, no. 399 (1990): 23. To be sure, some critics have suggested that the Haig-Simons definition is inadequate. See Walter Hettich, "A Theory of Partial Tax Reform," *Canadian Journal of Economics* 12, no. 4 (1979): 692–712. Further, at least one scholar has contended that Haig was a lukewarm advocate for using accretion income as the basis of a tax system, preferring consumption. See David Wildasin,

"R. M. Haig: Pioneer Advocate of Expenditure Taxation?," *Journal of Economic Literature* 28, no. 2 (1990): 649–54.

54. "New York State Tax Association Formed," *Wall Street Journal*, 6 June 1928, 15.

55. "To Assist Prof. Haig in Tax Study," *New York Times*, 25 January 1928, 31.

56. Anna Rothe, ed., *Current Biography: Who's News and Why, 1944* (New York: H. W. Wilson, 1944), 491–92.

57. Rothe, *Current Biography*, 569–71.

58. Quoted in "Preliminary Report of the New York State Commission for the Revision of the Tax Laws," Legislative Document No. 62 (Albany: J. B. Lyon, 1931), 3.

59. "Roosevelt against Imposing Sales Tax," *New York Times*, 18 November 1930, 26.

60. "State Farmers Meet, Seeking a Tax Remedy," *New York Times*, 6 November 1931, 21.

61. "Roosevelt against Imposing Sales Tax"; "Merchants Fights Sales Tax as Blow to Trade Recovery," *New York Times*, 20 November 1930, 1; "Retail Sales Tax Opposition Voiced," *Wall Street Journal*, 20 November 1930, 16; "Merchants Unite to Fight Sales Tax," *New York Times*, 7 January 1931, 25.

62. "Roosevelt against Imposing Sales Tax"; and "Roosevelt Opposes General Sales Tax," *New York Times*, 15 December 1931, 8.

63. Ralph Burnett Tower, *Luxury Taxation and Its Place in a System of Public Revenues* (Albany: J. B. Lyon, 1931), 15.

64. Ibid., 18.

65. Ibid. For an explanation of sumptuary taxes, see Cordes, Ebel, and Gravelle, *Encyclopedia of Taxation and Tax Policy*, 343–44.

66. Tower, *Luxury Taxation*, 19.

67. "Roosevelt Opposes General Sales Tax."

68. Franklin D. Roosevelt, *The Public Papers and Addresses of Franklin D. Roosevelt*, ed. Samuel Irving Rosenman, vol. 1 (New York: Random House, 1938), 457–68.

69. Ibid., 465–66; Leff, *Limits of Symbolic Reform*, 54–55; Bellush, *Franklin D. Roosevelt as Governor*, 141.

70. Bellush, *Franklin D. Roosevelt as Governor*, 141.

71. "Roosevelt Asks 100 Percent Increase in Tax on Incomes and Gasoline Sales to Meet Large Deficit Faced by State," *New York Times*, 13 January 1932, 1.

72. Roosevelt, *Public Papers and Addresses*, vol. 1, 118.

73. "Governor's Message on State's Financial Problem," *New York Times*, 13 January 1932, 20; "The State Budget," *New York Times*, 13 January 1932, 22.

74. "Governor's Message on State's Financial Problem."

75. State of New York, *Report of the New York State Commission for the Revision of the Tax Laws* (Albany: J. B. Lyon, 1932), 24–27.

76. Ibid., 27–28, 30–31; "$127,000,000 in Taxes Proposed for State to Cut Realty Levy," *New York Times*, 2 February 1932, 1

77. State of New York, *Report of the New York State Commission*, 30–31; "$127,000,000 in Taxes Proposed for State to Cut Realty Levy."

78. Twentieth Century Fund Committee on Taxation et al., *Facing the Tax Problem: A Survey of Taxation in the United States and a Program for the Future* (New York: Twentieth Century Fund, 1937), 421.

79. State of New York, *Report of the New York State Commission,* 124.

80. Ibid., 87–88.

81. Ibid.

82. Ibid.

83. Ibid., 176–177.

84. Ibid., 177–178.

85. Ibid., 205.

86. Ibid.

87. Ibid., 207.

Chapter 4

1. For a summary of the AAA tax provisions, see "Processing Taxes," *Tax Magazine* 11, no. 8 (1933); and Clarence N. Goodwin, "The Processing Taxes," *Tax Magazine* 11, no. 9 (1933). NIRA taxes are discussed in detail later in this chapter.

2. Groves, "Recent State Income Taxation," 107.

3. For an excellent treatment of local tax revolts in the early 1930s, see Beito, *Taxpayers in Revolt.* See also, Paul Hudson, "Post Haste," *Washington Post,* 4 January 1933, 6; and Paul, *Taxation in the United States,* 170.

4. Roosevelt, *Public Papers and Addresses,* vol. 1, 813–14.

5. Marriner S. Eccles, *Beckoning Frontiers: Public and Personal Recollections* (New York: Knopf, 1951), 95.

6. Roosevelt, *Public Papers and Addresses,* vol. 1, 797.

7. Ibid., 798.

8. For a discussion of early, quasi-Keynesian thought, see Herbert Stein, *The Fiscal Revolution in America,* rev. ed. (Washington, DC: AEI Press, 1996), ch. 7, and *Presidential Economics: The Making of Economic Policy from Roosevelt to Clinton* (Washington, DC: American Enterprise Institute for Public Policy Research, 1994), 27–63.

9. "President Declares against a Tax Rise; Asks People to Aid," *New York Times,* 1 April 1931, 1.

10. On Hoover fiscal policy, see Herbert Stein, "Pre-revolutionary Fiscal Policy." See also Herbert Hoover, "Annual Budget Message to the Congress," 4 December 1929, American Presidency Project, http://www.presidency.ucsb.edu/ws/index.php?pid=22022&st=&st1=.

11. Roosevelt, *Public Papers and Addresses,* vol. 1, 806.

12. Ibid., 798.

13. Franklin D. Roosevelt, "Campaign Address on the Federal Budget at Pittsburgh, Pennsylvania," 19 October 1932, American Presidency Project, http://www.presidency.ucsb.edu/ws/?pid=88399.

14. James C. Hagerty, "Governor Demands Slash," *New York Times*, 20 October 1932, 1.

15. Blakey and Blakey, *Federal Income Tax*, 336.

16. "Washington Tax Talk," *Tax Magazine* 11, no. 1 (1933).

17. "Washington Notes," *New Republic*, 28 December 1932.

18. Ibid.; "Post Haste," *Washington Post*, 20 December 1932; "Lehman Asks State Retail Sales Tax," *Washington Post*, 31 January 1933; "House Leaders Suddenly Veer to Sales Levy," *Washington Post*, 27 December 1932; Mark Graves, "New York's Retail Sales Tax," *Tax Magazine* 11, no. 7 (1933).

19. "Roosevelt Opposes Sales Tax Program," *New York Times*, 28 December 1932; "Sales Tax Doomed, Says Garner," *New York Times*, 28 December 1932; "Roosevelt View on Sales Taxes," *Wall Street Journal*, 28 December 1932; "Sales Tax Law Plan Believed without Hope," *Washington Post*, 28 December 1932; and "Democrats Balked in Revenue Quest by Sales Tax Doom," *New York Times*, 29 December 1932. See also, Blakey and Blakey, *Federal Income Tax*, 336; Freidel, *Franklin D. Roosevelt: Launching the New Deal*; Leff, *Limits of Symbolic Reform*, 56.

20. "Roosevelt View on Sales Taxes," *Wall Street Journal*, 28 December 1932; and "Washington Tax Talk." On the Hearst meeting, see Leff, *Limits of Symbolic Reform*, 56.

21. On the Civil War tax system, including its excise duties, see Brownlee, *Federal Taxation in America*, 31–36.

22. Ralph B. Tower, "Should the Consumer Pay Taxes?," *Tax Magazine* 12, no. 3 (1934).

23. "The Beer Tax Comedy," *Washington Post*, 10 March 1932.

24. "Plan No New Taxes to Balance Budget," *New York Times*, 2 January 1933; "Post Haste," *Washington Post*, 27 December 1932.

25. "More Taxes Invite Upset, Rainey Says," *New York Times*, 9 January 1933; "Rainey Stands Firm against Tax Increases," *Washington Post*, 4 January 1933.

26. According to Garner, Democrats would suggest that rates increase from 4 percent (on income up to $4,000) and 8 percent (on everything over that amount) to 6 percent and 12 percent, respectively. In terms of revenue, the gas tax would raise $137 million annually, while the beer tax would net $125 million. Lower exemptions and higher rates for the income tax would bring in $130 million to $150 million—perhaps even as much as $200 million. "Roosevelt and Congress Chiefs Agree on New Rise in Income Tax," *New York Times*, 6 January 1933; "Rise in Income Tax in Program of Democrats," *Washington Post*, 6 January 1933.

27. "The Democratic Program," *Washington Post*, 7 January 1933.

28. "Leaders Calm 'Rebels', " *New York Times*, 7 January 1933.

29. Ibid.; "Revolt Halts New Income Tax Rise," *New York Times*, 7 January 1933; "Democrats Despair of Fast Tax Action," *Washington Post*, 7 January 1933.

30. "Consider New Tax on Luxuries Alone," *New York Times*, 25 January 1933.

31. Ibid.

32. "Trial Balloons on Taxes," *Washington Post,* 26 January 1933.

33. Ibid.

34. Ron Chernow, *The House of Morgan: An American Banking Dynasty and the Rise of Modern Finance* (New York: Simon & Schuster, 1991), 367.

35. John Brooks, "The Millionaire and the Midget," *American Heritage,* October 1969, 34–35.

36. "Morgan Paid No Income Tax for the Years 1931 and 1932," *New York Times,* 24 May 1933, 1.

37. Quoted in Joel Seligman, *The Transformation of Wall Street* (Boston: Houghton Mifflin, 1982), 31.

38. "Personal Glimpses: Mirrors of Washington's Big Money 'Circus'," *Literary Digest,* 10 June 1933; Seligman, *Transformation of Wall Street,* 31.

39. "Let the Banking Inquiry Go On!," *Nation,* 7 June 1933; "Washington Notes," *New Republic,* 7 June 1933.

40. "Morgan & Co.," *Business Week,* 7 June 1933, 6.

41. Ibid.; "Where Morgan's Income-Tax Exemption Points," *Literary Digest,* 3 June 1933, 6; Harold M. Groves, "Yachts without Income," *New Republic,* 19 July 1933; Paul Y. Anderson, "The House of Morgan: With Comment on Its Retainers in and out of Congress," *Nation,* 7 June 1933.

42. *Stock Exchange Practices: Hearings Before the Committee on Banking and Currency,* pt. 1, 73rd Cong., 42–47 (1933).

43. Ibid., 53–54, 199.

44. Blakey and Blakey, *Federal Income Tax,* 341.

45. "Stock Exchange Practices, Part 1," 131–32, 198–200; Anderson, "House of Morgan: With Comment on Its Retainers"; *Stock Exchange Practices: Hearings Before the Committee on Banking and Currency,* pt. 1, 73rd Cong., 42–47 (1933).
Few critics seemed willing to acknowledge that Morgan's modest payments to the British treasury during the depression were balanced by equally modest payments during the prosperous 1920s. Since the British tax excluded capital gains from ordinary income, the partners had paid relatively little tax in the 1920s, at least compared to their U.S. tax payments. See Blakey and Blakey, *Federal Income Tax,* 341.

46. *Stock Exchange Practices,* 46–49, 78–87.

47. Ibid., 48. See also Chernow, *House of Morgan: An American Banking Dynasty,* 366.

48. Seligman, *Transformation of Wall Street,* 34.

49. John Brooks, *Once in Golconda: A True Drama of Wall Street, 1920–1938,* 1st ed. (New York: Harper & Row, 1969), 191.

50. "Personal Glimpses: Mirrors of Washington's Big Money 'Circus'."

51. "Roosevelt Backs Morgan Inquiry; Glass Threatened," *New York Times,* 30 May 1933; "Washington Notes"; Chernow, *House of Morgan: An American Banking Dynasty,* 359; Seligman, *Transformation of Wall Street,* 30.

52. Ferdinand Pecora, *Wall Street under Oath: The Story of Our Modern Money Changers* (New York: Simon & Schuster, 1939), 204–05.

53. "Morgan & Co."

54. Herman T. Reiling, "The Function of a Taxpayer's Ethics in Income Tax Liability," *Tax Magazine* 12, no. 6 (1934): 319–20.

55. *Stock Exchange Practices*, 199.

56. "The Week," *New Republic*, 7 June 1933; Pecora, *Wall Street under Oath*, 205. On the role of tax lawyers during the 1930s, including a somewhat hostile comparison to the activities of tax accountants, see Joseph J. Klein, "The Lawyer and the Income Tax," *Tax Magazine* 11, no. 2 (1933).

57. "Morgan & Co.," 6.

58. Blakey and Blakey, *Federal Income Tax*, 341; Groves, "Yachts without Income."

59. "Morgan & Co.," 6.

60. Anderson, "House of Morgan: With Comment on Its Retainers," 632.

61. Ibid.

62. Leff, *Limits of Symbolic Reform*, 59.

63. *Stock Exchange Practices* 879.

64. Anderson, "House of Morgan: With Comment on Its Retainers," 82.

65. Marjorie E. Kornhauser, "Shaping Public Opinion and the Law: How a 'Common Man' Campaign Ended a Rich Man's Law," *Law and Contemporary Problems* 73, no. 1 (2010): 126–29.

66. Anderson, "House of Morgan: With Comment on Its Retainers," 633.

67. Blakey and Blakey, *Federal Income Tax*, 339.

68. "Taxes and Public Works," *Washington Post*, 13 May 1933, 6; "By Another Name," *New York Times*, 15 May 1933, 12.

69. "Sales Tax Decision Left to Congress by the President," *New York Times*, 16 May 1933; "Sales Tax a Snag to Recovery Bill," *New York Times*, 17 May 1933.

70. "Tax Programs Suggested by Douglas for Bond Plan," *Washington Post*, 19 May 1933.

71. Ways and Means Subcommittee on Tax Revision, *Prevention of Tax Avoidance: Preliminary Report by the Subcommittee of the Committee on Ways and Means Relative to Methods of Preventing the Avoidance and Evasion of the Internal Revenue Laws Together with Suggestions for the Simplification and Improvement Thereof* (Washington, DC: Government Printing Office, 1933), 8.
The panel approved new normal rates of 6 percent and 10 percent, with the lower rate applicable to the first $4,000 in taxable income. They also recommended a variety of excise tax hikes, including a gas tax increase from 1 cent to 1.75 cents a gallon. "In the existing emergency there appeared to be no other commodity other than foods which would furnish a sufficiently broad base," the panel explained with apparent regret.

72. "Roosevelt's Aid Hailed by Pecora," *New York Times*, 30 May 1933.

73. "National Industrial Recovery Act Taxes," *Tax Magazine* 11, no. 8 (1933). NIRA tax provisions also included a new corporate tax on capital stock and excess profits.

Under the plan, companies would be taxed $1 for every $1,000 in the declared value of their capital assets; to dissuade companies from undervaluing their assets, it also taxed them on profits greater than 12.5 percent of their capital stock. In addition, senators tweaked the dividend tax, reduced the gas tax hike, and eliminated the increase in normal income tax rates.

74. Anderson, "House of Morgan: With Comment on Its Retainers."

75. For a classic examination of vertical equity, including the pitfalls associated with several standards, see Walter J. Blum and Harry Kalven, *The Uneasy Case for Progressive Taxation* (Chicago: University of Chicago Press, 1978). For an interesting critique, see Murray N. Rothbard, "The Uneasy Case for Degressive Taxation: A Critique of Blum and Kalven," *Quarterly Journal of Austrian Economics* 4, no. 1 (2001), 43–61.

On the notion of ability to pay and marginal sacrifice, one of the oldest texts is still one of the best: E. R. A. Seligman, "Progressive Taxation in Theory and Practice," *Publications of the American Economic Association* 9, no. 1–2 (1894). For a more modern discussion, see Mehrotra, "Creating the Modern American Fiscal State," chs. 1–2.

76. See Joseph J. Cordes, "Horizontal Equity" and "Vertical Equity" in Cordes, Ebel, and Gravelle, *Encyclopedia of Taxation and Tax Policy;* and Richard A. Musgrave, "Horizontal Equity Once More," *National Tax Journal* 43, no. 2 (1990). For a helpful description of this issue, and an exploration of its complexity, see C. Eugene Steuerle, "And Equal (Tax) Justice for All?," in *Tax Justice: The Ongoing Debate,* ed. Joseph J. Thorndike and Dennis J. Ventry Jr. (Washington, DC: Urban Institute Press, 2003).

77. Carlton Fox, "Compiler's Note Regarding the Legislative History of the Revenue Act of 1934," in *U.S. Revenue Acts, 1909–1950: The Laws, Legislative Histories, and Administrative Documents* (Buffalo: William S. Hein, 1948). For the Treasury response, see U.S. Department of the Treasury, "Preliminary Statement of the Treasury Department with Reference to Amendments to the Revenue Acts," also in *U.S. Revenue Acts, 1909–1950.* For useful summaries of the JCIRT report and Treasury's response, see "Proposed Income Tax Law Revision," *Tax Magazine* 11, no. 12 (1933); "The Treasury Department's Tax Revision Recommendations," *Tax Magazine* 11, no. 12 (1933).

78. "Lovell H. Parker, Revenue Specialist," *Washington Post,* 18 January 1961, B8.

79. Brownlee, *Federal Taxation in America,* 86–87.

80. Ways and Means Subcommittee on Tax Revision, *Prevention of Tax Avoidance,* 1–12. For an excellent survey of the reorganization provisions changed by the 1934 act, including an exploration of their political impact, see Steven A. Bank, "Tax, Corporate Governance, and Norms," *Washington and Lee Law Review* 61, no. 3 (2004).

81. Henry Morgenthau, "Statement of the Acting Secretary of the Treasury," in *U.S. Revenue Acts, 1909–1950: The Laws, Legislative Histories, and Administrative Documents* (Buffalo: William S. Hein, 1933), 1.

82. Roosevelt, *Public Papers and Addresses,* vol. 4; Blum, *From the Morgenthau Diaries,* 298.

83. Morgenthau, "Statement of the Acting Secretary of the Treasury," 1.

84. Ways and Means Subcommittee on Tax Revision, *Prevention of Tax Avoidance,* 4; Morgenthau, "Statement of the Acting Secretary of the Treasury," 3–4.

85. Morgenthau, "Statement of the Acting Secretary of the Treasury," 3–4.

86. Ibid., 13–14.

87. Ways and Means Subcommittee on Tax Revision, *Prevention of Tax Avoidance,* 7.

88. Morgenthau, "Statement of the Acting Secretary of the Treasury," 8.

89. For a summary of the House provisions—including its more preferential treatment of wage and salary income—see "The Ways and Means Committee Revenue Bill," *Tax Magazine* 12, no. 2 (1934).

90. 78 Cong. Rec. 2,510 (1934).

91. "Magill Appointed Treasury Tax Aide," *New York Times,* 24 November 1933; Franklin Waltman Jr., "New Treasury Aid Is Dropped by Morgenthau," *Washington Post,* 24 November 1933.

92. Paul W. Ward, "Henry Morgenthau and His Friends," *Nation,* 14 August 1935, 182.

93. "Prof. Magill in Capital," *New York Times,* 28 November 1933; Franklyn Waltman Jr., "Bank and Tax Aids Selected by Morgenthau," *Washington Post,* 28 November 1933; "Treasury Would Alter All Taxes," *Wall Street Journal,* 16 December 1933.

94. Raymond E. Manning, "The Federal Revenue Act, 1934," *Bulletin of the National Tax Association* XIX, no. 9 (1934).

95. Henry Morgenthau, *Morgenthau Diaries,* Book 1 (Bethesda, MD: LexisNexis Academic and Library Solutions, 1934), 26.

96. On the law's provisions, see Roy G. Blakey and Gladys C. Blakey, "The Revenue Act of 1934," *American Economic Review* 24, no. 3 (1934).

97. The bill tightened provisions on corporate reorganizations and consolidated tax returns and various deductions from gross income. It also introduced a new method for calculating capital gains, much as the Ways and Means Committee had recommended in its report. For a useful summary of the law, see "New Provisions of the Revenue Act of 1934," *Tax Magazine* 12, no. 5 (1934). On the capital gains provisions, which taxed gains differently depending on the holding period for the asset in question, see Arthur J. Hogan, "Capital Gains under the Revenue Act of 1934," *Tax Magazine* 12, no. 7 (1934).

Chapter 5

1. Blum, *From the Morgenthau Diaries,* 298; "Mr. Roosevelt's Men," *Fortune* 9, no. 4 (1934): 141.

2. Eccles, *Beckoning Frontiers,* 138.

3. Brownlee, *Federal Taxation in America,* 71.

4. For skeptical commentary about Magill's appointment, see Ward, "Henry Morgenthau and His Friends."

5. Craufurd D. Goodwin, "Martin Bronfenbrenner, 1914–1997," *Economic Journal* 108 (1998): 1776.

6. Ibid., 1775–80; "Treasury Orders Bank, Tax Studies," *New York Times,* 27 June 1934, 19; Martin Bronfenbrenner, "Instead of a Philosophy of Life," *American Economist* 32, no. 2 (1988); Arthur I. Bloomfield, "On the Centenary of Jacob Viner's Birth: A

Retrospective View of the Man and His Work," *Journal of Economic Literature* 30, no. 4 (1992).

Some of Viner's more famous works included *Studies in the Theory of International Trade* (New York: Harper & Brothers, 1937); *The Long View and the Short: Studies in Economic Theory and Policy* (Glencoe, IL: Free Press, 1958); "Taxation and Changes in Price Levels," *Journal of Political Economy* 31, no. 4 (1923); and Jacob Viner and Douglas A. Irwin, *Essays on the Intellectual History of Economics* (Princeton, NJ: Princeton University Press, 1991).

For Viner's inclusion in the Chicago School, see Gonçalo L. Fonseca and Leanne J. Ussher, "The Chicago School," http://homepage.newschool.edu/~het/schools/chicago.htm, and "Jacob Viner, 1892–1970," http://homepage.newschool.edu/~het/profiles/viner.htm. For Viner's disavowal of the label, see Bloomfield, "On the Centenary of Jacob Viner's Birth," 2058.

7. "Advise Borrowing to Balance Budget," *New York Times*, 19 January 1933, 27. Other signers, all at the University of Chicago, were Frank Bane, Paul Betters, Carl Chatters, Paul H. Douglas, S. E. Leland, R. A. Millis, C. E. Ridley, H. C. Simons, Donald Slesinger, and Leonard D. White. On Viner's general approach to fiscal policy, see Bloomfield, "On the Centenary of Jacob Viner's Birth," 2074. See also Eugene Rotwein, "Jacob Viner and the Chicago Tradition," *History of Political Economy* 15, no. 2 (1983).

8. "Advise Borrowing to Balance Budget," 27.

9. Jacob Viner, "Taxation and Changes in Price Levels." For a fine study on fiscal conservatism in the New Deal, see Zelizer, "Forgotten Legacy of the New Deal."

10. Bloomfield, "On the Centenary of Jacob Viner's Birth," 2077.

11. On the appeal of Groves, see Ward, "Henry Morgenthau and His Friends" and Franklyn Waltman Jr., "14 Are Named to Check All U.S. Finances," *Washington Post*, 27 June 1934, 1.

12. "Treasury Orders Bank, Tax Studies," 19; Blum, *From the Morgenthau Diaries*, 298; U.S. Department of the Treasury, "Press Service No. 2-7," press release, 24 June 1934.

13. Robert Murray Haig, Carl Sumner Shoup, Reavis Cox, Louis Shere, and Edwin Harold Spengler, *The Sales Tax in the American States: A Study Made under the Direction of Robert Murray Haig* (New York: Columbia University Press, 1934). For a study of the professional community surrounding tax policy, albeit during a later era, see Zelizer, *Taxing America*. Dennis J. Ventry Jr. offers a similar look at tax policy communities, focusing on their treatment of a particular tax issue, "The Treatment of Marriage under the U.S. Federal Income Tax, 1913 to 2000" (dissertation, University of California at Santa Barbara, 2001).

14. For Shoup's attitudes toward sales taxation, see Haig et al., *Sales Tax in the American States*. For more of Shoup's research in New York, see "The Income Tax in New York State: A Correction," *Bulletin of the National Tax Association* 18, no. 5 (1933) and "Possibilities of the Income Tax in New York State," *Bulletin of the National Tax Association* 18, no. 4 (1933).

15. Waltman, "14 Are Named"; U.S. Department of the Treasury, "Press Service No. 2-7."

16. Carl Summer Shoup, "The Federal Revenue System: Forword and Summary of Recommendations," Records of the Office of Tax Analysis; Box 62; Tax Reform

Programs and Studies; Records of the Office of Tax Analysis/Division of Tax Research; General Records of the Department of the Treasury, Record Group 56; National Archives, College Park, MD; full text reproduction available at http://taxhistory.tax.org/ Civilization/Documents/Surveys/hst23735/23735-1.htm.

17. Ibid.

18. Ibid.

19. On the influence of fiscal conservatives within the Roosevelt administration, especially Treasury Secretary Henry Morgenthau, see Zelizer, "Forgotten Legacy of the New Deal."

20. Stein, *Presidential Economics*, 31.

21. Shoup, "Federal Revenue System: Foreword and Summary of Recommendations." For a study of some aspects of regulatory taxation, see R. Alton Lee, *A History of Regulatory Taxation* (Lexington: University Press of Kentucky, 1973). On the oleomargarine tax, see the chapter by Adam Gifford Jr. in *Taxing Choice: The Predatory Politics of Fiscal Discrimination*, ed. William F. Shughart (New Brunswick, NJ: Transaction Publishers, 1997).

22. Shoup, "Federal Revenue System: Foreword and Summary of Recommendations."

23. Ibid.

24. Ibid.

25. Louis Shere, "The Distribution of Federal Taxes," (1934, R-VI) in Box 62, Tax Reform Programs and Studies, Records of the Office of Tax Analysis/Division of Tax Research, General Records of the Department of the Treasury, Record Group 56; National Archives, College Park, MD. As historian Elliot Brownlee has pointed out, the Shere memo represents one of the first serious efforts to assess tax incidence. Shere stressed the conjectural nature of his conclusions: "Anyone who uses the figures on tax burden here presented must exercise extreme care not to read into them a degree of accuracy and authority which they do not possess." The memo, he humbly asserted, "does not purport to be anything more than a highly conjectural description of the distribution of the tax burden." In general, the Shere memo offers a wealth of statistical data on the tax burdens imposed on various income classes. By and large, it does not make specific recommendations for changes to the tax system. Instead, the other members of the Viner study group used Shere's numbers to inform their own recommendations.

26. Exemptions increased from $1,000 to $1,500 for individuals and from $2,500 to $3,500 for married couples. See U.S. Department of the Treasury, Internal Revenue Service, "Personal Exemptions and Individual Income Tax." On Democratic proposals to raise exemption levels in the mid-1920s, see "Substitute for Mellon's Proposal Presented by Garner," *Washington Post*, 7 January 1924, 1; "Garner Tax Plan Is Branded by Mellon as Mere Politics," *Washington Post*, 20 January 1924, 1; "Garner Has Plan Relieving 3,000,000 from Income Tax," *Washington Post*, 17 October 1925, 1; "Democrats Offer Substitute Plan for Cut in Taxes," *New York Times*, 7 January 1924, 1; "Mellon Analyzes Garner's Tax Plan," *New York Times*, 20 January 1924, 1; and "Mellon Is Opposed to Taking the Tax Off $5,000 Incomes," *New York Times*, 19 October 1925, 1.

27. U.S. Department of the Treasury, Bureau of Internal Revenue, "Statistics of Income for 1932" (Washington, DC: Government Printing Office, 1934): 5.

28. On Democratic support for lower exemptions, see Leff, *Limits of Symbolic Reform*, 102–119.

29. Suzy Platt, "Respectfully Quoted: A Dictionary of Quotations Requested from the Congressional Research Service," http://www.bartleby.com/73/1788.html.

30. Charles W. Gerstenberg, "Exemptions under the Income Tax," *Bulletin of the National Tax Association* 20, no. 6 (1935): 176.

31. Mabel L. Walker, "Opinion of American Professors of Public Finance on Important Tax Questions as of January 1, 1935," in *Tax Systems of the World* (Chicago: Commerce Clearing House, 1935). For an excellent analysis of the survey, coupled with results from a similar survey in 1994, see Joel B. Slemrod, "Professional Opinions about Tax Policy: 1994 and 1934," *National Tax Journal* 48, no. 1 (1995).

32. On the General Welfare Tax League, see "The General Welfare Tax League," *Bulletin of the National Tax Association* 18, no. 7 (1933).

33. Roy G. Blakey, "Federal Income Tax (Certain Phases)," in *The Federal Revenue System: A Report to the Secretary of the Treasury,* ed. Carl Summer Shoup (Washington, DC: U.S. Department of the Treasury, 20 September 1934).

34. Ibid.

35. Alfred G. Buehler, "The Principles of Expediency and Justice in Taxation," *Bulletin of the National Tax Association* 21, no. 5 (1936): 131.

36. For an influential critique of benefit theories, and a defense of ability standards, see Seligman, "Progressive Taxation in Theory and Practice."

37. Blakey, "Federal Income Tax."

38. Ibid.

39. Ibid.

40. Income estimates for the years before World War II are notoriously unreliable, but contemporary estimates are drawn from National Resources Committee, *Family Expenditures in the United States* (Washington, DC: Government Printing Office, 1941), 1.

41. Blakey, "Federal Income Tax." Blakey described a variety of possible rate revisions. A 10 percent across-the-board surcharge on existing taxes would raise $44 million in a depression year and perhaps $180 million in prosperous times. Even more could be raised by hiking the rates for the "normal" tax. An increase from 4 percent to 6 percent would raise $60 million to $75 million during depression and perhaps $200 million during prosperity. A hike to 10 percent would bring in almost three times that much. Even at that much-inflated rate, the U.S. normal tax would still be less than half its British equivalent. If policymakers wanted to make the income tax more reliable, they would have to move boldly in the British direction, depending more on the normal tax and less on the surtaxes. Even steep hikes in the existing surtax rates would raise relatively little revenue, he warned. During depression years, surtax rates were particularly futile.

42. Blakey, "Federal Income Tax," emphasis in the original.

43. Shoup, "Federal Revenue System: Foreword and Summary of Recommendations."

44. Henry F. Walradt, "Federal Estate and Gift Taxes," in *The Federal Revenue System: A Report to the Secretary of the Treasury,* ed. Carl Summer Shoup (Washington, DC: U.S. Department of the Treasury, 20 September 1934), H1.

45. Ibid., H46–H47.

46. Ibid., H37–H38.

47. Adam Smith, *An Inquiry into the Nature and Causes of the Wealth of Nations,* 5th ed. (1776; ed. Edwin Cannan, London: Methuen, 1904), http://www.econlib.org/library/Smith/smWN21.html. Original cited in Glenn E. Hoover, "The Economic Effects of Inheritance Taxes," *American Economic Review* 17, no. 1 (1927): 40. Hoover also notes similar arguments in Frank William Taussig, *Principles of Economics,* 3rd rev. ed. (New York: Macmillan, 1921).

48. Walradt, "Federal Estate and Gift Taxes," H38.

49. Ibid., H39.

50. Secretary of The Treasury, *Annual Report of the Secretary of the Treasury for Fiscal Year 1924* (Washington, DC: Government Printing Office, 1925), 13, quoted in Walradt, "Federal Estate and Gift Taxes," H43.

51. Walradt, "Federal Estate and Gift Taxes," H43–H44.

52. Quoted in A. C. Pigou, *The Economics of Welfare* (London: Macmillan, 1920), 718–19. For Carver's own work on this subject, see Thomas Nixon Carver, *Essays in Social Justice* (Cambridge, MA: Harvard University Press, 1915). See also D. H. Robertson, "Economic Incentive," *Econometrica* (1921): 231–45.

53. Walradt, "Federal Estate and Gift Taxes," H43–H44.

54. Office of Management and Budget, *Historical Tables,* 32.

55. Shoup, "Federal Revenue System: Foreword and Summary of Recommendations."

56. U.S. Bureau of the Census, *Historical Statistics of the United States: Colonial Times to 1970,* bicentennial ed. (Washington, DC: U.S. Government Printing Office, 1975), part 2, 1107.

57. Shoup, "Federal Revenue System: Foreword and Summary of Recommendations."

58. J. Wilner Sundelson, "Felicitous Nomenclature," *Bulletin of the National Tax Association* 19, no. 1 (1933).

59. For a critique of excise taxes and a history of their imposition in the United States, see the various essays in Shughart, *Taxing Choice.*

60. See, for example, Thomas P. Slaughter, *The Whiskey Rebellion: Frontier Epilogue to the American Revolution* (New York: Oxford University Press, 1986).

61. Many of the Early Republic arguments over excise taxation drew on British antecedents; taxpayers in Great Britain had long decried excise duties, even as their leaders continued to impose them. The British tax system of the late 18th and early 19th centuries included a range of levies, such as a tax on successions (a forerunner of modern estate taxes) and a limited collection of luxury taxes. For more on the British precedent for complaints about excise taxation, see Levi, *Of Rule and Revenue;* Edwin R. A. Seligman, *The Income Tax: A Study of the History, Theory, and Practice of Income Taxation at Home and Abroad,* 2nd ed. (New York: Macmillan, 1921), 57–114; B. E. V. Sabine, *A History of Income Tax* (London: Allen & Unwin, 1966); and William Kennedy, *English Taxation, 1640–1799: An Essay on Policy and Opinion* (London: Frank Cass, 1964).

62. Reavis Cox, "Tobacco Taxes," in *The Federal Revenue System: A Report to the Secretary of the Treasury,* ed. Carl Shoup (Washington, DC: U.S. Department of the Treasury, 20 September 1934).

63. Shoup, "Federal Revenue System: Foreword and Summary of Recommendations."

64. Cox, "Tobacco Taxes."

65. Ibid., 116–17.

66. Carl Summer Shoup, "Manufacturers' Excise and Special Taxes," in *The Federal Revenue System: A Report to the Secretary of the Treasury,* ed. Carl Summer Shoup (Washington, DC: U.S. Department of the Treasury, 20 September 1934).

67. Ibid.

68. Ibid.

69. Carl Summer Shoup, "Excise Taxes" (1934) in Records of the Office of Tax Analysis, Box 1: Excise and Sales Taxes in General, General Records of the Department of the Treasury, Record Group 56; National Archives, College Park, MD.

70. Ibid.

71. Leff, *Limits of Symbolic Reform,* 19–30.

72. Shoup, "Excise Taxes" and "Manufacturers' Excise and Special Taxes."

73. Carl Summer Shoup, "Sales Tax," in *The Federal Revenue System: A Report to the Secretary of the Treasury,* ed. Carl Summer Shoup (Washington, DC: U.S. Department of the Treasury, 20 September 1934).

74. Ibid.

75. Ibid.

Chapter 6

1. Robert H. Jackson and John Q. Barrett, eds., *That Man: An Insider's Portrait of Franklin D. Roosevelt* (New York: Oxford University Press, 2003), 126.

2. Herman Oliphant, "Tax Program," in *Morgenthau Diaries,* Book 2, 275–86.

3. Hessel E. Yntema, "Herman Oliphant," in *Dictionary of American Biography* (New York: Scribner's, 1958); Mark Warren Bailey, "Herman Oliphant," in *American National Biography,* ed. John A. Garraty and Mark C. Carnes (New York: Oxford University Press, 1999); "Herman Oliphant Dies; Treasury Counsel and New Dealers' Expert on Tax Legislation," *Washington Post,* 12 January 1939; "Herman Oliphant of Treasury Dies," *New York Times,* 12 January 1939; "Herman Oliphant," *New York Times,* 12 January 1939. For the journalist's quote on Oliphant, see Joseph Alsop and Robert Kintner, *Men around the President,* 1st ed. (New York: Doubleday Doran, 1939). This quote, and additional discussion of Oliphant's role, can also be found in Lambert, "New Deal Revenue Acts," 175–77. See also "Mr. Roosevelt's Men," 141; and Blum, *From the Morgenthau Diaries,* 298–99.

4. For Oliphant's most famous exposition on legal realism, see Herman Oliphant, "A Return to Stare Decisis," *American Bar Association Journal* 14 (1928). On legal realism generally, see Laura Kalman, *Legal Realism at Yale, 1927–1960* (Chapel Hill: University of North Carolina Press, 1986), especially chapter 1; Brian R. Leiter, "American Legal Realism," in *Blackwell Guide to the Philosophy of Law and Legal Theory,* ed. William A. Edmundson and Martin P. Golding (Oxford: Blackwell, 2003). On the Veblenite roots of realism, see Daniel R. Ernst, "Common Laborers? Industrial Pluralists, Legal Realists, and the Law of Industrial Disputes, 1915–1943," *Law and History Review* 11, no. 1 (1993): 70–7. On the realist reconstruction of antimonopoly policy that occurred in the late

1930s (and which largely abandoned Oliphant's tax-based approach to the issue), see Alan Brinkley, "The Antimonopoly Ideal and the Liberal State: The Case of Thurman Arnold," *Journal of American History* 80, no. 2 (1993).

Legal historians disagree on which New Dealers can reasonably be called realists, but two of the more prominent candidates are James Landis and William O. Douglas; see Thomas K. McCraw, *Prophets of Regulation: Charles Francis Adams, Louis D. Brandeis, James M. Landis, Alfred E. Kahn* (Cambridge, MA: Belknap Press of Harvard University Press, 1984), chs. 5–6; Donald A. Ritchie, *James M. Landis, Dean of the Regulators* (Cambridge, MA: Harvard University Press, 1980); and Bruce Allen Murphy, *Wild Bill: The Legend and Life of William O. Douglas,* 1st ed. (New York: Random House, 2003).

5. In a generally warm review of Oliphant's 1923 casebook on trade regulation, his future colleague at Treasury, Roswell Magill, noted approvingly Oliphant's functional approach to a range of legal issues. While no realist himself, Magill recognized the utility to connecting sometimes abstract legal issues with their real-world application. See Roswell Magill, "Review of *Cases on Trade Regulation,*" *Michigan Law Review* 21, no. 7 (1923).

6. Oliphant, "Tax Program," 279–80.

7. Ibid., 277.

8. Jackson and Barrett, *That Man,* 126. Budget numbers from Office of Management and Budget, *Historical Tables,* 21.

9. Oliphant, "Tax Program," 280.

10. On fiscal conservatism in the Roosevelt administration, as well as a review of literature indicating a much broader, bipartisan consensus on behalf of such ideas, see Zelizer, "Forgotten Legacy of the New Deal."

11. On the pro-spending group of proto-Keynesians, see Stein, *Fiscal Revolution,* 56.

12. Oliphant, "Tax Program," 277.

13. David Joulfaian, "The Federal Estate and Gift Tax: Description, Profile of Taxpayers, and Economic Consequences," in *Office of Tax Analysis Papers* (Washington, DC: U.S. Department of the Treasury, Office of Tax Analysis, 1998).

14. Oliphant, "Tax Program," 280.

15. Inheritance taxes could also be graduated according to the relationship of the beneficiary and the deceased. Many tax theorists believed that close relatives should be taxed more lightly than distant relations or friends. For an excellent contemporary discussion of estate and inheritance taxes, including a comparison of their relative advantages, see Walradt, "Federal Estate and Federal Gift Taxes."

16. Oliphant, "Tax Program," 280.

17. Ibid., 281.

18. Ibid., 282.

19. Ibid. The Oliphant memo concluded with two final, less dramatic recommendations. First, he urged a thorough revision of oil depletion allowances—tax preferences that allowed petroleum producers to substantially reduce their tax liability by granting them deductions for the depletion of existing oil deposits. The allowance was first granted during World War I to encourage investment in this high-risk industry, but it had long since outlived its usefulness. Second, Oliphant suggested a constitutional amendment that would allow the federal government to tax the securities of state and

local governments (and vice versa). Treasury officials had been asking for such an amendment for well more than a decade; Andrew Mellon was a principal opponent of exempt bonds, insisting that they allowed wealthy individuals to escape their fair share of taxation, even as the bonds served to distort investment decisions. Expert opinion was almost unanimous in considering such bonds a pernicious tool of tax avoidance for the rich. "The amounts of tax exempt securities, Federal, State, and Municipal, embarrass us at almost every turn," Oliphant complained. See Ibid., 283.

20. "Tax Profits!," *New Republic,* 24 May 1933; "Wanted: A Philosophy of Taxation," *Nation,* 3 July 1935.

21. Shoup, "Federal Revenue System: Foreword and Summary of Recommendations."

22. See Nelson L. Dawson, *Louis D. Brandeis, Felix Frankfurter, and the New Deal* (Hamden, CT: Archon Books, 1980), 29–30, 159–61, 187. Brandeis outlined his tax ideas as early as 1922 in a letter to Frankfurter. For the 1922 memo, see Louis Dembitz Brandeis, *Letters of Louis D. Brandeis,* vol. 5 (Albany: State University of New York Press, 1971), 67–68. See also Nelson L. Dawson, *Brandeis and America* (Lexington: University Press of Kentucky, 1989), 48–49; Philippa Strum, *Louis D. Brandeis: Justice for the People* (Cambridge, MA: Harvard University Press, 1984), 383, 390–93. On Brandeis's satisfaction with FDR's 1935 tax message, see Michael E. Parrish, *Felix Frankfurter and His Times* (New York: Free Press, 1982), 248.

23. Ellis Wayne Hawley, *The New Deal and the Problem of Monopoly: A Study in Economic Ambivalence* (New York: Fordham University Press, 1995), 344; Lambert, "New Deal Revenue Acts," 179–80. On the influence of Brandeis and Frankfurter more generally, see Dawson, *Louis D. Brandeis, Felix Frankfurter, and the New Deal.*

24. On Frankfurter's role, see Blum, *From the Morgenthau Diaries,* 299. Brandeis had been agitating for some tax penalty on holding companies. See, for example, Louis Brandeis to Felix Frankfurter, 26 January 1932, excerpted in Louis Dembitz Brandeis, Felix Frankfurter, Melvin I. Urofsky, and David W. Levy, *"Half Brother, Half Son": The Letters of Louis D. Brandeis to Felix Frankfurter,* 1st ed. (Norman: University of Oklahoma Press, 1991), 474–75. Oliphant recommended a tax of 1 percent to 5 percent, insisting that such a burden was economically feasible, especially if phased in gradually. See Oliphant, "Tax Program," 280–81.

25. On the Frankfurter promise, see Bruce Allen Murphy, *The Brandeis/Frankfurter Connection: The Secret Political Activities of Two Supreme Court Justices* (New York: Oxford University Press, 1982), 159–60. Roosevelt asked Frankfurter to draw up plans for tax reform and later directed Morgenthau to consider them seriously. See Morgenthau, *Morgenthau Diaries,* Book 2, 332–35. In late January 1935, Roosevelt told Corcoran and Benjamin Cohen that he supported tax measures aimed at curtailing corporate size. See Murphy, *Brandeis/Frankfurter Connection,* 160. Murphy attributes much of the rhetoric in Roosevelt's eventual tax message of June 1935 to Frankfurter, but that seems unlikely, given the active and protracted role that others played in the development of that message. And Brandeisian overtones in the message were most likely the work of Oliphant and Robert Jackson, his assistant.

26. Franklin D. Roosevelt, Felix Frankfurter, and Max Freedman, *Roosevelt and Frankfurter: Their Correspondence, 1928–1945* (Boston: Little, Brown, 1968), 140.

27. Ibid., 139.

28. Jackson and Barrett, *That Man,* 119, 120.

29. Kirk J. Stark, "The Unfulfilled Tax Legacy of Justice Robert H. Jackson," *New York University Tax Review* 54(2001): 189.

30. "Mellon Brands Tax Suit 'Politics'," *New York Times,* 12 March 1934, 2.

31. "Andrew Mellon Is Exonerated; Grand Jury Votes 'No Bill' in U.S. Tax Action after Hearing Five Witnesses," *Wall Street Journal,* 9 May 1934, 6; Jackson and Barrett, *That Man,* 124–25.

32. Stark, "Unfulfilled Tax Legacy," 176–77; Jackson and Barrett, *That Man,* 126.

33. Blum, *From the Morgenthau Diaries,* 324; Morgenthau, *Morgenthau Diaries,* Book 5, 80.

34. Jackson and Barrett, *That Man,* 125.

35. Ibid.

36. Stark, "Unfulfilled Tax Legacy," 190.

37. Blum, *From the Morgenthau Diaries,* 325.

38. Morgenthau, *Morgenthau Diaries,* Book 2, 68.

39. Klaus, "Income and Income Taxes" (1935, 1) in Papers of Robert H. Jackson, Box 76, General Counsel, Bureau of Internal Revenue, Tax Studies—Income and Income Taxes; Library of Congress, Washington, DC. While Klaus did the writing, this study was prepared under Jackson supervision and guidance.

40. Blakey, "Federal Income Tax."

41. Klaus, "Income and Income Taxes."

42. U.S. Bureau of the Census, *Historical Statistics,* part 2, 1109.

43. Klaus, "Income and Income Taxes," 6.

44. Ibid., 15.

45. Ibid., 16. For the *Fortune* articles, see "Du Pont III: Delaware," *Fortune* 11, no. 1 (1935): 1; "The Corporation," *Fortune* 10, no. 6 (1934); "Its Management," *Fortune* 10, no. 6 (1934); "An Index," *Fortune* 10, no. 5 (1934); and "The Family Tree," *Fortune* 10, no. 5 (1934).

46. Klaus, "Income and Income Taxes," 17.

47. Klaus, "Income and Income Taxes."

48. Ibid.

49. Ibid.

50. Ibid.

51. Ibid.

52. Ibid.

53. Robert H. Jackson, "Effectiveness of Income Tax Law in Higher and Lower Brackets" (1935, 2) in Papers of Robert H. Jackson, Box 75, General Counsel, Bureau of Internal Revenue, Revenue Act of 1935; Library of Congress, Washington, DC.

54. Ibid., 2–3.

55. Ibid.

56. Jackson and Barrett, *That Man,* 128.

57. Robert H. Jackson, "Tax Changes to Improve Economic Structure" (1935) in Robert H. Jackson Papers, Box 75, General Counsel, Bureau of Internal Revenue, Revenue Act of 1935; Library of Congress, Washington, DC; George Haas, "Suggested Draft of Message to Congress on Taxation" (1935) in Robert H. Jackson Papers, Box 75, General Counsel, Bureau of Internal Revenue, Revenue Act of 1935, Washington, DC, Library of Congress; Robert H. Jackson and George Haas, "Suggested Draft of Message to Congress on Taxation" (1935) in Robert H. Jackson Papers, Box 75, General Counsel, Bureau of Internal Revenue, Revenue Act of 1935; Library of Congress, Washington, DC. All quotations are from this last version.

58. Jackson and Haas, "Suggested Draft of Message to Congress on Taxation," 5.

59. Ibid., 6.

60. Ibid., 7–8.

61. Franklin D. Roosevelt, *Complete Presidential Press Conferences of Franklin D. Roosevelt,* vol. 5 (New York: Da Capo Press, 1972), 33; Roosevelt, *Public Papers and Addresses,* vol. 4, 16–17, 36. See also Lambert, "New Deal Revenue Acts," 172.

62. Roosevelt, *Public Papers and Addresses,* vol. 1, 751–54, 766; Leff, *Limits of Symbolic Reform,* 131–32; Lambert, "New Deal Revenue Acts," 154–55, 180–81.

63. Raymond Moley, *After Seven Years* (New York: Da Capo Press, 1972), 308–09.

64. Raymond Moley, "Moley's Redraft of Tax Message" (1935) in Papers of Robert H. Jackson, Box 75, General Counsel, Bureau of Internal Revenue, Revenue Act of 1935; Library of Congress, Washington, DC.

65. Lambert, "New Deal Revenue Acts," 164–65; T. Harry Williams, *Huey Long* (New York: Knopf, 1989), 693; Alan Brinkley, *Voices of Protest: Huey Long, Father Coughlin, and the Great Depression,* 1st ed. (New York: Knopf, 1982); T. Harry Williams, "The Gentleman from Louisiana: Demagogue or Democrat," *Journal of Southern History* 26, no. 1 (1960): 8; Leff, *Limits of Symbolic Reform,* 123–24.

66. Hugh S. Johnson, "Pied Pipers," *Vital Speeches of the Day,* 11 March 1935, 354–60; Lambert, "New Deal Revenue Acts," 166; Leff, *Limits of Symbolic Reform,* 123–25, 148.

67. George W. Norris, "Redistribution of Wealth," *Vital Speeches of the Day,* 25 February 1935, 327–31. La Follette quotation from Leff, *Limits of Symbolic Reform,* 128. This discussion of congressional liberals, as well as Huey Long's tax proposals, relies heavily on Leff's excellent treatment of the subject.

68. "Mr. President, Begin to Tax!," *Nation,* 6 March 1935; "A New Outlook on Public Finance," *Nation,* 17 October 1934.

69. Paul Studenski, "Tax Program for the Future," *Nation,* 6 March 1935. Studenski recommended cutting the married couple exemption from $2,500 to $1,500 and the minor child exemption from $400 to $250.

70. Harold M. Groves, "A Tax Policy for the United States," *New Republic,* 24 January 1934; "Tax Profits!" For arguments that existing New Deal tax initiatives had placed a heavy burden on consumers and a relatively light one on business, see John T. Flynn, "Other People's Money," *New Republic,* 6 February 1935.

71. This section on conservative suspicion of Roosevelt, particularly with regard to tax policy, relies on Lambert, "New Deal Revenue Acts," 157–61; "Dr. Butler Scores Radicals for Talk of Wide Poverty," *New York Times,* 3 September 1934, 1; John C. Cresswill,

"The Redistribution of Wealth Ceases to Be a Theory," *Magazine of Wall Street*, 6 January 1934; George Wolfskill, *The Revolt of the Conservatives* (Boston: Houghton Mifflin, 1962), 130; Irving Brant, *Storm over the Constitution* (Indianapolis: Bobbs-Merrill, 1936).

72. Lawrence quotes are drawn from Paul, *Taxation in the United States*, 181–82.

73. Percy H. Johnston, "Our Overwhelming Tax Problems," *Vital Speeches of the Day*, 22 October 1934, 37–39.

74. Walter S. Landis, "The Hodge Podge of Tax Legislation," *Vital Speeches of the Day*, 11 March 1935, 369–70.

75. Mark Eisner, "Collecting and Spending the Tax Dollar," *Vital Speeches of the Day*, 6 May 1935, 510–11.

76. Samuel Untermyer, "The Greatest Obstacle to National Recovery—Our Destructive Income Taxes," *Vital Speeches of the Day*, 22 April 1935, 464–66; "Untermyer Urges Federal Sales Tax," *New York Times*, 17 March 1935, 25.

77. "Democracy Saved, Farley Declares," *New York Times*, 23 February 1936, 33.

78. Raymond Moley, *The First New Deal*, 1st ed. (New York: Harcourt Brace & World, 1966), 527–28, and *After Seven Years*, 308; Leff, *Limits of Symbolic Reform*, 134. On the Liberty League, see Frederick Rudolph, "The American Liberty League, 1934–1940," *American Historical Review* 56, no. 1 (1950); Wolfskill, *Revolt of the Conservatives*.

79. Blum, *From the Morgenthau Diaries*, 301.

80. Jackson and Barrett,*That Man*, 127–28. The quasi-Keynesian implications of this statement, including its focus on consumption and the danger of excess saving, seems out of character for this stage of the New Deal. Writing many years later, Jackson may have been projecting such motives into a period when they had not yet emerged.

81. Harold L. Ickes, *The Secret Diary of Harold L. Ickes* (New York: Simon and Schuster, 1953), 384, 472; Lambert, "New Deal Revenue Acts," 188–89.

82. Moley, *After Seven Years*, 310.

83. All quotations for the Roosevelt message to Congress are taken from Roosevelt, *Public Papers and Addresses*, vol. 4, 270–77.

84. Roswell Foster Magill, Lovell Hallet Parker, Eldon Paul King, and U.S. Congress Joint Committee on Internal Revenue Taxation, *A Summary of the British Tax System, with Special Reference to Its Administration* (Washington, DC: U.S. Government Printing Office, 1934).

85. Morgenthau, *Morgenthau Diaries*, Book 7, 15–15a. In fact, Morgenthau had spoken with Harrison the day before Roosevelt delivered his message and led the Finance chairman to believe that no new tax proposals were imminent. The Senate was then considering a joint resolution to extend expiring taxes, just as Roosevelt had asked in his annual budget message. "That is everything that we figured on," Morgenthau told him. "That is the absolute lowdown and you know that I never give you anything but that." See Martha H. Swain, *Pat Harrison: The New Deal Years* (Jackson: University Press of Mississippi, 1978), 107; "Widely Varied Views Greet Tax Proposals," *Washington Post*, 20 June 1935, 1.

86. Moley, *After Seven Years;* Patterson, *Congressional Conservatism and the New Deal*, 65–67; Turner Catledge, "Sturdy Pilot of the New Tax Program," *New York Times*, 7 July 1935, SM3.

87. Felix Bruner, "Message from Roosevelt Urges Levies on Huge Incomes, Gifts," *Washington Post,* 20 June 1935, 1; "Tax Move a Big Surprise," *New York Times,* 20 June 1935, 1; "Congress Planning Quick Tax Action," *New York Times,* 20 June 1935, 2.

88. "Congress Planning Quick Tax Action," 2.

89. For La Follette quotation, see "Widely Varied Views Greet Tax Proposals." For a detailed discussion of LaFollette's tax positions, see Leff, *Limits of Symbolic Reform,* 109–19.

90. "Text of Vandenberg Address on Tax Program," *Washington Post,* 8 July 1935, 7.

91. "Widely Varied Views Greet Tax Proposals," 1.

92. "Press Comment on President's Tax Message," *New York Times,* 21 June 1935, 3; Raymond Clapper, "Between You and Me," *Washington Post,* 21 June 1935, 2.

93. "Press Comment on President's Tax Message."

94. Quoted in Paul, *Taxation in the United States,* 185.

95. "Rates and Yields," *New York Times,* 12 July 1935, 18.

96. Turner Catledge, "New Mood of Congress Colors the Outlook," *New York Times,* 7 July 1935, E3.

97. Lambert, "New Deal Revenue Acts," 198–203.

98. "The Tax Fiasco," *Nation,* 10 July 1935; "Wanted: A Philosophy of Taxation."

99. All quotations from Lambert, "New Deal Revenue Acts," 191.

100. "Chamber Opens War on Tax Plan," *New York Times,* 12 July 1935, 8.

101. *Proposed Taxation of Individual and Corporate Income, Inheritances, and Gifts: Hearings Before the Committee on Ways and Means,* 74th Cong., 1st sess. 245–53 (8–13 July 1935).

102. Ibid., 128.

103. Ibid., 254.

104. Ibid., 199–200.

105. Ibid., 172, 173.

106. Fred G. Clark, "The Soak-the-Thrifty Tax," *Vital Speeches of the Day,* 15 July 1935, 677–78.

107. "Roosevelt Maps His Tax Bill Drive with House Chiefs," *New York Times,* 5 July 1935, 1. See also "Shouse Asserts Roosevelt Has Set Up Bureaucratic Autocracy for Government," *New York Times,* 2 July 1935, 13.

108. *Proposed Taxation,* 319.

109. Edward P. Costigan, "Taxes on Wealth," *Vital Speeches of the Day,* 15 July 1935, 673–76.

110. Edgar J. Goodrich, "House Bill Applies New Taxation Principles," *New York Times,* 4 August 1935, E3.

111. "Progressives Join to Pass New Taxes at Present Session," *New York Times,* 22 June 1935, 1; Blakey and Blakey, *Federal Income Tax,* 371–74.

112. Initial estimates suggested that the inheritance levy would raise $200 million, the new income tax rates another $100 million, and the corporate tax about $40 million. See Turner Catledge, "New Tax Program Pressed Despite a Revolt in House: Yield Is Put at $340,000,000," *New York Times,* 26 June 1935, 1; "Tentative New Tax Rates," *New York Times,* 26 June 1935, 1; Franklyn Waltman Jr., "First Part of Program for Taxes on Wealth Goes to Senate Today," *Washington Post,* 26 June 1935, 1.

113. "Incomes over Million Totaled 46 in 1933: Total for Corporations Was 2½ Billions," *New York Times,* 26 June 1935, 2; Blakey and Blakey, *Federal Income Tax,* 378–79; Morgenthau, *Morgenthau Diaries,* Book 7, 161.

114. Thomas I. Parkinson, "Undigested Taxes," *Vital Speeches of the Day,* 9 September 1935.

115. National Resources Committee, *Family Expenditures in the United States.*

116. Leff, *Limits of Symbolic Reform,* 144–45; Edgar J. Goodrich, "Big Fortunes Safe from Wealth Tax," *New York Times,* 30 June 1935, E11.

117. Moley, *After Seven Years.*

Chapter 7

1. Mark Hugh Leff, "Taxing the 'Forgotten Man': The Politics of Social Security Finance in the New Deal," *Journal of American History* 70 (1983): 360.

2. Ibid., 376.

3. Leuchtenburg, *Franklin D. Roosevelt and the New Deal:* 132–33.

4. On New Deal fiscal conservatism generally, see Zelizer, "Forgotten Legacy of the New Deal."

5. Schlesinger, *Coming of the New Deal,* 308.

6. On the use of trust fund financing to control expenditures, see Eric Patashnik and Julian Zelizer, "Paying for Medicare: Benefits, Budgets, and Wilbur Mills's Policy Legacy," *Journal of Health Politics, Policy and Law* 26, no. 1 (2001); and Eric M. Patashnik, *Putting Trust in the U.S. Budget: Federal Trust Funds and the Politics of Commitment* (New York: Cambridge University Press, 2000).

7. Quoted in Leff, "Taxing the 'Forgotten Man'," 374.

8. Ibid., 375–76.

9. Roosevelt, *Public Papers and Addresses,* vol. 4, 352–57.

10. Ibid., 392.; Roosevelt, *Public Papers and Addresses,* vol. 5, 17.

11. Roosevelt, *Public Papers and Addresses,* vol. 5, 17.

12. Leuchtenburg, *Franklin D. Roosevelt and the New Deal:* 171; Roosevelt, *Complete Presidential Press Conferences,* vol. 7, 103, 153; Lambert, "New Deal Revenue Acts," 268.

13. As one Treasury aide later observed, "The primary purpose of the undistributed profits tax was to obtain some $600 millions of additional annual revenues." See George Haas, "Rationale of the Undistributed Profits Tax" (1937) in Box 14, Corporations, Partnerships, and Sole Owners to Excess Profits and War Profits: 1936–1940,

Records of the Office of Tax Analysis/Division of Tax Research, General Records of the Department of the Treasury, Record Group 56; National Archives, College Park, MD.

14. U.S. Department of the Treasury, "Undistributed Profits Tax" (1937) in Tax Revision Studies, 1937; Tax Reform Programs and Studies, Records of the Office of Tax Analysis/Division of Tax Research, General Records of the Department of the Treasury, Record Group 56; National Archives at College Park, MD.

15. For a useful summary of economic opinion on business taxes during the Roosevelt era, see Gerhard Colm, "Conflicting Theories of Corporate Income Taxation," *Law and Contemporary Problems* 7, no. 2 (1940); and Paul Studenski, "Toward a Theory of Business Taxation," *Journal of Political Economy* 48, no. 5 (1940). Many problems associated with corporate income taxation had been under intense debate since World War I. For a noteworthy contribution to this debate, see Thomas S. Adams, "Fundamental Problems of Federal Income Taxation," *Quarterly Journal of Economics* 35, no. 4 (1921).

16. Shoup, "Federal Revenue System: Foreword and Summary of Recommendations."

17. For a useful overview of entity theory, see Steven A. Bank, "Entity Theory as Myth," 450. See also Reuven S. Avi-Yonah, "Corporations, Society, and the State: A Defense of the Corporate Tax," *Virginia Law Review* 90 (2004); and Marjorie E. Kornhauser, "Corporate Regulation and the Origins of the Corporate Income Tax," *Indiana Law Journal* 66 (1990).

18. While ostensibly designed to raise revenue, the 1909 corporation excise tax was actually a thinly veiled experiment in corporate regulation. Featuring a publicity provision that would have required corporations to disclose their tax returns to the general public, it was designed to promote transparency and accountability. The tax succumbed to a brutal assault from business leaders, who resented not its economic burden but its intrusions on corporate privacy. The best scholarly treatment of the corporation excise tax is Bank, "Corporate Regulation."

19. For a contemporary critique of entity theory see " 'Corporate Entity': Its Limitations as a Useful Legal Conception," *Yale Law Journal* 36, no. 2 (1926); and Maurice Finkelstein, "The Corporate Entity and the Income Tax," *Yale Law Journal* 44, no. 3 (1935).

20. Dividends were not subject to the "normal" tax, but they were vulnerable to the "surtax." Throughout the early 1930s, individual income above the exemption level was subject to a relatively low basic tax rate; in 1934, it was set at 4 percent. In addition, income above a certain level was also subject to a graduated surtax. The surtax was not only levied at higher rates but also included in its base certain kinds of income not subject to the normal tax, including dividends.

21. Carl Summer Shoup, "The Federal Revenue System: Individual Proprietorship, Partnership, and Corporation (Differential Tax Treatment under the Income Tax Laws); Imputed Income; Miscellaneous Tax Matters," (1934) in Box 62, Tax Reform Programs and Studies, Records of the Office of Tax Analysis/Division of Tax Research, General Records of the Department of the Treasury, Record Group 56; National Archives, College Park, MD.

22. Academic experts had long debated the issue of double taxation, with most concluding that it was best avoided through a restructuring of the individual income tax. For a contemporary discussion of the controversy, see H. L. Lutz, "The Treatment of Dividends in Income Taxation," *Journal of Political Economy* 33, no. 2 (1925);

Carl F. Wehrwein, "Some Aspects of the Double-Taxation Problem," *Journal of Political Economy* 44, no. 4 (1936).

23. Shoup, "The Federal Revenue System: Individual Proprietorship, Partnership, and Corporation (Differential Tax Treatment under the Income Tax Laws); Imputed Income; Miscellaneous Tax Matters." In this view, Shoup had support from other economists, who viewed ability theories skeptically when applied to business entities. See, for instance, Merlin H. Hunter, "Shall We Tax Corporations or Business?," *American Economic Review* 26, no. 1 (1936).

24. Shoup, "Individual Proprietorship, Partnership, and Corporation (Differential Tax Treatment under the Income Tax Laws); Imputed Income; Miscellaneous Tax Matters."

25. Ibid. See also Carl Summer Shoup, "The Corporation Tax and the Normal Tax," *Bulletin of the National Tax Association* 19, no. 4 (1934).

26. Raymond Moley, "Memorandum of May 19, 1932," in Box 282, Folder 3, Raymond Moley Papers, Hoover Institution Library and Archives, Stanford University (1932). Other members of the Brains Trust contributed to this memo, especially Rexford Tugwell. Elliot Rosen argues that Moley took the lead in crafting the proposal for an undistributed profits tax. See Elliot A. Rosen, *Hoover, Roosevelt, and the Brains Trust: From Depression to New Deal* (New York: Columbia University Press, 1977), 114–50. By contrast, legal historian Steven Bank has maintained that Berle was the principal advocate for the UPT. See Bank, "Corporate Managers, Agency Costs, and the Rise of Double Taxation."

27. Steven A. Bank, "Is Double Taxation a Scapegoat for Declining Dividends? Evidence from History," *New York University Tax Review* 56 (2003): 474.

28. Adams, "Federal Taxes upon Income and Excess Profits," 24–26. Lawmakers heeded Adams's advice, enacting an undistributed profits tax as part of their wartime revenue reforms. But the UPT of World War I proved ineffective. By granting generous exemptions for reserves used to finance productive enterprise, lawmakers rendered it useless. For that conclusion, see U.S. Department of the Treasury, "Undistributed Profits Tax"; and Benjamin Graham, "The Undistributed Profits Tax and the Investor," *Yale Law Journal* 46, no. 1 (1936).

29. Rexford G. Tugwell, *The Industrial Discipline and the Governmental Arts* (New York: Columbia University Press, 1933), 203–7; Gerhard Colm, "Conflicting Theories of Corporate Income Taxation."

30. Haas, "Rationale of the Undistributed Profits Tax."

31. This discussion of the "agency costs" associated with independent management of publicly traded corporations draws on the excellent work by legal historian Steven Bank. See "Corporate Managers, Agency Costs, and the Rise of Double Taxation" and "Rethinking Double Taxation's Role in Dividend Policy."

32. Adolf Augustus Berle and Gardiner Colt Means, *The Modern Corporation and Private Property* (New York: Commerce Clearing House, 1932). See also Gardiner Means, "The Growth in the Relative Importance of the Large Corporation in American Life," *American Economic Review* 21, no. 1 (1931); and W. L. Crum, "Concentration of Corporate Control," *Journal of Business of the University of Chicago* 8, no. 3 (1935).

33. Robert Weidenhammer, "Causes and Repercussions of the Faulty Investment of Corporate Savings," *American Economic Review* 23, no. 1 (1933): 40.

34. Moley, "Memorandum of May 19, 1932"; Rosen, *Hoover, Roosevelt, and the Brains Trust,* 142. While the propensity of corporations to oversave was widely asserted, the empirical foundation for such claims was weak. Beginning in the latter half of the 1930s, economists would bolster this case, offering data on the relationship between income and the propensity to save, both for companies and individuals. For discussion of this phenomenon, see Mordecai Ezekiel, "An Annual Estimate of Savings by Individuals," *Review of Economic Statistics* 19, no. 4 (1937); Donald W. Gilbert, "Taxation and Economic Stability," *Quarterly Journal of Economics* 56, no. 3 (1942); and Joshua C. Hubbard, "Income Creation by Means of Income Taxation," *Quarterly Journal of Economics* 58, no. 2 (1944).

35. Reavis Cox, "Memorandum N: The Processing Taxes and Taxes Imposed by the Bankhead and Kerr Acts," in Box 62, Tax Reform Programs and Studies, Records of the Office of Tax Analysis/Division of Tax Research, General Records of the Department of the Treasury, Record Group 56; National Archives, College Park, MD (1934). Echoing the party line among Treasury technical tax staff, Cox also insisted that taxes were a poor instrument for large-scale economic reform. "Social control and planning must necessarily be flexible, changing their procedures and immediate objective frequently, sometimes drastically," he wrote. "Fiscal administration, to be successful and efficient, requires above all stability and regularity." Clearly, Cox and his colleagues on Treasury technical staff were not inclined to support experiments in social taxation.

36. *Revenue Act of 1936: Hearings on H.R. 12395, Before the Committee on Finance,* 74th Cong. 927–28 (1936); Oliphant, "Tax Program."

37. Moley, *After Seven Years,* 310–12. It remains unclear whether Moley was ever a serious advocate of the UPT. Some scholars, like Steven Bank, have pointed out that the New Deal memo was a pastiche of economic theories, and Moley merely served to organize the project.

38. Morgenthau, *Morgenthau Diaries,* Book 18, 114–19; Lambert, "New Deal Revenue Acts," 272; Hawley, *New Deal and the Problem of Monopoly,* 350–51; Schlesinger, *Politics of Upheaval,* 507; Moley, *After Seven Years,* 302.

39. Morgenthau, *Morgenthau Diaries,* Book 18, 114–19.

40. *Revenue Act of 1936,* 889–90.

41. On Roosevelt's failure to seek broad consultation, see Arthur Krock, "Tax Bill Muddle Laid to Lack of Foresight," *New York Times,* 17 May 1936, E3.

42. Roosevelt, *Public Papers and Addresses,* vol. 5, 105. On Roosevelt's decision to stress fairness arguments, see Lambert, "New Deal Revenue Acts," 276.

43. Joseph Alsop and Robert Kintner, "Henry Penny," *Saturday Evening Post,* 1 April 1939; Moley, *After Seven Years,* 309; Lambert, "New Deal Revenue Acts," 287.

44. *Revenue Act of 1936,* 12.

45. Ibid., 19.

46. Ibid.

47. Robert H. Jackson, "The Proposed Revision of Corporation Taxes," *Vital Speeches of the Day,* 6 April 1936, 431–34.

48. Ibid.

49. Krock, "Tax Bill Muddle Laid to Lack of Foresight"; Paul, *Taxation in the United States,* 192. Republican members of the Ways and Means Committee fanned these

flames, raising doubts about any proposal that enjoyed support from academics like Oliphant and Tugwell. On worries about the influence of Roosevelt's advisers, see Lambert, "New Deal Revenue Acts," 297–99.

50. *Revenue Act of 1936*; Paul, *Taxation in the United States,* 194.

51. *Revenue Act of 1936*, 93. Seidman did not oppose the UPT in theory, but believed that it required further study. See similar comments in the testimony by Yale economist Fred Rogers Fairchild, Fred Clausen of the U.S. Chamber of Commerce, and Price Waterhouse partner George May: *Revenue Act of 1936*, 737; 202, 221; and 538–49.

52. "The Ship and the Rats," *New York Times,* 8 April 1936.

53. *Revenue Act of 1936,* 676.

54. Ibid., 207.

55. Ibid., 337.

56. Ibid., 204.

57. Ibid., 676.

58. Ibid., 320. Another witness, James Emery of NAM, compared business saving to old-age security. "If it be good policy for Government to compel reserves for security against the hazard of individual employment and age," he said with reference to the recent Social Security legislation, "it must be equally sound business policy to encourage rather than discourage the voluntary creation of corporate reserves against the continuous hazards of industrial operation, the casualties of which are written daily in the columns of business obituary." See *Revenue Act of 1936,* 680.

59. See comments by Fairchild, as well as those by R. C. Fulbright of the Southern Pine Association: *Revenue Act of 1936,* 208, 464–71.

60. Blum, *From the Morgenthau Diaries,* 312.

61. *Revenue Act of 1936,* 339.

62. Ibid., 28–37, 795.

63. Ibid., 225, 737–39, 221.

64. Ibid., 339.

65. Ibid., 650.

66. Ibid., 195.

67. For a summary of the House bill, see Roy G. Blakey and Gladys Blakey, "The Revenue Act of 1936," *American Economic Review* 26, no. 3 (1936): 471–72.

68. Revenue Act of 1936: Report of the Senate Committee on Finance, S. Rep. No. 74-1242, at 4.

69. Ibid.

70. On Upham, see Lambert, "New Deal Revenue Acts," 324–25.

71. Marriner Eccles, "Memorandum to the President," in *Franklin D. Roosevelt Papers,* office file 962, box 1 (Hyde Park, NY: Franklin D. Roosevelt Library, 1936).

72. For a summary of the law, see Blakey and Blakey, "Revenue Act of 1936."

73. The Treasury estimated that the tax added roughly 1 percent to the average effective corporate tax rate. It also helped boost federal revenue by almost $300 million

in 1937. Individual income tax receipts also rose by $400 million, and administration officials attributed the increase to a rise in taxable dividends. See U.S. Department of the Treasury, *Annual Report of the Secretary of the Treasury on the State of the Finances: Fiscal Year Ending June 30, 1937* (Washington, DC: Government Printing Office), 1–5.

74. Bank, "Tax, Corporate Governance, and Norms."

75. For critical comment by two legal scholars on the actual, versus the theoretical, application of the UPT, see John B. Martin Jr., "Taxation of Undistributed Corporate Profits," *Michigan Law Review* 35, no. 1 (1936); and Graham, "Undistributed Profits Tax."

76. *Proceedings of the National Tax Association, 1938* (Washington, DC: National Tax Association, 1938), 574–96. The NTA committee included several economists sympathetic to the Roosevelt tax agenda, including Robert M. Haig, who had served in the Treasury during the early years of the Roosevelt presidency.

77. Helvering v. Gregory, 69 F.2d 809, 810 (2d Cir. 1934).

78. In fact, there was even room for argument among lawyers about this distinction. See Lucius A. Buck, "Income Tax Evasion and Avoidance: The Deflection of Income," *Virginia Law Review* 23, no. 2 (1936); and Montgomery B. Angell, "Tax Evasion and Tax Avoidance," *Columbia Law Review* 38, no. 1 (1938).

79. Roosevelt, *Complete Presidential Press Conferences,* vol. 9, 399.

80. Gladys Blakey and Roy G. Blakey, "The Revenue Act of 1937," *American Economic Review* 27, no. 4 (1937): 703; Henry Morgenthau, "Memorandum to the President on Tax Avoidance and Evasion," 21 May 1937, in Box 43, Methods of Raising Additional Revenue, Records of the Office of Tax Analysis/Division of Tax Research, General Records of the Department of the Treasury, Record Group 56; National Archives, College Park, MD.

81. *Hearings Before the Joint Committee on Tax Evasion and Avoidance,* 75th Cong. 24 (1937).

82. Henry J. Morgenthau, memo to Franklin D. Roosevelt, 13 August 1936, in *Franklin D. Roosevelt Papers,* office file 137, box 2 (Hyde Park, NY: Franklin D. Roosevelt Library, 1936); and *Morgenthau Diaries,* Book 66, 72. See also Lambert, "New Deal Revenue Acts," 365; and Blum, *From the Morgenthau Diaries,* 362.

83. Blum, *From the Morgenthau Diaries,* 327.

84. Ibid., 329.

85. Morgenthau, "Memorandum to the President on Tax Avoidance and Evasion."

86. Ibid. Jacob Schick, founder of the Schick Dry Shaver Company, was the most notorious taxpayer when it came to such devices. As he had renounced his U.S. citizenship, moved to Canada, and created a series of Bahamian corporations, his tax machinations were under scrutiny by the BIR.

87. Ibid.

88. Ibid. On the exempt securities issue, see William R. Watkins, "The Power of the State and Federal Governments to Tax One Another," *Virginia Law Review* 24, no. 5 (1938): 475–506.

89. Morgenthau, "Memorandum to the President on Tax Avoidance and Evasion." For the "sporting" comment, see "Mr. Morgenthau's Exposition of Tax Evasion Methods to Members of Joint Committee," *New York Times,* 18 June 1937.

90. Franklin D. Roosevelt, *Public Papers and Addresses,* vol. 6, 238–39.

91. Ibid., 246–47.

92. *Hearings Before the Joint Committee on Tax Evasion and Avoidance;* Blum, *From the Morgenthau Diaries,* 329–32.

93. *Hearings Before the Joint Committee on Tax Evasion and Avoidance,* 10; Westbrook Pegler, "Fair Enough; Loophole Experts," *Washington Post,* 9 June 1937; "The Tax Expert Problem," *Washington Post,* 28 June 1937.

94. Roosevelt, Frankfurter, and Freedman, *Roosevelt and Frankfurter: Their Correspondence,* 422–24; Lambert, "New Deal Revenue Acts," 374.

95. Ernest K. Lindley, "Tax Dodgers on Parade," *Nation,* 12 June 1937; "A Drive against Tax Evaders," *Washington Post,* 30 May 1937; "Loopholes in the Tax Laws," *Wall Street Journal,* 29 May 1937; "Tax Laws and Morals," *Wall Street Journal,* 2 June 1937; "Plugging the Loopholes," *New York Times,* 2 June 1937.

96. "Taxing Called Question of Law by J. P. Morgan," *Wall Street Journal,* 8 June 1937; "Morgan Assails 'Moral Issue' Set Up by President on Taxes," *Washington Post,* 8 June 1937.

97. Commissioner. v. Newman, 47-1 USTC ¶9175, 35 AFTR 857 (2d Cir. 1947). Quoted in abbreviated form in Paul, *Taxation in the United States,* 206.

98. For an interesting debate over the morality of tax avoidance, see Roosevelt's exchange of letters with Alexander Forbes, a distant cousin and professor at Harvard Medical School. Forbes took Morgan's line on tax avoidance, further suggesting that New Deal profligacy only served to encourage aggressive avoidance. In his reply, Roosevelt dismissed Forbes as "one of the worst anarchists in the United States." See Franklin D. Roosevelt and Elliott Roosevelt, *F. D. R.: His Personal Letters* (New York: Kraus Reprint, 1970), 690–91.

99. For a summary of the law, see Blakey and Blakey, "Revenue Act of 1937."

Chapter 8

1. Economist Herbert Stein coined the "fiscal revolution" moniker to describe the intellectual and policy revolution surrounding Keynesian economics. He, too, identifies World War II as a pivotal moment in American fiscal history. See Stein, *Fiscal Revolution,* 169–96.

2. Herbert Stein points out that the changing fiscal picture resulted principally from introduction of the new Social Security taxes coupled with an end to the accelerated soldier's bonus. FDR's newfound commitment to spending restraint played a relatively minor role. See Stein, *Fiscal Revolution,* 99–100.

3. "Early Step Urged," *New York Times,* 29 October 1937. Not surprisingly, Morgenthau was reported to be "extremely dubious" of the tax. For Treasury plans to reform the tax, see Carl Shoup, "Undistributed Profits Tax Relief for Small Corporations," (1937) in Box 14, Corporations, Partnerships, and Sole Owners to Excess Profits and War Profits: 1936–1940, Records of the Office of Tax Analysis/Division of Tax Research; General Records of the Department of the Treasury, Record Group 56;

National Archives, College Park, MD; and U.S. Department of the Treasury, "Tax Revision Studies: Undistributed Profits Tax."

4. Committee on Ways and Means, "Proposed Revision of the Revenue Laws, 1938," ed. U.S. House of Representatives (Washington, DC: Government Printing Office, 1938); Gladys Blakey and Roy G. Blakey, "The Revenue Act of 1938," *American Economic Review* 28, no. 3 (1938): 448–49.

5. Blakey and Blakey, "Revenue Act of 1938," 450; Paul, *Taxation in the United States,* 212.

6. Roosevelt, *Public Papers and Addresses,* vol. 7, 214–18; and Blakey and Blakey, "Revenue Act of 1938," 451.

7. Franklin D. Roosevelt, "Address at Arthurdale, West Virginia," 27 May 1938, American Presidency Project, http://www.presidency.ucsb.edu/ws/?pid=15647. See also, FDR's message in late April on the concentration of economic power, in which he calls for UPT reform even as he acknowledges some of the large-scale reform goals implicit in the legislation: Roosevelt, *Public Papers and Addresses,* vol. 7, 318–19.

8. See, for example, Roosevelt's press conference statement of 21 March 1939 in *Complete Presidential Press Conferences,* vol. 13, 214.

9. See, for example, the Treasury's assessment on possible tax hikes for 1939: "In choosing among the limited number of possible tax sources, an important objective has been to avoid as much as possible harmful repercussions on the economy," wrote economist Roy Blough, then heading the Division of Tax Research. "It is believed that this can be attained best by increasing the estate and gift taxes and the individual income tax before resorting to additional taxes on business, and by imposing additional general business taxes before resorting to sales and excise taxes." While Blough and his colleagues still believed that consumption taxes were the least desirable source of federal revenue, business taxes were also considered a drag on the economy. See Roy Blough, "Methods of Raising Additional Tax Revenues," (1938) in Box 43, Methods of Raising Additional Revenue, Records of the Office of Tax Analysis/Division of Tax Research, General Records of the Department of the Treasury, Record Group 56; National Archives, College Park, MD.

10. On the conservative movement of the mid- to late 1930s, with a special focus on the late 1930s and widespread disaffection among rural lawmakers in both parties, see Patterson, *Congressional Conservatism and the New Deal,* and Kennedy, *Freedom from Fear,* 338–39.

11. See, for example, their investigation of business opinion on the UPT: Cy Upham, "Comments upon Reaction to the Undistributed Profits Tax Observed in Talks with Business Men" (1937) in Box 14, Corporations, Partnerships, and Sole Owners to Excess Profits and War Profits: 1936–1940, Records of the Office of Tax Analysis/ Division of Tax Research; General Records of the Department of the Treasury, Record Group 56; National Archives, College Park, MD.

12. Franklin D. Roosevelt, "Message to Congress on Stimulating Recovery," 14 April 1938, American Presidency Project, http://www.presidency.ucsb.edu/ws/index.php?pid=15626#axzz1VDwFxZQG.

13. For Morgenthau quotation, "Business Peace?," *New York Times,* 26 February 1939. On the business appeasement campaign more generally, see Felix Belair, "An Assuring Tone," *New York Times,* 18 February 1939; "Have No Fear, Roosevelt Tells

Business," *Washington Post,* 18 February 1939; "The Nation," *New York Times,* 19 February 1939; Arthur Krock, "Business Appeasement Now up to President," *New York Times,* 26 February 1939; Robert C. Albright, "Harrison Asks Budget Cut to Spur Business," *Washington Post,* 3 March 1939; and "Doughton, Harrison Ask Treasury to Map Tax Cuts," *Washington Post,* 4 March 1939. See also Blakey and Blakey, "Federal Tax Legislation, 1939," 699; and Paul, *Taxation in the United States,* 214–15.

14. John W. Hanes, "We Face a Test of Our Common Sense," *New York Times,* 22 May 1938.

15. Paul, *Taxation in the United States,* 215; Blakey and Blakey, "Federal Tax Legislation, 1939," 699–700.

16. Interview with Roy Blough, 15 September 1995 (notes in author's possession).

17. "Morgenthau Favors Revision of Taxes To Help Business," *Wall Street Journal,* 24 February 1939, 12; Paul Fredericksen, "Hanes—Student of Taxes," *New York Times,* 9 April 1939; Hanes, "We Face a Test"; George James, "John Wesley Hanes Sr., 95, Aide to Roosevelt and Corporate Chief," *New York Times,* 31 December 1987; Bernard Kilgore, "J. W. Hanes to Be Morgenthau's First Assistant," *Wall Street Journal,* 12 May 1938; Joseph Alsop and Robert Kintner, "New Deal's Bright Young Men Win Voice Again in Shaping Policies," *New York Times,* 3 June 1938; Alsop and Kintner, "Business Viewpoint on Taxes Seen in Treasury under Hanes Guidance," *New York Times,* 30 November 1938; Ernest K. Lindley, "New Deal Convert," *Washington Post,* 15 March 1939; Groves, "Yachts without Income"; "Hanes Nominated for Treasury Post," *New York Times,* 13 May 1938; "Tax Post for Hanes," *New York Times,* 5 June 1938; "Hanes Sworn In as Treasury Aide," *New York Times,* 2 July 1938; "Hanes Succeeds Magill," *New York Times,* 29 October 1938; "Hanes, Tax Expert, Leaving Treasury," *New York Times,* 22 December 1939; "President Praises Hanes for Service," *New York Times,* 23 December 1939; Felix Cotten, "Hanes Assails Eccles Views on Taxation," *Washington Post,* 17 November 1939; Paul, *Taxation in the United States,* 255.

18. For just a few of the most important works in this large and growing literature, see Stein, *Fiscal Revolution;* Robert M. Collins, *The Business Response to Keynes, 1929–1964* (New York: Columbia University Press, 1981); and Alan Brinkley, *The End of Reform: New Deal Liberalism in Recession and War* (New York: Knopf, 1995). Recent work on the rise of consumer-focused economics has also enriched our understanding of the fiscal revolution. See, for example, Meg Jacobs, *Pocketbook Politics: Economic Citizenship in Twentieth-Century America* (Princeton, NJ: Princeton University Press, 2005); and Lizabeth Cohen, *A Consumer's Republic: The Politics of Mass Consumption in Postwar America* (New York: Knopf, 2003).

19. On the important insights of pre-Keynesian economic thinking, see Stein, "Prerevolutionary Fiscal Policy."

20. Interview with Roy Blough, 15 September 1995 (notes in author's possession).

21. Roy Blough, *The Federal Taxing Process* (New York: Prentice-Hall, 1952).

22. U.S. Department of the Treasury, "Administrative History of World War II: Division of Tax Research" (1947) in Box 29, White Paper: U.S. Fiscal Policy in World War II, Records of the Office of Tax Analysis/Division of Tax Research, General Records of the Department of the Treasury, Record Group 56; National Archives, College Park, MD.

23. Ibid.

24. Ibid.

25. Ibid.

26. George Haas, *Tax Revision Studies,* vol. 1, *General Statement, Revenue Estimates, Summaries, and Recommendations* (Washington, DC: U.S. Department of the Treasury, September 1937).

27. Ibid.; and George Haas, "Tax Revision Studies: Income, Capital Stock, and Excess-Profits Taxes," in Tax Revision Studies, 1937; Tax Reform Programs and Studies; Records of the Office of Tax Analysis/Division of Tax Research; General Records of the Department of the Treasury, Record Group 56; National Archives at College Park, MD.

28. Haas, *Tax Revision Studies,* vol. 4. See also the more detailed explanation in the 1937 volume on income taxation: "Income tax revision must, therefore, be directed toward increasing the importance of the individual income tax in the Federal revenue structure to the level where it will be possible to relieve the low income classes from at least some of the regressive taxes, or in any event, to increase the individual income tax in the middle and upper brackets sufficiently to counteract the regressive taxes and thereby render the aggregate Federal revenue system progressive." See Haas, *Tax Revision Studies,* vol. 2.

29. Haas, *Tax Revision Studies,* vol. 2.

30. Haas, *Tax Revision Studies,* vol. 4.

31. Carl Shoup and Roy Blough, "A Report on the Federal Revenue System Submitted to Undersecretary of the Treasury Roswell Magill," 20 September 1937, in "The Birth Pangs of the Modern Income Tax—An Early Treasury Study, part 1 (27 February 1996)," Tax History Project, http://www.taxhistory.org/thp/readings.nsf/cf7c9c870 b600b9585256df80075b9dd/7555c9d686d69ae785256e430078dbfe?OpenDocument.

32. It is worth noting that significant tax research was also going on during this period under the supervision of the Temporary National Economic Committee. The panel produced three reports on tax issues. While none played a central role in shaping subsequent tax policy, they did provide an interesting critique of the existing revenue structure, as well as recommendations for reform. Specifically, the panel concluded that the tax system was regressive near the bottom of the income scale, proportional through the middle, and progressive at the top. They also concluded that corporate taxes were riddled with problems and did little to discourage the concentration of economic power. See Joseph Christopher O'Mahoney, *Taxation, Recovery, and Defense* (Washington, DC: Government Printing Office, 1941); O'Mahoney, *Who Pays the Taxes? Allocation of Federal, State, and Local Taxes to Consumer Income Brackets* (Washington, DC: Government Printing Office, 1941); and O'Mahoney, *Taxation of Corporate Enterprise* (Washington, DC: Government Printing Office, 1941).

33. "War Profits and Jokers," *Wall Street Journal,* 3 April 1935; Donald R. Kennon and Rebecca M. Rogers, *The Committee on Ways and Means: A Bicentennial History, 1789–1989* (Washington, DC: Government Printing Office, 1990), 330–32.

34. Kennon and Rogers, *Committee on Ways and Means,* 330–32; Zelizer, *Taxing America,* 36–37. On the growth of congressional expertise, see Blakey and Blakey, "Revenue Act of 1941," 819. The Blakeys pointed out that congressional understanding of tax legislation was lagging far short of necessity. "Very few Congressmen understand more than parts of the laws they pass," they observed.

35. "War Profits and Jokers."

36. Arthur Krock, "Move to End War Profit Tied to New Deal Timing," *New York Times,* 16 December 1934.

37. Warren G. Harding, "Inaugural Address," 4 March 1921, American Presidency Project, http://www.presidency.ucsb.edu/ws/index.php?pid=25833. Also quoted in Paul, *Taxation in the United States,* 260–61.

38. Hurley's tax would have been imposed on any corporate or individual income that exceeded a three-year average of prewar income. "War-without-Profit," *Time,* 24 December 1934.

39. Ibid. On the Vinson-Trammell Act, see "Seeks Profit Curb on Ships, Planes," *Wall Street Journal,* 3 February 1934; "Senate O.K.'s Navy Bill," *Wall Street Journal,* 7 March 1934; and "Warship Profits Limited," *Wall Street Journal,* 7 March 1934. The Vinson-Trammell law was amended several times, including during the war years when it was largely superseded by the excess profits tax. See Blakey and Blakey, "The Two Federal Revenue Acts of 1940," *American Economic Review* 30, no. 4 (1940): 729; and Paul, *Taxation in the United States,* 261–62.

40. "War Profits and Jokers."

41. Randolph Paul, "Federal Taxation in Total War" (1942) in Box 64, Tax Reform Programs and Studies, Records of the Office of Tax Analysis/Division of Tax Research, General Records of the Department of the Treasury, Record Group 56; National Archives, College Park, MD.

42. Paul, *Taxation in the United States.*

43. Ibid., 256.

44. Roosevelt, *Complete Presidential Press Conferences,* vol. 15, 518.

45. Revenue Act of 1940, Pub. L. No. 76-656, 54 Stat. 516 (12–14 June 1940).

46. Paul, *Taxation in the United States,* 256–60.

47. The Senate had approved an amendment that would have established very high upper-bracket tax rates should the United States enter the European war. Designed to prevent war millionaires, the amendment was considered an outgrowth of the Nye investigation. It failed in conference, as did a related amendment by Sen. Robert La Follette that would have established a true excess profits tax on corporations. See Blakey and Blakey, "Two Federal Revenue Acts of 1940," 725.

48. Paul, *Taxation in the United States,* 262–63; Roosevelt, *Public Papers and Addresses,* vol. 9, 276.

49. Paul, *Taxation in the United States,* 263. The bill allowed companies to write off defense facilities over five years, much less than normally permitted for that sort of investment.

50. Quoted in ibid., 264.

51. Quoted in ibid., 265.

52. Twentieth Century Fund Committee on Taxation et al., *Facing the Tax Problem,* 491–94; Alfred G. Buehler, "The Taxation of Corporate Excess Profits in Peace and War Times," *Law and Contemporary Problems* 7, no. 2 (1940). See also Carl Shoup, "The Concept of Excess Profits under the Revenue Acts of 1940–42," *Law and Contemporary Problems* 10, no. 1 (1943); Shoup, "The Taxation of Excess Profits II," *Political Science Quarterly* 56, no. 1 (1941); and Shoup, "The Taxation of Excess Profits I," *Political Science Quarterly* 55, no. 4 (1940).

53. See, for example, John Richard Hicks, Ursula Kathleen Webb Hicks, and L. Rostás, *The Taxation of War Wealth,* 2nd ed. (Oxford: Clarendon Press, 1942).

54. Blakey and Blakey, "Two Federal Revenue Acts of 1940," 733.

55. Blakey and Blakey, "Revenue Act of 1941," 816, and "Federal Revenue Legislation, 1943–1944," 329.

56. Treasury supported some of these relief provisions, notably the 80 percent ceiling. See Henry J. Morgenthau, "Statement Before the Ways and Means Committee of the House of Representatives" (1942) in Box 34, Defense and War; Records of the Office of Tax Analysis/Division of Tax Research, General Records of the Department of the Treasury, Record Group 56; National Archives, College Park, MD; and Paul, *Taxation in the United States*, 320–21.

57. Paul, *Taxation in the United States*, 271; Roosevelt, *Public Papers and Addresses*, vol. 11, 15.

58. Shoup, "Concept of Excess Profits"; Brownlee, *Federal Taxation in America*, 111.

59. U.S. Bureau of the Census, *Historical Statistics*, part 2, 1109.

60. Blakey and Blakey, "Two Federal Revenue Acts of 1940," 728.

61. Groves, "Appraisal of the Excess Profits Tax."

62. Morgenthau, "Statement Before the Ways and Means Committee."

63. On the incidence of business taxation, see Louis Shere, "The Distribution of Federal Taxes"; Maxine Yaple, "The Burden of Direct Taxes as Paid by Income Classes," *American Economic Review* 26, no. 4 (1936); Richard A. Musgrave, "Fiscal Policy in Prosperity and Depression," *American Economic Review* 38, no. 2, Papers and Proceedings of the Sixtieth Annual Meeting of the American Economic Association (1948); Groves, "Personal Versus Corporate Income Taxes" and "Appraisal of the Excess Profits Tax"; and Richard Goode, "The Incidence of the Corporation Income Tax: A Rejoinder," *Journal of Economic Review* 36, no. 1 (1946).

64. George Douglas, "Excess Profits Taxation and the Taxpayer," *Law and Contemporary Problems* 10, no. 1 (1943); Felix Cotten, "Fix 8% Sales Tax, NAM Urges House," *Washington Post* 13 March 1942.

65. Blakey and Blakey, "Revenue Act of 1941," 819–21.

Chapter 9

1. Brownlee, "Historical Perspective," 60.

2. To some degree, inflation also shaped the debate over corporate taxation, but the effect of business taxes on the overall price structure was the subject of much head-scratching among tax experts of the 1930s and 1940s. Most economists believed that corporate taxes had a modest influence on inflation, for both good and ill. See, for example, Groves, "Appraisal of the Excess Profits Tax," 135–36; and Sundelson, "Taxation during Inflation."

3. "Morgenthau Says Some Prices Rising Too Fast," *Wall Street Journal*, 14 January 1941, 2.

4. U.S. Department of the Treasury, "Treasury Anti-Inflation Tax Proposals" (1942) in Box 34, Inflation, Depression, Recovery; Records of the Office of Tax Analysis/Division

of Tax Research; General Records of the Department of the Treasury, Record Group 56; National Archives, College Park, MD.

5. Franklin D. Roosevelt, "Annual Budget Message," 3 January 1941, American Presidency Project, http://www.presidency.ucsb.edu/ws/index.php?pid=16081&st=&st1=. On the importance of consumption in 1930s political culture, including Roosevelt's role in promoting it, see Cohen, *Consumer's Republic*. On Roosevelt's support from other members of the administration, such as Jesse Jones, as well as from experts, see, "Jones Sees No Danger of Inflation," *Wall Street Journal*, 3 January 1941, 2; and Roger W. Babson, "Inflation Outlook: No Immediate Peril in Sight," *Washington Post*, 6 January 1941, 17.

6. "Henderson Sees 'Mild Inflation', " *New York Times*, 18 September 1941, 11; "Henderson Sees Living Cost Up 20% by Spring and Urges Price Control," *New York Times*, 3 December 1941, 16.

7. Paul, *Taxation in the United States*, 284.

8. For some of the best recent literature on the inflation and consumption debates of World War II, see Cohen, *Consumer's Republic*; Meg Jacobs, " 'How About Some Meat?': The Office of Price Administration, Consumption Politics, and State-Building from the Bottom Up, 1941–1946," *Journal of American History* 84, no. 3 (1997); and Jacobs, *Pocketbook Politics*.

9. Paul, *Taxation in the United States*, 283.

10. *Revenue Revision of 1941: Hearings Before the Committee on Ways and Means*, 77th Cong. 47 (1941).

11. Ibid., 82–88. Stam also suggested several shifts among "ability" taxes, placing more reliance on corporate excess profits taxes and less on the individual income levies.

12. U.S. Pub. Law 77-250, 77 Cong., 1st sess., 20 September 1941. See also Blakey and Blakey, "Revenue Act of 1941," 821.

13. *Revenue Revision of 1942: Hearings Before the Committee on Ways and Means*, 77 Cong., 7 (1942).

14. U.S. Pub. Law 77-753, 77 Cong., 2nd sess., 21 October 1942. See also Roy G. Blakey and Gladys Blakey, "The Federal Revenue Act of 1942," *American Political Science Review* 36, no. 6 (1942): 1075–76.

15. U.S. Department of Commerce and Bureau of the Census, *Historical Statistics*, 2.

16. Committee on Ways and Means, *The Revenue Bill of 1940*, 76 Cong., 3rd Sess., 10 June 1940.

17. *Revenue Revision of 1941*, 51.

18. Blakey and Blakey, "Revenue Act of 1941," 811.

19. "Tax on 1940 Income to Stand as It Is, Harrison States," *New York Times*, 30 November 1940; "Tax Program," *Wall Street Journal*, 6 July 1940; "Roosevelt Confers with U.S. Finance Leaders on Taxes," *Wall Street Journal*, 30 November 1940; Robert C. Albright, "Sales Tax Plans Still Considered in House," *Washington Post*, 4 December 1940.

20. *Revenue Revision of 1941*, 55.

21. "Federal Sales Tax for Defense Urged," *New York Times*, 2 January 1941; George Gallup, "Public Is Divided on U.S. Sales Tax," *New York Times*, 14 January 1942; "Pub-

lic Ready to Accept 2% Federal Sales Tax on All Commodities," *Washington Post*, 3 May 1942; "The High Cost of Morgenthau," *Time*, 18 October 1943.

22. *Revenue Revision of 1942*, 274, 510–11; Cotten, "Fix 8% Sales Tax"; "N.A.M. Advocates General Sales Tax, Lower Personal Exemptions, Cut in U.S. Spending," *Wall Street Journal*, 20 August 1941; "A.F.L. Protests Sales Tax Plan to Senators," *Washington Post*, 24 August 1941; "Manufacturers Favor Single Agency for Defense: Ask Federal Sales Tax," *Wall Street Journal*, 5 December 1941; "Sentiment Grows for the Sales Tax," *New York Times*, 11 January 1942; "Retailers Favor Sales Tax: NRDGA Will Back Proposal," *Wall Street Journal*, 25 February 1942; "48-Hour Week Asked by Small Business; Sales Tax Also Favored in National Poll," *New York Times*, 17 March 1942; Henry N. Dorris, "$3,680,000,000 Yield Seen in Sales Tax," *New York Times*, 17 March 1942, and "Retailers Line Up for 5% Sales Tax," *New York Times*, 1 April 1942; "Retailers Propose 5% Sales Tax to Raise $3 Billion," *Wall Street Journal*, 1 April 1942; Bernard S. O'Hara, "Wall Street," *Washington Post*, 3 April 1942; "U.S. Chamber Proposes Graduated Sales Tax and Flat 5 Per Cent Levy on Gross Incomes," *Washington Post*, 15 April 1942; Robert W. Langbaum, "General Sales Tax Urged," *New York Times*, 20 June 1942.

23. "Sentiment Grows for the Sales Tax"; "Sales Tax Gains Favor with House Committee," *Washington Post*, 9 January 1942; "The Sales Tax Looms," *Washington Post*, 10 January 1942; Donald A. Young, "General Sales Tax Considered Reluctantly by House Group," *Washington Post*, 11 January, 1942; Felix Cotten, "House Leaders Lean Strongly to Sales Tax," *Washington Post*, 3 May 1942; "General Sales Tax Is Advocated by Robertson of Ways and Means Group: AFL Hits Wider Income Base," *Wall Street Journal*, 18 May 1942.

24. "A Tax for Everyone," *Time*, 11 May 1942.

25. See, for example, Shoup, "Sales Tax."

26. László Ecker-Racz, "Some Considerations Respecting the Advantages of Increases and Additional Selective Excise over a General Sales Tax" (1941) in Box 1; Excise and Sales Taxes in General; Records of the Office of Tax Analysis/Division of Tax Research; General Records of the Department of the Treasury, Record Group 56; National Archives, College Park, MD.

27. Roy Blough, "Evils of the Sales Tax," in Box 44, Papers of Roy Blough (Independence, MO: Harry S. Truman Presidential Library, 1942).

28. Paul, *Taxation in the United States*, 325. In 1942, the Treasury predicted that a 10 percent retail sales tax exempting food would raise $1.7 billion; "Federal Manufacturers', Wholesale, and Retail Sales Taxes," in Box 44, Papers of Roy Blough (Independence, MO: Harry S. Truman Presidential Library, 1942). See also Ecker-Racz, "Some Considerations."

29. John L. Sullivan, address before the General Federation of Women's Clubs, Washington, DC, 24 January 1942, in Box 1; General Sales Taxes; Records of the Office of Tax Analysis/Division of Tax Research; General Records of the Department of the Treasury, Record Group 56; National Archives, College Park, MD. For similar arguments by Treasury experts, see Division of Tax Research, "Income, Sales, and Payroll Taxes and the Problem of Inflation" (1942) in Box 34; Inflation, Depression, Recovery; Records of the Office of Tax Analysis/Division of Tax Research; General Records of the Department of the Treasury, Record Group 56; National Archives, College Park, MD.
    Some Treasury tax experts were less certain that a sales tax would necessarily boost inflation, arguing that such concerns were overblown. See Division of Tax Research, "A

Retail Sales Tax and Prices" (1942) in Box 34; Inflation, Depression, Recovery; Records of the Office of Tax Analysis/Division of Tax Research; General Records of the Department of the Treasury, Record Group 56; National Archives, College Park, MD.

30. *Revenue Revision of 1942*, 913. See also Dorris, "$3,680,000,000 Yield Seen"; "A.F.L. Protests Sales Tax Plan"; and "Taxing Low Income Opposed by A.F.L.," *New York Times*, 18 May 1942.

31. Henry Morgenthau, "Statement Before the House Ways and Means Committee, 3 March 1942," in Box 34; Defense and War; Records of the Office of Tax Analysis/Division of Tax Research; General Records of the Department of the Treasury, Record Group 56; National Archives, College Park, MD (1942).

32. "Sentiment Grows for the Sales Tax"; Young, "General Sales Tax Considered Reluctantly"; Robert De Vore, "Treadway Predicts Sales Tax Adoption," *Washington Post* 7 April 1942; Cotten, "House Leaders Lean Strongly"; "General Sales Tax Is Advocated by Robertson"; Langbaum, "General Sales Tax Urged"; "Majority Backs Levy on Sales, George Says," *Washington Post*, 8 September 1942.

33. "Tax on 1940 Income to Stand"; "National Sales Tax Would Hold Back Prosperity by Reducing Consumption," *Washington Post*, 1 December 1940; "State C.I.O. Backs Labor Peace Move," *New York Times*, 1 February 1942; Henry N. Dorris, "President Says Tax on Sales Is Wrong; Murray Opposes It," *New York Times*, 8 April 1942.

34. "A Scheme for a Progressive Sales Tax," Papers of Roy Blough, box 44 (Independence, MO: Harry S. Truman Presidential Library, 1942); "Majority Backs Levy on Sales, George Says."

35. Paul, *Taxation in the United States*, 323.

36. "Congress Gives Orders," *Time*, 14 September 1942.

37. Henry Morgenthau, "Statement Before the Senate Finance Committee," in Papers of Roy Blough, box 6 (Independence, MO: Harry S. Truman Presidential Library, 1942).

38. Ibid.

39. Thomas S. Adams, "Fundamental Problems of Federal Income Taxation," *Quarterly Journal of Economics* 35, no. 4 (1921): 527–56; Irving Fisher, "The Double Taxation of Savings," *American Economic Review* 29, no. 1 (1939): 16–33. Many of the earlier plans for a spendings tax were designed to correct a perceived flaw in the income tax: the so-called double taxation of savings. The 1942 proposal recognized no such flaw, merely suggesting the spendings tax as a source of additional income during the war emergency.

40. "Proposal for a 'Consumption Expenditure Tax'," Papers of Roy Blough, box 6 (Independence, MO: Harry S. Truman Presidential Library, 1942).

41. "The Spendings Tax," in Papers of Roy Blough, box 6 (Independence, MO: Harry S. Truman Presidential Library, 1942).

42. Paul, *Taxation in the United States*, 294.

43. Morgenthau, "Statement Before the Senate Finance Committee."

44. Robert C. Albright, "Gallery Glimpses," *Washington Post*, 6 September 1942. Over the next year or so, Treasury did continue to study the levy, convinced of its virtues. But it never again received serious consideration.

45. U.S. Department of the Treasury, Internal Revenue Service, "Personal Exemptions and Individual Income Tax."

46. Carl Shoup, "Plans for Additional Revenue" (1938) in Box 43; Methods of Raising Additional Revenue; Records of the Office of Tax Analysis/Division of Tax Research; General Records of the Department of the Treasury, Record Group 56; National Archives, College Park, MD.

47. George Haas, "Methods of Procuring an Additional $500 Million or $1 Billion of Revenue, with Special Reference to Mr. Shoup's Proposals in His Memorandum 'Plans for New Revenue,' February 12, 1938," in Box 43; Methods of Raising Additional Revenue; Records of the Office of Tax Analysis/Division of Tax Research; General Records of the Department of the Treasury, Record Group 56; National Archives, College Park, MD.

A year earlier, Haas had made similar recommendations, although he also proposed an increase in estate taxes, as well as a special surtax on unearned income. See George Haas, "Supplementary Fiscal Requirements and Possible Tax Program, Fiscal Years 1936 and 1937," in Morgenthau, *Morgenthau Diaries,* Book 18, 91–95.

48. Roy Blough, "Thoughts on Increasing Taxes at This Time, 27 November 1939," in Box 43; Methods of Raising Additional Revenue; Records of the Office of Tax Analysis/Division of Tax Research; General Records of the Department of the Treasury, Record Group 56; National Archives, College Park, MD.

49. Shoup and Blough, "Report on the Federal Revenue System, 20 September 1937."

50. Morgenthau, *Morgenthau Diaries,* Book 134, 85.

51. Roosevelt, *Complete Presidential Press Conferences,* vol. 13, 423–24; Alfred Flynn, "Taxes for Defense," *Wall Street Journal,* 11 December 1939; "Broader Tax Base Studied by House Unit," *Washington Post,* 8 August 1939; "President Confers on New Tax Study," *New York Times,* July 8, 1939; "Garner for Cuts in Tax Exemption," *New York Times,* 25 June 1939; "For a Broader Tax Base," *Washington Post,* 18 June 1939; "President Says Income Tax Base May Be Broadened," *Wall Street Journal,* 17 June 1939; "President Suggests Tax Base Be Wider," *Washington Post,* 17 June 1939.

52. Turner Catledge, "President Favors Broader Tax Base," *New York Times,* 17 June 1939.

53. On the notion of sacrifice as a construct of American political culture during World War II, see Mark Hugh Leff, "The Politics of Sacrifice on the American Home Front in World War II," *Journal of American History* 77, no. 4 (1991).

54. "Tax Prospects: Sharply Increased Rates Likely on Corporation and Individual Incomes," *Wall Street Journal,* 7 January 1941.

55. "Asks Bill Halve Tax Exemptions," *New York Times,* 19 August 1941.

56. "Wider Tax Plan Backed in Survey," *New York Times,* 8 January 1941; George Gallup, "Voters Willing to Pay More Defense Taxes," *Washington Post,* 8 January 1941; Gallup, "U.S. Favors Defense Tax on Lowest Income Groups," *Washington Post,* 25 May 1941; Gallup, "Public Is Divided on U.S. Sales Tax"; Gallup, "Public Ready to Accept 2% Federal Sales Tax."

57. Labor leaders denounced several wartime laws for being regressive; the CIO called the landmark 1942 act a "soak-the-poor" measure. "C.I.O. Makes Target of Defense Taxes," *New York Times,* 18 July 1940; Turner Catledge, "C.I.O. Condemns Wider Tax Base," *New York Times,* 14 August 1941; "A.F.L. Tax Program Stresses Heavy

Levy on Surplus Income," *New York Times*, 20 March 1942; "C.I.O. Paper Assails Tax Exemption Cuts," *New York Times*, 2 September 1941; Catledge, "C.I.O. Fights Broadening of Income Tax Base," *Washington Post*, 14 August 1941; "C.I.O. Opposes Wider Tax," *New York Times*, 10 May 1942; "Sales, Wage Taxes Opposed by C.I.O.," *Washington Post*, 27 January 1942; "Sales Tax Urged by Taft as Need to Stop Inflation," *New York Times*, 24 August 1942; Thomas J. Hamilton, "Unions, Industry Criticize Tax Bill," *New York Times*, 30 July 1942; "C.I.O. Tax Proposal Attacked by Expert," *New York Times*, 14 March 1943; "CIO Asks Higher Tax Rates in All Brackets Over $3,000: Launches Plans to Reduce Plant Absenteeism," *Wall Street Journal*, 8 February 1943; "Taxing Low Income Opposed by A.F.L."; "Hint at Reducing Tax Exemption," *New York Times*, 24 August 1941; Hamilton, "10 Billion Increase in Tax Bill Urged," *New York Times*, 13 August 1942; "A.F.L. Decries Lowering of Tax Exemptions by Ways Group," *Washington Post*, 18 May 1942.

58. Revenue Bill of 1940, H.R. 10039, 77th Cong., 1st Sess. (1940), 7; Revenue Act of 1940, 33.

59. Revenue Act of 1940, 32. Only $14 million of the new revenue would come from the new taxpayers; the other $61 million would result from existing income taxpayers, who would see their liability rise as the exemption fell. In addition, Treasury believed that better compliance among existing taxpayers would raise perhaps $25 million.

60. Ibid., 35.

61. *Revenue Revision of 1941*, 48, 56.

62. "Roosevelt and Doughton Letters and Morgenthau's Note," *New York Times*, 3 August 1941.

63. Blakey and Blakey, "Revenue Act of 1941," 817.

64. *Revenue Revision of 1942*, 297–300; Paul, *Taxation in the United States*.

65. Paul, *Taxation in the United States*, 300.

66. Ibid., 301; Division of Tax Research, "Taxes Needed During Fiscal 1943 to Control Inflation" (1942) in Box 34; Inflation, Depression, Recovery; Records of the Office of Tax Analysis/Division of Tax Research; General Records of the Department of the Treasury, Record Group 56; National Archives, College Park, MD.

67. Franklin D. Roosevelt, "Message to Congress on an Economic Stabilization Program," 24 April 1942, American Presidency Project, http://www.presidency.ucsb.edu/ws/index.php?pid=16251#axzz1VDwFxZQG.

68. The Treasury prepared a series of reports on the $25,000 income cap, ultimately concluding that the tax would only affect about 11,000 Americans. Since it required a large pretax income ($50,000 for an individual and $185,000 for a couple) to have a *net* income over $25,000, the tax was never a threat to most people. See Paul, *Taxation in the United States*, 301–02; and Division of Tax Research, "A Supertax on Individual Incomes above $25,000" (1942) in Box 54; Super Taxes; Records of the Office of Tax Analysis/Division of Tax Research; General Records of the Department of the Treasury, Record Group 56; National Archives, College Park, MD.

69. For an excellent account of the Victory Tax, see Dennis J. Ventry Jr., "The Victory Tax of 1942," *Tax Notes* 75(1997).

70. Paul, *Taxation in the United States*, 319.

71. Ventry, "Victory Tax of 1942." As Ventry explains, credits included the lesser of 25 percent of the Victory Tax or $500 for single people, 40 percent or $1,000 for married persons, and an additional 2 percent or $100 for dependents.

72. After its enactment, Treasury spent the rest of the war trying to fold the tax into the regular income tax. See Division of Tax Research, "Integration of the Victory Tax with the Net Income Tax" (1943) in Box 51; Individual Taxpayers—General; Records of the Office of Tax Analysis/Division of Tax Research; General Records of the Department of the Treasury, Record Group 56; National Archives, College Park, MD.

73. Revenue Bill of 1942, H.R. 7378, 77th Cong., 2nd Sess. (1942), 15–16.

74. Blakey and Blakey, "Federal Revenue Act of 1942," 1071–72.

75. Brownlee, "Tax Regimes, National Crisis, and State-Building," 92.

76. Division of Tax Research, "Collection at Source of the Individual Normal Income Tax" (1941) in Box 54; Collection and Payment; Records of the Office of Tax Analysis/Division of Tax Research; General Records of the Department of the Treasury, Record Group 56; National Archives, College Park, MD.

77. *Hearings on Revision of Income Tax Payment Methods Before the Committee on Ways and Means*, 78th Cong., 1st sess. (1943) (statement of Randolph E. Paul).

78. Jones, "Mass-Based Income Taxation."

79. Roy Blough, "The Individual Income Tax as a Method of Inflation Control" (1944) in Box 52; Individual Income Taxpayers; Records of the Office of Tax Analysis/Division of Tax Research; General Records of the Department of the Treasury, Record Group 56; National Archives, College Park, MD.

80. Franklin D. Roosevelt, "Annual Budget Message," 6 January 1943, American Presidency Project, http://www.presidency.ucsb.edu/ws/index.php?pid=16375#axzz1VDwFxZQG.

81. Randolph E. Paul, *Taxation for Prosperity* (New York: Bobbs-Merrill, 1947), 331.

82. Secretary Morgenthau told Roosevelt, "The plan presented about $64,000 to an individual with a net income of $100,000 . . . for a man who had earned $2,000, only $140." See Jones, "Mass-Based Income Taxation," 129.

83. Paul, *Taxation in the United States,* 329.

84. Brownlee, *Federal Taxation in America,* 92, 116.

85. Paul, *Taxation in the United States,* 335.

86. Ibid., 346.

87. Franklin D. Roosevelt, "Letter to Congress on Tax Bills," 17 May 1943, American Presidency Project, http://www.presidency.ucsb.edu/ws/index.php?pid=16400#axzz1VDwFxZQG.

88. "Not Current but Eminently Quotable," *Tax Notes* 70(1996): 1045. The top 20, with incomes for 1940 and 1941:

1. Rockefeller, John D., Jr.	$5,280,923	$3,789,204
2. Dillon, Clarence	5,238,059	129,019
3. Richardson, S. W.	3,948,794	(264,498)
4. Fleet, Reuben H.	3,878,047	291,013
5. Mellon, Richard K.	3,861,678	4,069,178
6. Mellon, Paul	3,737,023	5,074,832

7. Scaife, Sarah Mellon	3,420,855	4,021,264
8. Hartford, George L.	2,730,076	3,140,642
9. Bruce, Ailsa Mellon	2,661,148	2,074,634
10. Ford, Edsel B.	2,408,556	3,483,889
11. Chaplin, Charles	2,354,277	<100,000
12. Palmer, Edgar	2,207,248	1,883,406
13. Milbank, Jeremiah and Katherine S.	2,194,144	211,628
14. Davis, Arthur V.	2,193,030	2,054,765
15. Hartford, John A.	2,106,390	2,819,498
16. Reilly, Minnie Hartford	2,039,313	3,029,144
17. duPont, Lammont	1,873,444	1,805,384
18. duPont, Jessie Ball	1,755,683	1,785,279
19. Noble, Edward J.	1,611,624	209,380
20. duPont, William, Jr.	1,522,022	1,458,160

89. Jones, "Mass-Based Income Taxation."

90. Witte, *Politics and Development*, 129.

91. Surrey and Warren, *Federal Income Taxation*, 15.

Chapter 10

1. The administration's proposed estate tax changes would have boosted rates, pushing them to 80 percent on sums more than $1.5 million. It would also have lowered the estate tax exemption to $40,000. Supporters insisted that the levy made only a small contribution to total revenue, and that rates in lower and middle brackets were still moderate. Indeed, while estate tax increases had been a fixture of wartime tax reform, they played a distinctly secondary role in the federal tax system; between 1940 and 1945, their contribution to total receipts dropped from 6.7 percent to just 1.3 percent. See Roy Blough, "Postwar Tax Structure" (1944) in Box 64; Postwar Planning; Records of the Office of Tax Analysis/Division of Tax Research; General Records of the Department of the Treasury, Record Group 56; National Archives, College Park, MD.

2. *Revenue Revision of 1943: Hearings Before the Committee on Ways and Means*, 78th Cong. 4–8, 11–16, 18–20 (1943).

3. Paul, *Taxation in the United States*, 356.

4. Ibid.; "The High Cost of Morgenthau."

5. Paul, *Taxation in the United States*, 358.

6. Revenue Bill of 1943, H.R. 3687, 78th Cong. (1943).

7. Ibid., 5; Committee on Ways and Means, *The Revenue Bill of 1943: Supplemental Views to Accompany H.R. 3687* (Washington, DC: Government Printing Office, 1943), 2.

8. "The Nation," *New York Times*, 5 December 1943, E2.

9. Franklin D. Roosevelt, "Veto of a Revenue Bill," 22 February 1944, American Presidency Project, http://www.presidency.ucsb.edu/ws/?pid=16490.

10. Ibid. Roosevelt singled out five provisions for special criticism: (1) Permission for corporations reorganized under bankruptcy protection to retain a high excess profits

credit and depreciation basis attributable to the contributions of stockholders. Since these stockholders were generally eliminated in the reorganization process, he asserted, the provisions redounded to the benefit of bondholders who had often purchased their bonds at a steep discount; (2) Extension of percentage depletion allowances to additional minerals, including vermiculite, potash, feldspar, mica, talc, lepidolite, barite, and spodumens. Roosevelt questioned the appropriateness of percentage depletion allowances in general, but he also pointed out that the War Production Board had refused to certify several of these minerals as being in short supply for war needs; (3) Permission for lumber companies to treat income from the cutting of lumber as a capital gain rather than as ordinary income. "As a grower and seller of timber, I think that timber should be treated as a crop and therefore as income when it is sold," Roosevelt said. "This would encourage reforestation"; (4) Exemption of natural gas pipelines from the excess profits tax. This provision, he warned, might be exploited by the oil companies eager for similar exemptions applicable to their pipelines; and (5) Extension of a tax subsidy on airmail contracts for commercial airlines.

11. Ibid. The next year, Congress and the White House would cooperate to pass a variety of simplification measures as part of the Revenue Act of 1944.

12. Paul, *Taxation in the United States.* 372–73.

13. Ibid., 373–74.

14. Among its various major provisions, the Revenue Act of 1943 left individual income tax rates, as well as exemptions, unchanged; left estate tax rates and exemptions unchanged; cut the Victory Tax rate from 3 percent to 5 percent but repealed credits allowed under the levy; raised the excess profits rate from 90 percent to 95 percent but also raised the exemption from $5,000 to $10,000; and raised a range of excise taxes totaling more than $1 billion in new revenue. For a summary, see ibid., 375–78.

15. Samuel Lubell, *The Future of American Politics,* 1st ed. (New York: Harper, 1952), 18–19.

16. On the postwar history of tax legislation, see Zelizer, *Taxing America.* For an interesting study on the importance of tax preferences to the political sustenance of the modern income tax, see Christopher Howard, *The Hidden Welfare State: Tax Expenditures and Social Policy in the United States* (Princeton, NJ: Princeton University Press, 1997). The literature on preferences is vast, especially among legal academics. For one of the seminal studies on tax preferences, see Stanley S. Surrey, *Pathways to Tax Reform: The Concept of Tax Expenditures* (Cambridge, MA: Harvard University Press, 1973). For an influential interpretation of modern tax history that emphasizes the importance of loopholes, see King, "From Redistributive to Hegemonic Logic." See also Brownlee, *Federal Taxation in America,* 116–17.

17. Office of Management and Budget, *Budget of the United States Government, Fiscal Year 2013.* Government Printing Office, 2012, 32.

18. Paul, *Taxation in the United States,* 422. Corporation taxes were, however, the subject of considerable dispute. Business leaders were eager for a major reduction in corporate tax burdens, with a special eye on the excess profits tax. Unlike the World War I version of this levy, the new profits tax was never seriously expected to survive reconversion. As Randolph Paul later noted, the tax had a short life expectancy. But even the regular corporate income tax was on the chopping block; its 40 percent rate in 1945 was considered an easy target for reduction.

Beardsley Ruml again emerged as a principal champion of tax reform, calling for a reduction in the tax on dividends. See Beardsley Ruml, Hans Christian Sonne, and the

National Planning Association, *Fiscal and Monetary Policy* (Washington, DC: National Planning Association, 1944). On the planning for reconversion, including corporate tax reduction, see Blough, "Postwar Tax Structure"; Gerhard Colm and Ralph E. Flanders, "Revising the Postwar Federal Tax System: Discussion," *American Economic Review* 34, no. 2 (1944): 39–43; and Groves, "Revising the Postwar Federal Tax System." For two very prominent efforts at outlining the postwar system, see Committee for Economic Development, *A Postwar Federal Tax Plan for High Employment* (New York: Committee for Economic Development, 1944); and Paul, *Taxation for Prosperity*.

19. Stein, *Fiscal Revolution*, 177–81. For comments on the propensity of saving increasing with income and wealth, see Hubbard, "Income Creation by Means of Income Taxation"; Gilbert, "Taxation and Economic Stability"; and Ezekiel, "Annual Estimate of Savings by Individuals."

20. Stein, *Fiscal Revolution*, 182–83.

21. Paul, *Taxation in the United States*, 384–86; Ratner, *Taxation and Democracy in America*, 519. In the process, it also established a rate structure that would remain more or less intact through the 1970s (the rates themselves varied somewhat over time, but relative burdens among the brackets stayed the same). See Edwin S. Cohen, "Reflections on the U.S. Progressive Income Tax: Its Past and Present," *Virginia Law Review* 62, no. 8 (1976): 1320–21.

22. Carl Shoup, "The Revenue Act of 1945," *Political Science Quarterly* 60, no. 4 (1945): 481–91.

23. Ibid., 487–89.

24. Ibid., 489.

25. Jerry Tempalski, *Revenue Effects of Major Tax Bills* (Washington, DC: U.S. Department of the Treasury, 2006).

26. Harry S. Truman, *Memoirs*, 1st ed. (Garden City, NY: Doubleday, 1955), 41.

27. Harry S. Truman, "Statement by the President Announcing Revised Budget Estimates," 11 April 1946, American Presidency Project, http://www.presidency.ucsb.edu/ws/?pid=12628.

28. Robert Young, "Find Only Bar to Tax Cut: The Democrats," *Chicago Daily Tribune*, 26 July 1946, 3.

29. Harry S. Truman, "Special Message to the Congress upon Signing the Second Price Control Bill," 25 July 1946, American Presidency Project, http://www.presidency.ucsb.edu/ws/?pid=12466.

30. John Fisher, "Truman Threat of Higher Taxes Irks Democrats," *Chicago Daily Tribune*, 27 July 1946, 3.

31. Gallup Polls (AIPO), January 1946 and June 1946, accessed 14 February 2010 from iPOLL Databank.

32. Gallup Poll (AIPO), September 1946, accessed 14 February 2010 from iPOLL Databank, http://www.ropercenter.uconn.edu/data_access/ipoll/ipoll.html.

33. William E. Leuchtenburg, "New Faces of 1946," *Smithsonian*, November 2006, http://www.smithsonianmag.com/history-archaeology/newfaces.html?c=y&page=1.

34. Ibid.

35. Gallup Poll (AIPO), November 1946, accessed 14 February 2010 from iPOLL Databank, http://www.ropercenter.uconn.edu/data_access/ipoll/ipoll.html.

36. "The Text of Senator Taft's Address at Republican Leaders' Dinner at Columbus," *New York Times,* 1 August 1947, 8.

37. Carolyn C. Jones, "Split Income and Separate Spheres: Tax Law and Gender Roles in the 1940s," *Law and History Review* 6, no. 2 (1988): 294.

38. Harry S. Truman, "Address at the Jefferson Day Dinner," 5 April 1947, American Presidency Project, http://www.presidency.ucsb.edu/ws/?pid=12859.

39. "NAM Is Insincere on Taxes, CIO Says," *New York Times,* 6 March 1947, 4.

40. Ibid.

41. Witte, *Politics and Development,* 133.

42. Harry S. Truman, "Veto of Bill to Reduce Income Taxes," 16 June 1947, American Presidency Project, http://www.presidency.ucsb.edu/ws/?pid=12670.

43. Roper/*Fortune* Survey, July 1948, accessed 27 February 2010 from iPOLL Databank, http://www.ropercenter.uconn.edu/data_access/ipoll/ipoll.htm.

44. Gallup Poll, March 1948, accessed 27 February 2010 from iPOLL Databank, http://www.ropercenter.uconn.edu/data_access/ipoll/ipoll.html.

45. Roper/Fortune Survey, March 1948, accessed 27 February 2010 from iPOLL Databank, http://www.ropercenter.uconn.edu.proxy.its.virginia.edu/data_access/ipoll/ipoll.html

46. Ibid.

47. Ibid.

48. Ibid.

49. Gallup Poll (AIPO), April 1948, accessed 28 February 2010 from iPOLL Databank, http://www.ropercenter.uconn.edu/data_access/ipoll/ipoll.html.

50. Leuchtenburg, "New Faces of 1946."

51. Ibid.

52. Harry S. Truman, "Special Message to the Congress on Tax Policy," 23 January 1950, American Presidency Project, http://www.presidency.ucsb.edu/ws/?pid=13545.

53. See, for example, Brownlee, *Federal Taxation in America,* 129. On some of the most important and expensive preferences, which tend to target the middle class, see Howard, *Hidden Welfare State.*

Chapter 11

1. On the nature of U.S. fiscal regimes, see Brownlee, "Tax Regimes, National Crisis, and State-Building."

2. Franklin D. Roosevelt, "Annual Budget Message," 5 January 1942, American Presidency Project, http://www.presidency.ucsb.edu/ws/index.php?pid=16231#axzz1VDwFxZQG.

About the Author

Joseph J. Thorndike is director of the Tax History Project at Tax Analysts, a visiting scholar in history at the University of Virginia, and a fellow of the George W. Bush Institute. He also teaches tax policy at the Northwestern University School of Law. Thorndike is a regular columnist for *Tax Notes* magazine and has also written for the *New York Times,* the *Washington Post,* the *Wall Street Journal,* Barron's, Bloomberg, Time.com, the Huffington Post, and various academic journals. He is the author, with Steven A. Bank and Kirk J. Stark, of *War and Taxes* (Urban Institute Press, 2008) and the editor, with Dennis J. Ventry Jr., of *Tax Justice: The Ongoing Debate* (Urban Institute Press, 2002).

Index